A JOYOUS TRANSFORMATION

Anaïs Nin at a lecture, 1969. Photo: Marlis Schweiger

A JOYOUS TRANSFORMATION

The Unexpurgated Diary of Anaïs Nin

1966-1977

Preface by Paul Herron

Introduction by Benjamin Franklin V

Edited by Paul Herron

COPYRIGHT INFORMATION

Cover photo: Anaïs Nin, 1973, Puerto Vallarta, Mexico, by Rupert Pole.
Frontispiece: Anaïs Nin, 1969.

Library of Congress Cataloging-in-Publication Data

Names: Nin, Anaïs, 1903-1977, author. | Herron, Paul (Paul S.), editor, writer of preface. | Franklin, Benjamin, 1939- writer of introduction.
Title: A joyous transformation : the unexpurgated diary of Anaïs Nin, 1966-1977 / preface by Paul Herron ; introduction by Benjamin Franklin V ; edited by Paul Herron.
Other titles: Diary of Anaïs Nin. 1966-1977
    ISBN 9781735745985 (hardback) | ISBN 9781735745954 (paperback) | ISBN 9781735745961 (ebook)
Subjects: LCSH: Nin, Anaïs, 1903-1977--Diaries. | Authors, American--20th century--Diaries.
Classification: LCC PS3527.I865 Z46 2023 (print) | LCC PS3527.I865 (ebook) | DDC 818/.5203 [B]--dc23/eng/20230203
LC record available at https://lccn.loc.gov/2023000163
LC ebook record available at https://lccn.loc.gov/2023000164

Sky Blue Press

State College, Pennsylvania

ACKNOWLEDGMENTS

The editor would like to thank the following for their contributions to the realization of this volume: the Anaïs Nin Trust, Benjamin Franklin V, and Jooyeon Rhee.

This book is dedicated to Rupert Pole and Hugh Guiler.

PREFACE

The original diary material used to put together *A Joyous Transformation* consists of approximately 1,500 pages, some written on loose paper, and the rest found in Anaïs Nin's bound, handwritten diary volumes. The diaries were found at Nin's home in Los Angeles, which she had shared with her lover (and literary executor) Rupert Pole, after Pole's death in 2006. Some of the correspondence and other materials were also found at the Los Angeles house, while the rest was collected elsewhere and inserted chronologically into this volume.

During the period of time that *A Joyous Transformation* covers, Nin often kept more than one diary at the same time, which means that some passages were written concurrently or overlapped each other. Therefore, in the effort to provide the reader with a smooth chronological narrative, text was sometimes drawn from more than one original diary—and the occasional external source—within the same edited passage. And, since some of the materials had become scattered during the years after they were written, Pole's meticulous photocopying of the originals served as a valuable guide in assembling this volume.

A note about Nin's final two bound and named diaries: initially, she intended to record the ravages of cancer in "The Book of Pain" and her contemplations of music, which acted as a psychological balm for her illness, in "The Book of Music." The initial entries from each of these diaries are so noted in *A Joyous Transformation*. However, as time went on, Nin used the "pain" and "music" diaries for other purposes, sometimes even convoluting the original themes, so the distinction between them becomes blurred. For the sake of chronology and flow, such passages are blended and incorporated into the rest of the text without notation of the source.

Paul Herron
State College, Pennsylvania
December 2022

INTRODUCTION

A*Joyous Transformation* concludes the publication of the diary Anaïs Nin (1903-1977) kept from age eleven until a month before her death. One of the most voluminous of all journals, it was published in nineteen volumes over more than half a century.[1] Not merely a log of daily activities, it records, among other topics, the author's thoughts and actions, dealings with friends, successes and failures, and reflections on herself. She expresses her beliefs, including the importance of relationships, the significance of the inner life, the superiority of emotion to intellect, and that personal liberation results not from collective action or politics but rather from individual growth. That is, the *Diary* tells the story of Nin's life from her perspective and details her convictions. The early volumes in particular attracted a large readership and inspired many women to consider Nin an ideal, a person worthy of emulation, though such adulation has not been sustained. Because the journals were published in three series in a non-linear manner (the first book, published in 1966, begins when Nin was twenty-eight years old; volumes dealing with her life from 1914 to 1931 appeared later) and because the volumes originally published came out subsequently in radically altered form, explaining their evolution is in order.

For three decades beginning in the mid-1930s, Nin wrote fiction—stories, novellas, novels, and a work generally characterized as a prose poem—that is experimental in the sense that it is mainly psychological in nature and little concerned with surface reality. Consequently, she had difficulty finding publishers, especially for the novels. When they appeared in print they attracted few readers; some reviewers derided them.[2] In commercial terms they were a failure, though in time they became valued. After writing her last fiction in 1964, Nin focused on finding a publisher for the diary.

No later than the 1930s Nin believed that the record of her life as presented in the journal merited publication. In 1937 a book of excerpts was announced as forthcoming, but it never appeared. Not until the mid-1960s did Nin find a publisher interested in it. On the recommendation of Hiram Haydn, one of its editors, Harcourt, Brace & World agreed to publish a single volume of selections from the typescript. First, issues had to be resolved, such as determining with which episodes to begin and end the book, establishing the editorial process, and deciding not only on the material to be included but also on the content that must be omitted for various reasons, especially legal ones. When all parties were satisfied, Harcourt—in conjunction with the Denver publisher Alan Swallow—published the book in 1966 in a modest press run of 3,000 copies. Spurred by many commendatory reviews, notably one by Jean Garrigue on the front page of the *New York Times Book Review*, it sold so well that a second printing was soon required and a contract was signed for another *Diary* volume, which appeared the next year.[3] These two books, which document Nin's activities in Paris from 1931 to 1939, formed the basis for the usually positive notice Nin received then and, less consistently, for the remainder of her life.

How excerpts from the diary would have been received in the 1930s cannot be known. Circumstances for a warm response were ideal in the decade beginning in the mid-1960s, however. It was a time of questioning, of challenging social realities. For much of this period society was in upheaval primarily because of protests—

including violent ones—against the Vietnam War and racial inequality. This was also the era of second wave feminism, when many women reacted negatively to sexism, a word that was then new. Rather than being limited too frequently to traditional domestic roles, they wanted to pursue their interests and develop their skills. They thought that working women must be paid what men earned for performing similar work. They craved sexual freedom, including access to birth control and abortion. They wished to determine their own economic destiny. And more. That is, they sought liberation from social restrictions. They were ready for— and were soon inspired by—*The Diary of Anaïs Nin*, which depicts a woman, Nin, leading a free, adventurous, romantic, and fulfilling life apparently on her own, without depending on a man for support.

Treating the years 1931-1974, the first series of the *Diary* was published from 1966 to 1980. In the first of the seven volumes, covering the years 1931-1934, the persona/narrator named Anaïs Nin meets and becomes friendly with the impoverished budding novelist Henry Miller, with whom she discusses writing and literature. Committing to a literary life, she quickly writes a study of D. H. Lawrence that was published in Paris. She desires experience, which Miller—he of voracious appetites—helps her attain. Among others who intro-duce her to new realities are Miller's wife, the beautiful and mysterious June, to whom Nin is attracted, and the psychoanalysts René Allendy and Otto Rank, who help her understand herself, as well as the actor and writer Antonin Artaud. In this book, then, Nin is in the process of self-discovery, which continues in the next volume.

Miller and Rank are also important associates in the second book, which deals with the years 1934-1939, while new personalities enter Nin's life. Most notable are a married couple identified only as Gonzalo and Helba, and Lawrence Durrell, like Miller an aspiring novelist. The Peruvian Marxist Gonzalo introduces her to the world of politics; Nin, Miller, and Durrell support each other's work to the degree that they refer to themselves as the three musketeers and commit to publishing a series of books, one by each of them.[4] Secondary friends include the writers Michael Fraenkel and Alfred Perlès, along with the astrologers Jean Carteret and Conrad Moricand. Nin remains dedicated to writing, as evidenced by her producing two manuscripts that were published in Paris. *The House of Incest*, her major work of fiction, appeared in 1936; *The Winter of Artifice*, which comprises three novellas, in 1939.

Alone and together, the first two *Diary* volumes are enhanced by a geographical focus (mostly in and around Paris), by the presence of Nin's engaging friends, and by a plot: What will next happen with Nin? The reader is curious about the people with whom she associates, the nature of her relationships with them, and especially about her character and behavior. In discussing the events and acquaintances depicted in these books, Nin charts her development from living a relatively ordinary life to one of excitement, from aspiring writer to published author, from innocence to experience.

The next five volumes are generally less artful and appealing than the initial two largely because the main characters are less interesting than the Millers, Allendy, Rank, Artaud, Durrell, and others; because the texts are more diffuse than those in the previous books; and because in time they rely increasingly on correspondence to drive the narrative. They may be summarized as follows.

In volume 3 (dealing with the years 1939-1944) Nin discusses her return to the United States and her attitude toward New York City (too harsh, yet redeemed by Harlem, jazz, and Greenwich Village), her establishing and operating the Gemor Press to publish her books (but also works by others) when commercial publishers were not interested in them, and her writing of erotica that would be published posthumously.[5] Among her friends are Caresse Crosby, Robert Duncan, and Luise Rainer.

In the next installment (1944-1947) Nin treats the Gemor Press; her relationship with Gore Vidal, a young editor at E. P. Dutton who was instrumental in having his firm publish several of her books; her befriending of young men partly because they are not prescriptive and stultifying, as is such a mature admirer as Edmund Wilson; and her discovery of and trips to the American West. She continues her involvement with Gonzalo, whom she employs at the press.

Because in the fifth volume (1947-1955) Nin travels back and forth between New York and California and visits Paris and Mexico, the book lacks focus. During this period both her parents die, her father in 1949, her mother in 1954. She engages the psychiatrist Inge Bogner in New York, is so frustrated by publishers' indifference to her fiction that she considers the yet-unpublished diary to be her major work, and takes LSD in a controlled environment. A tumor is diagnosed. Her friends include James Leo Herlihy and Maxwell Geismar.

In the period covered by the sixth segment (1955-1966), Nin perceives of her journal as primarily a "diary of others," by which she means that the narrative relies heavily on correspondence, though the persona/narrator's voice remains prominent. She writes the last two of her six novels (*Solar Barque* [1958], later expanded as *Seduction of the Minotaur* [1961], and *Collages* [1964]); establishes the Anais Nin Press to make available some of her previously published books and to publish *Solar Barque*; begins valuable relationships with Gunther Stuhlmann, who becomes her agent, and Alan Swallow, who brings her fiction back into print; continues seeing Inge Bogner; and is disappointed with Durrell's foreword to the English edition of her novel *Children of the Albatross*. Her fiction receives its first serious (and positive) analysis.[6] Most notably, the sixth volume announces Harcourt's decision to publish the diary. Renate Druks, Jean Fanchette, and Marguerite Young are among Nin's associates.

The final volume (1966-1974) documents the critical and popular response to the early installments of the *Diary*. It reveals that Nin spent an inordinate amount of time corresponding with readers who felt connected to her. During these years and slightly later, many feminists, including Kate Millett and Alice Walker, lauded her. Both her fiction and nonfiction were taught in college courses, she lectured widely, her books were published abroad, a newsletter was devoted to her, she was interviewed numerous times, and a documentary film was made about her. Concurrent with this success and adulation, Nin was dealing with cancer. Not wanting to end the account of her life with the suffering she endured in her last years, she insisted that the published text conclude on a positive note by recounting her 1974 trip to Bali. There she witnessed a cremation on a funeral pyre that inspired her to embrace the Balinese belief that death leads to "a joyous transformation" of the spirit.

Because of the nature of the persona/narrator and events depicted in these seven books, one can understand readers being so captivated by them that they overlooked issues that needed to be addressed. Specifically, these texts raise questions they do not answer. Some important ones in the first volume are these: What was the source of the money that permitted Nin to live a life of seeming independence and help friends, such as Henry Miller, financially? Was her relationship with Miller strictly platonic? Then, who was the father of Nin's fetus that was born dead in 1934?

The answers to these and other questions would be revealed in time. Before this occurred, Harcourt published Nin's *Early Diary*.[7] Appearing in four volumes from 1978 (two years before the publication of the last volume of the original sequence) to 1985, this second series covers the period from 1914 (arrival in the United States) to 1931 (in Paris). These books appeal because they portray Nin during her formative years, before becoming the woman who committed fully to writing. They document her withdrawal from school at age sixteen, taking classes at Columbia University, and dedication to reading and writing. They detail her working as a model, including posing for such notables as Charles Dana Gibson, thereby becoming a Gibson Girl, and Neysa McMein, whose representation of Nin appeared on the cover of the *Saturday Evening Post*.[8] These volumes show that though boys found Nin attractive, she was not fully smitten by a man until 1921, when she met Hugh Guiler, a recent Columbia graduate. Following a halting courtship they were married, in Cuba, in 1923. A banker, Guiler was assigned to Paris in 1924. There she took Spanish dancing lessons from a man who tried to seduce her, had an unconsummated affair with Guiler's former professor John Erskine, and became sexually voracious. At this point—as Nin, in Paris, is about to meet people who would expose her to new ideas and ways of living—the *Early Diary* ends.

The questions raised in the first *Diary* series began being answered in 1986 with the publication of *Henry and June*, a book characterized as unexpurgated, that treats the years 1931-1932, a period already chronicled in the 1966 volume. While the text of *Henry and June* repeats some material from the earlier book dealing with these years, most of it is new. It identifies the source of Nin's money: her husband, Guiler, who requested that his name be omitted from all installments of the original *Diary* sequence.[9] That is, Nin was not an independent woman confronting life without a man's assistance. She could not have lived as she did without the generosity and support of her spouse. Also illuminating is the nature of her association with Henry Miller. Nin was attracted to him because of his interest in writing and in literature generally, but their relationship quickly became physical. Her first adultery—which lasted for most of the 1930s—was with him. Chiefly to avoid her and Guiler's distress, Nin omitted these and other possibly embarrassing particulars from her initial depiction of this period. The unexpurgated book revived interest in Nin, whose reputation as a serious author had slowly declined over time. The text so appealed to filmmaker Philip Kaufman that he made a movie of it, *Henry & June* (1990).[10]

Henry and June and the unexpurgated *Diary* volumes Harcourt published in 1992, 1995, and 1996 (covering the years 1932-1939) constitute the first part of the third *Diary* series.[11] All four books contain revelations missing from the first treatments of these years. For example, the text of *Incest* discloses that the 1934 birth of Nin's dead child resulted from an abortion at around six months, not a stillbirth, and that Nin believed Miller had fathered it. This same book records what is probably the most shocking episode in Nin's life: consensual incest with her father in Valescure, France, in June 1933. Awareness of this event repulsed some readers to the degree that they turned against her. The final two volumes, *Fire* and *Nearer the Moon*, focus on her sex life, mostly with Gonzalo More on a houseboat on the Seine, but also still with Henry Miller plus, in *Fire*, with Otto Rank. In the last paragraph of *Nearer the Moon*, Nin provides insight into her behavior: "My only religion, philosophy, system, dogma, is love. Everything else I can only betray when passion carries me to a new world."[12] Guiler, a significant presence in all these unexpurgated texts, remains a constant in her life, an anchor.

Possibly because the last of these books, *Nearer the Moon*, concludes at a natural stopping point (with Nin's departure from France for the United States at the outbreak of World War II), perhaps because it is arguably the least captivating of the unexpurgated volumes, conceivably because her activities in the United States are less dramatic than those in France, but probably because, for whatever reason, its sales were disappointing, Harcourt published no more volumes of the *Diary*.

Realizing that journal entries written after late 1939 had not been published in unexpurgated form, Paul Herron perceived the need to have them made available in such a manner. Over time, therefore, he prepared this material for publication in four volumes. The books he edited constitute the second part of the third *Diary* sequence (the unexpurgated texts). In 2013, seventeen years after the publication of *Nearer the Moon*, the first of Herron's books appeared as *Mirages*. The next one was published as *Trapeze* (2017); the third, as *The Diary of Others* (2021); and the last, this present volume, as *A Joyous Transformation*.[13] Among other topics, the first three of these books deal with Nin's difficulty adjusting to life in the United States; her deteriorating relationships with Miller and More, both of whom had followed her to New York; her activities at the Gemor Press; her affairs; her involvement with Haitians; her frustration with publishing houses that were not interested in her fiction; her bonding with Rupert Pole (they were married from 1955 to 1966, while she was also wed to Guiler); her trip to and residence in California with Pole; and her flying back and forth between California (Pole) and New York (Guiler). Nin explains her important association with Alan Swallow. *The Diary of Others* ends with the publication of the first *Diary* volume.

The last book in the third *Diary* sequence, *A Joyous Transformation*, opens with Nin delighting in the publication of and warm response to the first *Diary* and concludes with the last entries she wrote as death approached. It contains significant material missing from the last volume of the initial *Diary* series, including specifics about the physical decline that followed her trip to Bali. She worries about realities relating to a film adaptation of her novel *A Spy in the House of Love*, a project that came to nothing; discusses her travels to Tahiti and Japan; and notes that because of the success of the *Diary*, university libraries want to buy the earliest versions of the texts. (They went to UCLA.) She charts her increasing popularity, which may be gauged by the number of people, mainly women, who adore her, as well as by the increasing scholarly interest in her work. Writing in her journal on October 1, 1975 after her health began to fail, she states that she was still at her best the previous year: "Will I ever be what I was in 1974—vital, radiant, not looking my age, making women feel hopeful and lose their fear of aging?" She would not.

Who could blame Nin for wanting her rendering of her life to end positively, not with weakness and illness? In fact, though, good things happened to her during her final two-plus years, despite her enfeeblement and lack of energy. She had a rewarding though wearing trip to Paris. Several young women became so close to her that she considered them her daughters. Because of the sale of her letters and typescript diaries and because she received substantial royalties from the sale of her books, she became financially secure enough to pay some expenses of her husband, who had underwritten her activities since their marriage in 1923. At a local community college she served as tutor for a successful independent study course. She received honorary degrees from Dartmouth College and the Philadelphia College of the Arts. Books and articles were written about her work. She wrote forewords to books by other authors. The *Los Angeles Times* named her the 1976 woman of the year. The *Journals* were being translated into several languages. She edited typescripts for the sixth and seventh *Diary* volumes. In her treatment of this period, Nin reveals attitudes she might not have felt comfortable articulating previously. She acknowledges, for example, that she was dissatisfied with what she termed "militant feminists."

One sympathizes when Nin asks, in a December 20, 1975 letter to Inge Bogner, "Why should cancer have come at the best moment in my life? When I had love, honors, enough royalties to not have to lecture?" She details her sad situation. She receives chemotherapy; wears a wig; suffers from indigestion, incontinence, and diarrhea; endures leaking colostomy bags; withstands pain that medication cannot moderate, let alone alleviate; deals with cataracts; and more. She withstands these ordeals with seeming grace, aided throughout by Rupert Pole. Though she has occasionally been accused of being a narcissist, her depiction of her life concludes, less than a month before her death, with concern for another person, Pole. She wishes they could return to Paris, not for selfish reasons but so she could expose him to its charms, as represented by a table outside her favorite bistro.

A few documents relating to Nin are appended to *A Joyous Transformation*. Most significant is the initial correspondence between Hugh Guiler and Rupert Pole, the most important men in her life. Despite having genuine feelings for Guiler, their marriage so dissatisfied her that she desired what she called "a loving release" from him. Reluctant to discuss this issue with her husband, she wrote him a letter (undated but probably written in December 1975) about the dilemma, but the message was not sent. Pole, whom she met in 1947, fulfilled her emotionally and sexually more than had any man. Contented at last, she lived with him in California for the remainder of her life, other than when spending time with Guiler in New York. She tried to keep each man unaware of her relationship with the other.[14]

On February 23, 1977, approximately six weeks after Nin's death, Guiler wrote to Pole, presumably to open communication that would be required for resolving estate issues. In his letter Guiler indicates that for over a decade he has known the nature of Pole's relationship with Nin. The letter is a masterpiece of civility. He does not air grievances he might have had; instead, he expresses gratitude for the happiness Pole brought Nin and for his assistance during her final illness. Within a week Pole responded in a similar manner, but with even greater warmth. Greeting him as

"My dear Hugo," he characterizes Guiler not only as the main person in Nin's life from the time they met until 1931, but also as having been heroic then. He flatters Guiler by suggesting he write the forewords to the *Early Diary*, which Guiler did not do; he praises the program honoring Nin that Guiler organized in New York; and he acknowledges Nin's enduring love for him. As evidenced by these two letters, Guiler and Pole were gracious, thoughtful, and respectful men grateful to each other for having enriched Nin's life. With this *A Joyous Transformation* concludes, as does the publication of Nin's diary.

Benjamin Franklin V
University of South Carolina
March 2022

Notes

1. *The Diary of Anaïs Nin* was published in England as *The Journals of Anaïs Nin*. I use *Diary* and *Journals* (and "diary" and "journal") interchangeably. I distinguish between the unpublished ("diary") and published ("*Diary*") diary.

2. Negative evaluations of Nin's fiction include Herbert Lyons, "Surrealist Soap Opera," *New York Times Book Review*, October 20, 1946, sec. 7, p. 16; Marvin Mudrick, "Humanity Is the Principle," *Hudson Review* 7, no. 4 (Winter 1955): 610-19; and Frank Baldanza, "Anaïs Nin," *Minnesota Review* 2, no. 2 (Winter 1962): 263-71.

3. Jean Garrigue, "The Self behind the Selves," *New York Times Book Review*, April 24, 1966, sec. 7, p. 1.

4. Named the Villa Seurat Series and published by the Obelisk Press, the books are Durrell's *The Black Book* (1938), Miller's *Max and the White Phagocytes* (1938), and Nin's *The Winter of Artifice* (1939).

5. Harcourt published the erotica as *Delta of Venus* (1977) and *Little Birds* (1979).

6. Oliver Evans, "Anaïs Nin and the Discovery of Inner Space," *Prairie Schooner* 36, no. 3 (Fall 1962): 217-31.

7. The text of the first volume, *Linotte*, was written in French. Jean L. Sherman translated it for publication in English.

8. See the *Saturday Evening Post*, July 8, 1922.

9. Nin does not mention Guiler by name in the first *Diary* series, though she refers to her unnamed husband in the second volume on pp. 32, 349.

10. With the publication of her erotica in 1977 and 1979, Nin again became prominent, though not as a thoughtful writer. The movie features Maria de Medeiros as Nin, Fred Ward as Henry Miller, Uma Thurman as June Miller, and Richard E. Grant as Guiler. It is the first film to have received the NC-17 rating.

11. Questions have been raised about the accuracy of Nin's account of events in the *Diary*. See, for example, Joan Bobbitt, "Truth and Artistry in the *Diary of Anaïs Nin*," *Journal of Modern Literature* 9, no. 2 (May 1982): 267-76, and Katha Pollitt, "Sins of the Nins," *New York Times Book Review*, November 22, 1992, sec. 7, p. 3.

12. More is the Gonzalo depicted in the expurgated volumes of the *Diary. Nearer the Moon, From a Journal of Love, The Unexpurgated Diary of Anaïs Nin, 1937-1939* (New York: Harcourt Brace, 1996), p. 375.

13. The first two of these books were published by the Swallow Press/Ohio University Press in conjunction with the Sky Blue Press; the other two, by the Sky Blue Press.

14. Nin apparently never told Guiler about her relationship with Pole. In 1966 she informed Pole that she was then and would remain wed to Guiler, an announcement that led to the annulment of her marriage to Pole. See Deirdre Bair, *Anaïs Nin, a Biography* (New York: Putnam's, 1995), pp. 482-83.

CHRONOLOGY

1903 Anaïs Nin is born in Neuilly, France to the Spanish/Cuban pianist and composer Joaquín Nin and French/Danish/Cuban Rosa Culmell, a singer from a wealthy family.

1905 Brother Thorvald is born in Havana.

1908 Second brother Joaquín is born in Berlin.

1912 Nin nearly dies from a burst appendix in Brussels.

1913 Nin's father abandons his family for a young lover; Nin's mother and the children stay with Joaquín Sr.'s parents in Barcelona.

1914 Nin, her mother and two brothers come to New York; Nin begins her diary, in French.

1920 Nin begins to write her diary in English.

1922 Nin becomes an artists' model to help with the family income.

1923 Nin marries Hugh P. Guiler, a banker, in Cuba.

1924 Nin and Guiler move to Paris where he takes a position with the Paris branch of his New York bank; Nin continues her diary and dabbles in fiction.

1927 Nin begins Spanish dance lessons with Paco Miralles.

1929 Nin has an unconsummated affair with American author and scholar John Erskine, which haunts her for years.

1930 Nin and Guiler move from a lavish Paris apartment to a more economical house in Louveciennes, a suburb of Paris.

1931 Nin meets controversial American novelist Henry Miller in Louveciennes.

1932 Nin becomes Miller's lover and is infatuated with his wife June; Edward Titus publishes Nin's first book, *D. H. Lawrence: An Unprofessional Study*; Nin begins psychotherapy with René Allendy.

1933 Nin reunites with her father, and they begin an incestuous relationship in the south of France that lasts for several months; Nin begins psychoanalysis with Otto Rank.

1934 Nin becomes Rank's lover; has a horrific abortion; comes to New York to help Rank psychoanalyze patients—Miller secretly accompanies her.

1935 Nin and Guiler move from Louveciennes to Paris.

1936 Nin self-publishes *The House of Incest* (Siana Editions); meets Peruvian communist Gonzalo More and begins a sexual relationship with him; rents a houseboat on the Seine for their trysts.

1937 Nin meets Lawrence Durrell; she, Miller and Durrell begin planning a series of books.

1939 Obelisk Press prints Nin's *The Winter of Artifice*; Nin and Guiler fly to New York to avoid oncoming war.

1940 Nin reunites with her two lovers, Miller and More, in New York; begins an affair with the young John Dudley.

1941 Nin meets the Viennese singer Edward Graeffe in Provincetown and begins a sporadic but long-lasting affair with him.

1942 Nin self-publishes the expurgated version of *Winter of Artifice*; breaks with Miller; begins psychoanalysis with Martha Jaeger.

1943 Nin meets Haitian sculptor Albert Mangones with whom she has a brief affair.

1944 Nin self-publishes *Under a Glass Bell* (Gemor Press).

1945 Nin and seventeen-year-old William Pinckard begin an affair; Nin self-publishes *This Hunger* (Gemor Press); meets Gore Vidal; begins psychoanalysis with Clement Staff; begins a brief affair with critic Edmund Wilson.

1946 Nin falls in love with Vidal; with his help, E. P. Dutton publishes Nin's *Ladders to Fire*; briefly resumes her affair with Mangones.

1947 Dutton publishes *Children of the Albatross*; Nin meets Rupert Pole and drives to California with him, beginning her "double life," dividing her time between Pole in California and Guiler in New York; breaks with More.

1948 Dutton publishes *Under a Glass Bell and Other Stories*, but, due to poor sales, ends its relationship with Nin; Nin and Pole travel to Acapulco.

1949 Nin and Pole rent an apartment in San Francisco, where Pole attends forestry school; Nin's father dies in Cuba.

1950 Duell, Sloane and Pierce publishes *The Four-Chambered Heart*; Nin lives part time with Pole in Sierra Madre, where he is assigned a forestry post.

1952 Hugh Guiler's long incapacitation due to back problems creates a crisis for Nin, as her bicoastal routine is interrupted and Pole and Guiler nearly encounter each other; Nin's friendship with James Leo Herlihy blossoms; psychoanalysis with Dr. Inge Bogner begins; Guiler makes *Bells of Atlantis*, his first important film.

1953 Nin and Pole attend a "come as your madness" party, hosted by Renate Druks, which was the inspiration for the film *Under the Pleasure Dome*.

1954 British Book Centre publishes *A Spy in the House of Love*, underwritten by Guiler; Nin's mother dies.

1955 Nin bigamously marries Pole.

1956 Pole leaves forestry for a teaching job in Los Angeles.

1957 Gunther Stuhlmann becomes Nin's literary agent.

1958 Nin tries LSD; self-publishes *Solar Barque*; Nin and Guiler travel to Europe for the first time since the beginning of World War II; Nin sees Lawrence Durrell in France.

1959 Nin self-publishes *Cities of the Interior* and becomes involved with *Two Cities*, a bilingual journal.

1961 Alan Swallow becomes Nin's U.S. publisher and publishes *Seduction of the Minotaur*.

1962 *Prairie Schooner* publishes the first scholarly analysis of Nin's work, by Oliver Evans; Nin rekindles her friendship with Henry Miller.

1964 Swallow publishes *Collages*; Nin readies her diary for publication.

1965 Putnam's publishes Henry Miller's *Letters to Anaïs Nin*; Harcourt agrees to publish the first volume of Nin's diary.

1966 Harcourt, in conjunction with Swallow Press, publishes volume 1 of *The Diary of Anaïs Nin* to popular and critical acclaim.

Los Angeles, May 1966

Suddenly love, praise, flowers, invitations to lecture. The same publishers who turned down my work beg for my comments on the new books they are publishing.

The *Diary* was like a cyclone; radio and television two or three times a day.

Harcourt is very pleased, but Hiram Haydn is too cautious. A second printing of 2,500 copies is too small as things are going now.

Starting my work on the West Coast (radio, television); will go to San Francisco for two days.

Letter from Millicent Fredericks (AN's maid) to Anaïs Nin:
May 1966

Dear Miss Hugo:

I watched you Sunday morning on TV, channel 3. On account of same I could not make church. It was delightful and wonderful! I called everyone and they watched and enjoyed. Even Regina and her mother and aunt. She told them you were French. They called me after and were happy they were able to see and hear you. They send congratulations for your success and pray you will go higher and higher and take your place amongst the great writers.

Love,
Millicent

Card from Oliver Evans to Anaïs Nin:
May 1966

You have risen to fame at last, on the wings of the *Diary*. And high time!

I think I was wise to advise publication of my critique *after* Volume One of the *Diary*. Now the way will be paved.

Love,
Oliver

Letter from Hugh Guiler to Anaïs Nin:
New York, May 21, 1966

Darling:

I almost missed the ad in *The New York Times* yesterday but went out to several places uptown today, Saturday, and got you nine copies—all they had.

Congratulations and also on the reviews. It is certainly rare to have such a consensus (LBJ will want to know your secret—tell him it is just being a good writer, radiant person and honest—he is none of these).

In haste to get this off.

Love,
H

Letter from Harriet Zinnes to Anaïs Nin:
New York, May 22, 1966

Dear Anaïs:

We have just watched your program on *Camera Three*. You did beautifully. I love how you read—with just the proper timing and such clear articulation. You really came through. And the whole feeling of the program was just right. *The director obviously understood you*; you were the great lady of letters—sitting, standing, reading. There was glamor inside and out. The kind of glamor that is the result of that shimmering kind of greatness that is really yours alone. We recorded the broadcast, so that we shall have it for all time.

Beauty, beauty, beauty—that is the city of the interior.

Love,

Harriet

P.S. Looking forward to your return to the city.

LOS ANGELES, MAY 1966

A good review by Marion Simon in *National Observer*. I thanked her. My scrapbook is gaining weight.

My Japanese publisher invited me to Japan to celebrate the publication of *A Spy in the House of Love.*

Letter from Nobuko Uenishi to Anaïs Nin:
New York, May 1966

Dearest Anaïs,

Unfortunately, Anaïs, I'll not be back in Japan when you will be there, but do see my family when you get to Kyoto or Osaka. And, of course, your [husband] situation is no problem. It wouldn't occur to them to ask you about any personal matter.

I'll write to my parents about your coming and they'll be delighted to see you whenever you wish. Tokyo, Kyoto, Kobe, Osaka...

I'll write to Mr. Marsura, the theater director whom Hugo used to know *if* it is acceptable to you. For Mr. M. is the best friend of Mishima (famous writer and playwright) and through him you'll meet many wonderful people.

Here in N.Y., at the International PEN Club, I may see the main delegates from Japan, including Prof. Ivan Morris. I'll tell them you'll be in Tokyo.

I'll send you the addresses of my father's offices and houses. You may stay at our mountain house, you and Rupert alone; I'll write about it to my mother.

Nobuko

Letter from Anaïs Nin to Hiram Haydn:
Los Angeles, June 3, 1966

Dear Hiram:

I was so pleased with the ad in the *Times*. And did you see the big ads in *The Village Voice*?

I am not returning to New York until all my engagements here are fulfilled. I hope you can send me the Harcourt check before June 20. Is it possible?

The reason I brought up the question of a paperback of the *Diary* is that the bulk of my readers are college students and artists, and they are the ones who can't afford $6.95 for the hardcover. All of them write me (my mail is staggering) to please come

2

out in paperback. Believe me, dear Hiram, I think it would be a good idea. Have you thought about it?

From experience now, and my mail, it seems the most useful thing I can do for the books is to go on TV. I am waiting for Gypsy Rose Lee's TV show in San Francisco.

Anaïs

Letter from Hugh Guiler to Anaïs Nin:
New York, June 4, 1966

Darling:

I think you should disregard the article in *The Village Voice*. Otherwise you would have to spend all your time answering the critics. I suppose this one might say something to the effect that somewhere along the line you yourself said that the novels were based on the diary, although, of course, you transmuted and transposed them as a novelist always does. Anyhow, there is no doubt that this article has helped sales. Perhaps you can answer the questions you object to in your radio and television talks, as it gives you a chance to talk about transmutation. I suppose even in the diary itself you saw the same facts differently after the passage of time, just as Proust did. The diary itself should not be labeled as realistic in the ordinary sense.

Glad you and Piccolo are well. I am fine too. If it continues to be sunny, I will go to the beach tomorrow. Prospects for business in Spain seem better, and the next ten days should tell more definitely.

Love, love,
Hugo

Letter from Hilda Lindley of Harcourt to Anaïs Nin:
New York, June 1966

Dear Anaïs:

Thank you for your kind letter, which I truly appreciated. I'm enclosing a review that you may not have seen from *Manhattan East*. The diary is continuing to sell exceedingly well and I'm sure that all of the things you are doing on radio and television are a real contribution to its success. I frankly don't see any point of you returning to New York this summer for radio or television interviews. First because you had the cream of the crop on your last visit here and second because summertime is a rather poor time for this sort of interview on radio or television. Most of the interviewers go off the air for the summer and many of the programs are reruns. The book is doing so well in the East now that it is rolling along on its own momentum.

I am glad that you are feeling well and I hope that you are not going to strain yourself with all of your activities on behalf of the *Diary*. I called Leo Lerman and he told me, as you know, that he loves the book and a review of it will appear in a forthcoming issue of *Mademoiselle*, probably September.

Take care of yourself and keep well. Fond regards, as ever,
Hilda

Letter from Hugh Guiler to Anaïs Nin:
New York, June 6, 1966

Darling:

After what you told me about the offer to go to Japan, I think this is an exceptional opportunity to make an interesting trip and also to further the sale of your books and perhaps to get another contract for the Diary.

Gunther [Stuhlmann] will be back from Europe in a few days. His assistant says she has a check from Harcourt but that she shouldn't endorse it to you as only Gunther can do that when he returns, but he will surely do it first thing then. Anyhow, she wants you to know that Harcourt has done its part.

She has no further news about France for you but says that Spain and Scandinavia are as good as gold and that Holland is also close to agreement.

My advisor says if my *Bells of Atlantis* is copyrighted, as it is, I can claim a share of the Barrons' profits on their science fiction film. Maybe I will look into this.

I just found out that Peggy Glanville-Hicks is to be operated on tomorrow for a very serious brain tumor at the Presbyterian Hospital. It will take eight hours and will cost $6,000—she has no Social Security or Medicare. I did call Peggy on the telephone and tried to express confidence. It is certainly lucky she was here and not in Greece.

It would be more convenient for me to settle the accounts with you on my return, even though I *have* collected the insurance. But if you need the money while I am away, don't hesitate to say so and I can arrange it.

Love,

H

P.S. Erika Freeman, who knows Japan, says you are the only Western woman who could be appreciated there, because you have the same kind of prettiness and exquisiteness that the Japanese women have.

LOS ANGELES, JUNE 12, 1966

Book signing at Gotham Book Mart in N.Y. Overflow of people.

W. Colston Leigh wants to manage my lectures.

Book signing at Cody's Book Shop, Berkeley. Ferlinghetti showers me with rose petals.

Saw Raymond and Lynne Weston.

Letter from Anaïs Nin to Hugh Guiler:
Los Angeles, June 13, 1966

Darling:

One reason why I hesitated at the trip to Japan was I could not synchronize it with yours to Europe. Departures of Japan Cultural Society Flights are subject to change—teachers, museum people, their families. There was one I could not make because of commitments in San Francisco and another at the end of the month. We have been separated so long I hesitated to add to it. As it turned out I could have returned to N.Y. but by this time you were leaving. That's why I'm in a quandary. I will call you up before you leave. I am writing while waiting for the Belgian ladies to take me to the airport. Joaquín will meet me in San Francisco.

Called up Gunther. Deals with France OK (Julliard). Italy OK. Spain/Catalan OK. Japanese publisher has money for me for the Miller letters and the *Diary*.

Darling, do you have enough for your trip? I can't understand the overdrawn account. I am so careful. Will stop using the National City account for a while—to clear it up.

Hope you don't have too much to do before leaving.

Peter Owen wants phone interviews! I have no phone—and what an absurd expense—as much as my trip. An interview from London! And not knowing how it would come out. Don't bother to see him. You wasted precious time on him and have little to waste.

When will you be back, darling?

Love,

Anaïs

Letter from Hugh Guiler to Anaïs Nin:
New York, June 15, 1966

Darling:

Looks now as if I may not be back before July 5, so I again urge you not to miss the chance of getting a free trip to Tokyo; we would be together after you return for the rest of the summer.

Love, and let me know your plans,

Hugo

Letter from Anaïs Nin to Oliver Evans:
Los Angeles, June 1966

Dear Oliver:

It seems to me that we get confused when you think I expect praise, and all the time what I am struggling to get is interpretation, not evaluation. That you should declare the novels a failure from an 18th century point of view of what a novel should do does not disturb me, because I know that this has been the source of all the misinterpretations. That a work as large as mine establishes its own point of view is also true. Have I done what I started out to do? I don't mind at all that you should evaluate as you believe. But I do mind when you literally interpret a work that, strangely enough, parallels Carson McCullers only in one respect, that if the surface realism is well done, the allegorical and surrealistic meaning has escaped all the reviewers for that reason.

A Spy in the House of Love could not be filmed because it was treated as a realistic novel. I gave you all the keys I could, not for your final evaluations, but for my intent: I based my work on the labyrinth of the subconscious and on surrealism— what lies above and beyond realism. So the drama takes place there.

Yesterday when you spoke of nymphomania it seemed to me you were being very literal, and if you were, that is not the definition of nymphomania: A nympho- maniac is a woman who, while having an orgasm, nevertheless needs several lovers a day. Not one line in *Spy* indicates such a state.

My novels are not mere novels, they are surrealistic and allegorical. Judged by all of America on a naturalistic Hemingway-ish basis, naturally they failed.

I trusted you as a poet, not as a traditional critic. The end of *Spy* is poetic, not classical drama, or stage drama, or action narrative. The literalness of critics who singled out the "freaks" in Carson's novels were just as much in error as those who spoke of lesbianism, homosexuality, incest, nymphomania, in mine. That was not stated. That I went beyond and above action, above narrative—that was my quest. So please stop your judgments.

Anaïs

Letter from Anaïs Nin to Hugh Guiler:
Los Angeles, June 19, 1966

Darling:

Last night Oliver Evans took me to an Englishman's house for dinner. I never saw as clearly Oliver's total insensitiveness to people, lack of empathy—he was pedantic, rude and perverse—shockingly so. And it crystallized all my impressions (you had them too) of an unfeeling person without insight. I dread reading his book about my work! Oliver got a Fulbright Scholarship to teach one year in Bangkok, but deep down he is dead and does not care about anything.

Today the beach.

It was the uncertainty of the Japan flight that had deterred me, but now that I am ready everybody is giving me advice, guides, addresses, letters of introduction, guidebooks, books to read, one of them Donald Keene's *History of Japanese Literature*. First thing you do is have your card printed in Japanese with your name and profession—very important to the Japanese—professor, writer, etc.

Will send you a night letter when I know the date of departure.

Address c/o Takao Kawade/Chiyoudaku/Tokyo/Japan.

I read that—30 years too late—France has decided that Pierre Jean Jouve was one of the greatest poets and possibly planted the seed of the anti-novel. And I fell under his spell all those years ago!

Love,
A

Letter from Gunther Stuhlmann to Anaïs Nin:
New York, June 20, 1966

Dear Anaïs:

Getting out from under my illness has taken a little longer than I had suspected but most of the things here are running smoothly again.

1. Still awaiting news from two publishers on the *Diary*.

2. Thanks for all the reviews. *The Village Voice* is a beauty. I'll check out the Flemish one for possible quotes.

3. I have some bidding started in Germany on the *Diary* with Fischer, who was here and is back in the race. This should strengthen our hand in dealing with Christian Wegner in Hamburg. They are for a Nin "plan" if we can agree on terms.

4. Japan: Kawade Shobo paid for the Miller letters, which should be coming out this July. Have not signed the contract for the *Diary* yet, so I think it will be best if you take the contract along to Japan for their signature to expedite things. I'll have them drawn up and get them to you before you leave. I think the fact of your arrival there will help expedite things, and you could then collect the money right there in Yen.

Talked to Haydn's office about all the orders that were not fulfilled and they promised to look into it. They claim that these must have come when they were temporarily out of stock before the next printing. I have to order more copies myself as I am all out.

How long will you be in Japan? While you are there you might also talk to them about the other books again. When I saw the Japanese publisher here they said they would like to do the novels but they don't answer direct questions.

IMPORTANT QUESTION: When would you like me to start working on the second diary volume? I want to plan out the rest of the year and if need be I will take off a few weeks to do work on nothing else—if you want me to and if I am required to write another intro, which should be easier this time. Let me know what you think about all this. I can make time and if we want to publish in the spring I should get busy before the summer is over. This time we could also make it a slightly bigger book, no?

Love,
Gunther

Letter from Anaïs Nin to Hugh Guiler:
Los Angeles, June 24, 1966

Darling:
Ready to leave for Japan at a moment's notice.

Hiram wants to sign the new contract before delivery of the MS—apologized for crankiness—sold 7,000 copies to date and no sign of letting up.

I didn't tell Ruth Witt Diamant of going to Japan as she is so possessive, so if she turns up in N.Y. and catches you (I told her you were in Europe to spare you a duty), say I didn't know when I was leaving, that I was on call for a museum trip.

On the 29th I sign books here at Yellow Rose Gallery. I told everyone I would be away one or two months to calm down the mail and invitations because it has been too much and detrimental to my work. The ballyhoo means nothing; only the serious reviews and the emotional letters do.

Jerry Bick says Robert Wise is still interested in *Spy* and in a woman script-writer he likes, and when she returns from England he will see her.

Love,
A

Letter from Hugh Guiler to Anaïs Nin:
Edinburgh, June 26, 1966

Darling:
Here I am after my sudden impulse yesterday morning in Paris. Everyone I knew had left the city, and my bills at the Crillon were running $30 a day without meals. Here they are $10 a day *with* meals, which are good.

The first thing I did was to go over to Edinburgh Academy and arrived about 8:30 PM when I miraculously found the students giving a concert—orchestra and choir. One of the teachers, seeing me looking in, and finding out I was a former student, asked me to come in, sit beside the rector, who, like everyone else here, was

7

very friendly and invited me to come to his office tomorrow morning. The concert, at least much of it, was first class, led by a most talented teacher who himself sang with a fine tenor voice. I spoke to him afterwards and told him how the concert had confirmed my memory of the broadness of the education I had received here. It was probably this, as well as your influence, that gave me my penchant for a variety of interests—artistic as well as practical. But what was important, as I now see better, was that the teachers became my real fathers, so close was the personal relationship with them, and this must have acted as a counterbalance to my Aunt Annie's severity, and explains why the harm she did was not irreparable. I am also trying to find the house where I lived with her, and have already forgiven her, which shows that I feel strong enough in the present. This also explains why I could not return sooner.

Tomorrow I go on for a night and a day in Ayr. Will actually stay at Burns' birthplace, where I lived. I hope I will enjoy it as much as I have enjoyed it here in Edinburgh.

Everyone here speaks with a musical lilt, which, with the friendliness, is very attractive.

I bought a little Instamatic Kodak and have taken quite a few shots.

I hope this reaches you before you leave and that you will have some of our dreams of the Orient achieved.

Bon voyage and all my love,

Hugo

Letter from Anaïs Nin to Hugh Guiler:
Los Angeles, June 30, 1966

Darling:

Last night my book signing at Yellow Rose Gallery—a waiting mob—a line down the street as for a movie star. Sold 70 diaries and 20 other titles—could have sold 100, but people couldn't get in. A blind woman came, who wanted to touch my face and listen to all my readings. Friends gave me gifts, poets their books. It was quite incredible.

So sorry, my darling, to not be home to welcome you and hear all about your trip. Hope you are not tired and that the goal you set for yourself was reached. I wish I could provide you with relaxation now, easing up in your work—not to play the guitar, but to enjoy yourself and save your energy. I am confident now I will never be a burden on you again. I may be able to help you with every expense.

So much to do yet—little things. Bathing and clipping Piccolo. I hope to get mail from you today.

Anaïs

Letter from Anaïs Nin to Hugh Guiler:
Los Angeles, July 1966

Darling—a note before leaving on Japan Air Lines. Will write often—excited by all I have been hearing and reading about Japan!

Gunther sent me the Japanese contract, so I may get 400 dollars while I am there.

Spend the health insurance money any way you like.

Love,

A

P.S. Signed contract with Harcourt Brace for volume 2.

Rupert Pole and Anaïs Nin at Imperial Hotel, Tokyo, 1966

JAPAN, JULY 1966

The beauty of Japan began in the airplane. It appeared in the form of a fan in the pocket of the seat, in the delicate design of the paper napkins and the writing paper. We arrived late, just in time to see the somber silhouette of the Imperial Hotel built by Frank Lloyd Wright.

The next morning I met my publisher, Tomohisa Kawade, only 28 years old and who inherited his publishing house from his father. I met Hideo Aoki: Nobuko had introduced him to me in New York. He speaks English. He too is only 28 years old. They took us to lunch at a Tempura restaurant of the highest quality. The women waited on us with such skill and silence, their footsteps unheard in their white socks.

The talk was laborious, slowed down by translations. Tomohisa Kawade's skin glistened like a woman's, fresh and transparent, his eyes like onyx, and his perpetual smile hospitable, but by our exchange I could not feel I knew him. The chef presided with ceremonious pride. He served fried shrimp, fried mushrooms, fried asparagus, string beans, eggplant.

Rupert delighted everyone by consulting his dictionary and offering the word for *delicious*.

After lunch we were taken to visit the publishing house, a small, intimate house, only two or three floors high. Tea was served in Mr. Kawade's office and we were shown the books that had been published. We admired them, although I found them gaudy in appearance, and the choice of writers from America was very conventional: Salinger, Hemingway. In Miller they seek the opposite of themselves, liberation from form, patterns, disciplines, tradition, elegance, the reserved and formal façade.

In the evening we were initiated to more dimensions in flavors of Japanese food. We were taken to a place where geishas sat next to us, a little bit farther back, and watched our sake cup, filling it each time. And in the empty room beside us they danced and sang, played the three-stringed *shamisen* directed by a governess. We were invited by other editors from the house of Kawade, and my translator, who spoke little English, asked me American-style questions: had I really taken moonbaths and what did I play with as a child. To the last I answered: Japanese dolls.

I told them how my father did not believe in giving us childish books to read and that one of the first books I remember reading was from the series *Voyages Autour du Monde*, one on Japan. I never forgot the illustrations. What I did not say was that during my rebellious years I thought I would not like Japan because of its formalities and discipline, but that after living in formless and uncouth America I found Japan elating. The dinner was a feast for the eyes as well as the palate. Color arrangements and flavors so subtle and so full of surprises, now sweet, now tart, now sharp and bitter, now bland, now stinging, now crunchy, now crackly, now melting and soft. They served cucumbers shaped like flowers, floating mint and tiny fern buds, purple leaves, honeydew on green dishes, fish as glistening as in a pond, tiny daisies in the clear soup.

We left Tokyo quickly. It was noisy, crowded, like any big city. We did visit a temple, which was neglected, the Ueno Park, the Mitsubishi department store and a strip-tease place where the women were beautiful.

We wanted to see Kyoto. It was disappointingly large, but its beauty was soon revealed. It is ringed by mountains. We stayed at the Miyako Hotel, in a Japanese-style room. It was my first experience sleeping on the floor, but the slender mattress was soft and I slept well. Everywhere there were polished floors, clean straw mats, shining lacquer trays, flower arrangements, windows open on the quintessence of gardens. Small and large trees, small and large stones. Green tea. White kimonos under black muslin transparent ones. Half the women in kimonos, half in Western dress. In Western dress they lose their charm.

Then we began visiting temples and gardens. In the Nijo Castle we saw a most amazing thing. The floor wood was linked underneath by hooks of metal in such a way that when people walked over it, it emitted a pleasantly musical tinkling sound to warn the Shogun of the approach of an enemy. As he ruled by power, he was hated. Walking on the beautiful floor with bare feet and hearing the floor singing like a nightingale was amazing. Even in the case of fear, hatred, danger, to express it by a pleasant chime-like sound! The courtiers wore long, long trousers, twice as long as a man that we had seen in the Japanese art films, impeding the walk very much as a Spanish dancer's long train might trip her, and which was always skillfully manipulated and intertwined. The courtiers were thereby hampered, and if they assassinated the Shogun they could not run away.

They planted many gingko trees because they do not burn easily, and fire is the nightmare of Japan that has destroyed many of their most beautiful wooden temples and castles.

The women of Japan are at once the most present and the most elusive inhabitants of any country I have seen. They are everywhere, in restaurants, streets, shops, museums, subways, trains, fields, hotels and inns, and yet achieve a self-effacement that is striking to foreign women. In the hotels and inns they are solicitous, thoughtful, helpful to a degree never dreamed of except by men, but this care and tender lavishness is equally given to women visitors. It was as if one's dream of an ever-attentive, ever-protective mother were fulfilled on a collective scale, only the mother is forever young and daintily dressed. They were laborious and yet quiet, efficient and yet not intrusive or cumbersome.

Being invited to Japan by my publisher and being a writer, I was allowed at the geisha restaurant where patrons are usually men only. A geisha kneeled or stood behind each guest, and my geisha noticed I did not know how to handle my fish with my chopsticks, so she operated on it with amazing skills. She first softened the fish with pressure from the chopsticks, and then suddenly pulled the entire bone clean and free. All this in an exquisite dress with floating sleeves which would paralyze a Western woman. Another geisha brought me her scarf to sign: "I have read Hemingway," she said. "He signed my scarf when I was fifteen years old."

They stood before you not a moment longer than necessary, and not one of them seemed to be saying: "Look at me. I am here." How they carried trays and served food and listened seemed a miraculous triumph over clumsiness, perspiration, heaviness. They had conquered gravitation.

Dressed as they were, in fresh, starched, embroidered kimonos, with their hair in the high classical coiffure, lacquered and neat, with their white socks and new sandals, it hurt me to see them follow us out into the street, in the rain, and bowing low until we drove away.

Outside of Tokyo, I saw them in their geisha quarter, rushing to their assignments, exquisitely dressed, the sleeves floating like the wings of butterflies.

I saw the women at work in factories. They wore blue denim kimonos, shabby from use but clean. They kneeled with their legs under them, at work with the same precision of gestures as their more glamorous counterparts. Their hair was not lacquered or worked into high chignons, but neatly braided.

The modern, emancipated Japanese women remained in Tokyo. During the rest of the trip the women I saw seemed to please the eye, to answer miraculously the need for a drink. Their costumes bound them, but their gestures remained light and airy, transcending the tightness of the obi. Their feet were as light as those of ballet dancers.

In the fields, the peasant women at work presented the same harmonious dress of coarse, dark blue denim uniforms, which were elegant even when worn out. The straw hat and the basket were uniform, and the women worked with such order in their alignment that it seemed like a beautifully designed group dance. I watched them pick up weeds, in a row, on their knees, with baskets beside them, and they pulled in rhythm, without deviations or fumblings. The women weeded gardens while the men took care of the trees or cleaned the ponds of surplus water lilies.

The softness, the all-enveloping attentiveness of the women. I thought of Japanese films, in which their delicacy could turn into fierceness if challenged, in which they startled you with a dagger or even a sword at times. What kind of woman would emerge from the deep, the masked, long-hidden Japanese woman of old? The whole mystery of the Japanese woman lay behind her smooth face, which rarely showed age except perhaps in peasant women battered by nature. But the childhood smoothness remained far into maturity.

The thoughtfulness could not be a mask, I thought, it seemed so natural; it seemed like a genuine sensitiveness to others. It seemed to come from identification and empathy.

Although my publishers were 28 years old, they did not introduce me to their wives. The wives were not invited to share in any of the dinners we had in restaurants or visits to the Noh plays and Kabuki. To console myself I collected a large number of novels, thinking I would then become more intimate with the feelings and thoughts of Japanese women. It was a woman, Lady Murasaki, who wrote the first novel and the first diary in the year [1000], and although the novel is a Proustian work of subtle and elaborate detail, and the feelings and thoughts of the personages at court are described, the woman herself remains an image. The works of modern Japanese women writers are not translated. And the novels, as a whole, did not bring me any closer to the Japanese woman. The same element of selflessness enters the novels. Very few of the women are dominant or self-assertive. There is a strong tendency to live according to the code, the mores, the religious or cultural rules. To live for a collective ideal. The one who breaks away is described as a monster of evil.

The children presented a different mystery: the mystery of discipline and love being dosed in such balance that they appeared as the most spontaneous children I had ever seen, and at the same time the best behaved. They were lively, cheerful, charming, outgoing, expressive and free, but their freedom never ended in sullenness or anarchy. I witnessed a meeting of Japanese schoolchildren being guided through a museum, who came upon an American child of their own age. They surrounded him gaily, twittering and speaking the few words of English they knew. The American child looked sullen, suspicious and withdrawn.

Through the gardens and the museums, they were responsive, curious. Their gayety was continuous but contained. In Kyoto, during the Gion Festival, which lasts for several hours, the children were everywhere but they did not disrupt the ceremony. They showed the most amazing combination of spontaneity and discipline. The heat did not wilt them, the crowd did not dirty them, their clothes did not wrinkle. Had they learned so early to defeat slovenliness and ill humor, to emerge fresh and gracious from the most wearing day? I thought of the gardens of Japan, the order, the stylization, the control of nature, so that they presented only an aesthetically perfect image. Had the Japanese achieved this miracle of aesthetic perfection? No weeds, no dead leaves, no disorder, no tangles, no withered flowers, no mud-splattered paths?

In Kyoto, after a day of the most lyrical and poetic beauty, after seeing the Golden Pavilion, which is unearthly and like a living fairytale, we went to a small, shady theater with a big stage. It was filled with young men (only one old man as in *Odd Obsession*). On the left side of the stage an orchestra played jazz badly. On the right there were mirrors and gauze curtains. In the center of the stage extended a ramp. The women came out in gaudy caricatures of Ziegfeld Follies costumes, feathers, Spanish and Gypsy dresses. Only one was in a traditional kimono. They danced badly, stripteased badly, but at the end came forward absolutely nude and began a series of poses to show their sexual parts, opening the labia with their fingers, and squatting a few inches away from the young men's faces who had gathered by the ramp. All of them pressed forward to see. One woman who looked like a beautiful female Buddha, not fat but voluptuous, exposed herself nonchalantly with an impassive, mask-like face. She lay on her side, with one leg stretched out, the other bent. If the young men came too close she ruffled her hair playfully. The young men were curious but quiet, cheerful, not vulgar and showed none of the Westerner's contempt or shame. But the last woman in her kimono let one of the young men unwind her sash, and she rubbed herself under the dress as if itchy, impatient. Laughingly, she stripped and slipped into a gauzy, transparent kimono. Then she came forward on the ramp and not only raised her very long, very black pubic hair, but opened the labia and inserted two fingers as if masturbating, shaking them inside. Then she brought her fingers to her nose, smelled them and then shook them as if to get rid of the drops clinging to them. She performed this partly on the right side of the stage where it was reflected in the mirror, and partly on the ramp where the young men could watch her.

This sight, superimposed upon my vision of the Golden Pavilion, which I could not forget—so serene, so golden, so fragile, so utterly beautiful—was one of the most extreme paradoxes I had ever experienced between aesthetics and animalism. The squatting of the women divested them of poetry; their exposure was almost clinical in its thoroughness. It was later, while reading the *Temple of the Golden Pavilion* that I came upon a similar juxtaposition. The monk is haunted by the Golden Pavilion. He visualizes it while visiting prostitutes. It interfered, he felt, with his animalism, and it rendered him impotent. He burned the temple, as if its destruction could have helped him accept his own physical ugliness and the coarseness of his desires. The beauty of the striptease women was admirable, but it was not erotic.

While in Tokyo we took the train to Yokohama to visit the Sex Shop described by the Willcox guidebook. From the owner's mimicry and broken English we learned his father had been put in jail, and the items we were interested in (among them a music-playing ball to be inserted in the vagina) were now all prohibited, but there were stimulants, pills to enlarge the penis, and we came away with a few colored condoms and a bar of stimulating chocolate.

Rupert was a skillful, active traveler. He took over the difficult tasks of reading maps, planning small trips, arranging tours, consulting the dictionary, gathering information. Alone, I would have settled in Kyoto and lived as deeply as I could my Japanese life. Alone I would have worked on the Diary and visited Japanese friends. I would have seen less, but more attentively. But Rupert wanted to see more— exploratory trips, he called them. By the time we left Japan we were hopelessly in love with it. No other country seemed as wonderful. It set a standard for good taste, architecture, food and personality. Japan was a unity. It had more meaning and more depth.

It made Thailand seem gaudy; Cambodia a sad dream of the past, asleep; Hong Kong vulgar; Singapore shoddy.

At Singapore we wanted to stay at the Raffles Hotel because of Somerset Maugham's legend, but it was full. We stayed at a cheap hotel that reminded me of Mexico, Cuba, Spain—a fan as big as an airplane propeller turning over our heads, mosquitoes, noises, shutters, tile floors, shaky plumbing, poor reading lights, infernally noisy streets. We took a rickshaw-tricycle and felt in danger of death, had lunch at the Raffles Hotel, a cold deluxe affair, a buffet, marvelous waiters, marvelous food, air conditioning, English, formal, but American tourists trampled tradition and appeared in shorts and loose Hawaiian shirts. I looked in on the bar where Maugham heard stories, wondered how much he really saw, heard, did, experienced.

The next day we discovered a beach and a hotel on the beach—trees. The night before we had walked through crowded street markets and saw a medley of races and costumes, saw the most beautiful Indian girl, unbelievably perfect, saw sarongs, Chinese pajamas, Western delinquent costumes.

Nature was sweeter in Malaysia than in Cambodia, where the rain forest is oppressive, large and without gaiety. Penang was full of flowers. The great rubber plantations and the houses were not sumptuous by American standards, but by Malaysian standards.

The beauty of the Malaysian women surpassed those of Japan, Cambodia and Thailand, because added to a perfect form was a tropical languor, a voluptuous motion. Waists very slender, hips full, lovely skin and hair, brilliant soft eyes. The hostess wore a *batik* dress—the fitted bodice, long-sleeved, and a sarong skirt. But she moved with her tray as if she were turning or undulating in bed on a hot afternoon, half-dreaming, half-prepared for caresses.

In Cambodia there were roots and powerful trees, but no flowers. The mood of Angkor Wat was dramatic, fierce. The mood of Penang was sweet. Thailand was sugary sweet.

Memories—no time for full writing. Hong Kong. The sail of a sampan. The children in Aberdeen begging, lively like Mexican children, but rapacious, fiercely poor. The woman who pushed the boat that took us to the floating restaurant in

Aberdeen used a pole twice as long as our oars. The floating restaurant was a monstrosity in red and green paint. While you eat luxuriously you watch thousands in the boats who show their hunger on their faces—the refugees from Communist China—three generations on a boat together, a woman pushing or holding the till while the men fished.

At the Hong Kong station we met Yonie, who was well-dressed and waiting for us at the airport as if he were a representative from our hotel—he paid the tip for the baggage and our taxi. But he was not sent by the hotel. Then he introduced himself. He was a tailor and asked if we wanted suits and dresses made. He called us every day, intercepted us when we walked out of the hotel. Yonie was a super salesman.

The streets were bedlam, the shops so full and so tricky that it took the pleasure out of shopping. But Rupert made me buy a blouse of ivory silk. I prefer the Malaysian skirt, which is long and graceful. I bought one at Antoinette's in Singapore.

Swimming in the Indian Ocean. The effect of history and legend and literature is so strong that it illumines and transforms. With closed eyes would I have known it was the Indian Sea? In old cultures you are immersed in the souls of the past.

I would gladly see it all again—only more slowly. I love the tropics with a passion—I am physically attuned to the great heat, to *grillons* [crickets], to odors and colors and lushness.

We returned to Japan—but always Rupert went too fast, was too greedy. He had to be on the go. We landed in Nara and he went off to shoot the rapids. We were in Kyoto and he left to visit Ise. I wanted to taste more deeply. But thanks to his restlessness, energy, curiosity and endurance, I saw much more—the jungles of Malaysia, the Indian Ocean at Pesiang, and we took long journeys by bus through Japan's southern landscape.

The Japanese were interested in Rupert's understanding of politics, history. I wanted him to get recognition as I did and led interviews to his informative mind on a subject that interests the Japanese. He talked about William Fulbright's speech and the Americans who were against the war in Vietnam. I did not want to be fêted alone as a writer. Rupert felt he had a role to play, but when my Japanese publisher gave him a model of a samurai headgear, and we were drinking together, tired, and talking over our day, he repeated: "I don't deserve it, I am not worthy." He was overwhelmed. He could not enjoy the solicitude of the Japanese hostess at the inn, who sat near us and was ready to help us in the art of eating Japanese food.

———

LOS ANGELES, JULY 20, 1966

Oliver Evans gave me the manuscript of his study of my work before I left, which I read on the way back from Japan. I was crushed by his lack of understanding. We exchanged bitter letters. He determined that I wanted his praise. He betrayed me because I let him interview me. He had all the collaboration he needed. But he used his Victorian academic point of view. I was appalled at the wasted time.

The Library of Congress asked me for a gift of the diary originals. I answered that this was the only capital I had because recognition had come so late and royalties are barely enough to live on.

When I returned from our fabulous fairytale trip I heard Eve Miller had died. I was sad. She was beautiful and talented. What happened? Henry said she was an alcoholic and that when she drank she was the opposite of the lovely self she was when sober. She took antibiotics for a cold with a whole bottle of gin. Did she want to die?

LOS ANGELES, SEPTEMBER 1966

In New York, Nobuko joined the Noh Theatre, and she writes and talks about its meaning, the inherited tradition of the Noh Master, the incredibly severe discipline, and how the discipline broke down in America.

I saw many friends in New York, including Mary Weir and Jerzy Kosinski.

I met May, a dangerous adventuress known all over Europe, once married to a wealthy man and who entertained all the celebrities. The husband repudiated her. In Italy she was a procuress. She knew Gore Vidal, Tennessee Williams, etc. She told a story about Gore. He was so eager that people should believe he made love to women (I know he never did) that it became a game for prostitutes or women who attended orgies. They would claim that Gore made them pregnant and got money for an abortion. She was full of such tales. She came as an interviewer, but in reality to beg for help. Once she called for me downstairs in the lobby at 9:00 AM. She had a black eye and obviously had been beaten. She talked about Kosinski, a group who had indulged in sadism. Finally this underworld repelled me and I severed the connection. She wanted credit for introducing me to Kosinski and Mary Weir.

The past has not left any bitterness or revengefulness. I face the love and tributes I receive with pleasure. I am as if a new woman, reborn with the publication of the *Diary*. This new woman is at ease in the world, because whatever shyness is left over from the past is helped by the fact that when I enter a room or a lecture hall, people know me already and they rush towards me. The warmth creates a climate in which I can open up, return the love, respond.

Georgiana Peacher: the problem with her is similar to mine with the *Diary*—people magnify our friendship beyond its genuine size. I hate to disappoint or hurt. I feel ungenerous not to be able to return in the same amount, with the same temperature.

We went to the beach with Dorothy Brodin. She is so vivid, full of life, and her husband Pierre is the very opposite. She loves to sail, to swim. He is an indoor, scholarly man, pale from reading books as I was at 16, 17, 18. The library pallor.

I saw Dr. Goldstein, who is psychologically depressing. I respected him because he is scholarly and reads musical scores. But he is overly watchful and creates anxiety. He over-watched Hugo until he almost made an invalid of him.

Roger Bloom is free from prison at last.

Editing volume 2, copying, numbering.

Meeting with Henry Miller about what concerns him in volume 2.

Letter from Joaquín Nin-Culmell to Anaïs Nin:
San Francisco, November 6, 1966

Dear Anaïs:

Have just written to Hugh and hope that my letter will clear up whatever misunderstanding you seem to feel has arisen. I know that Hugh knows how much I admire and love him and hence he must know that my [investment] questions are never doubts. He has taught me to question, and, as I wrote to him, I have learned my lesson well.

Looking forward to receiving the new diary manuscript and I will work on it with all of the admiration and love you can suppose. Thank you for suggesting that I fill in some additional information about my activities. Will do so if it suits and fits the text. I would hate to put hairs in your soup! In any case, many thanks for your confidence and many thanks for thinking of me as you do. You and Hugh must realize that any praise from either one of you is honey to my ears... I feel now as if all the bees in the world are trying to get into my ears!!

Working hard but more on my classes than on my music. Had the pleasure of hearing some of my piano *Tonadas* played superbly by a Spanish pianist called Alicia de Larrocha. Terrific. She is a tiny dynamo but with power and musicianship to spare. You would like her.

Nothing else to report. Raining and cold here, but the apartment is still most pleasant. Hope that you can see it sometime.

All my love,
Joaquín

Los Angeles, December 1966

I heard about Alan Swallow's death just after Thanksgiving Day. He died at his desk. Heart attack. Very affected by his death because he represented a unique attitude in publishing, a unique integrity. He was a unique human being, as poet, as writer, as publisher. There are only a few human beings who cannot be replaced. There was only one Alan Swallow.

Began work on volume 3.

Visit from Varda. He came with three young women—dancers—the Three Graces. The young love him. One young man learning to be a chef is working for him. Varda looks ruddy and strong although he had a stroke. He tells me this stroke delivered him of the fear of death. "I saw wonderful colors, like an LSD vision. It was beautiful. I had no sense of parting from the world, just dissolving in color."

Made friends with Dr. Félix Martí Ibañez, editor of *MD* magazine. I visited him. I told him *MD* had been my education. Dr. Ibañez has immense knowledge; he writes on every subject imaginable. He was wounded fighting against Franco and exiled from Spain. Came to America. Practiced psychiatry. Evolved the clever, successful *MD* magazine, which is sent free to all the doctors. The advertisers pay. But the magazine is full of articles on travel, biography, history, literature, essays on films, on personalities. I met his woman assistants.

Letter from Anaïs Nin to Lawrence Durrell:
Los Angeles, December 5, 1966

Dear Larry:

Stopped in the middle of copying such a beautiful letter from you written during the war from Greece, because I was once more pained by the great change in you towards me and would like to understand it before it is recorded in later diaries as a mystery. (Such a beautiful letter. I would like to quote it in *Diary* volume 3—working on it now—but I imagine you may want to edit some of it.)

The great contrast between your opinions, reactions, understanding and deep friendship, and later attitudes. In the *Diary* of 1934-1939, as I told you, all is trust and understanding. What happened?

When I became for a few years estranged from Henry, after he moved to Big Sur, everything connected with him was painful, and I felt he was essentially your friend and you his, and I ceased writing to you. Did I offend you then? I cannot believe the mere dislike of my novels could create such a chasm. Did you feel I had deserted you? In Paris when I invited you to come and see me, did I offend you by saying it could not be the Crillon because the Crillon bill was paid by Hugo's company, not by me, and was not within my means? By the time I came to visit you [in 1958] there was a wall of some kind. Vague remarks.

You thought I had been unkind to Henry (from the *Diary* you can see I was not). I tried not to see the misunderstandings, but they appeared clear when you wrote the parody of a preface [for *Children of the Albatross*] that so wounded me. And even then I thought perhaps you had disliked my books. But now the *Diary* has been published, the same diary you loved so much before, and you find nothing to love, nothing to respond to, you find only flaws in cuts which were humanly necessary …you are concerned about Fred Perlès, but were you concerned when Fred wrote such an absurd story of my relationship to Henry? Did you worry then about whether he was just? I think I was very kind to him. He caused me great humiliation and almost destroyed all my protection of Hugo.

You recently wrote to me about my vulnerability. You thought I had left it out as well as humor, playfulness, but in Paris you spoke of the tragic quality of my diary and did not expect comedy. If you know about the vulnerability, how could you then do everything which could possibly wound it? *Mystère.*

The second visit I paid you I felt something wrong. Tell me what happened. I know (I found out by accident) *The New York Times* asked you to write about the *Diary* and you refused. Henry did too. But Henry felt he was too close to it, too involved. Friends who visit you tell me of your reserved comments on me. Others bring me your love. The Three Musketeers, Henry, yourself and me; later it is Fred who claims to be the third.

Please be truthful, dear Larry, for the sake of the old sincerity. I do not wish to record sad changes, betrayals, some misunderstanding. Is it my fault? Have I been remiss?

I had hoped we would have a talk, but it looks as if I would not come to Europe again. I have found greater affinities with Japan, a deeper relationship with its writers, critics.

I thought you understood the human motivations for what I could not tell. Close friends were happy that I could publish any part at all, knowing otherwise the *Diary* would have been buried for fifty years.

Won't you take the time and patience to clarify and restore a friendship that was so precious to me?

Anaïs

NEW YORK, JANUARY 1967

New Year's Eve, Los Angeles: Rupert and I alone, by the fire. A bottle of champagne. My hand-made white wool rug I worked on in France, on which we lie and make orgiastic love.

So I arrived in New York on January 2nd—went straight from the airplane to the hospital. A recurrence of Hugo's hepatitis, a recurrence of days spent in Doctor's Hospital keeping him company, of myself being gravely ill. Hugo looks pale, but has no pain. It is a matter of rest, patience. He reads Konrad Laurent's *On Aggression.*

For three weeks, up at seven, working on last-minute revisions to volume 2, translating *clochard,* finding spellings of the language spoken by the Incan who wrote *Du Sang, de la Volupté et la Mort,* translating *merle blanc* [white blackbird], learning how to spell Dostoevsky. Errands for Hugo. Telephone calls to hospital room 631. What do you need? Stamps. Ginger beer. Envelopes. A file case. I arrive at Doctor's Hospital after lunch, loaded. I sit down with my work if Hugo is asleep— or we talk.

NEW YORK, JANUARY 5, 1967

At eight o'clock I go to St. Mark's church, to the Parish Hall, where a few writers meet to pay homage to Alan Swallow who died at his desk during Thanksgiving. A unique man, a man of integrity and courage. Walter Lowenfels reads poetry. Natalie Robbins is young and sweet.

Friday workmen replace the kitchen floor tiles. Millicent is home. She can no longer work—73 years old and arthritic legs. It was a difficult break. Vera has replaced her. Russian, 63, old-fashioned servant, obedient, humble, fanatically clean. We give Millicent a pension. We talk over the phone. Vera is neat—fat— wears a braided chignon over her hair, has innocent blue eyes and says her prayers before eating. She comes straight out of the Moscow Art Theatre.

I see Dr. Bogner. Hugo's illness always triggers an attack of guilt.

I talk with Marguerite Young. She complains of loneliness, but she is in a *cabine étanche* [impenetrable den] in her self-created world. People do not exist except as fictional. I am fictional. I am her beautiful mother, but giving her the attention and affection her real mother did not.

On Sunday, January 8, I go to a Sunday brunch at Erika Freeman's. She is a beautiful Viennese woman with a delicate face and voluptuous body. Her husband is a strong, colorful painter with the head of a prophet—a well-fed, content, earthly prophet. From there I go to see Hugo.

NEW YORK, JANUARY 10, 1967

I see Gunther. I take Varda's latest drawings to an art book publisher.

I meet Nobuko for lunch. She wears a black sweater with emerald-green stripes and a green velvet bow in her hair. She wears a sailor's coat—and she looks fragile. Ivan Morris is trapping her into a possessive, rigid relationship, into all that she was struggling to escape. I try to free her. "You can't grow with so many restrictions," I told her.

NEW YORK, JANUARY 12, 1967

Lunch with Hiram Haydn. He behaves gallantly, but I cannot forget that in the spring when we met at the Algonquin and I brought him Karl Shapiro's beautiful review of the *Diary*, he said, "I wish someone would write like this about *my* writing." The editor is displaced by the unsuccessful writer.

After the hospital I have dinner at Bettina Knapp's. She is writing a book about Artaud. She is intelligent and wrote about Louis Jouvet and Yvette Guilbert. She is a shrewd and meticulous biographer. It was Bettina, during her first visit with me, who solved the mystery of my quarrel with Artaud. I was telling her how it came about. I had returned from the South of France where I had celebrated my reunion with my father. I was telling Artaud about it when he burst into a tirade about the monstrosity of this love. A preacher's curse upon an unnatural love! I was offended by his moral judgment. He was at the time filled with his play about the Cencis—and so, Bettina said, he could only see what filled his own consciousness: Beatrice Cenci and incestuous love. He no longer saw me, but Beatrice Cenci. Yes, I knew this, but I didn't know why this had caused such anger in me. For him the unconscious *was* the truth. Clairvoyance. He read my story of unconscious, symbolic love.

NEW YORK, JANUARY 13, 1967

Talk with Henry Wenning, the rare book and manuscript collector, about the diary originals. If Hugo stops working I will have to sell them. In 1966 I earned $9,500 and spent about $3,000. It is not enough to take care of Hugo.

That evening dinner with Michael and Frances Field, Leo Lerman, and Jack Gelber.

Leo Lerman described his childhood at the end of one of Michael Field's lyrical dinners—Michael and I were listening while Leo ate several helpings of an incandescent dessert.

Leo's grandfather was a rabbi who said he came from Moscow (Leo later found out he came from Latvia but preferred to say Moscow). He was a terrifying old man—high-brimmed yarmulke, beard, sideburns, black suit—oscillating between religious moral fervor and tyranny and cruelty, prayers and beatings. The family lived in a brownstone house in the East 90s—the grandfather and all his children and grandchildren, besides other relatives who came from Russia. The newly-arrived young relatives worked, and so the household was well-served. No English spoken. Leo was born a blue baby who had to be spanked into breathing—he was frail and not expected to live. No one knew how the household survived or where the relatives worked. The grandfather went out, but Leo did not know where, except when he took him along to explore antique shops on Third Avenue and collect incredible objects as if to recover the lost land of Russia, as if to return into the past. Leo remembered most of all the collection of cut glass. Often one of the children would dream of escaping, would leave, but soon return, unable to survive in the outside world. Leo's own mother once left with Leo and a bag filled with her cut glass collection, but soon returned. Leo was placed in schools, which he hated, falling on the floor with convulsions; his mother was called to take him home. The household was filled with the best music as everybody played the piano, was filled with books too. Leo was filled with learning but spoke no English until he was five or six. One of the young nieces was using matches in the kitchen. She set herself on fire and ran towards all the children and died before their eyes. The grandfather came in, and all he said was: "See what happens when you play with matches?" Days of festivities when they went to the opera or to concerts. A world of their own. An aunt took Leo to a dance hall and danced, was found out and beaten by the grandfather. The couple who came home after midnight was beaten. Leo placed himself so vividly in his story that I could see him, small and frail with burning dark eyes, a Marcel Marceau art theatre face, caught between cruelties and pleasures, tea and hearty food and fires and whims and ardor and Russian excesses, and born in this was his gift for storytelling.

Jack Gelber was dressed in Edwardian style, narrow pants, narrow shoulders, wearing a jacket that seemed to belong to a younger brother, and always talked in a style of his own so that all he said seemed to have never been heard before and was unexpected. He was not, as I had expected, a tough person. With the hair curling behind his ears, and his eyes very round, he looked almost romantic—he was the author of *The Connection* and *The Brig*. We talked about Julien and Judith Beck, always about a disintegrated yet indestructible life, touring Europe without money, designing new plays without material, costumes without textiles.

His wife wore a minidress of grass-green wool, with a halter design that left arms and most of the shoulders and ribs exposed. She wore white lace stockings, prompting one to seek the garter line but discovering that they continued to become pants. Her eyes were painted in an ironic slant. She was dressed as neither woman nor child but some sprite playing with the body like a new collage, stressing new pieces, new assemblage, new focus, new allurements, part-masquerade, part-theatre, part-Roxy's ballet. Jack had frightening fingertips—wide and thick. An original mind off focus.

Leo had not written about the *Diary* for *Mademoiselle* as he had promised, but it inspired him to write his new book in that form—a book on antiques in England. "I became bored with it as a book and decided to turn it into a journal."

Edmund Wilson, too, was inspired by the *Diary* to do some of his own editing. Over the telephone admitted he had enjoyed the *Diary* very much but would make no comment—he no longer made any comments for anyone!

New York, January 14, 1967

I worked on the curtains for the apartment, worked on the Diary and visited Hugo. I felt depressed by his illness. I fed a nonchalant cat instead of an emotional Piccolo.

New York, January 15, 1967

Kept Hugo company—worked on the Diary in the hospital room, looked at the same river I watched when I was ill. Had dinner with the Brodins in a Japanese restaurant, which only made me long for Japan. Pierre Brodin looked devitalized, and their apartment was old-fashioned—the only gay notes were paintings from Haiti and a marvelous Siamese cat who lies on Dorothy's shoulder.

New York, January 16, 1967

Dr. Goldstein checked on my five gallstones to see how they were behaving.

No alarming changes. At six I talked with Bogner. I cannot change or control my desperate irritation with Hugo—and I hate myself for it.

At lunch Nobuko translated a beautiful letter from my Japanese translator Mr. Nakada and part of the long interview I had with Ōe Kenzaburō, which was published in its entirety.

New York, January 17, 1967

Hugo is getting better each day. Had a phone call from Barbara Turner who is working on the script of *Spy* for Robert Wise. Jerry Bick rattles her, interferes, wants to be the writer. She is only 28. I try to solidify her. Bill Barker calls up. He has finished a novel and spent seven months in a Greek jail for possession of hashish.

New York, January 21, 1967

Hugo came home at last.

In the evening Jack Jones and Vicki Lipton came. I had been corresponding with Jack Jones about Rank, and in response he wrote a review of the *Diary* in which he called me Lady Murasaki and which reached me when I was sailing on the *S.S. Murasaki* through the Inland Sea of Japan! Vicki Lipton also had written a review I liked, and we became friends. Jack Jones is deaf and has to read lips. He also has trouble with his eyes. But he is spirited, warm, dynamic, makes such great efforts to communicate. I was moved by his aliveness breaking through such barriers. He types his letters in capitals. He wrote the biography of Rank for a reference book.

His friendship was Maxwell Geismar's only gift to me because when the *Diary* came out Max was silent, and it was his only chance to make up for his shabby treatment of the novels. I had sought a reconciliation after I heard that he had been pained by the quarrel and had been very ill. But when I asked him about his silence, he answered that I have received *too much* praise!

Sunday Hugo and I took our familiar walk through the Village. Hugo's paleness worried me.

New York, January 23, 1967

Nobuko and I have lunch together. We discuss Ivan Morris's tyranny and possessiveness. For the first time the smooth, lovely face betrays anxiety. Her ambiguities remain invisible. She says: "Anaïs, may I ask you a brutal question? How did you and Hugo become free?" After answering her, I said: "Nobuko, may I ask you a brutal question? Do you have a grand passion for Ivan?"

"No, Anaïs."

"Well, then to be imprisoned with a grand passion is good and bearable, but otherwise it will merely give you claustrophobia."

She asked Ivan if she married him, could she get up at 6:00 AM to work on her novel. Ivan said no one could stir in the home until 9:00 AM—when he got up. He wants her to give up her job with Toho, give up entertaining producers (part of her work to affect the American exchange of plays with Japan), lecturing and teaching.

New York, January 24, 1967

I spent hours at the Brooklyn vault, filing letters and photographs.

Evening with Annette and James Baxter. They are Henry James characters. She is a vital Armenian with a refined intellect. Henry Miller introduced me to them because they helped June—he as a psychiatrist, together as friends, her "family." When we feared June's reaction to the *Diary* I went to see them. We felt instantaneous friendship. They read the diary manuscript, and I told them I would consider June's feelings. They felt I was not unjust to her in my portrait. They exerted great influence over her—controlled her. When she did react badly, the Baxters softened her. There was a moment of danger when a psychotic man called Dick met June and tried to tape her story—but she stopped after a while.

The friendship between me and the Baxters—lively, literary, human, sparkling—must remain unknown to June because they are her refuge.

Annette would have liked to write about me.

We had a gay dinner at an Armenian restaurant. Annette is teaching a course about women in the history of literary criticism. James is precise and a curious mixture of gentleman of the South, New England, pedantic in a charming, ironic way. A slender, stylized man—she is voluptuous and vital.

New York, January 25, 1967

I took a bus to Princeton where Anita Faatz met me and drove me to her home in Doyleston Bucks County. She and Virginia Robinson (83 years old) are retired from the Philadelphia Social School, where Rank taught, and are devoting their time to the Rank Society. A neat, clean house in a clearing, overlooking a pond and forest—a house filled with books, Rank's photograph on the table, a copy of the journal in which they printed a section of the *Diary*. We talked about Rank—their memories and mine. Complications prevent his books from being reprinted. I felt badly because Miss Robinson was at the Cité Univeristaire when I, in the *Diary*, described the lectures as tiresome and could not continue although Rank wanted me there. I felt I had been superficial in mocking the dullness of the classes.

The peace and scholarliness of the atmosphere pleased me—the meditative bus ride—but I felt depressed. Is it sad to see people seeking to sustain a man's work, to keep his ideas alive? I don't know why I felt heavy-hearted. Should I have sacrificed my writing to Rank's writing, my life to his work?

It was a foggy night as I returned to New York—so many busses, so many people, no time to *see* a face…so many faces.

How often we make this circular journey into the past, linking fragments of an incomplete puzzle, seeing a finished image. What emerges is the change in our vision, the changes in our character, the errors, the blind spots. As we make the return journey, it is not only to pass judgment on our past selves, but also to crystallize, reinforce, consolidate what we have gained. I see today what I could not see in the '30s when the intellectual life was ignored in favor of passion. I was only interested in love, not in psychology. It was only after the passion was over that I could clearly see the work of Rank and join forces with Anita and Virginia. I gave Rank a fiery moment—they are working for his immortality.

But this fragment was not wasted. Rank's work was part of his seduction. It outlived the seduction. A life is then a composite that finally reveals its meaning, its purpose. It was not an error to be cast out. It became a synthesis worth keeping. So we pick up what looks like a stone, a broken shell on the edge of the sea, and upon closer inspection is it a sculptured work of art.

NEW YORK, JANUARY 27, 1967

Lunch with Hilda Lindley—a lively, intelligent, vivid woman, head of publicity at Harcourt. A glowing, sparkling face—handsome. She tells me not to expect as much star billing for the second volume. Second volumes never receive as much attention. She asked, "What we can do to attract attention?" I said, "Let's have a party on a houseboat. In June it will be warm. The Gotham Book Mart will be hot and stuffy—not enough room." Mrs. Lindley thought it was a wonderful idea: "If I find one in the Yellow Pages." Our lunches are always lively. She feels it is easy to work with me, that I do not have a prima donna's tautness or exigencies.

It was morning. I had errands to do—shopping for Stephan Chodorov and his wife. He is so brilliant. This generation is gifted and unconventional. He travels to Yugoslavia on an assignment with his wife and baby. He is interested in LSD. They read widely, deeply. He is aware of past, present and the future. He visits Ezra Pound. He can read the *Diary* with gusto. He does his job, plans the programs—but dreams of other subjects, themes.

NEW YORK, JANUARY 28, 1967

I went alone to Marguerite Young's party. I don't know if it was my mood or her choice of friends, but I lived through a caricatural evening of detachment and distortion. Tom Harshman tells me how much he loves the *Diary*. I like him. I knew him first as a fairytale boy living with Stanley Haggart. He looked transparent, German. He painted and wrote. I remember when he stopped loving Stanley and fell in love with a girl from Germany. It happened in Harlem before my eyes. Then the luminousness went out of his face, and he became a successful designer, wrote a novel about Haitian folk tales, wrote another novel, became Marguerite's student and friend, had a child…but the *light*, where is this mysterious *light* that disappears —who extinguishes it, what kills it? His face is pale, tired. The eyes are pale. The *Diary* makes him feel intimacy, warmth.

I want to talk to the priests from Fordham, but I am detained by a friend of Truman Capote, who is drunk, who sticks to me, and an angry woman who attacks me—"So you are Anaïs Nin. I hate women who tell all."

"Perhaps because you have nothing to tell, or may not know *how* to tell it!" (I remember Proust getting out of bed to visit a friend to ask what kind of flower she wore on her hat 20 years before…)

I am not the first to track down a figure, complete a story, pursue a *dénouement*. I'm only excited when I find a clue that leads me to a new facet or a new version of a story… I live for the Diary.

I am not happy in Marguerite's apartment. It is like a child's room, a gypsy cart, a wax museum, all that a child dreams of—balloons, merry-go-round horses, red walls, dolls, tin soldiers, shells, angels, chimes, crystal balls, doll houses.

Marguerite's childhood. Her mother was very pretty, spoiled, not intelligent, shallow. Her father was scholarly and brilliant. The mother went off with another man, not even leaving a note for Marguerite's father. He then married a Greek woman. He had other children, two of whom are Marguerite's half-brothers, one a scientist, the other in politics. The mother married several times, lived in fantasy. Marguerite was brought up by a grandmother—unloved—in a dream world.

Outside it is snowing. I walk very fast along Bleeker St. on a Saturday night. It is crowded, rowdy, half-bohemian, half-criminal. The girls wear high boots, skin-tight pants, long hair, heavily made-up eyes, false eyelashes, pale lips. The men wear boots, tight pants, wide belts, long hair. When I get home Hugo's door will be closed. He will be asleep.

Sunday evening I will be in Los Angeles.

For the Fields I dressed up in my long skirt from Singapore. I dress up to show my invulnerability, a pose in the world—to pretend I was not hurt when Leo Lerman said on the day of publication of *Ladders to Fire* (in 1946): "Go and hide your head under a pillow."

When Hugo talks about the drama of Indonesian President Sukarno, the drama is the same—it always has its roots in the personal, a personal defeat, a personal humiliation. I study the personal and it applies to Sukarno, to Asia, to war, to the world, to leaders—to all! In the personal, there is more hope of learning why—but *never* in history. In the personal there is some hope of truth—*never* in history. To confuse the Proustian "I" with narcissism is absurd. The "I" here is merely the eye of the microscope.

Marguerite said the *Diary* was an evolving whirlpool, tales within tales.

Sara Berenson: "The *Diary* is a perfect balance to the novels, not that I felt they needed one when I read them, but the *Diary* does provide weight for them, anchors them in the world a bit more. And it made me go back to them and find them richer, just as they gave depth back to the *Diary*."

One night Louise Varèse called me up—she had just returned from a concert of Varèse's music perfectly played and was elated. She is writing about him. She talked about his death. It happened ten days after an operation for an intestinal obstruction. After the operation he had two days of euphoria—but after that he began a long monologue, memories, nightmares, a struggle against dying. He said once: "*J'ai peur.*" He did not accept death. He fought against it. He was angry and rebellious against death too.

"We had quarrels. But they didn't last. He was an angry man, hard at times. I was vulnerable. I would fight back. He would go out, banging the door. He would write me a note, signing it: '*Ton grand emmerdeur*' [your big pain]. Once we quarreled. He had been very insulting to someone, unjustly so. He was going to go out. When he got to the bottom of the stairs I called out: 'What are we going to do with that special bottle of wine you opened?' He laughed and came back."

He didn't want to die, but for two years he could not work. He had arterio-sclerosis. No memory. He would sit for hours before his work, unable to compose. He was a ham actor—always at his best for people—and never revealed how he felt. Louise alone knew about the sleepless nights, the asthma, the fear of flying. She recalled their first meeting at Patchen's.

"He intimidated me. I called him the Corsican bandit. A bandit with the wit of Blaise Cendrars and Leon Paul Fargue's verbal fireworks. He was a storyteller. He was also ferocious, and sometimes erratic. He was impatient with tradition, corny musicians, clichés, falsity. About Henry Miller he said: '*C'est un bon copain!*'"

Strange that his last project was *House of Incest*. He was sensitive to the anguish. He wanted voices that screamed the music. Was his vision of hell like mine? Anxiety—the nightmare. Death turned us into statues.

The relationship we have with the dead is an entirely new one. Some trait dies with them, the one that interfered with communion, with the flow of love. With my mother it was her belligerence, with my father his play-acting, and with Varèse it was his cynical mockery that surrounded him like a constellation of bows and arrows—they flew out of him, from his *herrissé* [bristling] eyebrows, his *yeux foudroyants* [menacing eyes], his artistic dictatorship, his trenchant statements. With Rank, and that may have been the cause of my depression the day I visited his devoted followers, it was his desire to possess me. With death all the alarm signals and interferences in reception disappear and one sees and hears the person more distinctly.

Renate Druks' relationship with her son Peter was, at first, one of desperate guilt. Was she responsible, first of all, for depriving him of his father? She caused the divorce. Was she responsible for his taking drugs, and before that for his conflicts between art and science, between bohemianism and bourgeois life? She felt responsible for his death. When she went to Europe with Ronnie Knox, Peter felt deserted and was sullen and disconnected. He tried bourgeois life with the Suttons, the family who wanted to adopt him and send him to college. He walked through our parties, masquerades and art games like a ghost—but he drew, wrote poetry, and when I designed *Solar Barque* with his drawings it gave him fulfillment as an artist.

So at first Renate wailed and almost lost her reason. Two years later she begins to discover what she had given Peter through a girl he loved at age ten, who tells Renate: "Peter and I were so close, almost married then—but his great worry was that I didn't *believe* in anything. He felt I should believe in something. He asked you to play the role of fairy godmother—to appear and offer to grant my wishes." Renate dressed up as a spirit and came to the window at night and whispered: "Make a wish and it will be answered." The girl wished to fly, and while the fulfillment of this wish was postponed, the apparition of Renate as a fulfiller of magic wishes made the girl believe. Renate stirred Peter's imagination, encouraged his drawing and writing. At 13 he asked her if he could sleep with her. "I like you better than the little girls at school."

Letter from Anaïs Nin to Roger Bloom:
Winter 1967

Dear friends (since now there are two of you):

I was so happy to hear about your marriage…

In March I will be in New York, lecturing at the Library of Congress, Long Island University, Brooklyn College.

The second volume of the *Diary* will be out June 23.

The death of Alan Swallow was a shock. There was no one else like him. He was genuinely interested in his writers. He was only 51. We had a service for him at old St. Mark's Church in New York, a church for the poor of the Bowery now taken over by the Beats. The room was full. We read poetry and tributes to him. Walter Lowenfels was there, an old friend of Henry's. And Victor Lipton, who wrote a wonderful review of the *Diary*.

The script of *Spy* written by the young actress is not good. Unlike the book. So we are stymied again by that.

My best to both of you,
Anaïs

Letter from Anaïs Nin to Hugh Guiler:
Los Angeles, February 8, 1967

Darling:

Yesterday I wrote you sketchily and chaotically about the *mess* of the *Spy* movie. I am simply bowing out. But someone here, a big producer friend of the Westons, who was a good poet once visited by T. S. Eliot, may advise me on finding a writer. I cannot suggest Chodorov because he has no name and because he would never work under these conditions with Jerry Bick's interference. What I realized the last few days is that somehow Jerry has got himself in well with Robert Wise and will constantly obstruct our communication with Wise because Wise does not know what he wants. And Jerry has the gift of gab.

Enclosing my article on diary editing requested by Mrs. Lindley for controversy purposes. Tell me what you think of it. I had to bring in Gunther as he is officially the editor. Very ticklish, not giving impressions of all that is left out, detrimental, difficult.

Love,
Anaïs

Letter from Gunther Stuhlmann to Anaïs Nin:
New York, Feb. 15, 1967

Dear Anaïs:

I am sorry to hear about all the film trouble—maybe we should get the whole thing away from Jerry—he seems to be the worst ambassador in the long run.

I am trying to find out more about the current Swallow Press situation.

You will have gotten the proofs of the diary photos meanwhile. I asked Hiram to see the jacket copy—particularly after our last experience with him, and I will pass it on to you as soon as it comes in.

Contract with Stock for *Diary 1* will follow. After a year's hassle we are back in the fold.

Love,
Gunther

Letter from Hugh Guiler to Anaïs Nin:
New York, February 15, 1967

Darling:

Gunther told me about the photo he arranged to get into *Newsweek*. It is a lovely picture and should help the *Diary*.

It was good to hear you on the telephone for my birthday, and Joaquín too, as I can't telephone you. I must just wish you now a happy birthday, darling, on the 21st, but if you call me over the weekend I can say it to you. You are still phenomenal, and now I feel more confident about your physical state, as Goldstein says he hopes to avoid another operation for you unless your precious stones act up.

For my birthday I worked extra hard at the office, handling complaints about matters at Hayden Stone. From what John Chase told me over the telephone after his return from Europe it looks now as if I will not have to leave H. S., of which I am glad since I was not looking forward to the big move, especially at this time.

The Deadly Affair, which I saw with Gunther and Barbara, was full of violence, and, after reading *On Aggression*, I can't bear violence any more than you can. Barbara was delighted with it, especially with the way Simone Signoret was killed, almost jumping with delight, saying she got a real kick out of that scene! So I refrained from saying what I thought. And the human story is used as a foil—the mystery is not convincing. The end is quite unbelievable.

I also saw *Blow Up* and thought it was utterly childish. Antonioni had an idea at the end—that it had all perhaps happened in the young man's imagination—but by that time the subjects of his imagination were so trivial that I was no longer interested. And, of course, again the homosexual reduction of women to the status of silly models, or silly teenagers, or just silly people. The colors were mostly garish pop art—nothing as subtle as *The Red Desert*—also silly as a story.

All my love,
Hugo

Letter from Hugh Guiler to Anaïs Nin:
New York, February 19, 1967

Darling:

Am enclosing two articles, one a review of Marguerite Duras' new novel and the other an article by Barry Farrell in *Life* on "The Other Culture." I read them both this morning and it struck me that there is a relationship between the "objectivity" of the new writers like Duras and the desperate search by the Underground to open up new areas of perception by making the "secret psychic" drama the collective experience. Farrell says in the end, after pointing out that the Underground is "anti-art," that "whether or not you approve depends on who you are and how well you like the life you're leading." This is obviously an international movement, and apart from charlatans like Andy Warhol, there is some sincere seeking in some of it. But I, for one, am not dissatisfied with "who I am," and while not all of the life I lead satisfies me, I do feel that I have had the privilege that few, except you, have had, not only opening up, but connecting new areas of perception into energy that we have been able to use creatively in both life and art. It would have been so easy for me to yield to all these collective movements—Dadaism, Surrealism, etc.—during the past 50 years, and the collective is the most dead-end of all—getting further and further removed from the real center in ourselves. They have just not had your courage to look into the individual self, as you said in the *Diary*.

All this is anti-art, but Duras is regarded as a novelist of quality. Once in a while she seems to have some sudden insights, but what the critic says here corresponds to the impression I had of Duras personally when I spent that day with her in New York—of a woman who knew very little about her own unconscious and so had ended up more of a victim of it than its master. Again, as in the Farrell article, I realize how privileged we have been.

Have just noticed, and read, the review of Genet's *Miracle of the Rose*. I know you admire his style, and I suppose to that extent he can be called an artist even though he must be pretty boring sometimes. But he is obviously, again, completely unaware of his sickness, and as an artist he tries to make of that sickness something rational and even beautiful. All that would be more justified if he had lived in the 19th century instead of the 20th of Freud and Konrad Lorenz, for he has represented the only valid revolution. And I know of only one poet of that revolution. Her name is Anaïs Nin.

All my love,

Hugo

P.S. Our friend May is back and has almost had another breakdown between anxiety over her son, who seemed for a while to have disappeared (later turned up in India), and Yurek [Jerzy Kosinski], to whom she foolishly turned for comfort in her distress, and who told her she deserved to lose her son—that she was just a "rich bitch," etc. Yurek is now revealed as the sadist that he always was and that I saw from his article interpreting his *Painted Bird*. But I hinted to May that she is perhaps acting out the counterpart masochistic role to his sadism.

LOS ANGELES, FEBRUARY 25, 1967

All of February I worked on the third volume of the *Diary*. As this includes the story of erotic writings, I thought of mixing the facts and fiction to make this a sensual book.

The transplant to America was the opposite of freedom, for in the air there was so much puritan disapproval, so much of the spectator and voyeur watching and being jealous of those who *lived*. Anti-pleasure.

In America, it is a sin to look inward, and that is why there is so much loss of identity. It is a sin to be personal, and that is why there is so much loneliness and alienation.

Someone said about Louis and Bebe Barron's music: a molecule that has stubbed its toes.

Rupert said once: "I always need a double dose of medicine, so I need twice as much LSD." Kent Cathcart said: "That's why you married Anaïs!"

Kent is a transvestite. He dresses like D. H. Lawrence—carries his phallus like a conductor's baton, writes about it, but the soft, yielding body of the woman appears under the disguise, something creamed and boneless. He is a desperate actor, covering his anxieties and fears, hiding behind a would-be priest's robes at a time when priests are rejecting abstinence. His alibi. Abstinence from women, debauchery with boys. I do not like how he forces everything. He is theatrical. When we are about to be natural and spontaneous, he makes a remark that is self-conscious: "You are a paragon," and it irritates me. I tore that down with no uncertain humor. I also attacked his talk of uniting Catholicism and sensuality—Catholicism having been the worst enemy of sensuality. Priestifying men and sanctifying women in niches. "Your poem is a black Mass." He can write—brilliantly—he is a poet, but his writing is theatrical, inflated. I do not accept his roles, postures, because he himself does not espouse them.

A few days later he and his wife Kathryn quarreled. He attacked her, beat her, tried to strangle her, tried to suffocate her with a pillow. She came today with scratches and scars over her face and legs. "He was not trying to kill me, Kathryn, but *woman*."

All that I did not like in him crystallized at this moment, but the ugliness killed her illusions and delusions—and cured her. The violence broke the marriage. Quarrels did not lead anywhere. "She is trying to cut off my balls." With that came jealousy and possessiveness. The housekeeper was so frightened by the scene that she called the police. Deena Metzger came and pacified them.

LOS ANGELES, MARCH 1967

When Kathryn Cathcart came to me, slim, in her minidress and high boots, and said: "I am going to commit suicide," I suggested she take up some work she liked instead. She said she would like to do a book on my lectures and notes on writing. I agreed. We signed a contract with James Wade at MacMillan. We began to work. I gave her all my notes. We spent long hours taping conversations.

We did not talk about her personal drama. She did not want to. She was terribly tense. I thought the work would help her as it helps me.

Letter from Hugh Guiler to Anaïs Nin:
Cuernavaca, Mexico, April 8, 1967

Darling:

Another letter from you yesterday (April 3). I am glad your lecture went well and that Gunther has done a good job.

This has been a strenuous week. Now something has come up with the woman who is still my best prospect here, that makes it necessary for me to stay over until Tuesday—so I will be back only Tuesday night, the 11th.

It was good having Chase's man with me. He was very impressed with the visits I lined up for him and the way I handled them, so he will take back a good report to Chase. And we all made a good team together. He says I am the only broker he knows who works with them in this way.

Net result is I have opened up a new field here and I will have to return from time to time. I have been getting the benefit of my two years' worth of study in Spanish and getting along pretty well. Mexico is about 5% pure Indian, but the Indian blood is spread throughout most of the rest of the population, so one always has to understand the way the *Indian* mind works to get along with the Mexicans.

Love,

Hugo

P.S. Chase's man had the *turista* [digestive illness] here, but I have not been troubled, so I seem to have found the way to avoid it.

Letter from Gunther Stuhlmann to Anaïs Nin:
Hamberg, Germany, May 1967

Dear Anaïs:

After my visits to London and Paris, a brief note.

Had a long session with Peter Owen and I hope I have straightened him out once again on how to progress on the *Diary* and the other books. We spent a long evening in talk and he was once more his happy and enthusiastic self. And he promised to handle things right in the future.

In Paris we saw Dominique and Christian Bourgois—the translation of the Miller letters is finished and they plan to publish in the fall. They got a very good young translator of 25 who did a fine job—I had a quick look at the manuscript—and he is also doing the first volume of the *Diary* and has started the translation already. André Bay sounded very good and enthusiastic. The contracts were signed on April 3rd and I have a photocopy of the complete contract. He was full of enthusiasm for you again, and he now feels vindicated in terms of having you at Stock. He will also do the second volume—we had a long, personal talk at his home—and he wants to push the novels.

More soon. I am seeing your German publisher today.

Love, also from Barbara, who is reading a proof of her own book right now.

As ever,

Gunther

LOS ANGELES, MAY 1967

Hideo Aoki came, editor at Kawade. He came to visit me and also to meet Henry Miller. We had a cheerful dinner with Henry at an Italian restaurant. Miller is a great favorite in Japan, a country so suppressed it finds him liberating.

I have met the Ohnukis. Mr. Ohnuki is a scientist at Cal Tech and Mrs. Ohnuki likes to translate English to the Japanese. She translated my interview in Japan. She brought a friend, Susie (Kazuko) Sugisaki, pale and self-effacing. She asked me how I had become free.

Later we took Aoki and Susie to a party, and Varda was there. We ate and drank heartily. Susie would not serve herself until Aoki had.

LOS ANGELES, MAY 1967

Susie Sugisaki came to our house to dance, framed by the pool and the lake. She appeared in a white kimono painted with red peonies—wistful eyes, the head bowed slightly like a rich flower. She carried two long muslin scarves sewn to fan handles. They were about three yards long and very light. She waved them in such a way that they undulated before, around and high over her head, sometimes slowly, sometimes swiftly, spiral in space—a river, she said, clouds, winds, breezes, waves filled with breath or trailing on the shore. Then she was still, holding the fan handles over her shoulder, the scarves hanging like a heirarchic cape. Meanwhile, as the head oscillated on her delicate porcelain neck, she arched backwards, holding her whole perfect body in graceful tension. Her body obeys a stylization, holds itself in control to design grace. When she bends her wistful face, she seems to be fragile and burdened. When she turns her back and half-kneels, her neck looks tender and delicate, but her legs are strong as she holds the pose of a Japanese print. Her hands rest on the edge of an open umbrella for another dance, long fingers undulating harmoniously, free, but reigned by the laws of the dance. Each dance is a song, a slow dream, a painting held long enough to be seen, suspended. The body serves the dream, is eloquent, fluid or static, free or fragile, to perfect obedience to the spirit.

Letter from Anaïs Nin to Hugh Guiler:
Los Angeles, May 5, 1967

Darling:

Aoki left Thursday morning. Everybody liked him. The last thing we did was to take him to the Theatre of Being (the Negro theatre where I saw Baldwin's *The Amen Corner* before). The play was called *The Loudest Noise Ever Heard*, and though it was inspired by *Waiting for Godot*, it brought in many different elements, vitality, humor, expressiveness, aliveness within the misery, not that deadly, dusty quality of Beckett. It was wonderful. Aoki seemed to appreciate the humor and indigenous quality.

I have not yet read the clippings you sent me; I was so anxious to get back to work on the Diary and was fearful of losing the thread, which I do at every interruption. Picked it up again. I write until my back aches, really.

Jerry Bick is corresponding with Jeremiah Brooks, his latest potential film writer, and I am waiting for Stephan Chodorov's letter. I heard also from a very brilliant, very young, very hip director who wants to do *Spy* imaginatively. I will meet him when I return to N.Y.

Renate and I are speeding through the script of *Collages*. She has a gift for dramatizing.

A

Los Angeles, May 9, 1967

Did a program at KPFK.

Saw *Ulysses*—extremely well filmed, a script by Fred Haines, faithful Irish actors, superb.

Saw Albee's play *The Delicate Balance*. I do not respond to him. It is too abstract. How cruelly the media has diminished Tennessee Williams, forgetting his past gifts to the theatre and greeting Albee with exaggerated praise.

Letter from Anaïs Nin to Gunther Stuhlmann:
Tahiti, July 4, 1967

Dear Gunther:

I sent Hiram Haydn the itemized list he asked me for, for his accountant. I trust your objectivity. I had a feeling that the publicity budget was small this year. Read my letter to Lindley. It you think it unwise, tear it up, but the points I made are true. The feeling I had was that they did less and let me carry a greater part of the burden. For example, Harriet Zinnes, whose copy I signed on May 21, received her review copy on June 28! So I had to go around giving the book to those who wanted to write their reviews, such as Anna Balakian, before going away for the summer! I guess I am tired. But when you sign the next contract (and I hope to god you get Scribner or some other publisher else interested, Goyen, anyone), I want to put in fine print that I am not to be charged for copies for public relations, because I did most of it. Robert Kirsch is a typical example. Hilda Lindley knows him well and could have found out he was on vacation. She said she would phone him about my article on editing, and didn't.

I don't think I am unreasonable. The pettiness is incredible. It may be I am tired of being the do-it-yourself kid.

Do please let me know if you saw William Goyen, or anyone else, before signing with Haydn. His last concern was that his own book was dead. Also I won't sign for the *Diary* unless he gives me a contract for the paperback of volumes 1 and 2. (If you agree with me.) Or let's do them with Bantam if he wants them.

Anaïs

Anaïs Nin in Tahiti, 1967

TAHITI, JULY 9, 1967

Left L.A. at midnight, and eight hours later Rupert and I landed at Papeete—described by Loti and Simenon—more beautiful than Acapulco in the dawn. Streets, people, markets very much like Acapulco. The members of the group I'm with, being no Playboy Bunny Club, are studying the entire island and the life of Polynesians, so we are island hopping—a few days on each island. We are in Moorea for three days. A million times more beautiful than Acapulco. A volcanic island, jagged peaks, lush vegetation—lagoons, palms, flowers. Native shacks. Ideal temperatures, but lighter than Acapulco in summer—a breeze that sounds like rain—birds, open palm-leaved cottages. Sleep under mosquito netting. The native girls are incredibly beautiful—perfect—graceful—not only perfect skin, eyes, teeth and ankle-length hair, but gracefulness and playfulness. Ravishing. A million stars in the sky. Too sleepy to stay up for dancing. French food—ample, good, combined with native dishes. Today, Sunday, people are lazy. But you can do a million things if you wish, rent a jeep and tour the island, sail, deep-sea dive, snorkel, bicycle, ride horseback, go canoeing, go shell-hunting, hike to the top of the volcanic peak. The sunset is even more subtle than Acapulco. Again there is a sense of serenity.

33

Tahiti, July 10, 1967

No phones. No mail. Temperature ideal—a fresh breeze. So much to see. Each island is different—rocks, coral reefs, amazing fish. The natives cook and welcome us. Each meal is wrapped in leaves and covered by hot stones.

The nights are fresh. Colors of the lagoon go from purple to green to blue to turquoise to snow-white in layers of currents where there is coral, and with seaweed, it darkens. But the beauty is due to the absence of buildings—like the Acapulco lagoon before it was ruined by big hotels. The French are clever—they have only thatched palm cottages that are beautifully designed for ventilation.

Tahiti, July 12, 1967

Today we were on a sailboat with a motor, holding twelve. We went to visit the atolls—reefs of coral said to have grown upon volcanic reefs that later sank, leaving only the coral. Here one can stay in several places—the Club, which is charming, designed by a Tahitian, with individual shacks and a collective dinner so at each meal we sit with different people. I'm writing this under a palm-leaf umbrella as in old Acapulco—the breeze is fresh. The cook is French and perfect.

Papeete is honky tonky and spoiled so no one goes there to stay. But on the 14th of July, there is not one hotel room available. It is the biggest of holidays.

Reading about the history of Polynesia during evenings. Mosquitoes love us as much as we love French cooking. Water is crystal clear, and with goggles you can see marvelous fish, corals, etc. People hunt for shells and scuba-dive with instructors.

Tahiti, July 13, 1967

Today I finally tried snorkeling. Clear water, Cousteau marvels—I can stand on white sand and look over coral banks. Amazing. People do it all day long. Tomorrow a trip to another island not far away—then back for a Tahitian dinner and the July 14th celebration.

I am a new person. All my nervousness is gone—it is as quiet and velvety as Acapulco.

Tahiti, July 14, 1967

The day began gaily. They set up a cardboard Bastille and divided young people into two camps, and they had a sandbag fight on the pier, captured the "aristocrats," doused them in red wine. The *pirogue* races—flowered boats with the incredibly beautiful girls. Then a buffet lunch, later a dance spoiled by rain. Two afternoons of rain.

The fiesta brought the natives, fat mammas, darling children, fat papas, hair down to the hips, flowers in the hair, crowns of white flowers. Each woman wears a pareo differently—different colors.

A bitchy review came in the mail.

Tahiti, July 16, 1967

Slept twelve hours yesterday. An hour of sun on the pier to avoid the mosquitoes (the only flaw here), a swim. Putting on a pareo and flowers for lunch.

Shopping for soap at a boutique and avoiding buying all the books on Polynesia for $5 and $6 each. Long line at the doctor's office—Americans with the *turista*, French with coral scratches. Some women are not sick at all, but the doctor is young and handsome.

Lunch is abundant and lovely. The dining room is open—no air conditioning— fresh, breezy, no perspiring. A *pirogue* is filled with giant fruit and flowers— children, wearing yesterday's flower crowns, offer them to new arrivals. At 2:30 I take a glass-bottom boat—a lazy way of seeing fish. Just like Cousteau's *World Without Sun.*

Tahiti, July 16, 1967

The *Kermesse* in Papeete: Coney Island à la Polynesian. Stands are draped with pareo prints, others in brilliant colors—like an Italian village fair. Population is colorful—Cuban taste in clothes. Gaudy. Mumus shaped like Spanish Sevillian dresses, flowered cotton, fitted, flounces, gay. Dance competition in a stadium like a Mexican bullfight ring, only covered with palm leaves and flowers. Soft songs. Drums. Babies.

At midnight we returned to the boat, but the boatman was asleep, drunk, and was not leaving till 8:00 AM! People lay on deck trying to sleep. Frenchmen went to wake up the director of the Club. One more man turned up drunk. The French doctor arrived to see what he could do. People were trying to sleep in lifeboats, on benches, on deck. At 3:00 AM all the lights were still on. Then fresh, sober crew-men came on and awakened everybody to collect tickets! I was half asleep. A trip in the dark, the mountains looming, the sound of surf on the reefs. Arrival at Moorea at 5:30. No bus. A native jumps on his motorcycle to awaken the bus driver. He comes. We arrive at dawn! Sleep until the last call for breakfast at 9:30. Will take a siesta.

Tahiti, July 1967

Exploration of Moorea—today in a Volkswagen. Incredible beauty. Jagged volcanic peaks, rain forests, flowers, birds, lagoons, breadfruit trees, coconuts drying in the sun, vanilla, fishermen in their canoes, lakes filled with purple iris. Rupert and I had lunch on the beach. Miles of quiet, deserted beaches like the little cove in Acapulco where Hugo and I found a man fishing, a woman splitting coco-nuts. The temperature is ideal. A lunch of breadfruit cooked by our Tahitian driver, who spoke neither French nor English. Papaya such as I never tasted in Cuba. An airport is being built, which will mean the end of miles and miles of native shacks, nature, peaceful life.

Tahiti, July 18, 1967

I am not a Tahitian, but I did the best I could. And under and beneath the romantic dream I can see other things: the American woman who went mad in the middle of so much beauty, the young French doctor who has to stay with her. Always, beneath the beauty, danger and evil and death.

The madwoman was taken to Papeete, drugged and put on a plane. Without the devotion of Club members she might have ended her days in a Papeete madhouse. The natives found her nude in the middle of the night washing a child's cloth in a bowl of water. When she was found, she said: "I died yesterday." Such a contrast to the beauty of nature, to the wit and joyousness of the French.

At night, the open hut receives the dank odors of the tropical earth through the loosely fitted boards of the floor. I smell the earth and the *sulphur* in the dampness. In the dawn the birds *trill*. The French have done everything to create an atmosphere.

The Tahitian dances are monotonous. They only have two steps—the rolling of the stomach and hips of the women in grass skirts, and the tinkling knees of the men as in African dances. But the conch shell melody is strange and the singing is performed with a *drone* as in bagpipes or Hindu instruments. Monotony—the theme of Polynesian culture—ritualistic sameness.

TAHITI, JULY 19, 1967

Whenever I leave Rupert alone I have quieter adventures—I decided to go on the bus (like a Mexican bus) rattling to the Chinaman's shop, the only shop in town. (The Chinese are the Jews of Asia—hard-working traders.) I wanted a nice pareo for the maid because we can't tip them with money. She leaves flowers and shells every day in my shack. We kiss and say *toi*.

After shopping I started to walk back—a fairytale land. Black birds with yellow beaks trilling away. Fiddler crabs scurrying into their holes. Shacks, naked children, pools, the lagoon, sailboats, giant ferns, kapok trees, pigs, cows, natives shelling coconuts, Gaugin girls in pareos on bicycles.

The pareo is made of colorful material, which they tie in different ways (once, for women, below the breasts—before the missionaries came). The road is made with a mixture of coral dust and shells—pock-marked and full of holes. Everything is so peaceful. Then a jeep came with a fat mama (originally French), a Gauguin girl at the wheel. They work at the Club. They were looking for a pig to roast at a picnic. Now I sit as in Acapulco watching the sunset and ocean waves breaking far away against the coral reefs.

TAHITI, JULY 20, 1967

A day of rain.

Things I have learned: They have bicycles and scooters, very few cars. There is a metal band a foot wide around each palm tree, like a silver wedding ring, to discourage rats from eating the coconuts. They slip on that. As the government pays peasants to put the bands on the trees, they often place them on dead trees. (Thieving is not a crime. It is natural.) The foot of the coconut tree looks like an elephant foot. In typhoons your life depends on finding a coconut tree—not too young and not too old—to strap yourself to during the storm. They are the last to be uprooted. The breeze has gradations—some rustlings—difficult to distinguish from rain on the roof. They have apples here. They have trees that produce a fruit like butter. There is vanilla and pepper. You can smell them. The coral reefs keep the sea out of the lagoon. The breaking of the surf is like a dream.

TAHITI, JULY 21, 1967

The wonderful names of Pacific shells: voluti; sunrise tellin; turban shells; tessellate cowrie; wide-mouthed purpura; joagoda; emperica volute; lurid cowrie;

China moon; teut olive; spiny helmet; miter shell; grinning tuu; pelican foot; bleeding moth; Japanese Babylon.

TAHITI, JULY 22, 1967

We were awakened at 3:00 AM—breakfast at four, bus drive, a 1½ hour boat trip at dawn to take the 8:00 AM plane to Los Angeles.

This place gave me all I had needed—the knowledge that somewhere one can escape the cruelty and ugliness of the Western world and live with just a small income. And here, until *we* came, they had no disease, a perfect balance with nature, a simple life, no concerns. We are the snakes in paradise. The war invited the Polynesians into our Western Hate Culture.

Last night Tahitian dances and songs.

At dawn I went for a swim. Breakfast is sumptuous—giant fruit and croissants. More sun and swimming. Now sitting in an Acapulco-like bar because the light is good for reading and drinking rum with papaya juice.

Rupert was passionate. We made love every day.

I offered him the freedom to court a Tahitian. He would not take it. I have conquered jealousy.

———

Letter from Hugh Guiler to Anaïs Nin:
New York, July 27, 1967

Darling:

Got a whole batch of letters from you. I suppose you will call me when you get to L.A. and let me know when to expect you back here. I sent you a direct cable today and hope you received it—and post restante Papeete.

I spoke too soon about the *turista.* It has taken me all this time to get over it, but I think it has stopped now, or I hope so. Have lost about 10 lbs.

Your descriptions of the trip are fascinating and I hope I can get there sometime. As a result of my physical state I have not been able to get to the beach except once, but I hope to make up for that in a day or two.

Reading *Proust: The Early Years* by George Painter and enjoying it as you thought I would.

I will be glad when you are back. I have a car for two months.

Louise Varèse says Varèse's unfinished symphony with your work will be performed at Tanglewood August 14 and asks if you and I would like to go. Let me know about this so I can answer her.

Love,
Hugo

LOS ANGELES, AUGUST 1967

Spent two weeks with Hugo in New York.

Letter from Anaïs Nin to Gunther Stuhlmann:
Los Angeles, August 12, 1967

Dear Gunther:

I was moved by your telling us about the war years in Germany. It was the first time I felt I knew you in the past as well as the present. It was an overwhelming and terrible story and you told it not only humanly but so well, like a writer. I may put it in the Diary, you know. Your portrait was incomplete. And it may be because you feel somewhat more rooted, married, successful, that you could tell it.

I think I forgot to give you this end piece to the review: "The *Diary* has beautiful, rich, profound prose" by *The Observer*, N.C.

Do I have to join the writer's guild? I don't see why, do you?

Please accelerate Bantam Books talks as I have many debts!

The best reviews are yet to come: a real essay by Marguerite Young in *Voyages* (the new journal edited by William Claire), one by Harriett Zinnes in a new magazine called *Works*, and Daniel Stern is deeply impressed and wants to do something.

I have many more reviews from which you can extract short comments. I should give you the folder, or, better still, do the extracting and you can choose.

Anaïs

Letter from Hugh Guiler to Anaïs Nin:
New York, August 31, 1967

Darling:

Went to the Au Coin de France bookstore today, which is what you called the Librarie Française. The books you wanted have been sold, but they have taken the order and will have them next week.

We had an unsuccessful test for the images on the redoing of the *Venice Etude no. 1* film due to some accident at Eastman Kodak. But the Harry Partch music came out splendidly and Leo Lerman is very satisfied with that.

Glad you are getting immune to the critics. My psychoanalysis could have done that. I am only seeing Bogner once a week now as she is busy. But I am feeling fine physically.

I am so glad you are less nervous since taking the estrogen and the thyroid medication. It was too bad that neither of us realized sooner that you needed these so badly and you went through a tough time.

All my love,

Hugo

P.S. I opened the envelope of the clipping service to take out any reviews that might upset you while you are away from Bogner. But here they are, all of them, because I think, except for the one who misses the point, they are very understanding.

Letter from Anaïs Nin to Kazuko (Susie) Sugisaki:
Los Angeles, September 1967

Dear Kazuko:

How like you to start your letter with the lovely allusion to our house! As I am deep in *The Tale of Genji* I feel I should send you a poem.

I am very light-hearted today because I received a letter from Mr. Nakada: "First of all I must tell you about Miss Kazuko Sugisaki who had been kind enough to see me a few weeks ago. Knowing that she is someone who understands your work and is contemplating a translation of *Collages*, I have agreed to her plan and want to assist her as much as I can. This is good news for you, which is perhaps at the same time good news for Miss Sugisaki. I learned that Mr. Takao Sugawara, one of the devotees of your work and who is an editor in the publishing department of Shi-chi-sha, intends to introduce as many Anaïs Nin novels as possible to Japan and asks me to supervise the work. Of course, I agreed. We must find excellent translators, and I have already started selecting some, including Miss Sugisaki. We have come to the conclusion that your novels must be published in a splendid binding of two volumes or more. Once our scheme materializes, people in Japan will look up to you as a great author more and more."

Isn't that wonderful? If this comes through then our trip to Japan next summer is certain.

Our house is the same, sunsets, heat and pool. Rupert is back to teaching. I have worked every day except our 28 days in Tahiti. Volume 3 is thorny and difficult because it takes place in America and I found the adaptation difficult. I am walking on cactus. I think some of the conflict came from the fact that in France I was only with artists. In New York I was with anti-artists.

Through my being on a committee for a tea ceremony school, I will be able to influence interest in Japanese literature. I hope to plan lectures and readings. My problem is getting good translations of articles by people like Nakada and other critics and writers. I think Japan has a great deal to give to America and could be a most refining influence.

I have met Mako, the Japanese wife of Sam Francis, a painter. Sunday we are having cocktails for them. Wish you were here with us, dancing for us.

My love to you,
Anaïs

Los Angeles, September 1967

At Robert Haas's cocktail, I met the editor of *Partisan Review*. He looked at me with amazement and said: "Nature has been very kind to you."

"In contrast to the *Partisan Review*," I said.

They became hostile to me when I answered truthfully that I was not a relative of Andrés Nin, the anarchist. There are many Nins in Barcelona. They thought I repudiated him because he was a Trotskyite. Ridiculous. But from then on they sniped at me whenever possible. In the '40s no one cared about writing, only politics. It was at that period I remember Lila Rosenblum wanted to abdicate from the Communist Party and three rough-looking men came to intimidate her and tell her she could not quit.

It was at that time that Gonzalo reported often to the party center and left me waiting in the street. Lila was selling the *Daily Worker* on street corners in the middle of bitter winters.

Letter from Lawrence Durrell to Anaïs Nin:
Sommières, France, Sunday, September 3, 1967

Dearest Anaïs:

Just back from a long journey of some four months around Greece for a *changement des idées* to find a desk full of mail including your new volume of the diary, which I am reading with the aching nostalgia such a document must revive in anyone who lived through that period, particularly as a very young man. I was terribly touched by the little dedication to me and hope sometime soon to redeem the charming epithet, which, in some mysterious way, seems to have foundered— though what went wrong, when and how, I have no clue. Sometimes one quite inadvertently hurts friends and loses them without meaning to, without wanting to, and spends the rest of their life in puzzled me-fulness, chewing the cud and wondering. Not me. *Toujours* here I am, your old friend.

This new volume moves out confidently, in the mainstream now, and all the uncertainties of vol. 1 (insisting too much on the manner of Proust's vol. 1) are ironed away. You are now the master of your audience and can move ahead confidently, recording the ebb and flow of your inner tides with brilliant insight and cunning female formulations—200 volumes would not be too much. Hurrah! A warm embrace. One feels the momentum now. I shall be seeing Henry on the 20th in Paris. Why not you too? It's been so long…

Much love,
Larry

Letter from Gunther Stuhlmann to Anaïs Nin:
New York, September 4, 1967

Dear Anaïs:

First of all, I have just put a check for $111.15 in the bank here, which constitutes royalties from Peter Owen up to June 30, 1967. This was again a check that took ages to clear but we just got the remittance advice this morning. So there is a little trickle.

Also this morning I got a very nice letter from the new editor of the Swallow Press, now in Chicago, whom I had seen here last month as I told you. He is very eager to pursue the one-volume complete *Cities of the Interior* idea, which I had originally wanted to do with Harcourt, but which Hiram procrastinated on. (I have meanwhile taken up the whole situation there with Jovanovich and expect some reaction soon. I am also pursuing the other people we spoke about.)

The Swallow editor writes: "I have thought through, since our conversation, the matter of *Cities*. From our talk and from a review of Alan's Nin papers, I can see no 'legal' reason why the volume could not come out under the new Swallow Press imprint, without a joint Swallow-Harcourt agreement. And in terms of practical reasons, I feel our enterprise could give *Cities* an excellent exposure and distribution. Our advertising program is already underway for the Swallow line. We project to spend during the coming year well over ten times what Alan was spending for advertising…in other words, as you and Miss Nin look forward to a one-volume *Cities*, I propose that you seriously consider letting us do the work for you."

I also had word from Japan that Kawade Shobo is seriously thinking of doing a Japanese edition of *Collages*—and I am standing by for further news. Aoki has not yet responded on the second *Diary*, but his assistant wrote to me about *Collages*.

First responses on Barbara's novel are very nice—Harry Moore gave us a long, enthusiastic quote and we are slogging along the hard road.

Hope all is well on your end. I saw the Harcourt store has a nice big display of *Diary 2* in their window. And the cumulative reviews make a very impressive showing. So on to *Diary 3*.

Love,

Gunther

Letter from Hugh Guiler to Anaïs Nin:
New York, Saturday, September 9, 1967

Darling:

Sorry to hear *Spy* does not work with Wise. It is really the lack of any unity in him and the people he chooses that make such a theme impossible for his kind of films. All he had to do was to put it in the hands of someone like Serge Bourguignon, who made *Dimanche et Cybele*, or someone of that kind of poetic comprehension. But carpenters cannot be expected to build lunar satellites.

I have noted to expect you around the 15th, which is next Friday, but you will let me know more when you know.

Stephan Chodorov has confirmed that they want me and my films on *Camera 3* very soon. Leo and I have been having considerable technical problems with *Venice Etude No. 1* and Part 2 of *The Gondola Eye*, but it looks as if everything should be ready within another week.

I've been told there have been sales of the films to colleges and libraries, which will bring in around $1,000 this month.

Am feeling better all the time. Beach today and I hope again tomorrow.

Bogner's new place has an arrangement similar to that of the other, so one feels comfortable in it. And it has a real garden leading out from the living room, now overgrown with grass, which makes it appear quite country-like.

All my love,

Hugo

SEPTEMBER 14, 1967
Left for New York.

Letter from Edmund Wilson to Anaïs Nin:
Wellfleet, Mass., September 23, 1967

Dear Anaïs:

I have just finished your second volume. I don't think it is quite as interesting as the first. Your friend Gonzalo except when he is talking about Peru. Henry Miller and your father are carried on admirably as characters. But of course there is really no sense in criticizing the separate volumes as a unit. The *Diary* as a whole is the thing. Will you be in New York this autumn and winter? Reading you has made me want to see you.

Love,

Edmund

P.S. Who is the man who writes your introductions, and are they really necessary? Surely not for every volume.

Letter from Anaïs Nin to Gunther Stuhlmann:
Los Angeles, October 13, 1967

Dear Gunther:

I am so eager for news on three fronts: film, paperback, Haydn. And my account is also overdrawn! I tried to phone you. I left a message. Perhaps you will call this weekend. I will be back October 26, and meanwhile I am working like a fiend. Scenario for *Collages* is finished and I sent it to you. My book on writing is terribly good. But please give me news.

I hope all is going well with Barbara's book. I gave my copy of it to a film director.

Love to you and Barbara,
Anaïs

Letter from Gunther Stuhlmann to Anaïs Nin:
New York, October 19, 1967

Dear Anaïs:

Just to clear up the Mysterious Orient Department and to keep you abreast of the latest moves, I wanted to fill you in on what I proposed to the two Japanese publishers.

I told Kawade they could have *Collages*, since they had spoken for it before we heard from the other house, and I have asked Aoki to make us an offer for *Diary 2*.

To Shi-chi-sha I suggested that we draw up contracts for the following books: *Ladders to Fire, Children of the Albatross, Four-Chambered Heart, Seduction of the Minotaur*, since they wanted four novels. (I reminded them that Kawade has already done the *Spy*, and I also told them that this was the order in which the books should be handled.) I also suggested that if they wanted to do other books they could perhaps do *Under a Glass Bell* and *Winter of Artifice* as a one-volume edition. They did not mention *House of Incest*.

They wanted to do editions of 2,000 copies each, and I have asked for an advance on each book of $250, which evens out if they sell out at their price of roughly $2 a copy, with a six per cent royalty to start with.

I'll keep you posted on their reply. Meanwhile, I return the letter from your friend—maybe Kawade would use her translation of *Collages*? Peter Owen contract follows.

Love,
Gunther

LOS ANGELES, NOVEMBER 1967

I see Kathryn Cathcart often. Deena Metzger. Much music. Cocktail with the editor of *Mankind*. We went to the beach.

I left for New York Oct. 26 and attended the Rank Society meeting on the 28th. My difficulty there is that social workers see the destructive side of the young, and my work only attracts creative young, the talented young, not the dropouts and drug addicts. So we clash—our images and interpretations are contradictory.

I gave a lecture at Philadelphia.

Letter from Hugh Guiler to Anaïs Nin:
Geneva, Saturday, November 11, 1967

Darling:

The Cinématèque Française is going to have a showing of my films next Friday the 17th. I am having Monique and Michele invited and suggested she write the friends she had in mind inviting to her house for the same things. This will be better, I think.

I see René de Chochor Monday morning and hope to straighten things out with him. Then Zurich Tuesday the 14th and back to Paris that night. Wednesday and Thursday hope to have the meetings—the most important object of my trip. Then London Sunday to Wednesday night the 22nd. Hope to sell at least one copy of the film.

The elevator man at the Crillon, along with everyone else, asks for you and Piccolo. I told them you would be in Paris in the spring, so you must try to do this. My own affairs are in good shape and if you need more money, I can send it to you. Let me know. I will be in Paris until the 19th, so you have time if this reaches you before you leave on Tuesday.

Love, love,
Hugo

Letter from Anaïs Nin to Hugh Guiler:
Los Angeles, November 28, 1967

Darling:

I want to explain to you what happened with the book on writing so you will understand why I have to stick to it. Kathryn Cathcart has done a lot of work, read all the books, marked passages, collated them, searched for sources, footnotes, quotations, typed all the tapes and reorganized the lectures (to avoid repetition), but when it came to doing the running narrative she became paralyzed. She did thirty pages, which sound stiff. So it was back on my desk. However, with all the material there, I can do a very fast job of running things together, supplying missing transitions, as I do not have to worry about sequence or organization. I took the first folder, and in one week wrote 60 pages. They are very good. They sound, as Kathryn begged me, like the Diary. Flowing, easy, confident. I have seven folders. Seven times 60 is 420 pages. The book was to be about 350 pages or so. At this rate, with continuity and concentration, I can finish it a month after the deadline of December 1 and receive my $2,500 due on delivery of the manuscript.

The only thing that bothers me is leaving you alone. Let's make up for that by going to Paris in the spring. Jerry Bick is moving to England and is producing two comedies with English filmmakers. They will have a home there and we can meet all the filmmakers. We can stay there.

Peter Owen wants me to come, so does André Bay, and Gunther tells me I have the biggest of German publishers. But Hiram Haydn has not yet signed me for *Diary 3* and I guess one of the reasons I want to bury myself in the writing book is that I have lost the impetus of finishing *Diary 3*—I get angry each time I think of Harcourt

Brace. On the other hand, I can't afford to lose my patience because changing publishers midstream with a sequence of volumes would be bad for the other two unless someone else bought them all together. Gunther can't shop around as it will get back to Harcourt (so don't speak of this to anyone). I called him up and he told me all this. I may write a personal letter to Goyen and Burroughs Mitchell. That I can do.

Meanwhile, as I type, Kathryn comes and types too. I had not intended to work so hard but I want to keep my deadline with MacMillan because I need the money and it keeps my mind off my Xmas neurosis (the only thing Bogner has not been able to cure).

I met a painter, Sam Francis, and his Japanese wife, Mako. He is supposed to be among the five best modern artists. His work resembles a light show and your filmic effects. He has designed a light show, and I asked him if he would do it when I read for a whole evening at the big UCLA auditorium in the spring. I have several lectures at $200 at this end around that time, and we will have money for Europe and maybe Agadir. How do you like that?

Mako is charming. Sam stole her from a prominent Japanese art dealer who had given him a show. They will have a baby. If the light show works with the reading of *Collages* I will bring it to New York. It may convince you to design one yourself!

Love, and please do not be disappointed, I will absolutely be home January 2, after the holidays, which I abhor.

Anaïs

Letter from Hugh Guiler to Anaïs Nin:
New York, November 30, 1967

Darling:

Received your letter this morning and understand why you will only be back after January 1. Will try to keep busy until then and will probably have no trouble what with the office and the film.

Temple University, as a result of your lecture there, has booked *all* of my films for March 15 and would like me to be there at the same time if possible. I cannot give a definite answer, in case I might have to go to Europe then (with you).

Roger Boulogne would like to have an approximate statement of your expenses incurred since the last one you gave him, and also of any income received or that you expect to receive before the end of the year. He says it would be better to *defer* receiving any further income until after Dec. 31st.

More later, in haste, love,

H

LOS ANGELES, DECEMBER 1, 1967
We moved Rupert's father from a hotel to a home for the old. There is no spectacle closer to Dante's *Inferno* than a home for the old. It has the dismal atmosphere of a hospital. They sit inert and in semi-comas before televisions. They are mere bodies. Reginald needed care. He lies in bed most of the time. His talk is rambling. He does not belong there, but he has forced himself there with his life in hotel rooms—he did not eat properly and he took devastating amounts of medicines, sleeping pills, asthma medicines, etc.

Joaquín came to visit. He and Rupert get along very well.

Letter from Hugh Guiler to Anaïs Nin:
New York, December 6, 1967

Darling:

Gunther says he has just signed the contract for vol. 3 of the *Diary* with Hiram Haydn and you will get an advance of $3,500, of which normally $2,500 would be payable now and $1,000 next year. But Roger Boulogne says it is impossible for him to give an opinion about when the $2,500 from Harcourt should be taken until he gets the whole income and expenses for 1967.

Am sending this to you special delivery in case it can get to you quicker that way.

In haste, love,
Hugo

Letter from Hugh Guiler to Anaïs Nin:
New York, December 10, 1967

Darling:

The money I had expected to receive two weeks ago was delayed, but I did not think, from what you had told me over the phone, that you needed it right away, as it was only to clear up the doctor's bill, which could, of course, wait. In fact, you did not say you needed anything until I offered it. Anyhow, I will speak to the bank about it tomorrow morning, when I deposit $500 to your account and try to see this does not happen again.

I have sent a contribution to the committee for the Democratic Alternative (see Bogner's name on the list). Try to get others to contribute. Several of these committees are going to work together, but I like this one the best.

I saw Eugene McCarthy on TV today and he has many things in common with Adlai Stevenson. He is also charming, intelligent, and he will get votes from women based on his looks alone. He cannot possibly win the nomination from Johnson, but if he gets a substantial vote in the primaries it might either attract Robert Kennedy to run or at least influence Johnson's idea about Vietnam. Anyhow, it is a satisfaction to have someone to work for against Johnson.

I will probably not get the new kitten for another week, as Leo will see it gets all its shots, which will save me a visit to the vet. I am thinking of getting a big bamboo birdcage to put the kitten in until Tiggy gets used to it. Meanwhile, as if he sensed something, Tiggy is being extra affectionate with me. I am like well-kneaded dough!

Have been catching up on my filing—bills, etc.—and will have everything done tonight if the cat stops licking my fingers.

Love, love,
Hugo

LOS ANGELES, DECEMBER 1967
Rupert and I spent Xmas with the Wrights and Hanukah with Deena Metzger.

Deena had set two long tables, one for the family, one for the friends. The children read the history of the Jews—persecution and exile. Each guest read a section in turn. The little round yarmulke looked oriental.

Lunch with Mako. The repetition of Nobuko's story. The Japanese women expect to be liberated by marriage to an American. It does not liberate them. Liberation comes from within. Her reproaches are vague, as vague as Japanese novels. Her husband stays out all night. To punish him she cuts her beautiful, long hair. He goes to bed with a pile of art books. She is pregnant. She telephones me like a woman drowning. She does not like what pregnancy is doing to her body: "I feel like an animal—bloated and stagnant."

NEW YORK, JANUARY 2, 1968

The morning I left Rupert, I placed his bedroom slippers at the foot of the bed with a card that I signed with "Love from one-who-tries-to-be-a-Japanese-wife." The other card signed with "Would-be Japanese wife" was placed next to a freshly-made coffee for his dinner.

I ask for $100,000 for the original diaries; Harvard is not interested in them.

I was nominated a Daughter of Mark Twain.

My books are being taught at Queens College in a program of avant-garde literature along with Woolf, Joyce, Beckett, Ionesco, Robbe-Grillet.

Invited to lecture at the Library of Congress.

Spoken Arts is bringing out my recordings.

I am now translated into French, German, Italian, Swedish, Japanese, Catalan, Danish, Hebrew, Finnish.

Talk at Princeton Public Library.

First letter from Richard Centing, librarian at Ohio State University.

In New York Hugo awaited me, driving for the last time at night because he is developing a cataract in his left eye, which impairs his vision. He was in a good mood, however, because he was obtaining business from Mary Wise and starting a new film. The cats had the flu and my first duty was to take them to the veterinarian.

Then began a hectic month. I received three marvelous reviews of the *Diary* from Daniel Stern, Marianne Hauser and Marguerite Young. I gave two evenings of film showings for Hugo. I saw Sandra Hochman, who gives me joy, who is like the sun, all gold and earth and warmth, though as a child she did not receive any love. I saw Frances Field who was ill, and her son Johnnie who has the same trouble with his parents as we had with ours—who responds to the *Diary* at 17 but cannot forgive Frances for denying him the study of dancing and hating his best friend (for fear of homosexuality).

NEW YORK, JANUARY 3, 1968

Work on writing book. Work on expenses and tax information.

NEW YORK, JANUARY 1968

Sandra Hochman is in the hospital after the birth of her little girl. A bed of flowers. The smell of a garden. Her face so sensual, her eyes those of a puma. Full mouth. She wanted poets to be the first visitors for her daughter. I was the first.

Daisy Aldan is receding into past. Eurhythmy: Hippies in costumes from the past.

Frances asks me to seduce her son. She is afraid he is a homosexual. He comes to see me. I now see Frances and Michael under a totally different light: as irrational parents—prejudiced—projecting their own wishes.

Letter from Durrett Wagner of Swallow Press to Anaïs Nin:
Chicago, January 19, 1968

Dear Miss Nin:

First, let me explain the enclosed copies of letters to Gunther Stuhlmann. I am sure he normally is in touch with you about business matters, but I thought that perhaps in these particular cases I should send copies to you in order that you are sure to see exactly what I said to him and how I said it.

The January 16 letter of mine is the culmination of a brief exchange between Stuhlmann and me about Marboro Books selling the British edition of your *D. H. Lawrence* in this country. I asked why. Gunther explained it was wrong and hoped we would go after Spearman, the British publisher.

Now on to your letter to me of January 15. I am certainly very happy for you to write me about any problems that come to your attention—distribution, etc.

I have earlier this month written City Lights and Pickwick and tried to set things straight and kill all false rumors. I will follow that up. (Speaking of rumors, I have just learned in the morning mail that some Swallow author is talking around that Alfred Knopf, Sr. is really the man behind our purchase of Alan Swallow's enterprise from Mae. Wow! *That* is not true. But so rumors go.)

Thanks very much,
Durrett

NEW YORK, JANUARY 20, 1968
Saw Kosinski yesterday. Tonight dinner at Mary Wier's—Sutton Place South. Extreme luxury. Antiques, brocades, silver, butler and maid. A pleasant pheasant displayed on a platter, feathers and all, beautiful wings spread, stuffed, holding a cherry in its beak. Took my appetite away. Pleasant talk with Richard T. Kennedy, Senior Editor at Delacorte Press. Mary is conventional.

NEW YORK, JANUARY 28, 1968
I become obsessed with the beauty of light shows. Saw an interplay in my own work that indicated a living, moving relation between the arts.

My book on writing is now 300 pages. Result of six intensive weeks in Los Angeles.

My window overlooks NYU, Washington Square, excavations for the new NYU library and lower Fifth Avenue. The Empire State Building is my beacon, its tip floating in the clouds.

For years, at the end of the day I played ostrich—took a glass of beer or wine, a pill, and went to sleep to have energy for the next day. This was the time I once gave to writing in the Diary, to reflection. I am trying to recapture this moment, not to become submerged.

Bogner talked of Marguerite Young's obsession with drowning as an obsession with the womb, the mother. I had interpreted it as an oceanic unconsciousness.

At 7:00 PM I call up Rupert. He has just come home from school. He has let Piccolo out into the fields and hills and neighbors' gardens. Piccolo will return with bluebells clinging to his white lamb's hair, like the dogs in Venetian court paintings. Rupert tells me about his father, about a quartet he heard, about a movie.

Hugo is filming his copper engraved plates. He has rediscovered their beauty while doing a program for *Camera 3.*

EN ROUTE TO LOS ANGELES, JANUARY 31, 1968

Airport at 4:00 PM. Arrive in L.A. 6:45.

In the subway I saw a very, very dark Negro girl with a platinum blonde wig admiring herself in the subway mirror.

LOS ANGELES, FEBRUARY 1968

Letter from André Bay—vol. 1 will be translated into French!

MD magazine is preparing a biography on me.

Letter from Anaïs Nin to Sam Eisenstein:
Los Angeles, February 1968

Dear Sam:

Someday when your writing becomes known you will understand why I cannot give your work the attention it deserves. You cannot imagine what it is to be bombarded with hundreds of letters a month all asking to be answered and sending writing to be read, to have my own work piling up, books waiting for me to comment on so that I no longer read what I want to read, friends' demands, old friends who have a right to demand, and trouble with my eyes.

Please understand and do not be offended.

Anaïs Nin

LOS ANGELES, FEBRUARY 1968

I had given Kathryn Cathcart an advance on *Novel of the Future.* She did not work on it. Gunther made her sign a release of all claims as I was going to have to produce the book alone.

One day Rupert and I drove to Venice to see why she was not working. We found her in a small apartment with several black musicians sitting around. Kathryn was under the effect of drugs, vague, detached. Her two little girls, blond and naked, were running around. We took back all the tapes and notes, and I began working on the book myself.

The first time I met Kent and Kathryn Cathcart at Deena's he gave me a first edition of a D. H. Lawrence novel and the usual homosexual exaggerated praise, which masks jealous hostility. Kathryn was quiet, self-effacing, with long black hair dressed with stylization, a chignon. They came to dinner. I objected to his idealization of me. They invited me to their house—there were two little girls dressed like dolls in pink. He wrote a brilliant, artificial, exhibitionist book, and although publishers prefer caricatures of sex, nobody wanted Kent's. Meanwhile, his marriage was imploding. He had intended to be a priest and she a nun. I thought she was a victim of his homosexuality. He beat her. I took her side. She seemed unstable, taut, quivering, but I thought it was sensitiveness. I misjudged her anguish. She came to visit me in such anguish that I played analyst to restore her confidence. She tried to commit suicide at Deena's. To distract her I talked of work and suggested she edit my lectures on writing. She had done a textbook for MacMillan, and they gave her a contract. MacMillan liked my idea. Kathryn was given a half of the $2,500 advance so she could give up teaching and devote her time to the book. She did not finish.

Daniel Stern reviews volume 1 in *The Nation*.

The novels are being transferred to the new Swallow Press.

Letter from Anaïs Nin to Gunther Stuhlmann:
Los Angeles, February 13, 1968

Dear Gunther:

Congratulations on total victory in France. I mailed back the contract instantly.

Had to write to Jim Wade because Kathryn is behaving like a psychotic and nobody knows what she will do next. To recapitulate, I have carbons with her editing, 95% not used. I have her slapped-together paste-up, with which no one could have written a book. So the comparison between the final book and her work will show the extent of her contribution. Just in case, I am bringing it back. Deena thought we should inform MacMillan because she may write to MacMillan (they met here when she did a textbook for them) or to Wade (she met him with me when he came West).

I should be back March 1 with the finished book. If you do not agree with my letter to Jim don't send it.

Deena introduced me to Kathryn and now realizes her condition. Her mother was insane. Her father a prison warden! We have all voted her the best actress of the year. Believe me, if you saw her you would be deceived. She is bright.

Back to work, affectionately,
Anaïs

LOS ANGELES, FEBRUARY 17, 1968
Finished the book on writing, *The Novel of the Future*. Had to explain to Hiram Haydn why I did not submit it to him. Contract was made with Kathryn Cathcart as editor.

Working for Barbara Turner's script for *Spy*.

NEW YORK, MARCH 1968
Party at Marguerite Young's.
Lectures at Library of Congress; Long Island College; Brooklyn College.

NEW YORK, MARCH 8, 1968
Met Benjamin Franklin V and Duane Schneider.
Reproachful letter from Daisy Aldan to answer.

LOS ANGELES, MARCH 27, 1968

Work on *Novel of the Future.*

Part of the Imperial Hotel in Tokyo is to be moved to Meiji Village with famous buildings of the Meiji era, 30 minutes by train from Osaka.

Wrote preface to *Under a Glass Bell* for the British edition.

Letter from Anaïs Nin to Koji Nakada, Japanese translator:
Los Angeles, March 30, 1968

Dear friend:

I'm so happy that recently I was able to help Japanese literature to get better in the United States. I introduced Nobuko Uenishi's story of the Noh Play in *Mademoiselle*, and Mrs. Ohnuki's translations of stories by Kenji Miyazawa, which will appear in the *Chicago University Magazine*. The editor is delighted with them. I am still planning to come to Japan July 15, but I am concerned about the natural feelings of Japan against America. Does Japan know how many of us are against the war in Vietnam and against Johnson? I hope so.

I recently read another remarkable book from Japan: *The Hunting Gun* by Yashusi Inoue.

I understand Hideo Aoki is coming to New York in June to open a branch of Kawade there, so I may have more news. Kazuko tells me she finished her translation of *Collages* but she also heard the *Diary* was not to be translated for some time. Perhaps she meant published. But your last P.S. is very clear. You had to abandon the translation of the *Diary*. And I am very sad about that. I do hope Aoki will be definite when I see him, for he told me he enjoyed American directness, the "yes or no." (When I was concerned that he might be offended by Americans' lack of tact, Aoki said no, he enjoyed knowing what everyone thought, everything being said in the open for a change, no mysteries.)

He went with me to a very open, frank, argumentative evening at a painter's house with Margaret Mead the anthropologist, who spoke her mind like a good middlewesterner, roughly, about opinions and ideas on everything. When I see you this time, I hope I will not be treated with formal ways, but enjoy your bohemian life. I made friends with Sam and Mako Francis and they told me about the easy-going café life in Japan. I love informality. Unfortunately, they are returning to America in June as he cannot take the heat. We will stay with Aoki and his wife as they built a new house and invited us.

As you know, Nobuko is now married to Ivan Morris. He has just published a translation of *The Pillow Book.*

Am sending you a book on my work by Oliver Evans, an American critic. It is the first academic study. I do not agree with all he says. He is a rationalist and I a surrealist... In October MacMillan will bring out my book *The Novel of the Future*, a collection based on lectures and tapes, on writing and American writers, etc. I will send you a copy. Is there anything you need from here? Any book you cannot get? Be sure to let me know.

I have not talked by phone with Henry Miller recently so I do not know his plans. Why did you think I would not care to see your article on Miller? Or Masako Karatani too? She sent me chrysanthemum petals for salads.

I am trying out a new electric typewriter for the first time and I am not used to it, so this letter is full of errors. I hope you can read it.

Why do we write? I don't know. For three months I worked on the writing book and did not hear the mockingbirds sing. Now I hear them again. It is like a fever, or a cold, an illness. One recovers, and one is free until the next book.

I am so glad you are writing me in English. I feel now I know you better.

Anaïs

Letter from Anaïs Nin to Ruth Witt Diamant:
Los Angeles, March 31, 1968

Dear Ruth:

Are you home? Time is going by so swiftly that I no longer know it as days, months, but as jet flights.

Confidentially, I will be in Japan from July 15 until the end of August. I have many friends there now. You may have met Sam Francis and his wife Mako. Millie Horton will be teaching at Osaka. Kazuko Sugisaki translated *Collages*, and I have also succeeded in getting short stories published, which had been translated from the Japanese in *Chicago University Magazine*. Finally saw Nobuko's story on the Noh Master in *Mademoiselle*.

Nobuko is the opposite of Mako. Mako is free and living sincerely. Nobuko has become a woman of society and position and is not free, or able to be herself at all because Ivan Morris is an insincere Englishman. The English are false. They live in a conventional, artificial persona. I like them less and less. I was on a panel with an English poet, and he was all false modesty, false humility, false self-effacement. He could neither read nor talk with acute self-consciousness and sought to obliterate himself, and the result was entirely negative.

Everybody is well. Hugo is making a new film. Rupert still loves his students and his garden is thriving. Marguerite Young is slowly getting recognition. Sylvia Spencer is working for the Parson School of Design. Next year their multi-media theme will be lights and costumes for a reading from *Collages*.

Let me know whom we should meet in Japan. No one knows I am going yet.

Love,
Anaïs

Letter from Hiram Haydn to Anaïs Nin:
New York, April 2, 1968

Dear Anaïs:

I am happy to tell you that we are ready at last to take the step of a paperback edition of *Diary 1*. My thought is that we proceed as we have with hardcover editions, first trying out volume 1 and seeing what the results are before moving on. I hope you are pleased at this. I will be back in touch again when the contract people have gone over the prospects. I hope you are feeling well.

Love,
Hiram

LOS ANGELES, APRIL 1968

On the 3rd I had an all-evening reading at UCLA.

At the death of Dr. King, I became hysterical. I could not bear the cruelty, the horror of it. I knew what a deep wound it would cause the Black people. I never espoused causes, but the cause of Black people affects me deeply. Attended a vigil for Dr. King at Pershing Square.

I was invited to visit a radio telescope by Eugene Epstein at the Aerospace Corp. radio astronomy program.

Lectured at Cal State College, Dominguez Hills, which was impressive. It is near Watts, and the student body is half Black and angry. Professors feel in danger of their lives now. I heard about Black Power on TV. They are too late, I think, for a cure. They talk of a sick society and wanting a separate culture. I'm so involved in this that I changed my lecture to one on sensitivity versus toughness. And the students responded. I dedicated the talk to Dr. King.

Also lectured and read at Santa Barbara; did a Poetry Center reading at YMHA in New York.

LOS ANGELES, APRIL 1968

Dream: The protestors against the draft are babies—5, 6, 7 years old. I look at them from a high-up place. People throw pieces of broken metal at them to cut them. I shelter them. I am waiting to see the doctor. I see a man horribly hacked to pieces; I ask the doctor to put him out of his agony. I am desperate. The doctor tells me I have cancer.

Lecture at UC Santa Cruz; I was invited to contribute to several college magazines; David Maddow will teach *Novel of the Future* in his class. It will be taught at Ohio University also.

Last night I read a study of the Japanese mind. Occidental Psychoanalysis. Japanese individualism, *dis*-individualism, duty, revolt, a hatred of foreigners, the repression of hatred—obedience. There is no crime, even in the insane. No violence. There are only rice paper partitions between the insane. They choose suicide rather than murder.

Louise speaks of the many selves of Varèse. He is difficult to write about—mercurial.

Mary Weir asks Hugo how he could give me so much freedom.

Daisy retrogresses: bad poetry, bad art (due to Rudolf Steiner, religion).

Sandra Hochman advances in life, but there is a danger in her popularity—her beauty, warmth, sensual magnetism, elegance, radiance—danger in her *fashionable* status.

My depression, once cured by passion, activity and ecstasy, is now permanent. No physical cause detected.

I discovered Rupert's letter to Susie Sugisaki by accident, in which he refers to their affair. I have no anger—ideal behavior—I am generous and understanding. But sorrow. Is it the beginning of the end? The first fissure. He says: "No, no, it was minor, not major."

Should I leave?

"No."

He looked frightened.

This happened two years ago! Last summer we went to Tahiti, but I noticed no change in him. He can wait. I could not have waited, if I desired someone. He planned patiently. We would ask Susie to accompany us in Japan, he thought. We would rent a car. I would have been caught in the middle. In the letter to her he said: "Anaïs cannot climb mountains."

But I, who committed a thousand treacheries, how can I condemn? I, who loved in dualities, triplicities, in fragments, of course cannot judge. I will accept, encourage. I tell Rupert to go to Japan alone. He will not. He cancels the trip to Japan without hesitation. "I was prepared for a sexual fling—a whim—not for a romantic episode."

I loved her. I write to her. I will let them meet. I need certitude. Anxiety is the enemy, the not knowing. I will not use my power to destroy this small love. I will let it live.

After the talks, Rupert was passionate, clinging, made love. I did not withdraw. A great victory over jealousy and fear. To remain open and loving is an achievement.

When I was in New York briefly, Rupert said over the telephone: "When you left I realized what my life could be without you." But nevertheless he protests too much. "I love you. I love you." Does he say it to persuade himself?

Depression.

End of passion?

End of life for me.

"You are not angry?" asked Bogner.

"How *can* I be? She is lovely and intelligent and sensitive. He is sincere. He does not lie. We *both* fell in love with Japan and the Japanese woman."

Letter from Anaïs Nin to Kazuko (Susie) Sugisaki:
Los Angeles, April 16, 1968

Dearest Susie:

This letter is a *secret*. It is written with love and understanding. By a freakish accident, a letter to you was returned, which I thought I had written and I opened to add to it. But it was Rupert writing to you. It was a love letter to you about seeing you in Japan. Because it was you, and I know your quality and loveliness, I could only be sad for the three of us. Because all of us are sacrificial and unselfish, it is even more painful. I do not want you or Rupert deprived of anything. At the same time I cannot go to Japan knowing this.

I begged Rupert to go to Japan alone. It is important that nothing should be denied and sacrificed. You know I believe that. I would never forgive myself for paining you or Rupert. I would never feel worthy or even sure of his love again. Of course, now he says he will not go. He will sacrifice this for me. And I don't want such a sacrifice. If this is deep, it must be lived out. I cannot even understand why Rupert did not plan to go last summer.

But you, Susie, are a woman, and women understand the needs of love. Please, dear Susie, treat me like a sister. I was concerned about the wistfulness of your face.

Can you help me to make a plan by which nothing will be sacrificed? Rupert will feel now he cannot go to Japan even if I plead with him and promise to be here when he returns. But will you come here? I would like you to come. I will help you to come. I will be sure to be away. Both you and Rupert deserve whatever happiness may come of this. You can stay at Bernard Forrest's house. He will be in Japan. You can see Rupert. I can find things to do.

I say this with love and trust and only ask you not to tell Rupert. Then, at least, we will know if it is a more important relationship than all others. I have lived by the rules of love alone, so I feel others should too. You do understand how guilty I would feel if this were ignored, and how this might estrange me from Rupert, far more than knowing I had been, accidentally, instrumental to the destruction of something alive.

Write to me at another address: 4255 West 5th St., Los Angeles 90005. I will be in New York for lectures May 3 so unless you answer me immediately, write me care of Gunther Stuhlmann, 65 Irving Place, New York City 3. He is my agent. If we do not go to Japan we can invite you here. Do you have a vacation? We were not even sure if you had any leisure. Do you teach all summer? As you probably know, Rupert's school ends June 20 or so. I can be away at any time you can come. Can you come?

I will keep this secret from Rupert. It will be our secret. If you tell me you want to come, I will send you a ticket. You can stay as long as you want to, as long as you can. I have lectures up until June 12. But there are many things I can do to be far away. I can go to Europe. If this is impossible, will you meet us in Europe, in Paris? I can also find ways to disappear. I want to be the cause of your happiness, not of your unhappiness. Rupert asked me where I wanted to go this summer. I can say any place but Japan, if you cannot come. I always dreamed that if Rupert had to love another woman it might be someone like you.

Anaïs*

Letter from Nobuko Uenishi to Anaïs Nin:
Spring 1968

Dearest Anaïs:

You are such a rare human being. I am awed and given confidence back.

Anaïs, I have never been so fundamentally depressed.

1) Dr. King's death. Death of hope in America...

2) Ivan cannot be my lover. Period. It is so, so heartbreaking that I stare into the face of this reality and not believe it.

3) Question: Shall I end then this false life with him? I keep on asking myself. Kindness, social preoccupations, to keep face, etc., get in the way...

Perhaps things will be better after both of us get over this weighty depression from the general social chaos, but no, the problems become deeper.

One kind of callousness can lead to another, and it spreads without end. The greatest callousness on my part is to think that it is all right to keep on pretending that a life shared with someone with whom I can't feel romantic or feel passionate fire is "manageable" or "permissible."

---

* For Sugisaki's responses to Nin, see Addenda.

I am not making Ivan unhappy by any means, but I always feel that there can be someone else who could make him happier. And this is a grisly thought: to feel myself so useless a burden on him, and so pointless an existence to anyone...it's horrid.

I might as well go to Bolivia and die for the poor peasants. To be useless disgusts me so that I can't even feel worthy of writing even a line.

Yet, life itself goes on lifting my thinking, probing feet off the ground. Parties, meetings, luncheons, appointments...

What an irony! He said, "Since we have accepted the invitation, a sit-down dinner on Friday, we can't get divorced before then..."

(The other day I strolled into a book shop on 89th street, and right on the front counter I saw the title: *A Spy in The House of Love* in paperback with a misty, greenish-blue photograph, very fascinating... There were several right on the front desk.)

What can I die for? I ask myself. Something positive. Self-pride is negative. I must not waver, flinch from confrontation. I think I will keep on asking myself...till I know.

Love?

The terrible truth is, Anaïs, that I could die right this minute practically for anyone. I could also live for anyone. I am indiscriminate...

I am running the risk within my life.

Much, much, much inexpressible love and admiration to you, Anaïs.

Nobuko

WRITTEN FOR A JOURNALIST, LOS ANGELES, SPRING 1968

Here are some more concrete facts about the elusive Miss Nin. Names of our trees: Canary Island Pine (tall and languid); Twisted Juniper (my favorite); Pittosporum (the bushes around the pool); bougainvillea on the walls; Lippia is the ground covering, a green carpet on which Piccolo likes to sit watching the birds. Ah, birds. I feed them. I really do. So I can watch them while they eat: linnets, mockingbirds, blue jays. The blue jays have a voice like Donald Duck and *demand* food; the ring-neck doves come from China, and they are gentle and coo. Some birds have black hoods around their heads, I don't know their names. Some have red breasts. They are fun to watch.

My love of costume has continued from the early Diary days. I brought back a Vietnamese dress, a Malaysian skirt, a Japanese kimono, and I love to wear them. My favorite designer is Rudi Gernreich because he is imaginative. I like many things about California that the East does not have—the glass chapel of Lloyd Wright, son of Frank Lloyd Wright, the Watts Towers, which the surrealists would have loved.

One may think from the Diaries that I live in the past. Not so. I am just as active with new experiences, new travels, new friends. I love light shows and am planning to read with a light show and paper dresses for Parson's school of Design. I have international friends, with a preference for Japan. I am on the Committee for the Tea Ceremony School, which is tied up with Zen. I love the hippies. I love underground films and student films. My best relationship of all is with the young. It is the young who read me and who visit me.

California is ideal for a writer.

Arrival in New York.

A bad translation of *Diary 1* by Stock. I rejected it. Stock answered I would have to find my own translation and pay for it. I wrote to Michel Fabre who had asked me for more details about Richard Wright for his biography. We had corresponded. He suggested a student of his now teaching American literature at the Sorbonne, Marie-Claire Van der Elst. It was a lucky choice. She was excellent — natural and exact.

A visit from Jack Jones. Incredible courage against handicaps. Deaf and mute. Crippled. Eyes not good. But he is a specialist on Rank.

Letter from Koji Nakada to Anaïs Nin:
Tokyo, May 12, 1968

Dear Anaïs:

I am writing this letter with regret.

I am deeply sorry to hear from you that you have dropped your plan to come to Japan while I have been expecting you.

I read your letters with regret and I have been, in a way, standing in two fires since February.

At that time, Kawade's editors wanted to publish my two novels—and I accepted their offers in January. But I then told the editors that unless they hasten to publish Anaïs's novels, I have to abandon the hope of my own—this happened in early March.

Incidentally, Miss Sugisaki sent me her translation of *Children*, which I immediately delivered to Kawade. At that time, I consulted Mr. Naguchi, the editor, whom you may remember from my talks with you, to see if he could handle the *Children* draft with the one Mr. Fukada made. Then he promised me to consider the matter. I wired the above fact to Miss Sugisaki, telling her that all seemed to be going well. No sooner than the above arrangement was made, Kawade faced a financial crisis.

I have no hope of my new novels being published through Kawade. I think that we had better find another publisher, although that is very problematic nowadays. Of course, I will do everything possible. Mr. Sugawara, of Shi-chi-sha, will translate only a few pieces of your short stories and intends to use a very minor publisher. After reading through his draft, I will assist him in every way.

As you already know, Mr. Kan Nakajima, a translator living in Osaka, has translated your short story "Mouse" and sent me the draft to get my view of whether his work was satisfactory or not. I read it thoroughly and was determined to introduce it to *Bungei*—but alas, the publication of *Bungei* will cease very soon. My endeavors are therefore in vain. How disappointed I am!

Dear Anaïs, please understand that I am always doing everything possible. Miss Sugisaki called me a few days ago, and I explained to her this unfortunate occurrence; she is very surprised and utterly disappointed. I shared the above fact with her, Mr. Fukada and others as well. No doubt they are also very sorry to know how discouraged you are!

Yours sincerely,
Koji Nakada

Letter from Gunther Stuhlmann to Anaïs Nin:
Hamburg, Germany, May 25, 1968

Dear Anaïs:

We got out of Paris (riots) just by the skin of our teeth and this is the first chance I have for a brief typed note.

As Marie-Claire already told you, I had a number of sessions with Stock on the translation of *Diary 1*, and they have agreed to one of two courses to improve the situation:

A) We could edit and rewrite the existing translation as much as we wanted to your full satisfaction.

B) We could commission a new translation with a translator of your choice—in which case, however, we would have to bear the cost.

André also suggested that we could get an independent appraisal of the translation in Paris—but I don't want to go into all the back and forth. In general, they were quite amenable to anything we wanted (they had a similar experience with Mary McCarthy, it seems). Personally, I think that it might perhaps be better to edit and rewrite the existing translation, since at least this is in hand. With a new translation, we might eventually have the same problem.

The new edition of the Miller letters was scheduled for June (Philippe Bourgois came forth with long apologies and took the entire blame upon himself) but, given the near-civil war and general strike in France, I don't know what will happen. Also, this may be the time to suggest to Stock a translator for the second volume. They are ready to listen to suggestions and to get samples.

The German situation of the Miller letters and *Diary 1* is well in hand. I had a lengthy meeting with both Wegner and Rowohlt, and they are going to cooperate with each other and bring out the books simultaneously this fall. You may have seen Mathias Wegner, meanwhile, in New York. I was able to check out certain questions with them and make a few changes. I also discussed with Wegner's editor a number of suggested cuts for the German audience on vol. 2 and I will tell you about this in detail. I see no problems there (we spent a good deal of time going over everything) and they want to contract for vol. 2. I also saw the jacket for vol. 1 in Paris (they are using an adaptation of the U.S. jacket, which is very nice).

I still hope to see you in New York when I get back so we can talk about all this.

I am very pleased with the careful way people here are working (I met the Rowohlt translator who did a careful index, etc.). We all hope to have a success here.

Am off now for the last lap of the journey and look forward to being back. Having some trouble with my back and leg, which makes travel less than a joy right now. But I am sticking to the schedule.

Best from both of us, also to Hugo,
Gunther

JUNE 18 TO JULY 1968

In Mexico with Rupert.

We stayed in Acapulco, which was suffering great changes from a fishing village to grand deluxe hotels, the pool life. But the beauty is still there. We worked at dawn, from six to eight, on revising volume 3 of the *Diary*; then, when the heat came, we swam. I had the same view I describe in *Minotaur*, swans and sunsets, the same winds and the same flowers.

In Mexico City we saw the most beautiful museum in the world, the new archeological museum, which is not only beautiful and noble and modern in architecture, but presents the history of man and of Mexico in a dramatic, living way. For example, the collection of instruments is never as in other museums, merely placed in a window. They are played upon by figures appropriate to the time and place, and the music that they created is played on tapes, authentic. Entire shacks of palm leaves are recreated, tools, gestures, costumes. There is space and per-spective, beautiful use of color backgrounds and effects similar to the Japanese in the windows giving on Chapultepec Park, with statues and temples outside. Beauty and drama, no dusty accumulation, each object placed within its time and in the present. Open tombs, dances, weddings, bones, silks, baskets, fishing nets, feather ornaments, enlarged photographs of temples and pyramids. One could spend a week there.

NEW YORK, AUGUST 1968
Returned to New York Aug. 21.

Spent time at the beach; saw Marguerite Young, Lili Bita and Robert Zaller; worked on fixing up the apartment.

Nearing the end of volume 3. Benjamin Franklin works on my bibliography with my collaboration. Worked on my preface to Bettina Knapp's book on Artaud.

Richard Centing is working to interest Ohio State University in the diary originals.

LOS ANGELES, SEPTEMBER 1968
Took part in Robert Snyder's Miller documentary at Henry's home. Saw Paul Mathieson, then Renate the next day.

Duane Schneider has hand-printed excerpts from vol. 1 that were left out of the *Diary* (at Hiram Haydn's request).

Wrote new prefaces to *House of Incest* and *Stella*.

Worked on volume 3.

Letter from Joaquín Nin-Culmell to Anaïs Nin:
Berkeley, September 9, 1968

Dear Anaïs:

Your welcome welcome note was duly received, but better still it was good to hear your voice on the 5th. You sound fine and optimistic in spite of the fan letters and too much work. As soon as I can settle down, I will write to Ayma in Barcelona and ask them why in hell they haven't sent you a copy of the Catalan edition of *Spy*. During my stay in Barcelona I bought a dozen or so copies, which I distributed to my Catalan friends. It's a limited public but one that reads enormously.

Let me know if I can help with volume 3. As for *The Novel of the Future*, I will wait for your plans in December to give you a "coming out" party.

Things are fairly calm here. Am giving a department bash on the 27th. 72 invited guests! It will be a catered cocktail party. More expensive, perhaps, but less wear and tear on the soft-wear like myself. All of it will be held on the patio at the back of the house, and I am praying for good weather.

Thorvald and Kay about the same. Thorvald seems to be having less trouble with his back. Ken is in boarding school and working for Nixon. (Don't throw up!)

Opera season begins on Friday. On Saturday I go to hear Teresa Berganza in *Il Barbiere*. Should be a fine performance.

Love,
Joaquín

LOS ANGELES, OCTOBER 6, 1968

Mike Steen, an actor I had met several times and now a neighbor, told me Tennessee Williams had taken a house in the hills and invited us for dinner. I had a strong desire not to go, remembering the Tennessee of parties, the artificial talk, the flippancy and hypocrisies—I had heard about his drinking, his depressions. Once he talked with me over the telephone and he was drunk. "I need you desperately." I refused several times.

Finally last night we drove up dark and torturous hills, looking at houses that expose only their garages and their cars and garbage cans. The air was pungent from damp earth and plants.

Mike opened the door. Mike is big and strong, and at first one thinks he is merely a physical athlete. But he has soft eyes, and at a party with Joanne Woodward and Gore Vidal he was the only one who remembered to give Tavi water. He was also the only gentle and natural one.

The last time I saw Tennessee was at a party after the opening of *The Milk Train Does Not Stop Here Anymore*. He was on his way to Italy. He seemed the same as he had always been. Last night when I saw him standing by a table in an ivory-colored embroidered Nehru suit, I received the full shock of the change.

He looked small, soft, a mixture of old lady and child. Small hands, soft. The head round, full, the eyes slightly protruding—but all of it as if about to disintegrate. He was making an effort to hold himself together, offering me a red flower in a tiny glass holder. His lips were pursed, drawn into a tight bud. We embraced. His hair seemed so much thinner. It was not the lurching oscillations of drunkenness. It was the underwater swimming of drugs. He walked carefully. He lisped. Southern accent. His eyes dissolved. There was a space between his words. "I can't see the aquamarine beautiful eyes in this light."

He spoke of the *Diary*. "So beautiful, so beautiful," he said. "I kept a diary too."

"Show it to me, Tennessee. Read to us from it. You owe me that."

Mike and two young men sat talking. Rupert faced us.

Tennessee and I were on the couch. Suddenly what I saw was all the aging, desperate women he had portrayed reflected in him, in the dissolved face, the soft hands. He went into his bedroom to bring out his notebooks. Three school notebooks. One black and white. He opened it and said: "No, these are notes for *Milk Train*." The second one was black—"Notes, too." The third one was the diary. He read about the blackout—the one after the Japanese attack on Pearl Harbor. Simple notations in pencil. Facts. About feeling adverse at the Claridge Hotel. He had not described the scene. He elaborated on it verbally. Two sailors attacked him and a friend with knives and beat them. A diary of facts—meetings—walking—seeing so-and-so. No elaboration. He closed it, though we wanted more. It was not a revelation. Then he talked about the Grey Goose who had come to see him. The Grey Goose was his mother, now 84 years old. He asked Mike to show us photographs. *La mère tigre*, who loved her sons more than her husband—and destroyed her three children. "My sister is schizophrenic."

Of Mishima he said: "He is a most *beautiful* man." The word "beautiful" was hissed as if uttered with hatred, lust, love. "He was in love with Frank. Did you know Frank? He died, you know. But I don't like his last book. It's *too* homosexual."

This was at the table. A stew cooked by the Argentine cleaning woman. All of us under tension, to entertain Tennessee. The three young men were rather silent. Hypnosis came up because someone had put Tennessee in a trance for 18 hours. He called him a guru. Mike called him an old con queen. I was entranced by Tennessee's face. When he did not like the food, it was that of an infant—spoiled. When he talked of Mishima, it was lust. But at times his mouth seemed more prominent as if he had difficulty in modulating the words or as if he couldn't control it. His smile was a leer. There was theatrical puppetry, an unconscious show that did not match his words. His mind, memory and sense of the present were at odds. The features were at odds. The tender, soft, childlike expressions mingled with a wolf-like grin.

On our way to the dining table he had stayed behind with Rupert, and I could imagine him saying: "You are too beautiful to live with a woman," but what he did say was, "Anaïs is so beautiful, take good care of her, you are so lucky!" He had said to me: "You are more beautiful than ever," and kissed me, but today I distrust the admiration of homosexuals. Why should it concern him? The shock of compassion did not wear out. I saw him so vulnerable, counting his loves. "Oliver Evans was in love with me for so long." But the paranoia is there. "They want to kill me." And Ruby, the pug dog, worried him. "She whines. Her ears are icy cold."

I said, putting my ear to her nose. "She's wheezing. She's allergic to smog. She's not ill."

"She is very ill."

Mike could not help saying: "You're projecting, Tennessee." He had to be reassured. "We know a wonderful veterinarian who loves his animals. He once sheltered an old toothless lion the neighbors reported because they were afraid. He was doing no one harm. He lived in the garage, and when he roared his master spoke to him through the intercom and he would go back to sleep."

We had seen *Boom*. "A terrible film. They massacred the script—and when I first saw it, they had handled the camera like a bird—it swung, flew here and there. At the opening all this was gone. I have never liked any of my films."

Between the words there were drugged pauses—fade-outs—meltings, silences. It was like sitting by a sick person having dreams and nightmares, and I suddenly understood how all these years we had been witnessing Tennessee's nightmares. He was given so much by the world, but the nightmares engulfed him. The last one was about a dying old woman and the Angel of Death.

His face lay as it might be in sleep—the eyes not seeing you but filled with ghostly visitors. At times the grimace of lust, the tongue curling as if before a feast, or one of anguish—or the pursed lips seeking the small kisses of childhood.

He yawned. The Seconal pills and the drink were sending him into drowsiness.

As we left, outside Mike said: "He must have taken a Seconal and one of Jacobson's injections. He is utterly dependent on them—he gives them to himself. They are Methedrine."

"Are you sure?"

Suddenly my last visit to Jacobson was clarified. I had been stunned by the change in Jacobsen's appearance—he was bloated—an unhealthy fat—enormous. He did not know what he was doing. He faltered with giving me his injection. I could not understand. The nurse had to remind him that there was a patient waiting.

I had once seen an item in a paper about the wife of an actor who had reported to the police that her husband would get up in the middle of the night to get an injection from Jacobson.

What happened? He began with potent vitamins. He attracted people under stress—from the theatre, concert halls, opera, TV—who *had* to perform. When did he begin to give out drugs and to take them himself?

Mike's solicitude, his effort to bring people around who would understand and help Tennessee—all this was explained. It was this or a sanitarium. His sister is in an asylum. A doctor from UCLA lives nearby.

The damage to Tennessee? Was it done by alcohol or drugs?

Now Mike admits that his associates are becoming secretive.

Why did he have to disguise himself as a woman, the woman who went mad, the woman who inhaled ether, the woman who howled for her dead love, the woman who had tantrums, the woman enslaved by gigolos, the woman denied, outraged, used? I see the changing face of Tennessee, not the smiling face of the social Tennessee, but the baby fat and the woman fat softening, dissolving in the anguish of nightmares. The mask is shattered. Ruby moans—he moans. Tennessee does not want clear vision. He is flooded and invaded by his own theatre of hysteria, with the poet's madness at times inspired and at times infinitesimally small—a round-faced child.

Letter from Anaïs Nin to Gunther Stuhlmann:
Los Angeles, November 1968

Dear Gunther:

Danièle Suissa, the Canadian producer, writes me that she wants an option on the *Spy* movie and has Jeanne Moreau's approval of the part of Sabina. She wanted to know whether she should buy the option from Trianon immediately or wait until it expires.

I cabled that you had advised to wait until Dec. 27 (much as I hate to wait), so now we shall hold our breath for I want so much for the film to be done in France.

About the diary film. Of course Ellis Marcus was startled by the $2,000 he said he must spend on lawyers for a contract, etc. So he will offer $1,000. I guess it is better than nothing. And for some perverse reason in this perverse town, having an option impresses them, the mere idea someone else might want it...remember *Spy*. So please, dear Gunther, let us expedite this. I suggested the best way to obtain releases from Henry and June was to promise that the script would be faithful to the *Diary* portraits such as I made them. But I feel the bird in the hand is Danièle. They have a French script already, being translated. I can't call you up because of the answering service.

Love,
Anaïs

Letter from Anaïs Nin to Danièle Suissa:
New York, November 7, 1968

Dear Danièle:
   I now have definite news. My option with Trianon ends December 27. I believe the film was not made because the script by Barbara Turner was not good. If Moreau is interested, it would be marvelous timing, because in June they will be filming *Tropic of Cancer* in Paris, and the limelight will once more be on that period. A young script writer you will like immensely will be there. He did the script for *Ulysses*, and now *Tropic*, and then *Steppenwolf*, etc. Or were you thinking of writing the script? I love the idea of our working together. I truly believe this film can only be made in France. Always felt so, and you remember at one time I liked the camera work of *La Fille Aux Yeux d'Or*. Where will you be? Where will you make your friend's novel (which I still have among my books)? In France or Canada? Do write me. Do you need books? Have you read the *Diaries*? Gunther is still in Europe but will be back the end of this week. It was his wife who gave me the data from the contract. Tracey Roberts' brother-in-law is taking an option on *Diary 1*. If you answer me I can take care of all this before I leave New York November 26 for Los Angeles. After that write me 4255 West 5th, Los Angeles. And who knows, we may meet in Paris again. Let me know if you intended to write the script, whether you liked *Ulysses*, whether you have talked with Moreau. Marguerite Duras once wrote a script for Robert Wise, but she is comfortable in her own moods and work, and was thrown off course by the impersonality of Hollywood directors. She had never worked with an invisible director and did not know English, and it was all very distant and foreign to her. The script was always the stumbling block. I have an immense admiration for Moreau the actress and the woman. If you want to telephone me, I have a private phone: 254-0352.

Love,
Anaïs

NEW YORK, NOVEMBER 25, 1968
   Gotham Book Mart Book Party, 350 people, for publication of *Novel of the Future*.

LOS ANGELES, NOVEMBER 28, 1968
   Arrived in L.A. yesterday; beach today with Rupert.

Letter from Anaïs Nin to Bettina Knapp:
Los Angeles, December 12, 1968

Dear Bettina:

I had so many frustrations with reviews that I did not want to write you. It is terrible that a writer should depend on such a politically corrupt system as that of reviews. I am going through a depression about the way things are run. MacMillan saying they ran out of review copies and omitting my loyal and friendly and selective list of reviewers, 30 or 40 of them, and I having not only to buy the books but spend three days mailing them, an unprofessional gesture, a gift. Then a reviewer from *The New York Times* saying my *Novel* book was too much about French writers, and, not taking an excerpt, they let someone write about Cendrars who is not an expert on him, and gave the Cendrars book to nobody at all to review. No wonder Nona Balakian is depressed. I am beginning to agree with the dropout hippies!

I am detained here by film possibilities that are not yet concrete (options). Have met Herbert Blau, a big theatre man now in charge of California Institute of the Arts. I have much work, but a feeling we are combatting a Goliath Computer told to make money only...but I know this will pass.

Love,
Anaïs

NEW YORK, DECEMBER 29, 1968

Returned two days ago; helping Hugo film. Saw Danièle Suissa, Marguerite Young, Tana de Gamez, Daniel Stern, Frances Field, Nobuko, Bogner.

LOS ANGELES, JANUARY 1969

Returned to California Jan. 15. Saw Joaquín's concert; at his cocktail for me saw Ferlinghetti, Ruth Witt Diamant.

Lectured at the Berkeley Extension; saw John Pearson. Lectured at Santa Barbara.

R. W. Newcomb of Stanford Electronics Laboratories uses as a letterhead my words: "Only when the poet and the scientist work in unison will we have living experiences and knowledge of the marvels of the universe as they are being discovered."

Oliver Evans sells my letters to him.

Finished vol. 3.

When Fred Haines scripted *Ulysses*, I became friends with him and his wife Frances. They invited us over, and we found them drugged. They gave us some cookies and watched us eating them innocently. Suddenly I felt dizzy and detached and I wanted to leave.

The drive home was a nightmare. Rupert was afraid to lose consciousness and asked me to talk to him. Time seemed endless; it seemed like hours between one red light and another. It is a miracle we reached home. We lay in bed. Each one of us had the feeling of dying, and held on to the other. "Hold me, I am going away, I am dying."

I was deathly ill, vomited to the point of exhaustion. A nightmare. I don't know how long it was before we fell asleep.

Letter from Durrett Wagner to Anaïs Nin:
Chicago, January 20, 1969

Dear Miss Nin:

Received your letter today from Berkeley. Yes, I too am sorry that the Swallow-Nin-Stuhlmann relationship has skewed off into the strained tension that has developed. I deeply regret it, and even more deeply hope that we can re-establish a relationship of genuine cooperation and harmony—as I strongly feel we should and can.

Mr. Weisman does come on curtly sometimes, and perhaps he has at times been a bit brusque. On the other hand, I suspect that all the shortness and tactlessness has not been on Mr. Weisman's side. Gunther has not been the epitome of gracefulness at all times either. I have been privy to all the Weisman-Stuhlmann correspondence and I can understand Mr. Weisman's impatience with Gunther; I have been impatient myself. From our point of view, we have waited *ever* so long for a contractual clarification of the whole Swallow-Nin matter. The controversy seems really to have revolved around two issues, which from the outside must appear terribly simple: 1) certainty and clarification about Swallow-Nin titles, etc.; 2) subsidiary rights on Nin titles. It is simply the case in regard to the latter, for example, that Gunther made curt, blanket assertions about this matter that we do not understand or agree with from our reading of the contracts in hand. Yet we have yet to receive from Gunther any unambiguous clarification or argument or reassertion or counter-assertion about the matter. Perhaps if Gunther's European trip and his illness had not come when they did, everything would by now have been settled and we would all be living happily together. But it didn't and we aren't...

Also, I think you will appreciate the fact that at least from our point of view we have indeed been waiting an incredibly long time—since August 1967 when we took over Alan's line—that's about 1½ years—to receive from Gunther contracts on the titles, of which we have none. In the meantime, we have reprinted practically all our Nin titles; we have redesigned (and hopefully improved) most of the covers; we have advertised Nin titles in journals and on the back covers of other non-Nin Swallow books, etc., etc. In other words, we have, with all the good faith and all the money we could muster, gone gung-ho with the Swallow-Nin titles, certainly doing as much as—and more, I think—than Alan did with them. So it is, again from our point of view, a puzzlement and a frustration why we cannot get from Gunther the simple satisfaction of contracts and clarification we have requested.

It is out of this frustration and impatience that perhaps Mr. Weisman sounds harsh and rude. Certainly we do *not* want our relationship with either Gunther or you to be harsh or rude or strained in any way. Good luck to us all as we happily and quickly—I hope—wrap this matter up in the next few weeks.

I am also sorry this flap spoiled the atmosphere and kept you from the Swallow party last month. If Swallow doesn't have another big one soon, I, at least, promise a little one! Wagner, Stuhlmann, et al. can have our own small and sedate bash when we have depolluted the psychic air—OK?

Thanks also for the *Voyages* tip. Bill Claire and I are on very friendly terms; he was at the N.Y.C. Swallow party, for example. So Swallow and *Voyages* will keep in touch properly. Please continue to drop such hints my way, however; the next one will probably be a journal or a person I am not in constant correspondence with.

I appreciate your writing me your letter of January 16.

Cordially,

Durrett

Letter from Gunther Stuhlmann to Anaïs Nin:
New York, January 20, 1969

Dear Anaïs:

Hiram seems happy about the additional changes for volume 3 and I told him you would get some of the releases he has asked for.

Also, he asked whether you had a schedule of your lecture engagements, so he would know where to reach you if anything came up. This might also be valuable to have for tying in some publicity when the paperback of vol. 1 comes out. It has been announced in the Harcourt spring catalogue. I told Harcourt that if and when you are at some college campuses they should make sure that copies are in the bookstores and perhaps set up some autographing situations.

I heard this morning from Mort Weisman of Swallow, who wants to bury the hatchet (though he still threatens with law suits), and I will now get him some contracts for Swallow Press to put things on an even keel again. I don't like his attitude, really, but at this point we have not much of an alternative. He tells me he wants to promote the books in 1969 and keep after the stores, etc., etc., etc., and I guess we will just have to ride hard on him whenever we find stores without copies.

All the best,
Gunther

P.S. The German edition of vol. 1 has gone into a second printing after two months and we have gone over 4,000 copies already. They are pushing.

Letter from Anaïs Nin to Hugh Guiler:
Los Angeles, January 21, 1969

Darling:

It took me two days to recover from the San Francisco trip. Joaquín's ballet was more modern than Falla, more subtle, and quite beautiful. Nobody realized he barely touched on Spanish dance themes and developed a subtlety. But I was depressed to discover his vulnerability to rudeness and lack of savoir-faire. He was invited to a reception for the symphony on the same day—an oversight. As a member of the university, they should have made some gesture of celebration. Boorish people—unable to praise or admire anything.

Joaquín's friend is very kind and helpful. He is an architect. He takes care of the garden and advised the house as a solid investment. Beautiful view. Very comfortable. Joaquín is a very thoughtful, devoted host brought me coffee in bed. The lecture went terribly well.

After the lecture, so many people surrounded me that there was a cry. Joaquín whisked me away. His neurosis was blatant. He suffers from a lack of recognition, yet when a gesture is offered him, as when he was asked to stand up for applause, he refused; the same at my lecture—the introduction included him and he was ungracious. He stood up without a smile and would not look at audience—deprecating. Whereas, thanks to Bogner, I can establish a real intimacy with the audience, even playful and humorous, and when they demonstrate response and stand up, I smile and accept it.

Thanks be for Bogner. It made me sad to have had the kind of help Joaquín did not have.

Although I am between books, I seem to have as much work as ever. Tomorrow I go to Santa Barbara. Rain and windstorms have been exceptional. We circled for 2½ hours over a plane that went down on its way to Denver.

Love,

A

Letter from Anaïs Nin to Luise Rainer:
Los Angeles, January 22, 1969

Dear Luise:

I made all the elisions and changes you asked of me, but Harcourt Brace still wants a formal signature. It is absurd, but they are pedantic and literal. I hope you don't mind. I would send you a final copy, but I already spent $70 on Xerox copies, time in mailing, and would have to take back the final copy from Harcourt to cut up and send you your section and make another $70 copy for them.

I can't remember if I wrote you that all our references to June were from the novel and the Diary. You mention you did not know her. True. But we were talking of literary characters as symbols, not of people we both knew. Different as you are from June, it was strange that you had the same birthday. You are creative and positive and a real artist, wife and mother, and June must have been all negative. Astrologic signs express the highest development of the personality and also its opposite.

Anyway, *Diary 3* is in. *The Novel of the Future* is appearing in England, *A Spy in the House of Love* will be filmed by a French-Canadian company, with Jeanne Moreau as Sabina, but, alas, not in Europe. In New York.

My publisher fell in love with my portrait of you! What a charmer, he said.

Love,

Anaïs

Letter from Anaïs Nin to David Pepperell:
Los Angeles, January 23, 1969

When I don't write it is because I am drowned in work or am very, very weary! As a writer, you sing your ballad, and suddenly, when the world answers, it overwhelms you! I lecture and the students treat me like the Beatles! I'm swamped in correspondence. It is wonderful in one way; in another it is like the sorcerer's apprentice—he summons forces that he cannot control. I enjoy your letters but cannot always answer. Can do so today because I'm forced to lie still to recover from two lectures, interviews and a hundred new friends at Berkeley University and Santa Barbara.

When I went to the Santa Barbara campus by the sea, my friend warned me they were a sleepy, lethargic lot, too comfortable, dazed by the violence of events, and might not awaken. Awaken they did! We could have dialogued for the entire night. There is a new generation of Americans nobody knows. They are caricatured as hippies—but that is not exact. They are enormously intelligent, loving and sensitive. America was too big a monster to fight, and so they turned to the East.

When I began my lecture a few hours ago I used the symbol of pouring teakwood oil on my spirit house from Thailand (the Thai people build a miniature duplicate of their home for the spirits to live in), and the young audience understood.

I asked a bookshop to mail you Henry's latest books—did you receive them? Did Henry answer your letter? He will be in Paris in June for the filming of *Tropic of Cancer.*

Diary 3 is in and will be published next September. What is keeping me busy is the excitement over *The Novel of the Future.*

A Spy in the House of Love will be filmed by a Montreal company, with Jeanne Moreau as Sabina, and Jean Aurel directing. I'm very happy.

I will send you the recordings when I get some money in. At the end of the year I had $48.00 in the bank because MacMillan made me pay for the 50 books I had to give friendly reviewers and another 50 to friends who could not afford to buy it. (I sent you one but it was returned due to a dockers' strike for shipping—it will have to wait.)

You *do* understand, or better still, feel, D. H. Lawrence. He was my first love.

I can see you better in a bookshop than as a tram conductor! So many writer friends of mine are there, with books in hand!

Anaïs

Letter from Anaïs Nin to Gunther Stuhlmann:
Los Angeles, January 1969

Dear Gunther:

The letter from André Bay is Jesuitical and hypocritical. There is nothing to be gained here but failure, as the reviews of the Miller letters show every day. Miller showed me reviews ridiculing the translation.

I am corresponding with Christiane Pauvert, who is interested in Éditions de la Jeune Parque. I cannot afford to gamble $1,500 on a translator I don't know. I prefer to return the $2,000 and be free of the anguish Bay causes me. I prefer to not be published. I trust you, but in this case this has a particular personal meaning for me, and I have a right to refuse such a shabby situation. I am not acting behind your back, but please consider my wishes this time.

Anaïs

Letter from Anaïs Nin to André Bay:
Los Angeles, January 1969

Dear André:

I did not rely on my own impression of the translation of the Miller letters. I consulted with trusted friends, such as Pierre Brodin, director of the Lycée Française, several French writers, a professor of French at UCLA, a Frenchwoman who writes historical books and teaches at Santa Cruz. The translation by Alieu is amateurish.

There is nothing in your attitude to indicate that you are a friend. You washed your hands of the responsibility. I have too much work to do. I wrote two books last year, my reputation is established, and I don't have time to repair a schoolboy translation, a translator whose French is as bad as his knowledge of English. The

67

behavior of Stock towards me is unbelievable to people I have discussed it with. I have only one wish and that is to cancel the contract altogether. You once ignored a contract you had signed. I do not believe in your friendship. I have never been handled by the most cynical of American publishers as I have been handled by you.

If you can seriously try to ruin my work in France by trying to persuade me Alieu is no worse than any other translator, I would prefer to cancel the contract.

I will naturally refund you your advance.

I kept myself from writing you because of my disillusion and shock. But 18 months later, after I wrote you not to use Alieu because everyone knows the translation of the Miller letters is a disgrace—I am still unable to trust you. You are not a friend.

Anaïs

Letter from Anaïs Nin to Gunther Stuhlmann:
Los Angeles, January 24, 1969

Dear Gunther:

I would like to know about Doubleday regarding a preface for Anna Kavan's *Ice*. I should be paid, or I will not do it.

What of the Swallow Press contract?

I'm disappointed at the delay on *Diary 3*, but I rely on your judgment. Haydn once said they needed six months to produce a book. Why couldn't it be out by September?

I would like to know what Harcourt will do for *Diary 3* when the *Los Angeles Times* let a psychotic subway-spitting girl "spectorate" on me, as Mrs. Sitwell said. And Harcourt should have advertised vol. 2 so California would know it was out.

I let Swallow and Harcourt and Spoken Arts know about all my lectures. A lot of books were sold at Berkeley and at Santa Barbara—I was literally mobbed by the students in both places. I could have stayed hours after the lecture.

So sorry you had the flu!

Love,

A

Letter from Anaïs Nin to Durrett Wagner:
Los Angeles, January 27, 1969

Dear Durrett:

I'm glad you wrote me as you did. It justified my feeling that *we* could talk peacefully. I think our two combatants have decided to make peace. I do believe Gunther had at first asked for time and a trial period to see if the books were properly distributed. A few of Mr. Weisman's demands seemed really exaggerated, such as $500 for my quoting from my own books and royalties from MacMillan, or royalties on the *Diaries*, etc.

I saw my Swallow books at Berkeley bookshops—and at Santa Barbara. People will tell you halls are filled and students surround me with books to sign and to ask more questions. The next two evenings should be good too, at Immaculate Heart and Jewish Community Center (Feb. 9 and 10).

How are your relations with Pickwick? Everybody goes there but they never have any of my books.

I was sorry you gave up your Varda collage as he has recently been put on the map in a film made by Agnès Varda called *My Uncle Yanko*, shown at every museum and film club and art film theatre—and he appears in a documentary film on Henry Miller at a gallery exhibit, the three of us talking together.

For the next edition of *Collages* I might suggest a preface by Deena Metzger, who places the right focus on it.

Anaïs

Letter from Hugh Guiler to Anaïs Nin:
New York, January 29, 1969

Darling:

Congratulations on your triumph at Berkeley and glad Joaquín was there to rescue you. It meant you have really broken the sound barrier.

Also congratulations to Joaquín on his success, with the hope he may someday take pleasure in it.

Danièle came this afternoon for an hour and a half. She has been seeing the top Paramount man and says he has given his verbal OK, which will be confirmed in a couple of weeks. She seemed satisfied that the first step has been taken and is sure that the film is now on its way. I said I hope it would be shown just in France. She agrees, but that will be Paramount's decision to make.

To her surprise they told her that Jeanne Moreau's name is *not* a big drawing card here ("bankable" is the technical word). But she wants her to have the role anyhow. Her own wish would be to bring the film out at the Cannes Film Festival, if possible.

I showed her my new film and she was quite enthusiastic about it. And she gave me a very good idea—to add shots of *hands* to those of faces and feet. I agreed at once. She will return to N.Y. in ten days or two weeks, and I have arranged the gallery to be available so I can work with Danièle and Nobuko and Lo. Danièle has beautiful hands and I think Nobuko has too. I don't remember Lo's. Do you? And, of course, I will film your hands when you come. It would, of course, be best to have two sets of hands. But I could do much with a right and left hand of one person.

I was very pleased that, without my saying anything, Danièle got the point of the change of mood in the last part of the film, immediately after the "demonic" eyes. I am also starting and ending with the bird in flight.

By the way, when I asked Danièle if my film would be acceptable in France to go with a feature, she said "yes"—provided there is some narrative. She agreed that you might well take something from *Spy* and adapt it to the film. We might do this in a French language version.

No word from René de Chochor. I had to call him Sunday, after which he agreed to write the next day, but no word yet. He is most inconsiderate. I just wish this transition were over quickly, but that may now take longer than I had imagined. Bogner is helping me to be less impatient about it. But now I have an additional reason for leaving, for a friend has recommended to his wealthy brother to open an account with me, but only after I leave Hayden Stone.

Sunday, Gunther and Barbara came and they liked both the engraving film and the new film very much. Gunther even had a special good word for the narration.

Love,

H

LOS ANGELES, JANUARY 31, 1969

Gunther signed a contract with Danièle Suissa.

Letter from Gunther Stuhlmann to Anaïs Nin:

New York, February 1, 1969

Dear Anaïs:

I just had a note from your German publisher, Dr. Mathias Wegner, who writes: "I would like very much to invite Anaïs Nin for a visit to Germany this fall and to organize various meetings with the press and the book trade. A short round-trip would also result, probably, in some interesting talks and meetings for Miss Nin with her readers and admirers here. Naturally, I would personally accompany Miss Nin everywhere and look after her during her entire stay. Would you ask Miss Nin whether the idea would appeal to her? I would think the best time would be around the Frankfurt Book Fair. Such a visit would be an enormous boost for her work here and very valuable."

He would like to know what your thought on this is—since Peter Owen also would like to see you in London, one might combine the two things or merely concentrate on Frankfurt and the Fair when publishers from all over the world will be there. This could help in other countries, I'm sure. And I think you would like Wegner, who is a very nice young fellow.

I'm going after Hiram for a fall date for vol. 3.

Love,

Gunther

Letter from Anaïs Nin to Gunther Stuhlmann:

Los Angeles, February 1969

Dear Gunther:

Hiram called me yesterday in his usual, oily, ponderous, false way. He said book production takes eight months. A year is too long. Eight months from January is September or October. I was firm in my objections. I also told him that I do not know what he is really fussing about.

The logic is that I can't get a release for every minor character, or even major ones, before I have proofs. He asked about letters. I have consents for the major part of portraits, along with requests for minor changes. I explained that the release he gave me was too brief and people would not sign a blank statement. Luise and her husband mailed signed releases provided I had made changes indicated in her letter.

My intuition tells me (damned women's intuition) that Hiram is *stalling*, and if they are going to engage in pusillanimous pussy-footing around the *Diary*, I want to know.

Or should we let him quibble and squabble and pay no attention?

I'm having a real Vietnam conference here with Henry to sign—bad psychology on Harcourt's side. Can you talk to our dumb Hiram Haydn?

About the preface for Anna Kavan's novel. It is true I did not ask Peter Owen to pay for this in the English edition, but then he is my publisher and I owe him a courtesy—but Doubleday is not my publisher, and I am glad you insisted on payment.

I get letters every day asking for vol. 3. One more point I forgot to make with Hiram. Two books are being written on my work, and they could include vol. 3 if it were out. Otherwise not. Such books by multiple professors can bring in many readers.

Did you send my letter to Bay? He is such a hypocrite—sly.

Did I tell you I pulled out of the Ellis Marcus talks? He was going to make the *Diary* sound like *Confession* magazine—and invent scenes and characters. Characters from Hollywood producers would not do the *Diary* justice!

Miller's documentary film will be a success. He is a natural actor, storyteller. Will be shown in April at UCLA. I have a nice part in it.

It would be wonderful to go to the book fair and to meet my German publisher. Would they finance me? In some combination with England? When is the Frankfurt Fair? Let me know so I won't get tied down by lectures. I'm not keen on England, but I suppose I have to go. Peter has been decent.

I do hope you pin down Hiram. I'm getting a chorus of protests about the delay of the *Diary*. And now they are on required reading lists of several colleges.

Gunther, you charged me very little for editing. I know how much work you did on vol. 3. I appreciate this at the moment as my finances are low and Hugo's film has been a drain, but someday I hope to be more concretely appreciative.

I once told Hiram that the one quality I do not possess is *patience!* I hope you are with me in this.

A

Letter from Anaïs Nin to Hugh Guiler:
Los Angeles, February 7, 1969

Darling:

We were both writing about *waiting*. A month of waiting. I am glad you had the film to distract you from the change of jobs.

As I received the checks from the two lectures and another from Harcourt, I can return part of what you loaned me. You deposited $100 and loaned me $200 when I left. I had to catch up with bills and so I am sending you only $200. (Gunther, of course, keeps ten per cent, and this time he took a reasonable $100 for editing the *Diary*. He spent a lot of time on that.) And I spent so much preparing the *Diary* for publication. No Danièle check yet.

When I call you at an inconvenient time, darling, all you need to say is you will not accept the call. I would like to find out if I could charge my calls to my own phone in N.Y. instead of to you.

At last a sunny day. Resting up for a reading at the Jewish Community Center to three hundred persons. Typical that they charge $2 entrance, pay me $50, and take 30 per cent of books and recordings sold. But Immaculate Heart makes up for this with $500.

It seems I am a success in Germany, of all places. They want me to come for the Book Fair in the fall. It might synchronize with one of your trips.

My scientist friend at Stanford is giving a seminar on the relation between integrated circuits and the poetry of Anaïs Nin! That floored Louis Barron! How many years back did you talk about poetry and science?

Will call you Saturday or Sunday.

Love,

Anaïs

Letter from Anaïs Nin to Hugh Guiler:
Los Angeles, February 10, 1969

Darling:

All went well last night at the Jewish Community Center, which is like the YMHA in New York. About 300 people—and I sold $65 worth of books. Two actors read "The Party" better than at the Living Theatre. I signed books for an hour. Found out a woman was teaching *Collages* at UCLA.

Forgot you could not deposit the check I sent without knowing the number of my account. What I should have done is make it over to you as part of the $100 more I owe you.

Won't send any more. You have enough to do.

Tired today.

I read well but was nervous at the beginning. An endless never-to-be-won battle, but professional actors feel this.

Love,

A

Letter from Hugh Guiler to Anaïs Nin:
New York, February 11, 1969

Darling:

Was just about to throw away the Sunday *Times* when I saw your face and the enclosed article. Congratulations, and I am glad it is such a good photo.

I spoke with Danièle twice over the weekend by telephone, and she said without my asking that she was to have had an answer from Paramount before the end of this week and that was when she had been hoping to come to N.Y. Now she fears the storm has made a delay in everyone's plans, and she will probably not come before sometime next week. I gathered she remained confident everything would be OK.

Thank you for the check, which arrived today. But, as it happened, I received $1,000 more from Hayden Stone for January. They should owe me more, but they say I will have an accounting in a week.

The film: I believe I can use one of the shots of you that I had discarded because you felt it showed lines. I have an idea these will not show in *superimposition*, so I want to experiment. If that does not work, I have the shot from Acapulco of you opening your eyes. And for hands, I have a very good one from the footage I shot at the water's edge below Fort Lee.

All these ideas came to me while I was filing footage in five metal filing drawers I bought at Woolworth's.

Very interesting about the program "Anaïs Nin and Integrated Circuits." The word "integration," it seems to me, is a key word at this particular "conjuncture."

Love, love,

Hugo

Letter from Anaïs Nin to Gunther Stuhlmann:

Los Angeles, February 1969

Dear Gunther:

Very much cheered up by my meeting with Ilse Lahn of the Paul Kohner agency, the biggest and most international of all, tied to all the filmmakers we like, the actresses, the Italian, Swedish and English productions, etc. She is Viennese, very well read, and was tremendously encouraging. Said the time was right, that people were tired of violence, and wanted stories on two levels. She thought *Minotaur* would be the easiest to do, then *Children of the Albatross* and *Collages*. She genuinely likes them. And also, unlike Jerry, she believes in selecting people capable of reading the book itself, and all that the writer has to say rather than a dried-up synopsis or an already fabricated treatment. A few years back, she said, she would not have taken me on. She is sorry that the books are done by such a small publisher. So hard to buy and find. She could not get copies. This brings me to your problem with Swallow. I do understand how you feel, that you wanted to test them as distributors. They are better than Alan, but not big enough to make such big demands as film rights, etc. They never advertise. Aside from that announcement of my books in *Publisher's Weekly* once, I have never seen any ads. What has been happening with them? Meanwhile they are reprinting the books at a mad pace. Recently *Four-Chambered Heart*. Do they send you copies of the new books? At the Jewish Community Center (like the YMHA) I sold books, but I had to do it all myself—order the books, take them to the bookshop, see they are on display, take back the unsold ones. Don't they have a salesman here in California?

I have not received any reviews of the *Novel* from you. Only two clippings from my service. When will the paperback be out?

Hiram wrote me sweetly, so I guess all is well; one always hopes to overcome the facts. I once took the trouble to explain to him why I had *no more patience*. After the two surgery episodes I received the jacket of the *Diary*, felt I had almost missed its publication, and might have died with a total sense of failure. This taught me not to wait anymore. (I once remember Dutton wanting to wait two years between books when I had three already written.) Your solution is always the best. Mediator. With a few galleys (Hiram took care to tell me how expensive they are) we can sustain the interest of the critics. Will Hiram object to *Diary 3* being written about in an academic study before its publication?

I hope you are out of the snow.

Anaïs

LOS ANGELES, FEBRUARY 1969

We went to see the raw footage of the documentary on Henry made by Bob Snyder. He has been at work on it for a long time. I participated one afternoon by talking with Henry in the garden.

Bob's best quality is his enthusiasm. Nothing discourages him, deters him. When he left college his first wish was to film Martha Graham. For this I like him. Other traits are discouraging: he is chaos personified. The footage showed a kind of *cinéma verité*—disconnected scenes, no coordination, none of the tensile strength of genuine free association. Henry was a perfect subject: he is natural, relaxed, humorous. The film was very faithful to Henry's changing moods, his storytelling, his recollections. Bob shot so much film, 13 hours, I believe, that he asked me how one could edit such a quantity of images. I suggested that as he had begun in the style of *cinéma verité* he had to remain faithful to an unstructured, free-flowing assemblage.

We saw the film in many stages. It was not the way Henry wanted it. Henry wanted a surrealist, Dadaist film. He did not want a plain, faithful documentary.

Henry has a secretary called Gerald Robitaille. He is a somber and bitter man. Thinking that he was homesick for Quebec, we tried to be friendly to him.

Letter from Hugh Guiler to Anaïs Nin:
New York, February 17, 1969

Darling:
Congratulations about Mrs. Lahn. This sounds like a real new start for you on your long quest.

Gunther has turned up a new distributor for Danièle, in case Paramount should hesitate. It is United Artists, where a friend of his has expressed interest. He did not, of course, mention Paramount. Gunther and Barbara were here last night when he told me, so as I had to call Danièle about the film I put him on the phone and she was pleased. She has no news yet from Paramount and says she is getting impatient. But she fully expects the deal to go through and to be in N.Y. for that this week.

I got a nice telephone call from Joaquín for my birthday.

Are you purposely delaying your arrival to avoid celebrating your birthday?

I have told John Chase about my decision to leave Hayden Stone. He approved entirely and promised to help me find the right new firm. I would hope he would send me some new accounts to help me get started. Anyhow, his being in the picture should be some protection against René and the others choosing a second-rate firm just to suit themselves, which is what I have been concerned about.

But I am well and able to face all of this. Bogner leaves for Puerto Rico the 25th and will return about March 10th.

Love, love,
Hugo

Letter from Anaïs Nin to Christine Saxton [after a talk on "The Dream in Literature"—Immaculate Heart College, Los Angeles, Feb. 19]:
Los Angeles, February 1969

Dear Christine Saxton:
I am glad you admitted me like an intimate friend into your night world—your moods, uncertainties and quests. They reminded me of my early journeys. I don't

know if you were aware that you ended your description with the word *light*—the same with which I ended *House of Incest*. But I thought I had made clear that I was not luring anyone into the nightlife but in the richness of combining and fusing them. The two worlds are necessary to each other. To deal with the pressures, despair and chaos of the outer world, we need a strong core. I spoke for this resistant inner core. Perhaps I did not make this clear. I wish you would read *Novel of the Future*. It is hard to give all in one talk. You caught the ephemeral quality of my talk, but not its solidity or the solidity of my life based on interrelations between *all* worlds. You placed me only as a dreamer and not as one who has put dream into action. Not your way, you say. Let me know when you have found your way.

Anaïs Nin

Letter from Gunther Stuhlmann to Anaïs Nin:
New York, February 21, 1969

Dear Anaïs:

Dr. Wegner in Hamburg is totally delighted that you would like to accept his invitation, and he has just sent me a brief itinerary that would give maximum chances for this being a successful trip:

Thursday, October 9: Arrive in Frankfurt.

Friday, October 10: Meetings and interviews with major TV, newspaper and booksellers.

Saturday: Rest day with maybe a visit to the Book Fair, etc.

Sunday, October 12: Flight to Munich and press conference either Sunday night or Monday, reception for you, etc.

Wednesday, October 15: In Hamburg where they would plan a major reception with the most important journalists and critics.

Thursday and Friday would be in Hamburg for sightseeing or visits to editors, bookstores, etc.

This would be the official and hard part, and you could still spend the weekend in Hamburg, or maybe go on to London for a short stopover, or Paris, whatever we can arrange.

How does this sound to you?

Wegner plans vol. 2 to be ready for the Fair (October 8-13) and will do *Spy* early in 1970, he just wrote.

If these dates are all right with you he would start setting up the machinery.

Best,

Gunther

FEBRUARY 25, 1969
Return to New York.

Letter from Joaquín Nin-Culmell to Anaïs Nin:
Berkeley, February 27, 1969

Dear Anaïs:

Many thanks for the letter and news about L.A. You worry about me in

Berkeley and I worry about you in Los Angeles! I must say I would rather cope with the rain than with the fundamental dishonesty of the so-called activist "students." They are out to destroy, but they won't admit it, or take the consequences, or accept the fact that their ideals are negative ones. A far cry from the "pure anarchist" of bygone days... We are surrounded by establishments, a real political struggle for power and for nothing else. At least the older structure had a conscience and a bumbling desire to make changes and to accept responsibilities. I can see no future for these boys who will be swept away at the first opportunity of the "new establishment." And so it goes...in this veil of tears... *Plus ça change...* How long I can go along with this is another matter. I am sorely tempted to chuck it all out the window and retreat to some kind of peace and quiet. Unfortunately, I do not believe that there is such a thing in the world today, and as long as this is so, why make a change?

I hope you are enjoying your stay in New York. How is Hugh and how is his new film? He told me a bit about it when I telephoned him on his birthday, but you know how it is when a Catalan calls a Scot on long distance...

The Sánchezes are still fighting over the few trinkets Tia Anaïs left when she died. Anaïs complains that she has been left out. Ana María and Cuca are not talking and Ana María blames Graciella (who doesn't answer her letters), etc. Please forget I told you, but it depresses me to think that families can grow old and learn nothing. In any case, the complaining one is Anaïs as per usual. What a *costumbrista* [way to live]!

Love,
Joaquín

Letter from Anaïs Nin to Gunther Stuhlmann:
New York, February 27, 1969

Dear Gunther:
Are you ill? I tried all day to get you, and the answering service said you did not pick up my message at all. I hope you do not have the flu. In any case, I am sending you a special delivery because I had lunch with James Wade. When I was so disappointed at waiting a year for the *Diary* I called him up and asked him, as a friend, whether MacMillan would like to take the *Diaries* over. He answered instantly: "As an editor, of course I want them; as a friend I think it may be difficult to change midstream." Then you persuaded me to wait. But at least with Wade we have honest communication, no pompous game-playing. He said during the lunch that he considered me a valuable property, that his practical self wanted very much to have the novels, that only ethical considerations and knowing Haydn prevented him from grabbing at the *Diaries*. It was time to have a little talk with you. I said in the message it was urgent because I know sooner or later we have to sign with Swallow. And it would be vital to discuss this with Wade. In this case of MacMillan, Kaplan, the president, and Wade really believe in me, whereas Harcourt Brace Jovanovich recently turned down a suggestion by the Ohio University professors for a Nin reader, an introductory selection like the one made of Miller by Durrell. You remember how scathing Jovanovich was when I thanked him for consenting to the paperback and my intuition, after he turned down the novels, that he was not for me. Who was the bearded editor I met at the party—is he in charge of paperbacks? Hiram

is so unctuous and intriguing and not straightforward. Hiram once told me he and Jovanovich saw eye-to-eye on everything, yet I know now this is not so. I hope you will be able to talk to Wade.

Anaïs Nin, ca. 1969

Dear Gunther, while I am in N.Y. and so intensely active, is there a set hour at which I know I can phone you that will be convenient? I try not to call you for unessentials, but I get desperately frustrated when I can't reach you at all, ever. The mails are so unreliable and slow. I would like to know what Wade has in mind, whether they mean to try only one novel, and whether that will sour the Swallow people, or whether they will take them all in some way, which would put an end to that Mafia Swallow style of gangster threats on your life!

Danièle is on her way to France tonight, to push things there. She evidently did not meet the top man at Bantam's outfit, just a minor type who had never even heard of Jeanne Moreau.

It is evidently definite that Doubleday will not pay for the preface. So that is solved.

Marlis Schweiger will mail you both the better print of Hugo's engraving and a better photo of Varda. I have things to show you that I cannot mail. I would like to see you and get the letters that were returned to you. I would also like to see the photos and sizes and which ones they selected at Harcourt for the cover, etc.

You can always get me at dinner time, or in the morning, so please call me or call Wade if you are OK.

Anaïs

Letter from Anaïs Nin to Peter Owen:
New York, February 27, 1969

Dear Peter:

You may already know my German publisher has invited me to the Frankfurt Book Fair, and I have accepted. So I will see you there. As you know, I have been very reluctant to go to England because I find their reviews absolutely obnoxious, like the American reviews in the '40s, old-fashioned and petty. I would rather not go. And judging from the kind of journalists Marguerite Young met when she was there, the lack of serious critics interested in American literature seemed rather like prejudice. Do you think it is absolutely essential I come? In any case, *Diary 3* will not be ready and so there will be nothing new to celebrate. I have time to discuss this with you. How is the paperback of the *Diary* going? And when things are started with *Spy* can you get them to do the *Spy* in paperback on that occasion?

On this end, things are expanding beautifully. The reviews are positive. *Novel* is being used for teaching. Harcourt had more prepublication orders for *Diary 1* in paperback than any other title they have. The novels are part of literature courses in many colleges. And two more academic studies are coming out. A seminar is being given at Stanford, California, in September, taking my work and linking it with Poetics of Science, and I may be an artist-in-residence at UCLA, etc., etc. So many events I can't list them. One of the most indicative symptoms is the fact that collectors have bought all there is to buy; university libraries have cleaned out Gotham Book Mart.

Here people do not have much confidence in newspaper reviews. What is taken more seriously are the essay reviews in college literary magazines. Each college has one. *Prairie Schooner, 20th Century Thought*, etc. That is where the best critiques appeared. *Chicago Review*, etc. Is there a similar outlet in England? And what of the underground papers? Here they have given me the best reviews, long and very brilliant. Do you send them review copies? They have an influence among the young.

I believe I wrote you asking you to send review copies to Harriet Zinnes, who is now in Switzerland for a year and writing for the papers there (her husband is a scientist invited to conferences for a year). She has been one of my best critics, but she would be interested in other writers to review for the Swiss newspapers. Please send her *Novel of the Future* and any other book you wish reviewed. The *Diaries* have been unavailable in Switzerland. She found *Under a Glass Bell* by chance.

Now I start work on the script for *Spy* and on *Diary 4*. Plus reviews and articles. Let me know your plans. Otherwise I will see you at the Fair.

Anaïs

Letter from Anaïs Nin to Wayne McEvilly:
New York, February 1969

Dear Wayne:

I feel prompted to answer your letters without meditation or leisure, particularly about Marguerite Young. Yes, the great, mysterious, unconscious genius is there, the mysticism, but she is such a familiar friend that I want to make her visit to you as utterly familiar. She is the most comfortable, earthy, natural, easygoing friend I have.

She is playful, ordinary, everyday in her love of little things, homely events—I wish I could convey this. We rarely talk about ideas or writing. We assume that we agree on the basic essential *point de départ*. We talk about little things. Where to find a new dress in the Village, Long John's program on the radio. She reads the papers faithfully, the news, the elements you talked about when you spoke of the small and the big in Zen. If these are the materials and the things that she later transforms, transfigures, and make her immense spiritual world, as I believe, it is also true that she enjoys them in their untransfigured state. Her book is there. But we never ascend into these spheres in talk.

I can feel in your letter that you have such a visionary way of looking at people, as I have, that they occasionally become transparent (I *closed* my eyes to see Henry), but at some point or other I felt this visionary life robbed me of the small things, of the earthy things. And I turned to the earthy people. Yes, balance. I know you have that, and are that. But more and more as an artist, I realize that the balance is there, but that the vast world the artist creates (or recreates from small things as the birds make nests with twigs, etc.) is not always in their lives, and as much as one wants this world understood and appreciated, the awe of it hurts both. Perhaps because of this my best friends were those who did not know anything about me, and liked me as a neighbor, as the one who took care of their children in a crisis.

Marguerite has much of the child too; her apartment is full of dolls and angels and antiques, and as long as one starts by loving her, not wounding her, she is the easiest person to know, to feel at home with, to relax with. It may also be why sometimes I protest the mysticism. I do not want it to rob me of my very human life. I want to be treated like anyone. Probably because when I am not at work, not talking, not inspired (a beautiful word), I love to swim, to walk with the dog, to walk on the beach, to go to the neighborhood movie house to see a not-too-good film, to be anonymous...

I am so deeply grateful for your understanding, your familiarity and response to the unconscious Anaïs, as for the unconscious Marguerite, but also love how you feel about snow, how you named your child, how you write about music, and how I imagine you are as a teacher. I have no doubt your students are fortunate. We three are able to liberate and set others creating. I just wanted you to enjoy Marguerite on the small side of herself, after having loved the big one. Our human life is small like an igloo at the North Pole; it is vulnerable like the birds I feed every day, or the dog who never knows when I am coming back… Marguerite's whole secret is that she is not sure when she will be loved, but once assured, she takes off her shoes, makes herself comfortable. You will have a beautiful time. As if she had no particular gifts.

Anaïs

Letter from Anaïs Nin to Nobuko Uenishi:
New York, March 10, 1969

Dearest Nobuko:

Morbid is not a valid criticism [of your article]. One could apply that to Dostoevsky, Kafka, down to present-day writers. Coming from *McCall's* it means nothing because they represent the middle class and are full of hypocrisies. Please pay no attention. Mailer is morbid (*An American Dream*); Albee is morbid. Pay no attention to *McCall's* or you will only achieve a mediocre work. Be yourself, utterly sincere and truthful. I'm glad somebody will take care of the mechanics of your writing. Hugo did that for me with a saint's patience. He would say, "You can't say that in English." I would say, "Why not?" And today I am considered a stylist.

I tried to phone you but was not sure it was your phone. Call me. I hope you can go to Japan. Formed a club—Japan Society. I would love to go with you. Alas, I have so much to do.

Love,
Anaïs

Letter from Anaïs Nin to Lila Rosenblum:
New York, March 1969

Dear Lila:
Yes, our connection is still there. I admire your courage. But the break was not your fault at all. There were many reasons—one is that I came for shorter periods to New York, had to make up for my absences to Hugo (attend to *his* life, films, friends) with a diminishing energy. There were greater demands on me as the *Diaries* came out—a staggering correspondence. More profound than the external overactivity was that when a dear friend is handicapped, one feels a shame at being active, of one's travels, as if it were unfair (and it is). Even more subtle than that, I felt very badly when you had to meet the debts incurred by our magazine-to-be. I felt we should all have shared the debt—and couldn't. Guilt. So you see, we both felt the same mysterious, incurable guilt! So let's begin anew—and erase all that. The only thing which is real is that I am overburdened. I, too, enjoyed our talk!

Love,
Anaïs

Letter from Anaïs Nin to David Pepperell:
New York, March 10, 1969

Dear David:
You ask me about Eve Miller. She divorced Henry to marry a sculptor, a neighbor at Big Sur. I never met her, but everyone said she was wonderful. She drank. She had a cold and drank a quart of gin with antibiotics—or sleeping pills. No one knows. Suicide? Accident? Henry does not know. He does not talk about her. All he said once when I said I had heard she was wonderful was: "When she drank she was the opposite of what she was when sober."

June returned to New York, married the lover she had confessed having...then divorced, spent time in an asylum, became arthritic, rheumatoid, which ruined her beauty but stabilized the mental imbalance. She was cared for by a couple I know, the Baxters, one of whom is a psychiatrist. They became my friends, and I am equally devoted to both. They helped me with the *Diary* so June would accept her portrait even though she has transferred all her hostility to me as having separated her from Henry, which of course was not so. Their life together was hell—they were both trying to break. She sent Henry to Paris because she had a lover, and he went because he could not write when she was near. She is relatively well, holds a job in welfare, but talks uncontrollably and as fancifully as before. She invents half of what she tells—Henry visited her a few years ago and he ran away, shocked by her appearance and the sameness of her talk. She will not see me. I offered her reconciliation.

I'm glad you feel as you did about *Tropic of Capricorn*. I like it, and *Black Spring*. I do not like *The Rosy Crucifixion*.

Diary 1 is published in paperback too.

It is bitterly, bitterly cold. From the 14th floor I see New York University, a library being built, a few small galleries, the *Eye* magazine headquarters; and to the left Bleeker Street, heart of the Village, with a movie house, nightclubs, rock and roll, boutiques, and as many politicians as hippies!

Anaïs

Letter from Anaïs Nin to Duane Schneider:
New York, March 13, 1969

Dear Duane:

Although you came to interview me, I felt I became better acquainted with you. As in all these situations with limited time one feels one has only begun to talk.

I wanted to talk more with you about the relation between literature and social welfare. So many people do not believe they are essentially connected.

About politics—even if the power-obsessed men win and not the good men (Eugene McCarthy or Dr. King) we still have to act, don't we?—or it will be the Dark Ages. Power and money are stronger, but we still have to oppose them. Do you agree?

I enjoyed our talk. Next time let it be Duane Schneider who speaks!

Anaïs

NEW YORK, MARCH 1969

Music comes first, and quite possibly I wrote because my father's severity barred the way to music. Writing as imagery. Films. I love films.

Harcourt makes a horrendous cover for the paperback edition of *Diary 1*. As Gunther said: "It makes her look like a ghoul in some horror movie."

APRIL 1969

Return to Los Angeles.

Letter from Joaquín Nin-Culmell to Anaïs Nin:
Berkeley, April 1, 1969

Dear Anaïs:

So glad to hear about Hugh's new film and the change from Hayden Stone to St. Phalles and Co. Isn't the latter firm situated in Lausanne? I seem to remember the name. I most certainly will congratulate him when I see him.

Congratulations, also, on the paperback edition of the *Diary*. I know what you mean about "hideous covers" and how little one can do about them. I had a beautiful and inexpensive cover suggestion for the *Tonadas* but they felt they needed a keyboard and so a keyboard it is... I'm surprised, however, that your agent wasn't given the cover for his and your approval. Publishers being what they are, I shouldn't be surprised at anything. I recently gave an illustrated lecture on all four volumes of my piano *Tonadas* and the sponsoring group asked for some copies to sell. After much bickering and several telephone calls from me they finally sent forty copies with all kinds of ungracious conditions. Not only were all forty copies sold, but a new order was placed for a dozen or so more copies. You would think that a note of thanks might have been in order since they get $2.25 per copy and I get $.25 per copy or less. Not a word. *Sicut transit* [so it goes with] publishers...

As for the Hales, forget about them. They are most uninteresting and I wouldn't think of prodding them with a note from you. They finally invited me to a very dull cocktail party and thanked me profusely for sending them the *Diary*. What they said isn't worth repeating, but it is obvious that they are among those who have eyes but read not, have ears but hear not, and mouths but speak not. May they rest in the peace they deserve. No heart, no sensitivity, no nothing.

I'm fine but tired. Rested all this week but consequently am terribly behind in my work. House and garden are beautiful (thanks to Ted) and student fever is at its usual level. I fear that the crying of "wolf" is going to bring on the real wolf and that we shall all be devoured together. I pity the wolf that will get me to chew! I'm tough!

Love,
Joaquín

Letter from Anaïs Nin to Gunther Stuhlmann:
Los Angeles, April 8, 1969

Dear Gunther:
Your preface is beautiful. I read it twice—once for myself, as what I would like said about the *Diary*, another for what *needed* to be said. I can say with certainty you focused it exactly for those who might not see the overall themes. It is difficult for me to stand outside and read it impersonally. It is really a study—a critique—a review. In a way, I hope it will help the critics. I hope they won't get hung up on the America versus Europe syndrome. Perhaps the only missing point is that I *did* make friends in vol. 3. I don't want to stress isolation or disappointments. Have you shown it to anyone? You did a most careful and thoughtful synthesis.

I'm coming back May 1. I wrote Bay that I have a translator.

Did you ever find out if Bay paid for vol. 1? That would be funny!

The librarian of Texas University wrote they were interested in the original diary manuscript and hoped Andreas Brown would find a way to buy it... I don't know what the next step is. I wrote to Brown. Perhaps you might call him. I asked for $100,000.

Let me know the reaction to the preface.

Do you know an agent for ordinary cheap novels, the kind that sell? I have two pests on my hands.

Henry had a prostate operation. Doing well.

If you have an extra copy, will you show the preface to Hugo?

Gratefully, love,
A

Letter from Gunther Stuhlmann to Anaïs Nin:
New York, April 11, 1969

Dear Anaïs:

Thanks for your note of April 8th. I was glad to have your reaction to the little preface. Hiram Haydn liked it very much and it's in the works now.

A check in the amount of $744.43 I sent to you on March 21st you must have deposited into your account.

Bay and his accountants are still trying to solve the mystery of the first advance. I wrote him that you had a translator, but I've heard nothing further. I'll probably meet Fabre next week.

As for Texas University I am wondering about the Andreas Brown you mentioned, since the official or semi-official buyer for Texas here is Feldman. Please let me have Brown's address.

What kind of cheap novels are your two pests writing? There are a lot of cheap novel publishers in California now, and if I had some idea about the material I'd be glad to give you the names of a couple people.

With best regards,
Gunther

Letter from Anaïs Nin to Gunther Stuhlmann:
Los Angeles, April 11, 1969

Dear Gunther:

Thank you for the check from Peter Owen. I feel so badly that I will miss seeing Wegner in New York. I was held up here by the writer's workshop, the Miller film (at last being shown on the 12th), by a meeting at UCLA, and by the time I am ready to return Hugo has several trips to make, so we agreed I should not come until he is back from Europe. I wanted very much to meet Wegner. He sounds wonderful. He is not coming west? I can introduce him to Isherwood, Laura Huxley, Miller, Harold Norse, or take him to the biggest telescope in the world, meet the scientists who photographed Mars, visit Lloyd Wright the architect, visit Watts, the Negro poets, etc., etc. We will give a party for him.

Now that I am not returning until May 24, please, dear Gunther, write me about Swallow Press, about James Wade, MacMillan, Danièle Suissa's agent (no word from Danièle).

I am glad Hiram liked the preface. What always makes me nervous is not how I feel about it, but if they will twist it against me as they have on other things (the dramatic encounter with America, which you brought out). I never know what to play up. The answer is if they want to find a bone to pick, they always can. In the old days they knew I had studied psychoanalysis, so they decided all the novels were case histories. Hiram is pretty nationalistic, and if he was not offended, I guess your tact won out. For you are tactful. And that was the theme of this Diary.

I gather from hearsay the paperback is doing fine. I wish they would let me know. Bozeman, Montana ordered a hundred copies.

Will you buy (and charge to me) a copy of *20th Century Thought* from Russell Sage College with two of the best critiques of the *Diary*? Renate translated the German review she is mailing to you.

If you have Negro friends who want to teach, there are ten open jobs at Buffalo University. Herbert Blau told me about it. I can give you details.

You can make all the arrangements with Wegner you wish. As you had first mentioned a plan with small breathing spaces in between big events, it was fine. Were you able to include the photo of Frances Field? Does Hiram know I am going to the Frankfurt Book Fair, and if *Diary 3* comes out in October I will get a lot of publicity? Will you be coming? It would be so much better if you were there.

Anaïs

Letter from Anaïs Nin to Gunther Stuhlmann:
Los Angeles, April 12, 1969

Dear Gunther:

Daniel Mauroc showed the *Diary* to Christiane Pauvert of Éditions de la Jeune Parque. She was very much taken with it, she writes me, but was debating the various technicalities involved. Would it be so difficult to change, if she is genuinely interested? I have totally lost confidence in André Bay. What are the technicalities involved, since I am paying for the translation?

Do please phone me collect as I can never get you, especially Sunday when it is cheaper. I may try this Sunday. I know that this is the only time I have been rigid (about Bay). Usually I yield to your advice. We felt the same way about Peter doing all the wrong things, but finally accepted him. But Bay... I never had time to tell you the whole story. First he lost the translation of *Ladders to Fire* (free and labor of love by Anne Metzger) for *six years*. Then he found it. He paid Metzger $100 for translating *Spy*. He gave Duras the wrong book and set her off on another theme by the time we arrived in Paris! He wanted to cut the *Diary* in two, and the Miller letters. He said like a gangster: "I will see to it that Gallimard does not do the Miller letters. He and I went to the same sanatorium." And he did. It would give me so much pleasure to break with him.

Your preface is so good; I wish it would come out as a critique.

I don't imagine Hiram had anything brilliant to say about it. Poor Hiram. *Voyages* is going through with a tribute to him. I have to write my own piece, only because he was so ill and wept once at lunch!

Anaïs

Letter from Anaïs Nin to friends in Paris:
Los Angeles, April 14, 1969

Dear friends:

I imagine you have been caught up with new friends and more work on the *Cancer* film, for I have not heard from you. I thought of you especially when I received a delicious fan letter from Julio Cortázar, one of my favorites, who lives in Paris.

I thought of you missing Los Angeles, motorcycle rides, the guitar, Silver Lake, our talks...was all that left behind? Where will you be in October? I hope in Paris, for my German publisher has invited me to the Book Fair October 9 to 15 and I will pass through Paris to see you and Cortázar. What is happening?

As you know, Henry had a prostate operation, and was not well enough recovered to attend the documentary of his life made by Bob Snyder. The film came off. At the same time I saw what Agnès Varda did in a film of Varda in Sausalito. What a place and what an atmosphere. There will be a second part to the Miller film and I hope you will see it.

It is spring, all the flowers are open, the mockingbirds are singing continuously night and day. The mail is bulkier and bulkier and Cortázar is right when he says it is an agonizing choice each morning, whether one is going to answer all the letters, some of them so moving, or work at one's book. It is the *Apprenti Sorcier* [Sorcerer's Apprentice] story: the writer writes a letter to the world, and when the world answers he is flooded.

Diary 1 is out in paperback. The tragic things I won't mention, they are all in the papers. A revolution at Harvard. Unusual there.

Do you have books to read? Have you connected with Tony Miller, who deserted the army and is in Paris? I gave him the name of an American woman who would help him with the technicalities. I hope Henry sent it on.

I offered one of your cigarettes to Sam Francis, who is involved with the most beautiful light show in town. I told you I slipped out of the Tracey Roberts and her brother-in-law combination, which would have ruined the *Diary*.

I imagine Henry will be well by June. I hope he separates from Hoki Tokuda, his Japanese wife who is tormenting him with indifference.

I wish we had loaned you our camera while you were in Paris. I thought of it afterwards. In the Miller film there was a photo by Brassaï of cobblestones. Just cobblestones in a circular pattern. Are there any left? Are the river banks ruined with traffic and no longer fit for lovers?

Anaïs

Letter from Anaïs Nin to Hugh Guiler:
Los Angeles, April 15, 1969

Darling:

I have given up on letters. I look at the pile each morning and feel trapped. I once wrote you every day, and you have suffered too from the overflow and fatigue. Yet I can't afford to call up as often as I would like to.

Agnès Varda is the worst filmmaker I know. I saw *Les Creatures*. Skip it. It is unbelievably bad. *Le Bonheur* too. But *My Uncle Yanko* she did charmingly, under his influence. It is playful and amusing and yet shows his work and gives his flavor. Could not help thinking what you could have done with it. Try to see it. The houseboats are enchanting, the set marvelous.

The workshop was more work than I expected because I don't know how to shake off the students. One of them has to drive me home, and that becomes an excuse for showing me more work.

Alarmed by my loss of memory, I cut out the hydrochlorate or chlorohydrate or whatever. Slept fitfully, but determined to stop use of it. I feel better today. It is possible that with my low blood pressure it affects me differently than you. But I got tired of that fuzzy feeling and loss of memory to an abnormal degree.

I have used the new movie camera, but don't know yet if I have anything good. Can't wait for the film. Are you taking it to Paris?

I realize what was not good about your documentary of me was that you were not able to play with it. With the same images you had for Mrs. Lindley, once you start getting imaginative, you would do a better job than Agnès Varda did for Varda. On your own documentary you were able to play with the images and prove your point as a filmmaker.

Love,
Anaïs

Letter from Anaïs Nin to Gunther Stuhlmann:
Los Angeles, April 18, 1969

Dear Gunther:

I heard from Danièle. She was apologetic. She did not want to write until she had something definite.

The new Diary, at least, should be out while *Cancer* comes out as a film. And the *Miller Odyssey* will be shown, I am sure, on TV. Snyder feels it is not slick enough for regular theatres, but more for campuses. He is working on a second part. The general criticism is that as a film of Henry it is superbly interesting, but that it is much to the detriment of his friends. Henry upstages them. Don't know if it lies in the editor's hands. It is obviously hero-worshippy. Or his own personality may be best as a soloist. I wish you could see it.

We sold 600 recordings without fanfare, did I tell you? (I write so many letters I don't know what I have written sometimes.) I think that's pretty good. I helped a lot, with my list of fans, etc. I hope to hear from you today. Going to the post office now.

The spring is beautiful here. I got up at six to tape the singing of the mocking-birds. I am surreptitiously, quietly, secretly filming a bit here and there. I am hooked…

Anaïs

Letter from Hugh Guiler to Anaïs Nin:
New York, April 19, 1969

Darling:

I got your letter of the 15th just the day before yesterday, but, as you know, I have been under great pressure this week, with my energy low because of the trip and a cold.

I worked late at the office yesterday, to 6:00 PM. Today at 9:00 AM I had to take the cat to Dr. Sterling and got back just in time for my massage at 11:45. Then I made lunch for Olga and myself and was just coming out of my siesta when you called.

Darling, I have always thought that these telephone calls are unsatisfactory, and I also agree with you about the expense. So I suggest that in the future we limit them to real emergencies and resume writing postcards or short letters to each other as often as we are able to.

I read Gunther's preface, and it is good. I just wondered whether he did not overemphasize your "confrontation" with the U.S.A., especially in his opening sentence. And whether, if this has to be emphasized, it should not be tied in more with the fact that young Americans are now engaged in this same confrontation and that you are showing how it can be done in a constructive, rather than a destructive way, as Lili Bita's "quiet" husband advocates in the article you sent me today.

Gunther does point out how your solution was the creation of an inner life that is common to all nationalities. I just think that so long as it is a preface he might throw a ray of light onto the significance of this achievement as it turned out in the future (i.e., the present).

I may talk to Gunther about this, but fundamentally a preface is always less important than the living diary, which it inevitably must distort, so as to attempt to do the work the critics should be doing for themselves.

Love,
Hugo

Letter from Anaïs Nin to Hugh Guiler:
Los Angeles, April 29, 1969

Darling:

Sunday was a very blue day. I missed the telephone calls, as we are writing less. It seemed like a very long month. You seemed very far away. Are your plans the same?

Sunday I saw Beatrice Blau do the Beckett play *Happy Days*, which we saw in New York (the mound of sand rising to the neck of the woman, her husband just saying a word now and then), and which we found so depressing. She is a great actress, and, as it happened in the Gallery, one could see her face so well, it became a virtuoso act and a staggering piece of subtle work to hold an audience for an hour and a half in such a static situation. Herbert Blau, her husband and future director of Theatre Arts at California Institute of the Arts, suggested that stasis was necessary in order to stop and go deep (my theory, yes, is to suspend action, but Beckett's theme is death in life). On a beautiful warm Sunday afternoon it was cruel to be shut in with Beckett. This may have added to my blueness. Otherwise I have been infinitely better, since I threw away the chlorohydrate. Less tired, and no depressions, and my skin has ceased burning.

I am very sad to think that just because you are a man, you had to be in business and could not give all your time to filmmaking. And I, just because I am a woman, was able to give all my time to writing. What drives me to work as much as I am doing, trying to establish usefulness as a teacher, is the idea that when you tire of business, I may free you just to make films. It saddens me how many opportunities the young have, all the equipment, all the help, fellowships.

Will you let me call next Sunday?
Anaïs

Letter from Anaïs Nin to Hugh Guiler:
Los Angeles, April 30, 1969

Darling:

I was sad when I read your letter this morning. I felt that it was the red kite you destroyed as a child again, because it was *my* fault (or rather the fault of campus unrest) that I got tied down in April, but I could have been home in two weeks to help to see you off on the 14th. I could have been home the 27th. I had two lectures that would have paid for the trip. I knew there was something wrong, but I did not realize you would resort to the old way. You were disappointed at the practical difficulties of a weekend in Los Angeles, disappointed at my delay so you punished us both. I was uneasy, anxious, but not able to guess what it was. Dumb Anaïs, who always thinks we all change and do not use the same methods or have the same reactions. Yes, I was dumb, but you punished me. I felt an impulse to call you but felt this was too delicate to discuss over the telephone... So April was my responsibility, but May is yours.

I know how you feel about my absences, darling, but I thought we had accepted each other's way of life. I never question your trips, and I am working for an objective, and sometimes this work ties me down more than I wish it to, simply because here there are fewer colleges to choose from, and those in the East make me feel less welcome. I do not want to go into this now. It is something for Bogner. I am not unaware of your objections and your change of attitude. But at the moment I don't know how to cope with it, and will have to bring this to Bogner.

I thought my work and my relieving you of a part of the economic burden, my being partly self-supporting, meant something to you. But let us not go into things while we need all our energy for our work. You need your strength for Europe, and your attitude recently caused me days of depression and fatigue, which were purely emotional. I have to get the *Spy* script done.

Thank you for information on the camera, but I do not want to get involved with filmmaking. It is expensive. I have played with it, but it is too costly.

Will write you tomorrow when I get cheerful again.

Anaïs

Letter from Anaïs Nin to Hugh Guiler:
Los Angeles, May 1969

Darling:
First day of work on the *Spy* script with Danièle Suissa Monday. I was nervous about it. But it went extraordinarily well. After working with Jerry, with Tracey, with Barbara Lawrence, with Renate Druks, I found suddenly that Danièle and I are on the same wavelength, but even better, we balance each other's weaknesses. She has a French logic within the irrationality; she has continuity and doggedness. She stands in the room and acts everything out. A real actress. We wrote an outline, chronology, and solved the lie detector problem instantly. We type, or I type, and I may say to describe thus-and-so in detail in one spot, then I do this alone from the novel. I have never had anyone who understood the book so well. It will go quickly. She comes at ten in the morning from her motel. She rented a car. We work until we drop, around four... Then I swim, eat, and write letters or read. She has things to do in the evenings. She runs around with the son of Irene Selznick, Danny. She has friends. So I do not have to worry about her. She is quite a character. Quite thoughtful. When we first went to a hotel she did not like, recommended by Selznick, she would not tell the woman she did not like it but came back with a friend to say she had found someone to stay with... She saw Tracey (I met Danièle

through Tracey). She is quite practical too. But now the sun refuses to come out and she told her family she came in part for the sun and swimming. She is quite run down, eats little, does not look well...

It seems she has money tied up in Paris, which belongs to her...she may be able to pay my translator there...and I give her money here. Perhaps you could help her in this. I don't know. I am sure that is why she delayed my payment...and her father is kicking in expenses, such as for coming here. She is returning to Paris in June. If we finish sooner, she might catch you at the end of your trip. But what can you do about tied-up money? She talked about this in saying she would have our script done beautifully in Paris (they will make it look like a printed book), where she could pay for it with funds she could not get at... In June she'll be in Paris. Otherwise I would have gone with you to visit her father as a business contact for you.

All my love,
Anaïs

Los Angeles, May 1969

Age of absurdities.

In dress it is a masquerade. Nothing is new. The flower children wear their grandmothers' dresses from trunks in the attic, or all the items of Oriental bazaars —Greek, Turkish, Spanish—a masquerade. Never *themselves*. A toreador. A gypsy. A Swedish sailor. A Guatemalan Indian. A Mexican wedding dress. There is something of the baby doll in fashion, the little girl, the adolescent. Never warmth. Rudi Gernreich does invent the new, with new textiles. I like the plastics, the new materials, the science fiction dress.

June 1969

Return to New York.

Letter from Anaïs Nin to Wayne McEvilly:
New York, June 1969

Dear Wayne:

It was like a consultation with the *I Ching*. You wrote me "I am suffering," and while I was thinking about how to answer you, I was correcting the French translation of *Diary 1*, and the answer was there. Of course, at about the same time in light years, you were caught between inner riches and inner expansion, and the ambivalence of the hypersensitive to life... Of course ambivalences, but ambivalences can be painful. Of course you are hurt by jealousy or envy or even lack of full appreciation. Of course you are vulnerable to people and the absence of generosity. But to live in spite of this, to love life so much, one is willing to be wounded.

Marguerite seems to feel you were lonely. At once a perfect intimate world was created, without needs, and yet the collision with Marguerite (inner space) and with me, by contrast with Marguerite, and in relativity only, outer space...must have had on you the same exhausting and exhilarating effect that my meeting with June and Henry had. I recognize this kind of nervous exhaustion, the giving and the need of shelter, the wishing and the need of serenity. The outgoing and incoming.

Marguerite sees all your gifts and suggests a plunge. I see your gifts and I don't know what to say, for I know you need your retreat like a snail needs its shell, and you need a balance between your riches and their practice in a bigger world. The wounds can come from such little people, in the most sheltered corners, among mountains, lakes, snows, flowers...a petty man in school, and there you are. Can I say do not be hurt? No, because one cannot be both sensitive and invulnerable. Being emotional, you are doomed to vulnerability.

Meanwhile...my schedules. July 4 to August 15 I will be traveling, will be far from correspondence, renewing my strength, going from place to place...and by August 15 I will be in New York where Hugh has to have a cataract operation and will be nearly helpless for six weeks... On October 9 I have to fly to the Frankfurt Book Fair, invited by my German publisher because the *Diary* has been such a success there. Also on October 9 the French edition of *Diary 1* will come out, *Diary 3* will appear in America, and will also appear in England. So if you should drive in with your family late August or early September, I will be in New York. But if it is too hard, I promise to visit you personally on one of my returns from Los Angeles next winter...

Never mind the honors program, and do not be concerned about reception. I have often encountered hostility in unexpected places...it is inexplicable, but it has to be faced. Only recently, at Immaculate Heart, one girl said out loud: "Dreams are boring..." So do not be over-protective. Marguerite is more vulnerable because her writing is her whole world. Mine is not. My loves are there to give me strength...

She came last night for dinner and to see Hugo's new film. She was still within her book. She was having dinner with Ambrose Bierce, not so much with us. But all artists are obsessed this way, as in pregnancy—they cannot separate themselves from their work.

I wish I could help you at this moment. We are all, in turn, wounded, by someone, something. Yes, I feel as you do about the Power Men, Mailer, Vidal, Roth, hateful all...but invulnerable, because they want power and get it. What we want is far rarer and more difficult. But in the end, in the end, power is ugly and never, never wins love. Miller never, in the end, received love; the adulation of the world, yes, but not love. Because only love begets love.

Anaïs

JULY-AUGUST 1969
Trip with Rupert.

NEW YORK, AUGUST 17, 1969
I dedicated myself to nursing Hugo from the day I arrived from Turkey, Saturday, August 2nd. First there was the hospital, where I was surprised to see him up, with a white cotton patch over his left eye. He was cheerful because the day after surgery he could already see more than he saw before surgery. Bogner's cable reached me three days too late, three days after the sudden surgery (the cataract had unexpectedly ripened to the dangerous point where it might crumble as it was pulled away). Jennie Hamilton, a fan of mine, who had been at the apartment to see Hugo's films, was there as a private nurse (her profession) and lightened the atmosphere. She said Hugo was easy to nurse as he gave back so much and was so interesting.

He gave the caretakers his most patient, cheerful self.

After a few days he came home. Then it was a matter of dressing the eye, giving drops, changing the bandages. We sat in the garden. I read to him. We walked through the Village to pass the time, book-browsed, shopped, did errands. Hugo had only one visitor—he does not seek any—Bob Hanson, the photographer, telling of his trip through the United States.

Long days—during which I had too much time to think of Rupert.

Anaïs Nin and Rupert Pole, summer 1969 trip

The trip was a disappointment. The Agadir Sea was cold, there was fog, and Rupert caught bronchitis. We responded in the same way to Morocco, to its beauty, its vividness. But two flaws stand out, which make Rupert a bad traveler. He cannot take vicissitudes, waiting, mishaps, delays, complications, which are a part of travel. He either loses his temper and antagonizes those who might help him, or he frets, fusses and fumes instead of applying his wits to solving problems. Then he constantly worries about expenses—again, a part of travel. If a bar overcharges for beer or mineral water, he is not easygoing, tolerant or understanding. This, added to my underlying concern over Hugo, did not make for a happy trip.

I dreaded the moment when I would have to tell him about Hugo's surgery. Before I left, the date had been set for August 14th and I was to leave from Athens the 11th just when Rupert was leaving for a tour of the Greek Islands. But having to rush from Foca, near Izmir, was a complication. It took me two days and two sleepless nights, four plane changes. But Rupert behaved generously about my need to return. "I did promise to be there when he is in distress."

I exaggerated the urgency—the problem. I made Hugo older—75, not 71. It was a double cataract, not a single.

During this slow, becalmed life I feel anxiety and restlessness. Hugo enjoys being becalmed. As soon as he could read a little, he was immersed in papers.

He is planning a new film. His last one was beautiful—extraordinarily beautiful and modern.

He is growing deaf. I have to raise my voice. His memory, which was always bad, is worse. Business and filmmaking take all the energy he has. In life he is a zombie.

I was anxious about the ice-cold water of Foca in which Rupert snorkeled. I was anxious about his taking planes, his not knowing French and his inability to make friends. I have a gift for obtaining help, advice and friendliness when in trouble during trips. Rupert expects perfection.

Any day now he will be home, as will I in a week or ten days. Hugo's eye can be uncovered for two hours a day now.

Note from Rupert Pole to Anaïs Nin:
Foca, Turkey, August 1969

Tragedy here: the Vietnamese yoga teacher drowned. I assumed she had a heart attack. She had been in the sun for hours and then dove into the cold water. But the scuba instructor tells me she would go into a trance while under water and have to be pulled out! The whole Club is very upset.

Looking forward to Athens again and boat rides—strangely, the boat came back to Turkey—to the Greek ruins at Ephesus!

But I'm looking forward now to being home again—and having you beside me again—in our own environment—the more I see of the world, the more I appreciate what we have and have created together.

Love always,
R

Letter from Anaïs Nin to Rupert Pole:
New York, August 18, 1969

Welcome home, darling—the loveliest place of all!

I'm still tied down—eye drops every two hours, a change of the bandage. We take off the bandage for exactly 60 minutes a day—tomorrow for an hour and 20 minutes. Clocks. Routine. Care. All necessary to healing—but the healing is going well. Aging is a tragic thing, an incurable illness! I'm as sad as you are after spending time with Reginald.

Love, love,

A

Letter from Anaïs Nin to Lili Bita and Robert Zaller:
New York, August 24, 1969

Dear Lili and Robert:

All is well. Hugo is healing slowly and will be back at work next week. Rupert returned safely home. I will be in Los Angeles by the end of the month.

I received a clipping on your new book. I hope to find it waiting on my desk at Los Angeles.

Wondering how *you* are. I received *one* letter post restante in Athens. I'm afraid I lost the rest unless they gave them to you. Without you, Greece was not what you embody. I needed *history* (the theme, the lure of the trip). Will you see the Greek publisher of Henry Miller? He is still in Paris. Robetaille says the *Tropic of Cancer* film is bad.

During this becalmed month I read, read, read, between nursing Hugo.

New York decided to turn on the sunshine and give a real summer to Hugo—he could stay outside.

Wonder how you are, where you are.

Tuesday is Marguerite Young's birthday.

I remember the ferry boat crossing the Delphi, the drive up the mountain, the beauty up there—but the past was too heavy—everybody living in the past. Is it true?

Wish we could talk.

Love,

Anaïs

S**EPTEMBER** 1969
Return to Los Angeles.

Letter from Anaïs Nin to Gunther Stuhlmann:
Los Angeles, September 10, 1969

Dear Gunther:

Is there anything we can do about this silly write-up of the *Diary* I found? Everything is wrong. If they are going to give dates and facts they should read your preface. Is this by Harcourt?

Please let me know when my second option with Danièle was due. She became worried when some publicity came out in Paris. She will write you to be sure it has not lapsed!

Les jeux sont faits. Everything now depends on how Danièle and the others get along on revisions. She wants Aural in the picture—as an experienced director-consultant. I will see Moreau again.

Texas University's Dr. Roberts will come and see the contents of the Diary files in October, but Samuel Goldberg told me the Miller letters are worth one hundred thousand dollars. We should find out ahead of time. You remember he had helped Gotham's Miss Steloff. He told me Andreas Brown really took advantage of him financially and is ruthless.

Affectionately,
Anaïs

Letter from Anaïs Nin to Hugh Guiler:
Los Angeles, September 10, 1969

Danièle is in Montreal and beginning to worry about the overdue second option payment. Moreau I saw once again; I brought her my second Malaysian skirt she fell in love with, to wear or copy as she pleases. She embraced me and said: "Danièle, Aural and I will revise the script together. You will see it in October." And she gave me her home address. All we need is the official agent confirmation. I have done all I could.

Now my Science Seminar.

My schedule for October:

Oct. 1 to 8: Texas University man will visit vault with diary manuscripts. Oct. 8-16: Germany. Oct 18-22: Paris. Oct. 25: lecture Rank Society.

Will call to see what the doctor says about your eye and how you feel. Thanks for the mail.

My cousin Luis de Nin wrote to Gunther from Barcelona asking for my address.

Love,
Anaïs

Letter from Anaïs Nin to Danièle Suissa:
Los Angeles, September 12, 1969

Dearest Danièle:

I was a little sad tonight collecting and pasting letters for the June diary to find your loving letters. I felt you were less close to me than when we were working together. I felt a shadow. I feel perhaps you still think I lacked faith in *you* when I never swerved from the statement I made in my letter to your father. It is the businessmen I have no faith in. I feel that only when one has independent means can one do everything one wishes. The new wave was created by three or four filmmakers who had independent means. I believe you are highly gifted in many directions, but what I said to you over the telephone was that I was anxious that distributors and bankers would not give money without strings attached. That was not a lack of faith in you, but in the system. I know also you were deeply disappointed not to be working with an actress of your generation. I hope the shadow I felt and your sudden irritation were not due to anything between us. Reread my letter to your father. The very first time I realized you were not independent and mentioned studios and distributors, you remember I expressed my feeling that everything wonderful was done in spite of the bankers.

Much of this shadow may have been due to a year of stress and overwork and over-travel—I hope so—because I have not changed.

Love,
Anaïs

Letter from Gunther Stuhlmann to Anaïs Nin:
New York, September 15, 1969

Dear Anaïs:

The 12-month option with Danièle expires January 13, 1970 and can be renewed for 6 months upon payment of $500. I have not heard from Danièle nor received payment on the screenplay money she owes you. Should I push her directly in Montreal?

Your publishers in Europe are going full steam. Wegner has already published a short brochure about your visit and will cooperate with Rowohlt to push also the Miller letters. He says your ticket is waiting for you at the Pan Am office here in N.Y. I told André you could be in Paris till Oct. 23. This would also be exactly 14 days from your start. He speaks of major promotion, a full page in *Le Monde*, *Figaro Littéraire*, *Nouvelles Littéraires*, and he conveys enthusiasm.

Good news too: Wegner will do *Spy* in German in a new edition this spring. Will have the contract ready when you get back here. No statement from Swallow yet. You will need to gather strength before Europe. Seems like a full program.

Love,
Gunther

Letter from Anaïs Nin to Henry Miller:
Los Angeles, September 30, 1969

Dear Henry:

I'm so glad you agree with me about George Wickes. He is so humorless, literal and tactless. I wondered why he was chosen to edit your correspondence with Emil Schnellock. I am enclosing an offset of the chapter in his book in which he says all the clumsy things. I'm glad you reassured me about the letters. With the Durrell-Miller letters there was a misunderstanding. I never meant for you to leave *me* out altogether, but only what may concern Hugo, that was all. I leave for Frankfurt Oct. 8 or 9. I will be in Paris from the 18th to the 23rd—no longer because publishers are paying my trip and my hotel and I cannot afford it on my own.

While I'm away you may receive a copy of *Diary 3* in which I made all the changes you requested.

Henry, I would like to warn you about Oliver Evans. He is cold and cynical—he uses his friends and sells letters almost *before* they are written! Please do not trust him. Nobody likes his book on my work; it is petty, literal, unfeeling.

I will be back November 1 to work on vol. 4! Keep well.
Anaïs

Letter from Anaïs Nin to Hugh Guiler:
Los Angeles, September 30, 1969

Darling:

It is 6:00 AM. I tried to call you yesterday but no answer. I hope that when you disconnect your phone you remember to reconnect it, as I often forgot. I will try again today. But I want to write you in detail about Moreau. She came with Danièle Friday evening. I loved her immediately. She is smaller than she appears in films; she is in good form now, rejuvenated by her first film in America with an actor she respects, Lee Marvin. She is, of course, intelligent and well read. But best of all, she is in love with *Spy* and Sabina, has been for three years since she read it. (She does not know Danièle has been hunting around for a younger star and failed to get one; I hope she will never know.) Aurel had mentioned the book to her. She had asked several people for introductions to me. She asked Miller in Paris. We talked about Dinesen, about Lesley Blanch, about acting. Her eyes are very expressive. She is strong but in a velvety way. There was a good rapport.

It is good I came, because Danièle is the one who is not wholeheartedly happy about Moreau. I analyze this as part of Danièle's lesbianism and her age of 28 years. She wanted to direct a woman her age. She may be afraid she would be unable to control Moreau (even sexually, I imagine). She wanted someone more beautiful, she said.

Of course, I am happy. I admire Moreau and she alone could do this. Another wonderful point is that she is no longer interested in novels, in fiction, only in psychological books, biographies, etc. She is in a psychological phase. She read the *Diary*. I had been anxious, as you know, but she is willing to be directed by Danièle with Jean Aurel as technical co-director...but she does not insist on that as she agrees there is a woman's point of view that male directors do not get. We talked about women's vision. She even said she wanted to direct her next film on the friendships between women, real friendships, which men do not believe in. I can make a friend of her.

She is now reading the script that Danièle had not wanted to give her. But she knows the book by heart, which is more important. Danièle's lack of absolute adhesion to Moreau is the only weakness here. And my coming may have been of the greatest importance. Danièle will be very active, but I can see that what she is saying is avoiding control, which, given her dependence on her father, I understand, but which is a flaw.

Danny Selznick is here: he would love to produce...and so on.

I hope I can talk to you today. I think about you a lot. I promise you that the day I make 50 thousand dollars or so I will stop running. Enough to retire on...

Anaïs

OCTOBER 9, 1969
Arrived at Frankfurt.

Letter from Anaïs Nin to Rupert Pole:
Frankfurt, October 10, 1969

Chiquito:

Until today I could not write. Until today I had no definite address. What adventures! Arrived at midnight. My publisher, Dr. Wegner, was there, young and refined, with his beautiful young wife Christiana. He had a bandaged finger from an infection. He drove to the hotel he planned for me. The secretary made a mistake—there was no room. No room in all of Frankfurt! We drove to *his* hotel, where there was no room, but a housekeeper took pity and offered to take me to her home! We drove for an hour in a pea-soup fog! It is a small but new workman's house like any small standard American tract home. But her husband was paralyzed, in bed. So she sleeps on the ground floor and gave me their best room and her *wedding* nightgown.

The next day I had two interviews in the morning. Lunch. Then a book-signing party at an elegant bookshop. I signed hundreds of books! I was told beautiful things in faltering English. So much respect for the writer! So much love of *literature*. They all had the two volumes! Then to a small hotel, where I changed for a big reception at a literary magazine headquarters. A crush! Twice as many people as were invited or expected. Luise Rainer was there with her German-American publisher-husband. There were newspapermen, two television cameras and at least 10 photographers. Again a speech, and so much awe and admiration that I almost wept! Until midnight I met people, they made their speeches. I stood. It was hot and so crowded some people could not get in! Champagne—and finally sleep. My guide, translator, constant companion is a girl who looks like Marlene Dietrich, but so modern and intelligent—beautiful eyes, boyish hair, the famous cheekbones. It is 7:00 AM. I can rest till 10:00—then visit the foreign booths at the Book Fair, the French, Japanese.

Oh, I forgot… Yesterday we drove to Darmstadt, to a bookshop, 40 minutes by freeway, again a wonderful crowd. An actress read from the *Diary* in such beautiful German I almost understood. And we had a talk, a discussion. The bookshop man said (translated): "I was so nervous about meeting a famous writer, but you cured me. I feel relaxed." We laughed. I said I knew they wanted to know all that was *not* in the *Diary*.

Back to the Fair, where I was signing books all the time. And who turned up but Fred Haines, the producer of *Steppenwolf*, his wife Frances, and Bob Snyder. I invited them to dinner as they all looked seedy and tired. Fred and Frances were absolutely ill—yellow. My German publisher was interested in them—they talked books. He is publishing Leary. But the vulgarity of Snyder bothered me. After talking with the Germans, it seemed so crude. My idea of Germany is totally changed. They are so unashamedly serious and deep.

I'm sending you a night letter today as this will take five days. Today will be easy. It is a strenuous time, but far more interesting than I expected. The whole city is full of banners with book titles. The interviews are intelligent. Reviews were 100% good.

I'm lonely for you. Believe me, my sweet, all the praise in the world does not make up for closeness to you—the real one.

Your wife who loves you deeply,

A

Letter from Anaïs Nin to Rupert Pole:
Munich, October 14, 1969

Darling:

I'm glad you pushed and encouraged me to come. It has been a wonderful experience. It seemed as if I rediscovered the Germany of the fine composers you play and of fine literature. And their attitude towards my work has been overwhelmingly warm and deep. How they treat their writers! Like movie stars. My hand has been kissed to shreds—flowers in the room. Such a response to the *Diaries*. Hildegard Knef, the actress, was in the audience.

My publisher and his wife are great friends. My publisher took the *Diary* because he loved it, thought it might not sell, but did not care. But it *is* selling and the press has been wonderful. I'm a little dazed. I think of you at night when I return to my room, and am grateful for your love, and for the genuine love of the Germans.

They read deeply, seriously. They ask about America. "Why are there not more writers like you?" America sent Jacqueline Susann of *Valley of the Dolls* to the Book Fair. Their best seller, not their best writer, and the press is making a film on her.

It made me sad to see Americans occupying Stuttgart—you can't imagine a lovelier town, river and parks. The center was bombed so they made a park with a theatre and opera buildings. The hotel is next to the park. Modern, comfortable, clean. Was given a book on it, which you will see. The only frigid spot: the American Woman's Club. Wives of Americans. Not one book sold! Cold and wooden.

So many plans—interviews—too tired to write. This morning I have 15 minutes before the plane. Will finish another letter on the plane.

Love love love,

A

Letter from Anaïs Nin to Rupert Pole:
En route to Hamburg, October 1969

From Hamburg I will send you a second night letter. I don't trust cables or the post office. I hope you receive it. Forgot to tell you I received yours, which helped me, cheered me. What's more…you would love the many parks, the freeways all planted and fringed with trees—no signs—no ugliness—not a spot unkempt. Politeness and love of nature almost like Japan. The formality is old-fashioned, but full of exquisite thoughtfulness—really the opposite of the caricature of Germans and more like the German piano player in *So Little Time* or Oscar Werner in his earlier days. The contrast between our ruthless military and their intelligentsia is almost as sharp as the Samurai and tea ceremonies or paper flowers. At first they liked me as part of Henry Miller's life—but with the second volume they like me for myself. I spoke spontaneously all day, and every evening.

During one evening there was a comic incident. A young rebel, a short-haired hippie, protested formality and wanted me to come out and sit in a café with him and his friends. It caused a stir. I was in a tight spot. My diplomacy got me out of trouble. The young do not have the power, the freedom, the voice as they have in the U.S.A. They are steeped in tradition, like the Japanese. But they are 100% political—and leave literature to the parents. As a result of only sending bestsellers, America has a poor reputation. I should come back to talk about American writers—but together, you and I can talk about Frank Lloyd Wright—or science—if you want to drive. Ideal driving country—lots of little cozy inns! But it's tiring: people,

people, people, and my aptitude for reading faces and expressions put me in good stead.

Three of the best German actresses read from the *Diary*—one very young, one red-haired and dark-eyed, about 30, and the oldest read the best.

Hildegard Knef sings now and acts on TV. There are no German films—not good, they tell me. But TV has ads only from 8:00 to 9:00 AM—and that is all!

Dr. Wegner believes he will sell as many *Diaries* here as in America. The Miller letters sold poorly. The big publisher who kept me waiting for four years and then said *no* to the *Diaries*—Rowohlt—is astonished. But they cooperate. They only invite a writer every two or three years.

I think of you, my love, when I return to my maiden bed. Wish I could tell them my present life is *better.*

Love,

A

Letter from Anaïs Nin to Rupert Pole:
Hamburg, October 1969

Chiquito: Sitting in a hotel room filled with roses, waiting for my publisher. It seems that the small interviews I made on TV so many times impressed their biggest show *Portrait of an Artist*—something like *Camera 3*, and they will spend two days of careful work—Saturday and Sunday—and I get paid $250. My publisher is delighted because it will help sell books.

But they are very considerate about rest—I slept all afternoon before my reception tonight.

Danièle phoned me. Monday evening we will meet.

It's so relaxing, though, to deal with such high-level journalism. Gunther had told me they are never out to get you like *Time* magazine, etc. So I have been very spontaneous. Hamburg is beautiful with many rivers, parks, lakes, trees. Great order and cleanliness. Being in the world like this makes me appreciate even more what I do have—my intimate, personal life. I said I love the present best when they asked me if I found Paris to be my peak—so I said publically what I tell you every day.

I expect your night letter soon.

All my love,

A

HAMBURG, OCTOBER 17, 1969

Hair washed. Ten o'clock interview; one o'clock interview Schnappauf. Sitting alone in the restaurant as I must go to bed early to work all day for a TV show.

HAMBURG, OCTOBER 18, 1969

At 10:00 AM I recorded a television show at a historic house and park—the last two days were spent on TV. They took me to the port, along the beach, through parks, in a historic Patrician mansion—hours of care and technicalities—a real film. They will use part of the recordings, and the rest will be a German translation of what I say. I learned such fascinating things about Germany. The young, as usual, opened up to me and were amazed that I was formalized by the mature ones. What cities—half *parks*—for this reason they are always beautiful. Quiet, low-voiced, exquisite manners and *care*—the waiter cares, the taxi driver cares, the policeman cares, the journalists care, the TV people care—they all bought the *Diaries* like mad, even the desk clerk!

Letter from Anaïs Nin to Rupert Pole:
Hamburg, October 18, 1969

Darling:
    Sitting alone in the restaurant—lonely—no night letter from you in Hamburg, but the service is abominable—phoned six telegrams—so I'm resigned and only hope you receive mine.
    Success unbelievable. People mob me with both volumes. Last night a Press Club—best German actresses reading—eight photographers. Then I was asked if it seems it is a privilege—to do the equivalent of *Camera 3*—which goes all over Germany—I had to accept for the sake of my publisher. They chose a historic mansion, which was winter cold. But for the bitter cold, I would have enjoyed it. Talking, walking. The best scene reminded me of Ionesco's *The Chairs.* I spoke about my guests on the right, Paris, on the left, America. I mentioned Lloyd Wright, the scientists, the hippies, the man in jail, the Negro writers. *Comédie Humaine*—stressing the scope, range, unknown as well as famous. Came back at 4:00 PM, had no lunch, was frozen—went to bed with *gluhwein*—hot grog—after a hot bath.
    My publisher has been so sincere and devoted I don't know what to do.
    Sending you a night letter today, Saturday.
    Thinking of you, my love.
    A

HAMBURG, OCTOBER 19, 1969
    Monika Shubert deserves special attention. Short, tousled blond hair, the charm of her manner. Warm, spontaneous. She took charge of me, organizing, deciding, but always gaily and thoroughly. I enjoyed her presence. I let her make decisions, translations, help me inscribe books. Making the TV film, she wanted to interview me rather than the woman who had been assigned to. She was the luminous point—she and Dr. Wegner, whom I didn't feel like calling Mathias though he was young—because one doesn't do that in Germany.
    Monika's father died in the war. He was a doctor. Monika is 28 and unmarried. She had too absolute a concept of marriage—she frightened herself, as I told her. Once she took me to dinner at a beautiful small restaurant, all wood, beams, fireplaces, antiques, low ceilings, intimate. Small lamps, as in a country home. And the music came from a music box—a big music box with large copper disks with holes. The last night we went to another small, smoky, winey place. I saw her apartment—all white, clean, modern, a big picture window facing trees. She put on records. She fixed a salad. Her young man arrived from Berlin. She gave me a list of books to read. We talked a good deal. She wanted to know why politics did not play a major role in my work, and I answered because politics were not a cure for

war. I put my faith in the cure of individual hostilities. I turned my whole attention to psychology as a cure for hostility.

Watch me making my alliance with Germany, combatting in myself a past image, a past trauma (the war, Nazism); watch me connecting with deep, serious, intelligent Germans.

Of course, I was receiving love and homage, and my impressions were colored by this. In the park, when we were filming and Monika asked a German Sunday stroller not to come down the path I was going to take, he refused angrily and looked contemptuously at the cameras.

But the cousin of Gerd Bucerius, who owns all the papers and magazines, came to sit beside me as if she had known me all her life to talk about her son who was in a mental hospital.

PARIS, MONDAY, OCTOBER 20, 1969

Hugo and Danièle meet me at the airport. Hugo carries a bag full of small gifts: a clipping from *Le Monde*, bath salts. I have been delayed by the television show—so the weekend is gone and Hugo has to leave the next day for Zurich. He is in Paris on business and staying at the Crillon. Stock has reserved a room for me at the Pont Royale.

I like the hotel. It is small. My window opens upon a huge stained glass window of a church. Flowers from Danièle. Telephone messages. A journalist is waiting downstairs. I had lunch with Hugo (on my expense account), red wine. We laugh at the situation, each in a different hotel. In the evening, dinner at Charles Orengo's, the head of Éditions Stock. He is vital, positive and incisive. I like him as much as I dislike André Bay. When I arrive, Dominique Aury tells me how much she loves *Diary 1*. Madame Jacqueline Piatier of *Le Monde* too. André says he is surprised the young like it; he had thought it would touch only those who lived through that period. The young editor Christian de Bartillat protests. He is young and loves the *Diary*. Charles Orengo regrets the photographs that were not used, and the missing titles of my many books. André only listed *two*.

The next day at André's apartment too—elegant and refined, with works of art in a glass buffet—Chinese, Mexican, Greek. I meet Robert Kanters, the critic. But after Germany I feel depressed. The intelligence is dry and heartless. Intellectual *pirañas*. It is all too clever, too quick, and too abstract. Suddenly my dream of France is shattered. Refined, affected, artificial.

I prefer my publicity girl—Danièle Mazingarbe. She is in her twenties. We talk sincerely. She has organized my time. I cannot see my friends.

Journalists. They are all writers, and we can talk. They come with tape recorders. I go to a radio studio—as new and sterile as those in New York.

Letter from Anaïs Nin to Rupert Pole:
Paris, October 22, 1969

Darling:

Today I sent you a night letter. I was happy to get yours when I arrived.

Schedule here: Interview at 10:00 AM. Interview at 11:00 AM. Radio at noon —lunch with Moreau and Danièle—at 3:00 a radio interview—at 4:00 Prof. Lefebvre, who got me a translator. A formal dinner—I go to bed early tonight. All I have seen is the church window my own window looks out on—views from taxis— modern TV and radio buildings. Danièle's house you know. A chichi lunch. Moreau was dressed like an astronaut by Cardin.

Success is fine—but when I return to the room at night it feels empty. But the French are raving over the *Diary*—reviews all favorable. Journalists here are novelists—writers—one can talk books. The head of Stock is not Bay but a man far more intelligent. He says the next printing will have photos—and a bibliography. Tomorrow an interview (and, as always, a photographer), a formal lunch with big critics, an interview on the radio. A quiet dinner with Danièle. I miss you. This is real work—hard work! I miss our phone calls, hearing your voice.

Love love love,

A

Anaïs Nin at Pont Royal

PARIS, OCTOBER 1969

My Swedish interviewer, a camera and a tape recorder. I took my only walk— along Pont Royal, down the stairs where the houseboat was. No change here, but the clock of Gare D'Orsay, which timed lovemaking, love meetings, love partings, is dead. On the opposite quay cars drive along a freeway to decongest traffic. The sun is out. The weather is mild. The beauty of Paris moves me as always—these islands of peace in the heart of a city, trees, water, the arrows of cathedrals, the homogeneity, harmonies, symmetries. My Swedish interviewer, with whom I have had a sporadic correspondence, is so affected by our meeting that he swallows pills for his heart. He looks tall, strong, in his prime, but has had a heart attack. So we walk slowly, sit on a bench. At the hotel again, over a coffee, he tells me he believes women can reconstruct the world, that he is writing a book about remarkable women.

A lunch at Danièle's father's house. Luxury. Servants. Formality. He is a clever businessman, swollen ego, not a father. He dwarfs Danièle.

Jeanne Moreau—soft, relaxed, eating a pomegranate a cell at a time, leisurely, gourmande, her skin fresh, her fawn eyes clear, her smile sudden and absolute. The color of her skin is beautiful, slightly golden. Her agent is there.

So is Paula Rothschild, now Countess Rohan-Chabot (the Count lives in New York with a boy, and Paula, once Danièle's love, is now Françoise Sagan's).

Paris has refined Danièle's father, but not enough to prevent him from boasting of all the important people he knows, that he can never be taken in, that he is too shrewd.

PARIS, OCTOBER 1969

Dinner chez Marie-Claire's family. Blvd. St. Germain. A clan. A visit to a great-grandmother, a specialist on Proust's Empire furniture. The young people are quiet.

PARIS, OCTOBER 1969

9:15 AM interview; 9:30 interview by L'hoste for France Culture.

I felt powerful and alive, and it was contagious. As tired as I was, I was over-flowing with life, faith, new currents. People responded to the aliveness.

Letter from Richard Centing to Anaïs Nin:
Columbus, October 23, 1969

Anaïs:

Good news! Final approval for the newsletter [*Under the Sign of Pisces: Anaïs Nin and her Circle*]! I enclose a contribution from Benjamin Franklin, who will supply bibliographic articles concerning publications of your work, works about you and the Circle, etc.

You and your friend-contributors will produce the new fire that will light up the academic newsletter world.

Also, I have an invitation to the Gotham for Oct. 29. I would like to come. Will you have any time Oct. 29, 30, 31, Nov. 1 or 2 (morning)?

First issue of the newsletter is set for Jan. or Feb. 1970. Committee insists I have contributors for a few issues before going to press.

Richard

Anaïs Nin at a release party for the third volume of the *Diary*, 1969

NEW YORK, OCTOBER 25, 1969
Rank Association at 4:00 PM—negativity from Miriam Waddington.
Came back worn out. Fighting sinus infection.

NEW YORK, OCTOBER 29, 1969
Arden massage
4h Gunther
Gotham Book Mart party

Letter from Anaïs Nin to Peter Owen:
New York, October 1969

Peter:

I have heard that you have sold our correspondence to University of Texas without consulting with me as to the consequences. I consider this a breach of confidence. This is the last letter you will ever receive from me, and I will not come to England.

I would like to know the conditions of this sale, whether the letters will be open to the public, etc.

Anaïs Nin

NOVEMBER 1969

Return to Los Angeles.

Letter from Anaïs Nin to Gunther Stuhlmann:
Los Angeles, November 10, 1969

Dear Gunther:

When you receive the Robert Kanters review of volume 2, which was wonderful for him, as they say he is usually grouchy and mean, you will see why we must think of a way to cope with the wild speculations as to why I edited the *Diary*. They are going so far out! I am in love with my father, it is the House of Incest, who is the father of the miscarried child, etc. No one notices the statement in the preface. I will have to make a sharp, clear statement, isolated, as to why I could not publish everything. It has to stop. I should have discussed that with my publicity girl, who is very intelligent and charming. You'd think the French would be more discreet. While I was there they talked about how Julien Green adds a few lines to every new edition…I thought they were sophisticated…they are worse than yellow journalists.

I have had a devilishly hard time being active here in Los Angeles: Harcourt never sent the ten new *Diaries* for my activities here, which were charged to me. They never sent one to Murrah Gattis for the *L.A. Times* but it now has gone to Robert Kirsch. Review copies only arrived a few days ago.

I still have to give a copy for each activity: one to KPFK for an hour radio talk, one to an interviewer for an hour in French, etc. So it goes. My expenses, which I just did for Boulogne, are frightening. I am not sure the tax people will accept the cost of translation.

I will be back at the end of November. Have two lectures in the East.

Think about our problem. I will make a statement for volume 2.

Do you know anyone who cares about Tennessee Williams? Mike Steen did a book of tributes, *A Look at Tennessee Williams.* He interviewed me. If you know anyone who would care to review it, let me know.

The book signing party on Nov. 21 should be good. Then Stanford Nov. 24.

Anaïs

Letter from Anaïs Nin to Hugh Guiler:
Los Angeles, November 12, 1969

Darling:

Spent a whole day doing my accounts for Boulogne, then writing him a letter explaining about the cost of the French translation, the expectation of $5,000 for a script (no news of Danièle), the lectures in December, $600 and $200, the money from Stock (I asked Gunther to give you facts and the name of the bank). But I hope all my bookselling and book signing activities will pay off next year! The real aim, as you know, is raising the value of the original diaries. Dr. Roberts' visit from Texas was an indication. A day of bookkeeping. My expenses for stationery alone are frightening!

As a reward today, a summer-like day, I took a day of rest. Went to the beach.

Next year I'm planning to devote myself to showing your films. What discouraged me were the technical problems—bad projections, errors I could not remedy.

I hope you turned my phone off. The German TV crew who filmed me should be on their way to Cape Kennedy for the moon voyage. I don't want you saddled with my duties! They were the German equivalent of your *équipe*.

Love,

A

Letter from Anaïs Nin to Henry Miller:
Los Angeles, November 17, 1969

Dear Henry:

I find it easier to write about this than to talk about it. As it is quite clear I will never be a bestseller and will have to continue lectures to earn my living, I would like to ask you if you would make me a gift of your letters (the personal ones I did not publish) as you did for the first batch, which were published. If you would, write to Gunther Stuhlmann, 65 Irving Place, just giving me the royalties—with the same understanding, of course, that any publication plan will first be submitted to you for approval. This is only for the future, as they cannot be published until after the death of Hugo.

Is Sunday at five or six OK for you?

I have messages from Hildegard Knef and French reviews that may interest you. Also want to tell you what I said in Germany about you.

Call me only if Sunday is not good.

Love,

A

Letter from Anaïs Nin to Gunther Stuhlmann:
Los Angeles, Tuesday, November 18, 1969

Dear Gunther:

I sent you the Harcourt Brace bill for the books, so I have no way of checking whether or not they will credit me for the 140 copies. I have learned my lesson. I am not giving away any more copies, though I still feel it was a wise public relations activity, and I hope in the next contract for volume 4 you might demand 100 copies at cost, for just such a purpose. I do not want to discuss this with Hilda or Hiram anymore.

I am glad you called me. Sometimes when I am working my head off, for the bookshop party, for KPFK, and all I get is two weeks of silence (from France and Germany and you) I begin to lose courage. Everybody is sitting and waiting for their gift copies of the *Diary*. This time I bound one and am passing it around to those who can't afford it. But in Europe I was asked to send about 20 copies because of the demand they have for photographs. And by the way, Gunther, were those homemade copies of big photos serviceable for diary editions? Could we send them to France?

I write to Charles Orengo now, as he is still barely polite to my translator. I sent him a constellation of names, and as he is the one who said he wanted the photos, please send them to him. I explained to him why I wanted to be in touch with him. We sympathized with each other, and I merely said I had not been happy before but trusted him. He is positive, and forward-looking. Danièle Mazingarbe told me Bay has no faith, no energy, no real belief in anything. That is why they keep bringing in people to run the place when he is the oldest one there.

Anaïs

Letter from Anaïs Nin to William Trotter:
Los Angeles, November 18, 1969

Dear William Trotter:

I am very grateful to your grandmother for sending me your review and your address. So many times when I have read a sensitive review I have wanted to write a note of thanks, but when I write to the newspaper I do not believe my notes are forwarded. If my memory is right, you wrote a review of volumes 1 and 2, didn't you? This one is very beautiful, both in understanding and in response. I am not surprised that you are a writer. You have a rare quality, empathy, and, besides, you are not ashamed to respond, as so many reviewers are. I am grateful to you and touched that you seized upon the essential purpose and meaning of the *Diary*.

Please tell me about your writing.

If ever you come to New York, let me know.

Sincerely,

Anaïs Nin

Letter from Anaïs Nin to Gunther Stuhlmann:
Los Angeles, November 1969

Dear Gunther:

I want to explain to you why I would like to sign contracts with Swallow as soon as possible. Nothing else has come up. Too much time is passing. But all this is not as realistic as the fact that this year I have had more expenses than income. If anything comes in now, it would help me a great deal. You once said that on signature I would get an advance on royalties. I never ask you to do anything you do not want to do, but I feel we have waited long enough, and I am uneasy seeing all the editions coming out, one after another. They have done better in distribution. The books are everywhere, even better than with Harcourt. (There are no *Diaries* anywhere in Los Angeles!) So please, Gunther, let's make our peace with Swallow. Any change will spell trouble and delays. It is the delays, year after year, which I cannot take. The cheap paperback publishers are fly-by-night affairs. At the Frankfurt Fair the only one who greeted me with a complaint was Bantam, that they had not done well with *Spy*. I told them it was because it is not displayed anywhere. As far as a hardback with reviews goes, that is the only thing we might hold a right to, separately, as you once suggested. I know very well you are overworked; I have seen the pile on your desk. Out here in tranquility, I can think about all this quietly. And I can think of what I need. What I need now is something to explain all my expenses this year. You must be staggered sometimes by the post office and telephone bills.

That is why I accepted a lecture at Harvard, finally, because they promised to feature the *Diary*. The West Coast is totally ignored by Harcourt. So I am on my own. And no *Diaries* to work with!

I am seeing Henry about giving me the rest of the letters. He is enjoying *Diary 3* after putting us through hell about it!

I will send you a letter soon from Harry Moore complimenting you on the editing and preface. I'm having it copied.

I will be back at the end of November.

No stone-faced professors since Oliver Evans. Stanford's Dr. Newcomb I have not yet seen. He wears a red beret. I go there November 24.

The review copies were sent one week before the Gotham Book Party. Daniel Stern told me. Yet Hiram was ecstatic about the Gotham turnout...

But don't you agree that now we can relax, that I am beyond reach of the snipers such as *Kirkus*? Sign with Swallow, and let's relax. No word from Danièle Suissa. I will phone her today.

Love,
Anaïs

Letter from Anaïs Nin to Gunther Stuhlmann:
Los Angeles, November 1969

Dear Gunther:

Henry appreciates your considerateness because now he is having trouble with George Wickes who is editing the letters to Emil Schnellock and who is being obtuse and very tough, saying to Henry he had no right to edit out this or that. As you may know, Wickes wrote a clumsy book on writers in Paris during the '30s, which is refutable at every step—dull and incorrect. But New Directions likes him.

Henry said he was writing you a letter about giving me the rest of the letters—the same arrangement as before—I naturally said in my letter they would be subject to his approval, etc. Do please see that the letter is a sufficient gift assurance—as before.

For the first time Henry asked me for the real story of the Bourgois edition of his letters to me. His own agent (now that Paris has totally accepted the *Diary*—I have 15 clippings, Danièle tells me) Georges Hoffmann is in shock that Henry's name covers the title page and that mine is as small as possible.

Incidentally, I was to get $1,000 for the TV show in Germany. I worked hard for two days—hard.

I was also to be paid in France for three hours of recording by Pierre L'hoste of *France Culture*, which they will run in several segments. But no word from Stock. Should I let you follow up?

I finally received six copies of *Diary 3*; no review cards—no gift list to check. And all the people in Europe are aching for American editions of the *Diaries* because of the photos!

A

Letter from Anaïs Nin to Bern Porter:
Los Angeles, November 1969

Dear Bern:

I do the editing of the *Diaries*. I have explained to you before that I have *human* and *personal* reasons for what I left out. If you are a real friend you should under-stand that. The rest will come when certain people are dead. This has been true of *all* the diaries published in the world. Perhaps you feel, as Miller does, that it does not matter who is hurt by revelations—but I am not of that school. Human beings are vulnerable. Be happy for what I give now.

Anaïs

Letter from Anaïs Nin to Miriam Waddington:
Los Angeles, November 1969

Dear Miriam:

I was saddened by the discussion on the novel at the Rank Association meeting. I enjoyed your humorous and clever treatment of influences when you read your paper. But I, in the talk afterwards, felt a negativity, and this led me, as I have always reacted the same way, to try to restore hope and faith. I know that we talk from our own experiences, and I was sorry that the discussion led us to affirm opposite positions when I respect your poetry and you have written so discerningly about the *Diary*. I don't know why it happened except that I feel people need a life-giving faith. Social workers have a grim life. Literature for me has always been a con-solation and an enlightenment. How did we get into such contradictions? Afterwards I realized questions in general are unsatisfactory. Virginia Robinson was right to put an end to them. They come to us, the social workers, to get inspiration, to open their horizons. Later in the car, driving home, I felt that what we impart to others is always subjective, that perhaps your own temporary unhappiness you wrote me about affected your views. And I had just had a positive experience. Because of what you write and who you are, I wish you to be happy and fulfilled. I wish there was some-thing I could do. I asked Virginia about you. I was so often, in my life, in an atmo-sphere that was restricting and suffocating. Is it the teaching? The place?

You wrote me after you returned from England, which, I gather, did not give you the warmth and life you needed. England, I am sure, is the wrong place for that. You are alone for the moment, but I am sure not for long. I wish you could find a livelier place to teach, where the students would bring you life instead of just receiving what you give, where you could have friends. It concerned me when you said, "They do not read." I am trying to say, clumsily, that I was sorry we disagreed.

That I hope it was not as disturbing to you as it is to me. I have some impossible ideas of alliances and harmonies and cannot bear dissent.

If I can help you find a better place, school, or life, let me know. I realize you are at a crossroad. Women's lives seem to depend so much on the man. In any case, even though we look at the novel differently and I have to defend its life-giving potentials, please believe that I am your friend.

Anaïs

Letter from Anaïs Nin to Duane Schneider:
Los Angeles, November 1969

Dear Duane:

With the trip to Germany and France, and then New York parties for volume 3, I have not yet caught up with letters. I have also been delayed because Richard Centing came to New York, and I have a great deal of writing to do for the newsletter, copying out names, sending information, etc. Also because Benjamin Franklin's illness shocked me, and I keep writing to him. You must miss the collaboration.

When I was in New York I also found out that George Plimpton, who is never straightforward, asked Daisy Aldan to do an interview with me, and, indirectly, I realized he was not going to use yours. He has always prevaricated and always hedged as far back as I know. He told Daisy (whose attempt he also turned down) that he wanted a purely colorful action-personality interview, and Daisy has focused on the novels and short stories. I hope this will enable you to withdraw yours and use it somewhere else. As you spent time and labor on it, could it be incorporated into your book, perhaps? The newsletter, being only eight pages long, will not be able to use good pieces like that. I wish we could. I'm keen on the newsletter. Are you?

How is your book going? The first thesis on my work is being done at the Sorbonne (up until now one had to die first), and I promised the young woman your book. She is also my French translator. Meeting her family in Paris was like going back in time. Her apartment in St. Germain is old-fashioned, grandiose, dusty, elaborate, with plants and statues and lace doilies, 18th century furniture. And she is trying to free herself (via the *Diaries*).

Volume 1 is on the required reading list of Harvard's autobiography class. But you will read about all this in the newsletter!

Give me news of yourself. What are you doing on the printing press? Ask Richard to send you a duplicate of my mailing list for your next book.

Anaïs

DECEMBER 1969
Return to New York.

DECEMBER 3, 1969
Rochester Institute of Technology—lecture 8:00 PM.

Letter from Joaquín Nin-Culmell to Anaïs Nin:
Berkeley, December 3, 1969

Dear Anaïs:

The third volume of the *Diary* arrived yesterday and I have already read it from cover to cover (and back again!) in a series of determined sittings. How do you do it? It is tremendous. Falla used to say—with a bit of wry humor—that when his *Nights in the Gardens of Spain* was first performed, people would say: "Ah, yes, but I prefer your *Seven Popular Spanish Songs.*" Then when the *Amor Brujo* appeared: "Ah, yes, but I prefer your *Nights in the Gardens of Spain.*" Then when the *Sombrero de Tres Picos* appeared: "Ah, yes, but I prefer the *Amor Brujo.*" And so forth until his very last work. The important thing was to prefer the previous work and the important thing for the composer was—added Falla—to keep writing. All three volumes of the *Diary* are different, and all three of them are better than each other in terms, precisely, of their differences. Some of the characters (do they really exist?) become more human (Miller), others remind me of those poor animals caught in a spiraling cage (Gonzalo). I found your comments about Frances absolutely breathtaking and moving at the same time. Some of your spoiled brats I would have liked to have been able to swat. On the other hand, I found myself reciting the nursery rhyme about the lady who lived in a shoe and who had so many children she did not know what to do. Your shoe was a manner of Noah's ark, and as long as it rained outside they were quite willing to sail along with you. What a source of energy you must have had to have survived—and how brilliantly—this deficit spending of your powers, sympathy, encouragement, observations, clarifications, etc. To say nothing of what you gave of your own inner patrimony. You invented atomic energy before the atom was split. And so we both knew Colette d'Arville during her Waldorf Towers period, and the Rosens (Venice and New York) and Pierre de Lanux (Middlebury) and many others that I recognize more or less. Did they really exist or did we make them up to amuse ourselves or to frighten each other? In any case, I must make my typical Virgo comments: the editing is better in that there are almost no repeats. Brava! There are many more comments I should like to make but we would need to read it together... Now I sound like one of your passengers in the ark! Many, many thanks, also, for the dedication. You are the only one who can call me Joaquinito and get away with it. Moreover, I like it. There is no doubt in my mind but that you are the genius in the family. One to a family, you know. Anything else would be capitalism. Brava, genius, and all my love, always.

Joaquín

DECEMBER 5, 1969

Harvard—interview; Henry Miller film presented—criticism from Women's Lib.

Letter from Anaïs Nin to Marguerite Rebois:
New York, December 1969

Dear Marguerite:

I can hardly believe myself that I spent three days in Paris inside a Hotel Pont Royal room constantly interrogated by journalists. I went out only with my publicity agent to my publisher's home to meet more critics or to go to the radio station. If I had called you to say I could not see my friends I would have felt worse. It was my German publisher who invited me—the three days were left over as a courtesy from him. Then I had to be in N.Y. Oct. 25 for a lecture and a publication party for vol. 3 and in Los Angeles Oct. 30 for a book-signing party, back in N.Y. Dec. 1 for five college lectures, a radio talk, etc. Personal friendships, home life sacrificed to public life—but as this is against what I believe, I will learn to control it. By nature I am not fond of public life, as you know. But I am so happy to have received all a writer can dream of—all the love I gave has been returned. Because of the response to *Diary 1* the second one will come out in March.

It is vitally important that you tell me now what I asked you a long time ago: shall I change Jean Carteret's name? Is there anything in vol. 2 that would injure him? I have no desire to hurt anyone. Did you ever show him vol. 2? He can read the French version now by Marie-Claire Van der Elst. I am writing to her. She's at the Sorbonne doing her thesis on my work. If you do not want to contact Jean, please give me his address and I will write to him—I remember being concerned about this when vol. 2 came out.

Who would have thought the only walk I wanted to take, along the houseboat's place on the Seine, would be with a journalist carrying a tape recorder and a camera? This is not good for the real artist—and it is the danger of succeeding. One has to have the courage to refuse and return to work and privacy.

Do you want a copy of the French vol. 1 for a friend who can't read English? I'll send it anyway.

Affectuesement,
Anaïs

DECEMBER 9, 1969

Lecture at Clarion State College.

Letter from Gunther Stuhlmann to Anaïs Nin:
New York, December 9, 1969

Dear Anaïs:

First of all, a deposit slip is enclosed for the German advance payment on *Spy*, which I sent to your bank.

Hope to have a signed contract and money from Germany for *Diary 3* in the next few days. I also expect the Harcourt contract for *Diary 4* shortly. Told them you needed the advance this year.

Thanks for the German review—this is the first one I have seen—all the other stuff Wegner sent is publicity material from your visit. No reviews. The publicity stuff would not interest anyone, really. Let's wait for the reviews.

The Kirsch review is really marvelous!

When you have all the goods, let's hit Harcourt. I think it would be good to get the facts to Ed Barber, the editor-in-chief, who is an admirer of your work.

Love,
Gunther

DECEMBER 11, 1969

Lecture at Smith College—failure.

NEW YORK, DECEMBER 1969

Someone writes: "Volume 3 is a continuous stream of consciousness into humanity...femininity is felt, sensitively rendered. Intelligence and emotions weave in and out, entwine, intertwine with the subtle perceptivity of a hush—yet such strength."

The lectures are frustrating. They are the opposite of personal and intimate friendship. Only a passing glimpse of persons one would like to know better. The public life is the opposite of what I believe in.

This year was all life in the world, and I long for quiet to work on volume 4.

I feel destructive criticism can no longer prevent me from communicating with the world.

Psychologist Sarnoff Mednick of the University of Michigan developed a test for creativity based on the ability to make associations between things that might not appear related at first thought. A drive towards novelty creativity; I have an aversion to novelty—it is anti-creative.

There are children named after me.

Someone says: "Your special gift to the reader is a rare articulation of what the nerves feel."

Letter from Anaïs Nin to Gunther Stuhlmann:
New York, December 1969

Dear Gunther:

Let's first keep a file of items—but not present them yet—John Ferrone tells me Mrs. Lindley is really implacable when crossed and is very powerful. I honestly believe since they persist on wasting copies on morons like *Kirkus* and John Barkham, I have to get my 100 copies and do it all myself. We will hire a secretary and do it all in one day—no fuss.

Love,

A

DECEMBER 20, 1969

Return to L.A.

Letter from Sharon Spencer to Anaïs Nin:
New York, December 20, 1969

Dear Miss Nin:

I have recently completed a dissertation on "experimental" fiction at NYU; it is going to be published perhaps this spring, more likely next fall by the NYU Press. My research advisor was Professor Anna Balakian, and I believe she has mentioned me and this project to you, not only because *Cities of the Interior* is discussed in the chapters, but also because the topic should interest you generally. I admire all of your books, including *The Novel of the Future*, and I have had great success teaching *House of Incest* to college juniors.

I should very much like to send you Xerox copies of the two chapters that concern your work. I should also, if it is possible, very much like to meet you sometime. I know several people (my husband is one) who have either met you or have seen you at a public gathering of some sort—and each one has said that I resemble you! Anna Balakian is one of those who saw a resemblance.

I am sending you the two chapters to you in case of a MacMillan reply soon.

Yours very truly,

Sharon Spencer (Maljkovic)

Letter from Anaïs Nin to Sharon Spencer:
Los Angeles, December 26, 1969

Dear Sharon Spencer:

I do hope MacMillan will forward your two chapters. I have received your letter, which was sent to my agent Gunther Stuhlmann. If your manuscript went to him, I will write him. When I return to New York, I will gladly see you and we will talk.

Meanwhile, do you have *Collages*, my most experimental or surrealist work? And *Seduction of the Minotaur*? And the *Diaries*?

Let me know. I'm here in Los Angeles working quietly.

Sincerely,

Anaïs Nin

LOS ANGELES, DECEMBER 1969
The mail pours in. It is all love, praise, or learned interpretation.

I write to Susie Sugisaki—lovingly—I would betray my understanding of the rightness of love to "punish" her. It made Rupert happy that I did not revile her, cast her out (and with her a part of Rupert). I left her answer as a gift to Rupert. I conquered jealousy, which is selfish. Rupert said: "I love you for the way you treated Sugi."

Rupert spoke of how he would die if I did—that we must die together, on a plane, while traveling.

I wanted to preserve Susie for his life without me.

But the idea that I may not live long clarified that Rupert was my life and happiness. And Hugo my unhappiness. It is interesting that no beauty came from Hugo himself during the wonderful moments, but from his films, his art. The image of dancing gondolas, the colors of Venice.

In art, he creates beauty, ecstasy, dreams—but none of that is in his life or in him.

Letter from Gilbert Chase to Anaïs Nin:
Clarion, Pa., December 29, 1969

Dear Anaïs:

It's incredible, positively incredible, how you got through to the students. I have some 150 in four classes, and I have slowly been reading over what they had to say about you. "How does Anaïs Nin envision the novel of the future?" was one of the questions I asked them on a test in World Literature (you came after Dante's *Inferno*). Here's a typical answer:

"Anaïs Nin envisions the novel of the future as becoming an integrated circuit of subjectivity. Since coming to America, uprooted from her home, she felt the need for self-awareness—to find some quiet place within herself that she could turn to. But she felt that America was working in quite the opposite direction. Americans feel that after something has happened—wait awhile till it cools, so you could become objective about it—and this would result in the truth. But she never really believed this, and because she felt that there was no real and true objectivity, she tried both methods. She began to write a diary, under the assumption that no one would want to read it. This assumption allowed her to write honestly and freely what she felt. As she continued she became more sure that to be subjective was better, because from the past you find courage—courage in its images; whereas in the present, although it is warm and living, it still makes one despair. So she continued, as her diary is still growing. Her diary is read now, but she feels she can't lose her authenticity, because she is too far into the habit of saying what she feels. She feels that the youths today are becoming more aware of themselves and that they will help bring about this change from the objective into the subjective. To grow, you must integrate yourself, your ideas and your life's incidents; and to do this you must go into yourself and put it all together. And as you find yourself, you become better able to help and understand others."

You were a smashing success during your talk, despite my dear friend and his always defective mics. The students dug you deeply. You were even closer to them than Alan Watts last year.

Give Henry my best wishes for a long and happy life. I had a tape made that I mailed to you yesterday. Had hoped to bring it to you to N.Y. before Christmas, but the horrendous snows (1,000 cars in one spot buried in snow in Pa. last week) kept us from going.

What a joy to see you again.

Yours,

Gilbert

LOS ANGELES, JANUARY 1, 1970
A sad New Year's Eve.

LOS ANGELES, JANUARY 2, 1970
Bleeding.

LOS ANGELES, JANUARY 8, 1970
Named "Daughter of Mark Twain" by Mark Twain Society in recognition of outstanding contribution to literature.

LOS ANGELES, JANUARY 16, 1970
Newsletter published: AN and her circle [*Under the Sign of Pisces*].

Los Angeles, January 21, 1970

Tests at Kaiser Permanente Dr. Ebbert.

Los Angeles, January 24, 1970

Kaiser gives diagnosis of cancer.

January 25, 1970

Return to New York.

Letter from Anaïs Nin to John Pearson, photographer:
New York, January 25, 1970

Dear John:

I was told that I have a tumor that is dangerous to operate on and they will try radiation. This means I have to curtail all my activities, conserve my energy, and cannot keep my promise to see you. Forgive me! I was only told yesterday. I was looking forward to seeing you, to seeing Dr. Stone and the others. I had made notes on the Forgotten Feminine.

I will be here in New York c/o Gunther Stuhlmann for a few weeks. I will let you know.

If you have time, do take photos of my brother. I wanted that for his Xmas present!

Radiation means reduced energy and intermittent stays at the hospital. This detailed letter is for you only. Officially, say only what is necessary to explain my absence.

Anaïs

New York, January 26, 1970

Dr. Parks.

New York, January 30, 1970

X-ray at 9:45; Bogner; Dr. Goldstein; radiation treatments.

New York, February 2, 1970

When I arrived in New York I felt doomed. But when I saw Dr. Parks, the gynecologist who operated on me a few years ago, I felt more hopeful. Surgery was not possible, so Dr. Parks decided on radiology treatments. The tumor was small, contained, and my general health was good, no loss of weight or fatigue. I had a 75 percent chance of being cured by X-ray. Slowly I grew calmer. I saw Bogner. We discussed illness and my image of the tumor as "worry" or "irritation." I said my psychological state was so good, it would help.

When I arrived at the Presbyterian Hospital it was the children's hospital in whose cellar the X-ray machine was located, so I suffered to see children in wheelchairs, hairless heads, black pencil marks on their bodies where the radiation must be focused for tumors, cancers, etc. As I was wheeled to the radiology department, I passed beds with old, sick, infirm people who looked near death.

At 9:15 I entered the radiation treatment room. It was a yellow room. The machine is huge. The nurse cheerfully focuses it on my pelvis. Then she turns it on. It is deafening. From the first day I decided to close my eyes and help the radiation. I close my eyes and visualize it just like a motion picture, all the happy moments of my life—Acapulco with Rupert, Tahiti with Rupert, Japan, Thailand, Malaysia with Rupert, all the trips to Mexico, the beach always, the sun.

I was hoping I would not run out of images. Every day, for six minutes, for three weeks. I called Rupert at the same hour, 6:15 AM his time, Rupert who hates to awaken early, who "meditated" to help the radiations.

Letter from Anaïs Nin to Lili Bita:
New York, February 15, 1970

Snow. Every day a trip to the X-ray machine for six minutes of radiation to avoid surgery for a tumor. I'm responding to treatment and hope to be back in Los Angeles Feb. 22 to rest and work on vol. 4. I help the radiation by *rêves éveillés*, picturing only beautiful or beloved moments, and very often every scene of Morocco! You and Robert are the only ones I would like to see or imagine in Morocco. No one else fits, or belongs. We could buy a white house in Marrakech one day, with a courtyard, pool, patio and fountain.

You do not lack talent, remember that. You are blessed with a fire for living, but for writing, this fire has to be contained or it burns the words—it should not be repressed, but simply contained so the words do not explode. In poetry you do just that. You sculpt. In the novel that will come too—how not to kill the life with words, but also how to respect words so they do not disintegrate. I had many troubles with English at first—how to make it more supple, fluid, free. Yes, Greek gives people a stature that does not exist in English. The Greeks make grand figures by an excess *natural* to them. English *reduces*, puts down, as we say in slang. You will find your own measure with words.

Love,
A

Letter from Anaïs Nin to Richard Centing:
New York, February 18, 1970

Dear Richard:

About psychoanalysis: *Yes*. It is the spiritual discipline of today, more important than any religion; it is the only way for us to achieve wholeness and growth, to relate conscious and unconscious as they once were by faith. I believe in it as a philosophy and metaphysics. What violence could never achieve, understanding does. It is not a luxury. It is a matter of finding the right person (as we once had to find the right guru, or priest, or wise man). There are clinics. I consider it the most beautiful of experiences next to love, the key to all other experiences.

About Samson de Brier. He does not belong in the circle, believe me! He never knew me in Paris. He is a *mythomane*. He is a "procurer" for homosexuals. I met him through Kenneth Anger—spent the rest of my time eluding his parties. He *is* a character, but... He acted in Kenneth Anger's *Pleasure Dome*. We could have a

newsletter dedicated to con men I have known, or the Lower Depths of Pisces—
Pisces willing to walk into these worlds but escape in time!

Love,

A

NEW YORK, FEBRUARY 1970

The first volume of the *Diary* is on the list of best books 1969 in *Comité du Syndicat des Critiques Littéraires.*

Discount records—The Doors steal the title of *Spy. Morrison Hotel*, Electra Records. "I am a Spy in the House of Love." Jim Morrison. I telephoned them. They said titles of books were not copyrighted.

MARCH 1, 1970

Return to Los Angeles—rest and correspondence.

Letter from Anaïs Nin to Henry Miller:
Los Angeles, March 2, 1970

Dear Henry:

All those meditations and mantras you mentioned have been effective for I am on the way to recovery and by April may be all well. Thank you for helping the radiation. While under the fearsome X-ray machine with a fearsome noise for six minutes a day I was able to pretend it was a projector, close my eyes and run a film of only beautiful or happy images. The fourth week I ran out of images and was worn out!

Don't you remember we read *The Bright Messenger* long ago? That is what I called the young astrologer (the one in the Diary).

I'll have to send good radiations for your problems now!

Anaïs

LOS ANGELES, MARCH 4, 1970

David Korn writes a vulgar movie script for *Spy.*

LOS ANGELES, MARCH 6, 1970

Tony Miller asks for money for conscientious objectors in Canada; Sylvia Ruggles tries to interest Harvard in diary originals; after Ed Faucher left *Village Voice* they ignored me.

Letter from Anaïs Nin to Sharon Spencer:
Los Angeles, March 7, 1970

Dear Sharon:

Your pages came yesterday. I'm very happy with them and proud to be in your book. I am returning them reluctantly, for fear you may need them.

I feel better every day. Will return to N.Y. March 23.

118

I feel you did a subtle job on *Collages*, not easy to summarize or interpret. Your approach by way of modern art and technology and thought is the right one. You make the experimental quality of all these works a definite form to match changes of thought, environment, speed, etc. That is the true critic's role.

Love,
Anaïs

Letter from Sharon Spencer to Anaïs Nin:
New York, March 10, 1970

Dearest Anaïs:

I was so pleased to hear from you—and very glad you like what I wrote on *Collages*. I am now teaching *House of Incest*. Many of the students ask questions about the author; the very "hip" ones cannot believe this book was written in the '30s! (They think they are the only "modern" ones!)

I am returning the pages on your work. Please keep them—they are for you.

I wonder if you are feeling stronger and more cheerful in the sun and warm, dry air! And whether you are writing now. Some people create preoccupations. I am not one of them—and I suspect that you, too, need tranquility and a sense of calm in order to write your finest things. In any case, you are well away from New York City at this somewhat dreary time of year. There is a general sense that everyone is holding his breath until the first forsythia appears.

If there is *anything at all* I can do for you, please let me know. I should like very much to visit you, providing, of course, that you are allowed guests and feel like receiving them.

My husband is beginning *Diary 3* tonight; there is so much in it that I believe will help him fortify himself against the sense of the brutalities of New York.

Very lovingly,
Sharon

Letter from Anaïs Nin to David Barron:
Los Angeles, March 1970

Dear David:

I want to explain something so you will not suffer what you may believe to be indifference. When a writer is unknown, he is free, he has leisure, he has time for his family, his friends. The reality you refuse to look at is now that you have discovered me, thousands of other people are making the same request. The mail becomes multiplied, the pressure, demands, schedules, lectures, public appearances. The family and the close friends suffer from neglect. Also, *it is too late*. The world is slow, obtuse, full of obstacles. Subnormal critics prevented you from knowing of my existence. Retarded publishers and indifferent bookshops are still reluctant. I believe in your sincerity, but it is a request I cannot fill anymore. As hundreds of people wait, I meanwhile have three main conflicts. I have to find energy and time to continue my work; I have to find time for my family life; the relationship to the world comes when my energy is dwindling.

My gift to you is in my work. It means find friends as I did, make your own world; my friends were not famous when I met them. I never asked to share the life of D. H. Lawrence or Cendrars or other already-famous writers.

Anaïs Nin

Letter from Anaïs Nin to Félix Martí Ibañez:
New York, April 4, 1970

Dear Dr. Ibañez:

As I am writing you during a night of insomnia, I must tell you I am well again. The X-rays worked and soon I will have my energy. Two months wasted on illness! I know how impatient you must get with your eyes, as you love to read and write. I hope your eyes are better.

I heard you were highly praised by Dr. Otto Neurath, who spoke of your vast learning, the beauty of *MD* magazine, the incredible people in your books. Did I tell you I read all of your *History of Medicine*? I never would have read that if it were written by someone else, but your gift as a writer makes history colorful, and I love all the themes you weave around medicine, such as the chapter on Utrillo. Today I think you are the only Renaissance man I know. How do you find time for all this learning, besides practice? Now I have to work on vol. 4. I am way behind.

Just wanted to wish you all blessings and admiration.

Anaïs

NEW YORK, APRIL 6, 1970

Casting of *Diary* play by John McLean in Dallas. Joaquín refuses to have his music used as background.

Lili Bita translates *Spy* into Greek.

LOS ANGELES, APRIL 1970

Return to Los Angeles.

John Pearson prepares a beautiful book of photographs and quotations from my work: *Kiss the Joy While It Flies*. He also quotes a writer I admire, Loren Eisley. A French study of *House of Incest* is being translated. I did a long interview for *Mademoiselle*.

LOS ANGELES, APRIL 1970

Work on vol. 4—reached page 35.

I ask Hilda Lindley not to waste money advertising my books in *The New Yorker*, which has consistently denigrated my work.

John Tytell and Harold Jaffe include me in an anthology of short stories.

Letter from Rochelle Holt. Friendship.

Vol. 4 is concerned with my faith in the young.

Letter from Anaïs Nin to David Sapp:
Los Angeles, April 1970

Dear David Sapp:

Nothing ever pleased me more than your spontaneous, informal *Diary* review, the warm response and mingling it with your houseboat life, and moods. I enjoyed it as I do not enjoy academic reviews. It was the way to write a review, tasting, eating the book, dissolving it through one's own personal life. Thank you for *responding* rather than analyzing.

When I get to San Francisco, I'll come and see your houseboat. I may come in December to hear my brother Joaquín's composition (he is a music professor at Berkeley). You must know my friend Varda and his houseboat. How lucky Harcourt sent me a Xerox of your article—they rarely do. Forget about the drowned mother—I resuscitate every day and my best friendships are with the young because we see and feel the same way.

Anaïs

Letter from Anaïs Nin to Bettina Knapp:
Los Angeles, April 8, 1970

Dear Bettina:

Friendship made me say yes, and I read your manuscript of *Jean Racine: Mythos and Renewal in Modern Theater. Your* own work of interpretation, *your* creative reading, all that I admire, but I felt repelled by Racine, who represents everything I dislike—one-dimensional action characters taken from Greek sources. I cannot, cannot sponsor him. I feel you used your talent and imagination to reinvent him, heighten him. I have a responsibility to my readers—this is now a large number of people. I can't point to a writer who is the opposite of all I believe in—I could not even finish the book. I was so repelled by all the classic clichés. Forgive me. It would not be doing you a favor, for whoever would read the book would know I was betraying my belief in modern literature, or else the reader, if deluded by my name, would not be the kind of person who would appreciate Racine. Here I would be completely insincere. We must find someone adequate and devoted to Racine. Surely there must be someone. You put a lot of yourself in it trying to make him interesting. You made suggestions for theatrical effects. But nothing will revive him. I could inquire of Harry Moore. You praise Racine so in your introduction. Forgive me, but I know you would not want me to betray all I believe in.

Anaïs

Letter from Anaïs Nin to Roger Klein:
Los Angeles, April 17, 1970

Dear Roger:

Soon after I received your letter I was seriously ill and until now had no energy even to write. Your letter touched me, and I remember you so well, even though I did not see you after.

It was a difficult decision to publish the *Diary* during my lifetime when so much had to be left out—but strangely, it is that which brought people close to me while the rest of my work estranged them. Vol. 2 is appearing in French on June 1 and I will be in Paris. For the French edition I had to change Gonzalo's name because of Helba. Vol. 3 is out and if you enjoy reading English I will send it to you.

What is your life now? You do not speak about yourself. Are you far from Paris?

How I would like to talk with you one day. I hope Stock, who is inviting me, will leave me time for my friends.

Anaïs

Letter from Anaïs Nin to Monsieur Chateau:
Los Angeles, April 29, 1970

Dear Monsieur Chateau:

I have been so long away from France I can no longer write in French. I hope you can read English. I want to thank you for your letter, which only illness prevented me from answering sooner.

I am grateful for your appreciation of the *Diary* and hope you will like vol. 2 as well.

I did my own editing and Gunther Stuhlmann the final edit—the objective one. It is difficult to know what to leave out; too much editing might spoil the spontaneity. No, I do not wish to convert the *Diary* into a memoir because immediate impressions have a life that memory cannot recreate. I never tamper with what I felt at the time. It would falsify everything. I hope my editing will grow easier with each volume. Are you a writer since you know so much about pruning? I like your saying I seek *transparence* rather than the truth.

Thank you for writing me.

Anaïs Nin

Letter from Robert Zaller to Anaïs Nin:
Athens, May 1, 1970

Dear Anaïs:

Your letter arrived just as Lili and I were both thinking very hard about you; it must have been drawn by energy waves. Lili is typing up the Greek translation of *Spy* for the publisher, which seems to be almost as arduous for her as making it. As for myself, I was in the middle of writing a preface for the book. The publisher suggested that I do it, and naturally I was delighted. I hope it will please you, and not seem too terse. I was limited to 1,000 words, but my mind was writing 10,000.

To your magnificently generous offer about the royalties I truly do not know what to say, except to offer our great gratitude. I think it is for Lili to reply. But I will say what she would not, that she has slaved and battled for the book, and doubtless her battles are not finished. (At least I won't believe anything until I see it with my own eyes.) But if she accepts anything, I will insist that it go to build a house on a Greek island where you and Rupert can come and spend a summer with us.

Last Monday Lili and I were on television, interviewed. Lili was forbidden to mention the name of Kazantzakis—which is roughly equivalent to censoring Shakespeare in London. My hair exceeded regulation military length, and everyone was very upset about it. They pinned it back with bobby pins and plastered it with spray. Still there was a scandal; no one had read Lili's poems, and an actress began to recite a vivid passage on masturbation. Horror in the control room, and they nearly cut us off. For us, it was all comic opera, but it isn't funny if you live here. Today, my sister-in-law's parents called terrified from Serres, their village. The police wanted to know why she hadn't voted in an election. She hasn't lived in Serres for twelve years. We heard that the man who rented us the house in Kythera where Lili translated *Spy*, a good friend, spent three weeks in jail. So a thousand tiny acts of persecution and terror numb one's courage and sap one's will.

Still, America! Your letter disturbed us very much; it means something when someone as unflappable and life-asserting as you draws such conclusions. And now [the bombing of] Cambodia. I have been sick all day and trying to work off my rage in writing. If I were home I would surely be in some mob, trying to tear down anything I could get my hands on. But finally any action seems absurd. It passes all credence this time, and beggars all response.

What else to say except that we are well in our bodies and—yes, there is nature. But who would dare these days to watch a sunset or look a flower in the face? I have seen the very pavement flinch from human steps.

Oh well. That's more than enough of me. I do hope you like the preface; it has helped to keep me sane; I'll leave the rest to Lili.

Love,
Robert

Letter from Sharon Spencer to Anaïs Nin:
New York, May 7, 1970

Dear Anaïs:
Forgive my typing. I am so rushed...and slightly hysterical today because so much that is dreadful is going on in the colleges [protests]. I am still trying to get together all the permissions for the book; we are haggling over reprint rights and have not yet signed the contract, and I can't get anything done. Every other minute the phone rings: someone wanting to know whether the college is closed, whether exams are being given and so on.

First, I am so glad you are feeling completely well and are getting strong. That is marvelous, though no surprise and the best possible thing I could have heard from you! Continue to recover and build up strength in the sun and, I hope, tranquility where you are.

I have written to Swallow in Chicago for permission to quote from your books, but there is one small problem regarding *Realism and Reality*. I notice that it was published in Yonkers, N.Y. (is that right?), in 1946. If you do not own the rights, could you let me know who does so I can write to them?

One last thing—thanks very much for the material about *Rediscoveries*, which I will return to you on Friday. I like David Madden's selections very much, assume that you do too. I wonder whether he would like to have an article on *Collages* or *Cities*. Perhaps I'll write to ask him. That's what I would most like to do at this point, and I believe I could easily make his September 15th deadline.

Drop me a card if you like.

With love,
Sharon

Letter from Masako Karatani to Anaïs Nin:
Tokyo, May 8, 1970

Dear Miss Nin:

It is a great pleasure to write and tell you that the translation of *The Novel of the Future* has almost been completed and that it will be published by Shobunsha in a few months.

I think I should introduce myself to you now. I am a 29-year-old female teacher of English and American literature and drama at a women's college in Yokohama. I used to concentrate on English literature, particularly on Shakespeare and Laurence Sterne, but now I am more interested in modern American literature for such reasons as, perhaps, I find stated quite eloquently in *The Novel of the Future*. I have been writing about Edward Albee and am now planning to write about you and *A Spy in the House of Love*, which, as well as *House of Incest* and *Stella*, is already translated into Japanese. Besides teaching and writing, I have only begun my career as a translator, and *The Novel of the Future* is my third assignment.

I have heard that a Mrs. Ohnuki was eager to translate it, with your own permission and encouragement, and was much disappointed to let the chance slip by only because of her not going through the legal procedure about obtaining the copyright. I feel, in spite of my innocence, very sorry for her and, curiously, psychologically indebted. I hope Mr. Nakamura, editor-in-chief, did his best to explain and persuade her into a kind concession. Please tell her when you see her next how I feel and that I shall be much obliged if she can help me with difficult points.

I am now intent on making commentary and introductory notes covering as many newly introduced writers, artists, psychiatrists and others mentioned in the book as I can, and I must ask for your help now in identifying the persons I list below:

1. Dr. Robert Haas
2. Dr. Robert Lindner
3. Daniel Stern
4. Jerzy Kosinski
5. Hideo Aoki
6. Simon Rhodia and Watts Towers

I shall be very happy if you can give me a brief introduction on each of them.

I shall be even happier if you find it fit to write for the Japanese version *a dedication* to the Japanese readers in place of sensitive Americans. It doesn't have to be preface-like, just a dedication which all of us shall appreciate a great deal.

I enjoyed reading about four years ago the literary talk between you and some Japanese men of literature in a magazine. I wish that when you come to Japan again you will have a talk with female writers and critics. I believe it will bring forth a very urgent issue on women's writing, a part of which, incidentally, has been discussed by a few prominent female writers on the latest issue of a literary magazine. I am sure *The Novel of the Future* will induce much argument among us and I hope to do my best to render it as perfect as possible in Japanese.

Looking forward to hearing from you and with a prospect of writing you again.
Sincerely yours,
Masako Karatani

Letter from Anaïs Nin to David Pepperell:
Los Angeles, May 10, 1970

Dear David:

There is no break, is there, even when the letters stop. I had my own desert voyage—two months of illness with no energy even for letters, but I am well again now and working on vol. 4. A friend I have, your age, a teacher of Zen, and writing a book, and I agreed that when we were writing a book, no letters! And Cortázar writes me about an agonizing choice between answering a letter or working! I live in a country that is in a state of continuous revolution. I was shattered by the killing of four students and by war in Cambodia. Whenever you read a paper, listen to the radio or watch TV, there is horror and hell. So we seek solace in work.

We saw *Women in Love* of D. H. Lawrence on film and were excited. I read Gaston Bachelard, the French philosopher, now obtainable in English. Jeanne Moreau is arriving tomorrow and the new script for *Spy* is ready, and when that is settled I go to London and Paris on a publicity tour for vols. 2 and 3, invited by publishers, which means work, no leisure, no friends—the public side of a writer's life I do not like, but it brings me new, genuine friends. I'm sending you *Diary 3*.

Henry is not happy. He has decided not to travel anymore...

Am I in love, you ask—always, but with the same person who has all I need.

When I do not answer it is because the only thing I ever run out of is energy!

I will send you an interview with Miller to bring you up to date. But you should see the film made about him. Robert Snyder is now charting one on me.

It is good to get your loving letter and poem in a war-mad country where hate predominates. The young are the best we have—they have a sense of values and are ready to fight for justice. They are heroes.

Love,
A

Letter from Anaïs Nin to Sharon Spencer:
Los Angeles, May 10, 1970

Dear Sharon:

Events have been shattering. It is a nightmare and a madness, and it has affected you directly in your college. I can understand how you feel.

I own the rights to *Realism and Reality* and I give you permission to quote from it.

If you will still be in N.Y. June 10 I may see you when I return from Paris.

My trip to England is May 25 to 31. France June 1 to 7—unless I'm so over-whelmed by friends and critics that I may have to stay over at my own expense. Some critics have become friends I want to spend time with, like Diana Fernandez who is a psychologist doing her thesis on Rank.

I wore your beautiful Indian scarf.

Working hard on vol. 4—up to p. 120, one fourth of it. I often talk about you. I think your book is going to change the vision of modern criticism. When I think of you writing *and* teaching, I'm ashamed. Writing takes me all day (perpetual duties of a writer added) and all my energy!

Love,

Anaïs

Letter from Anaïs Nin to Robert Zaller and Lili Bita:
Los Angeles, May 10, 1970

Dear Lili and Robert:

Rupert and I read your letter together at the beach. The preface—beautiful! It could not be more understanding and incisive. So pertinent to present problems of women. And beautifully and clearly stated. I'm proud of it. I knew Robert was a clear-minded historian, but here you related the two—the personal as symbol of a bigger drama. I would like to see it appear in the newsletter from Ohio State University, which has 300 subscribers and goes monthly to universities. I ordered a guide to Grants for Writers but it may reach you too late.

There is a permanent revolution here. I do not know what news you get. Many campuses are closed—some want to close till June—protest marches and violence. Richard Centing opened the library to students so they could wash their eyes from tear gas bombs and attend to minor burns.

If your publisher has written to Gunther, fine. If he sends a check I will send it to you. If he finds it hard to export money tell him I want you to have it for trans-lation. It is I who should be grateful to you. It is much harder work to translate than to write a book.

We were amused by the story of your TV show! But I can see for your sister it is not the same.

I do not know my plans for the summer. All I know is that in July Rupert and I will take a vacation. He has been shattered by a teachers' strike—he didn't believe in either side.

I'm working hard on vol. 4.

I'm very proud of the preface, and grateful.

Love,

Anaïs

Letter from Anaïs Nin to Masako Karatani:
Los Angeles, May 13, 1970

Dear Miss Karatani:

I was very pleased to hear from you. I have explained the situation to Mrs. Ohnuki. I will try to help you with the footnotes to names and titles I allude to:

Dr. Robert Haas is Director of Arts and Humanities at USC, Los Angeles.

Daniel Stern is a modern American writer who has written several novels, lives in New York and is an accomplished cellist. I am including a full review of his novel.

Jerzy Kosinski is a modern writer, author of *The Painted Bird* and *Steps*, which someone is now translating into Japanese.

Hideo Aoki once worked as editor for Kawade Shobo.

Simon Rhodia is a legendary character, similar to Facteur Cheval, the French mailman who built a fantastic miniature castle with stones he picked up during his walk as mailman. Rhodia was an Italian mason who picked up leftover broken tiles, bottles, teapots, etc. and built fabulous towers in the center of the Watts area of Los Angeles (the poor Negro area) and was visited by artists.

I sent you a package of books, all but the ones that were published in Japan, which I never received from Mr. Sugawara. I would like to see them. I hope you can use the same phrasing in the dedication of *The Novel of the Future*, which I wrote in the preface to *House of Incest*, where I say I did not know Japanese literature before I wrote my novels, but if I had I would have been profoundly influenced as I feel a great affinity with it, with its subtle psychological observation, the sense of aesthetics, of nature, of mood, of inner journey rather than direct and violent action. Now I have read everything available in English, from the ancient *Tale of Genji* to the modern. I do not have this preface with me, but I feel what I said there might do. Would you mind? Then I could add that the book is dedicated to the sensitive writers and readers of Japan. Mr. Sugawara tells me critics have commented on my books but did not send me any critiques. I have Japanese friends here who could read them to me. As you may know, there are many Japanese living in Los Angeles.

I am glad you mention my meeting Japanese women. I was not introduced to a single one while in Japan. Of the Japanese women friends I have here, one is married to Ivan Morris, the well-known translator of Japanese literature, the other to Sam Francis the painter. And there is Mrs. Ohnuki, whose husband is a scientist.

I hope my information, though incomplete, will do.

With my warm greetings,

Anaïs Nin

Letter from Anaïs Nin to Duane Schneider:
Los Angeles, May 14, 1970

Dear Duane:

Finished signing the books of our interview today. They will go out over the weekend. I hope you don't mind if I send them by regular book post as the special delivery was high and I thought the first hundred would keep you going.

My problem is mostly people doing their theses in foreign countries who want to quote and read studies...and the difficulties of sending money from abroad. I was wondering, too, if you could not include the interview in your critique book so as to give it a more permanent form. It seems fitting, don't you agree?

I hope it will sell well.

Summer has come and will really cure me for the two weeks of relentless publicity in London and Paris. But there is another side to that—I made interesting friends in France. Did you see *Women in Love*? It is worth seeing. But stay away

127

from the *Satyricon* by Fellini. It is a Dante's *Inferno* of the most grotesque distortion. As my classical scholarship is limited, I do not know if it is Fellini or *Satyricon* that is madness and grossness as I have never seen. It also has a homosexual distortion of women, which is not beautiful.

I will leave for London May 25 for a week of publicity and a week in Paris, for the same, until June 7.

My love to you and your family,

Anaïs

Letter from Anaïs Nin to Takao Sugawara:
Los Angeles, May 15, 1970

Dear Mr. Sugawara:

Everyone has his own code of ethics. If you had written to me from the beginning that you had no money, that your press was small, that you intended to do this on your own, etc., it would be different, and I might have considered it. But this is not a personal problem. It concerns all American writers and will ultimately make American publishers damage Japanese writers in the same way. So the problem of taking books that have been in print ten years (like *House of Incest*) after which they are public domain will be taken up by the PEN club.

It also upset me that you could write me several letters before getting the book in print and once it was done, no more letters, no books. Yes, I know what it is to be ill, but you found time to write a long letter to Mrs. Ohnuki. If Kawade Shobo is still sending me royalties for *Spy in the House of Love*, it must be that there is interest in my work in Japan. Also, *The Novel of the Future* was handled in a normal way with Gunther Stuhlmann, my agent, and I am corresponding with my translator.

I still feel the attitude you took is not fair to writers. Writers live from their work. You say Mr. Nakada and Mr. Aoki tried in vain to get another publisher for my work, but I have found other publishers who are corresponding with Mr. Stuhlmann.

One is a matter of principle and ethics, the other is that if you had told me how you intended to work and it had been understood, I would have not have felt betrayed. Yes, everyone has his own kind of pride. Mine consists in trusting, and when I saw the quality of your letters, I trusted you. Then along comes my agent who says: "You are foolish to say yes before a contract." It was a wrong principle.

I would like to have copies of the books anyway. I have many Japanese friends who would like to see them. I would like to know how many were printed, as you understand this affects my contracts with other Japanese publishers.

I have not mentioned this to anyone but the PEN club, as the subject has been discussed in American papers only.

Yes, I understand how you used the phrase "good literature belongs to everybody." Mrs. Ohnuki and I have cleared up the misunderstanding.

Kindly send me copies to Box 26411 Los Angeles 26.

Sincerely,

Anaïs Nin

Letter from Anaïs Nin to Rupert Pole:
London, May 26, 1970

Darling:

Waiting for my first journalist at 10:30. The big plane was not so bad as they added extra personnel—but no quicker speed. Came in six hours! Peter Owen met me. Speedway all the way. A tiny pot with five posies in my tiny room on Sloan Square! But a sunny spring day. I have five journalists to see, about an hour each! That is all today. Tomorrow five more and a reception at Peter Owen's. Thursday a press reception at noon. Interviews by hippie papers. Evening an 8:30 TV taping for a 10:30 show, so I will come back to the hotel to see it. Friday more interviews, and I plan to leave in the evening or else I will be trapped by Luise Rainer (possessive) or Jerry Bick or someone else.

I slept fitfully, concerned over Reginald, Piccolo and you.

Peter Owen and Anaïs Nin, London

Peter has taken over *Spy* from the publisher who gave no royalties for three years! In honest England.

Days in N.Y. were useful.

No options without money, said Gunther, so I wrote Emily Stevens. Danièle must return the projector and Mrs. Weston's gypsy dress. The tape will be delivered by Moreau's chauffeur on June 1 when she goes for an appendicitis operation. That may be why she did not look well. Hush hush—Danièle said it is a big secret.

I love you,

A

Letter from Sharon Spencer to Anaïs Nin:
New York, June 4, 1970

Dear Anaïs:

I had hoped so much to be able to talk to you or see you after your return and before our departure. But our sailing date has been moved forward from the 17th to the 11th! And since we are sailing from Norfolk, Virginia, we will have to leave the city very early on the morning of the 10th. I hope your visits to London and Paris have been exciting, but not too wearing. Also that you accomplished the work you wanted on *Diary 4*. I am just in the process of sending *Diary 1* to a friend who, I feel, is suffering a lot of confusion about the female role and all that such confusion entails. I have recommended *Diary 1* or loaned it to many, many students. The response is always quick. Students find much in it to inspire them and give them courage.

Gunther Stuhlmann gave me some excellent advice regarding my contract with the NYU Press. I had to fight very hard, but I did get an "out of print" clause added to the contract. This means that when NYU has ceased printing the paperback, control of the rights reverts to me, and I can then place it with another publisher as a "quality paperback." In any case, the director of the press did not like *Poetics of Space* as a title. We are stuck with *Space and Structure in the Modern Novel*. Dull. Pedantic-sounding. Wholly lacking in euphony. What's done is done, in this regard, and there is nothing I can do about it. I am going to write to John Ferrone to thank him again for reading the manuscript and to bring him up to date on the status of the book.

At my college, at least, the Kent State massacre and the extension of war are producing a calm and reasoned reaction in the form of an organization whose purpose is to end the war and to change priorities in terms of national expenditures and generally of values. A group of seminars will be given next week on a voluntary basis. I'm going to try to speak on "Radical Style in Art, Politics, and Personal Creativity." My plan is very, very loose; much will depend on which students come and what their response turns out to be. I intend, among other things, to make the students aware of Dada and Surrealism and of the many factors that make the twentieth century so drastically different from the nineteenth.

I was quite thrilled at your suggestion that I might do the introduction to the reissue of *Cities of the Interior*. If that is still a possibility, do let me know as soon as you have a chance.

You did not mention your health, and so I am certain you must be regaining your strength rapidly after the ordeal of the winter. Where will you go after you return to New York in June? I can't picture somehow your spending the summer in the Village.

I think I forgot to tell you that I made a very slight revision in one of the chapters of the dissertation so as to mention Ian Hugo's name specifically in connection with the illustrations of your books. His films made a very deep impression on me, and I am going to rent them for use at the college next fall. I hope that you will give him our warmest regards and tell him again how extraordinary we feel his films are.

Do, please, write soon.

Much love,

Sharon

Letter from Anaïs Nin to Rupert Pole:
Paris, June 1970

Darling Chiquito:

Felt so badly today reading about war a few kilometers from Angkor Wat.

Today I see Marguerite Rebois for a walk and lunch—then I must say hello at least to my cousin, Eduardo's sister—a rest—and André Bay and his new wife will take me to dinner. I never stay up late. Monday and Tuesday are heavy days. Wednesday and Thursday are TV days and then I'm off.

Diary selling over 20,000—big for France and a bestseller in Geneva.

Another nice day. Thinking of our house, pool, beach, Piccolo and *us*—how I could be having an Acapulco siesta with you—but try to think this will enrich our life—indirectly.

Yesterday was spent at the radio station again. I am getting to handle it all expertly.

American literature is a great favorite here. I have not seen shops or clothes! I have had 100,000 photos taken—at cafés, walking, etc. No fun to be on stage. Love you and our life more than ever.

Yours,

A

Letter from Anaïs Nin to Rupert Pole:
Paris, June 1970

Darling:

I didn't send you a night letter because I write you every day, but I will tomorrow. I was so happy with your cable that all is well. It gave me courage. I rested all Saturday and Sunday—so I was ready for today. The magazine *Elle* has color photos of me walking along the Seine—a two-hour interview. Rest from four to six. Dinner, interview with Diana Fernandez, a woman who has written well about vol. 1. The difficult job will be TV shows on Thursday and Friday—one at a studio, the other visiting Paris haunts—and a third one on Monday, but in general everything has been successful; only one bitchy woman from the *London Times*— really bitchy. But I have decided no more personal interviews—they are really harassing—from now on just reviews. Instead of talking about what is *in* the *Diary*, all they want to know is what is left *out*. But I have managed rests, don't worry. I'm better at saying no.

I miss you, my sweet home and happy life so much. It will be my reward.
Love,
A

Card from Anaïs Nin to Rupert Pole:
Paris, June 1970

Darling:
One more day of work then I leave for N.Y. Thursday. Sad not to have news of you! The result of my trip is that the three *Diaries* will come out in paperback. Stock did more publicity than Harcourt! TV today all day—on a barge, walking, sitting at a café, etc., then all over again (two programs, half hour each). Radio-Canada insisted on a TV interview because the *Diary* is selling there and they are printing Canadian publications.
Love love love love,
Anaïs

Card from Anaïs Nin to Rupert Pole:
Paris, June 1970

I'm sad not to have had a second night letter Sunday—a week after the first one. I miss news of you and tried to write you every day. Today two hours of radio: a 4:30 radio show, and from six to eight a journalist. But the *Diary* is almost a best seller! Marguerite Rebois sends her love. We took a walk Sunday, had lunch. Traffic is like that in Mexico City—wild, noisy.
Love,
A

JUNE 8, 1970
Return to Los Angeles.

Letter from Gunther Stuhlmann to Anaïs Nin:
New York, June 22, 1970

Dear Anaïs:
Enclosed please find a check for $25 from David Madden for your Marianne Hauser piece. I had sent him the signed contract and he forwarded the check to me.
Thanks for the signed copy of the option amendment from Danièle which I have added to the file. She now has an option to January 15, 1971.
Spy contract for Peter has already come back from him, signed. He is getting set up with Penguin. He is still chipping away by changing ten free copies to eight!
Thanks for the Schneider interview. He sure has a neat operation.
Best,
Gunther

Letter from Anaïs Nin to Henry Miller:
Los Angeles, June 1970

Dear Henry:

Working hard on volume 4.

You won't have the chore of reading these 400 pages as the mentions are few. I will send you a carbon of them in September just the same—only those referring to you (1944-1948).

Do you by any chance have any photographs of Varda's barn at Monterey (where I first met him) or Varda and you? I mention your piece on him—the most lyrical you wrote.

I hear you feel well.

Peace and love, as the hippies say.

Anaïs

Letter from Anaïs Nin to Richard Centing:

Los Angeles, June 23, 1970

Dear Richard:

What a coincidence, which the surrealists called concordance. You take an interest in Anna Kavan and write wonderfully about her. I go to London and hear about her death. I talk with Peter Owen—I meet a man who has written a fascinating portrait of her, her life, her work. We are too late to delineate numbers of the newsletter to her, but your article sounds marvelous, and I'm so pleased you are writing it.

Yes, I will write something for you, for the newsletter—on the Women's Liberation question, or whatever. But this month and July, I need to get on with vol. 4 as I lost three months to illness and one to publicity.

Dear Richard, about coming here: I would prefer to see you in New York. Los Angeles is a difficulty. One is entirely dependent on a car—or a willing friend—or a chauffeur. Henry is capricious and unreliable about visitors. One day he says yes, the next moment he calls it off. He is not too well and not too happy. I could not make your stay as free and mobile as in N.Y.

I am not surprised at the English review. They have always been obtuse about my work (as they are about women in general), and there I met the neglect of all women journalists. Even my visit did not dispel my impressions, except for, again, the young. A young man from the Cambridge magazine and your underground paper—a different breed.

I don't drive and I hate automobiling so I am in sympathy with you. I love walking. I will phone you.

Love,
Anaïs

Letter from Anaïs Nin to David Pepperell:

Los Angeles, June 29, 1970

Dear David:

Yes, I understand duality in love; yes, I understand multilevels and multi-facets; yes to all you say: to LSD, to wonder, to what gives you faith in America, to the music, to the young. I will someday give you a full account of my LSD experience (it's coming soon, in the *Diary*). A writer only becomes miserly when he is working... I wrote part of the LSD experience in *Collages*—gave it to Varda's daughter.

So much to say—I understand your life, your moods, your loves, your enthusiasms. I thought of showing your letter to a beautiful young couple who want to go to Australia. Will you let me? He is an actor, an astrologer; she is gracious. They named their little girl Anaïs. I said first: But Australia! That is the desert—banned books, banned Negroes, banned Orientals—like the early West. Anne Baxter wrote a book about her four years there, married to a cattleman. But then I thought: Well, at least David is there. They will find one interesting person.

R. D. Laing—how did you discover him? I admire him.

Was in London, Paris, Montreal for the *Diaries*. Paris has accepted me, young and old. U.S.A, only the young...but I love them...they come every day. They send poems, tapes of their music...

Quiet summer—up at seven to write—the best time. Swim, see movies, friends...

I cannot remember if I sent you *Diary 3*. Will you tell me? It would take six weeks.

No, you do not appear literary or philosophic—you always balance your human life, love, moods, work, ideas. Well-mixed, yes, lyrical and alive—the mixture is good and fertile.

Anaïs

Letter from Anaïs Nin to Lili Bita:
Los Angeles, June 30, 1970

Dear Lili:

I must confess I was shocked at Gunther's attitude. He has changed over the last year—his profession is hardening him; he was once very lenient and easygoing and good-natured about the things I did that did not pay. In this case I told him I wanted the advance for you, for your translation, as I did not believe I would ever receive royalties (for you). I explained to him all the work you did. The incident of the ten dollars shocked me. It was petty. It cannot be that this makes it legal. And a great irony: because he had been so cross with my various non-paying activities, I had sent him $25 for his commission as if he had received a $250 advance, for his work on the contract, etc. I guess New York life does things to otherwise nice people. It is true that so many of my activities are not remunerative. In Japan they simply appropriated *House of Incest* because their law says a book published more than ten years ago is public domain. This was recently changed, but not retroactive. Please let me take care of this ten dollars, which is my affair. You have done a tremendously generous thing in giving all your time to the translation without even knowing if it would be published. I do not want to become like Gunther, losing faith in publishers!

Paris really welcomed me in a grand style. Next month *Elle* will publish the "Under a Glass Bell" story translated into French.

Did Stuhlmann help Robert with his article on Greece? Did you receive newsletter 2, the one published at Ohio State University Library?

I don't know the university rules, but if contact with friends of mine in universities can serve Robert, please let me know. Mine are all in the English Department. If Robert says yes I will send him a list.

Also, I want you to accept an *advance* on Greek royalties. When they come to you then you can return it to me! It is a loan, on faith that the publisher will come through. Just to bring you luck.

This year has been good to the writer. *Spy* will be done in an English paperback. *Diaries* in French paperback. Let me advance you your Greek royalties... please. I know of no one else who would sit and do a difficult job of translating as you did. You belong to some generous world that seems on the verge of disappearing. I am really quite sad about the change in Gunther, because I also feel I should not do things without telling him. I gave my permission to a theatre group to do the *Diary* in Texas; they did a fine job (no money), but now they will have to see Gunther to legalize things. I gave permission to a wonderful young photographer in Berkeley to quote me in a new book of his photos...no pay. That is why Gunther gets mad at me. But I can't change. I hate money and what it does to people.

I am working all day on volume 4, which is due in December. And then I will take a pause...a rest, really. I have been racing through time, with a feeling of it being short...

Love to you, Robert, the children,
Anaïs

Letter from Anaïs Nin to Renate Druks:
Los Angeles, Summer 1970

Dearest Renate:
I was delighted with your letter describing the voyage to the Vatican—delighted with your new cycle, your new story.

Was sorry you did not leave your films in care of someone in L.A. We all felt helpless. Raven called me. She has not yet found a distributor. I suggested Grove Press.

As soon as I came back from Europe I went to work on vol. 4. I feel well. A big success in France—genuine—the Critics Prize, the mature and the young. The *Diaries* are going into paperback. But London is as petty and peevish as ever. They are stingy with everything, words, love, etc. The young are wonderful; the men are old maids. But Paris—walking the streets for two days with television cameras, to houseboats, cafés, Villa Seurat—is lovely. Beautiful summer days.

We sit at the beach now and I read your letter to Rupert. Piccolo died suddenly and painlessly of a bleeding ulcer at eleven—very old for a poodle—while I was away. I cried for two days. But Rupert immediately found a baby poodle, whom we call Piccolino—four weeks old and who looks like Piccolo's child.

We are not traveling for the moment. Enough excitement. The American *Spy* script is terrible.

Do you have your camera with you? You must be glowing, healthy.
Love,
Anaïs

Letter from Gunther Stuhlmann to Anaïs Nin:
New York, August 25, 1970

Dear Anaïs:

You sound like you are really deep in the new *Diary*—it sounds very exciting, and I look forward to getting the rough draft when you are ready—will you send the manuscript before you go to France on Sept. 3? Or after you come back?

I would like to do the book of essays, and, if you want to, I can try to pin down Swallow for a contract. I would not think it wise at this point to ask anyone to expand the material till we really know what we want, what should be involved. Sorry to hear about Benjamin Franklin's illness. Is he dropping the newsletter?

Will send you the contract to sign for Peter Owen, for *Diary 4*, before you leave. Peter will be here in October, but I want to get it done now so you have some income. Peter wants to move the accounting to a yearly basis, which I am fighting since I don't want you to have to wait for a year to get royalties, and why should he collect interest on the money he owes you? I have taken a firm stand on this—so if he tries to weasel on you, don't let him!

Love, also from Barbara…

Gunther

Letter from Anaïs Nin to Gunther Stuhlmann:
Los Angeles, August 29, 1970

Dear Gunther:

Richard Centing is here drumming up business for the newsletter. I would like to know if there is anything I can do in Paris. I heard *House of Incest* was out of print. I would like to clear that for the Belgian edition Alain Valery Albert wrote you about, or at least prevent Dominque de Roux from reprinting since he never sent us royalties. I will get paid by *Elle* for "Under a Glass Bell" while in Paris. I will let you know how much. I will see Dominique Aury who had expressed interest in the other short stories. (She once did the Artaud story, remember.) If there is anything you want me to do let me know.

Anaïs

SEPTEMBER 1970
Return to New York en route to Paris.

Letter from Anaïs Nin to Lawrence Durrell:
New York, September 17, 1970

Dear Larry:

May I ask you a favor, which is very easy to respond to? Hugh has chosen to be out of the *Diary*. He also prefers to be known as the filmmaker Ian Hugo. He was never rich, or a *mécène* [patron]; he worked in a bank; Louveciennes was rented, not owned; we supported several relatives. He is distressed by your repeated references to him in a most trivial way which is not necessary to your recollections—of his wines or his non-existent fortune. It is not really much of a detail which would please him (and of course also Anaïs who has had to refute this legend for years). I know those considerations don't weigh much in your friendships. If you must really mention [your short stay at Hugo's London apartment] could then spell his name HUGH GUILER, or as an artist then IAN HUGO.

Your reference once more in your [essay "Shades of Dylan Thomas"] offends Hugh and Ian and me as it is pure fiction.

Please.

Anaïs

Letter from Rupert Pole to Anaïs Nin:
Los Angeles, September 1970

My darling:

A strange, frustrating day—went all over the city looking for a relief map (which shows mountains and valleys in three dimensions) of L.A. Valley—each store sent me to another, only to have an old maid clerk confide in me that the government has taken them all off the market—can't imagine why—there is no military significance. I wanted one to show my students why smog is so bad in L.A. Valley.

Many, many phone calls. I should have disconnected the phone. Mike Steen called to say Tennessee was there and *must* talk to you—I started to explain you were away, but Mike put Tennessee on the phone. Tennessee, sounding great, said he was off to Bangkok.

Piccolino is giving me a hard time—he's so damn active—and I have a terrible time getting out the door with him—but he's good in the morning, lets me sleep for what must seem to him a very long time.

He misses you—and the house misses you—and I read the calendar, counting days until my other half returns.

Watching terrible fires—on TV—and thinking how glad I am you helped me to leave the Forest Service, to build the house, and to go into teaching, which I like and can do well for the rest of my life. Watching these men on the fire lines—it is just too hard physically and with both *smoke* and *smog* and simply not enough oxygen.

Terrible smog still (glad you're out of it) and have had to give up the beach because of asthma—at least now I know why.

I worry about you flying so much with all the hijacking going on—but I suppose it's the price we pay for violence in the jet age—all international flights should be run non-profit by the UN so countries could not strike at each other through their airlines. But of course no country will give up any part of its sovereignty or its airlines or its profits. Won't really feel secure till you get back in your secure, tight little home to be guarded by your favorite watchdog—at present Piccolino watches everything, but only chases flies and doves.

I love you more and always,

R

P.S. Trying to get this off at the post office on way to cleaners and then back to school. Trying to do everything at last minute—*como siempre!*

Reg is giving everyone a very hard time now—his paranoia is worse—thinks his nurses are against him—wants me to move him! Mrs. Scott thinks the solution is to move him back to the old wing and get him to mix more with other patients. Hope it works.

Bea Wood writes that she met the curator of Eastern art at Museum of Natural History in N.Y. who said she has a record of your reading and "when she found I knew you, she touched me as if I were gold." In the same letter—"Art moves me so that when I look at it, there is an ecstatic feeling that lifts me to realms where nothing else matters, only the ability to create beauty, and man falls away."

P.P.S. Piccolino more impossible than ever, if that's possible!

Letter from John Ferrone of Harcourt to Anaïs Nin:

New York, September 1970

Dear Anaïs:

I went off to Europe for the first three weeks in August—to the south of France, near Grasse, and to England. It seems ages ago. I came back to relative quiet here at the office, but there were a few disturbing bits of news to face. For one thing, our paperback sales manager has left the company, which saddens me a good deal. He was lively and bright and knew what was going on. He won't be replaced until the first of the year. But our small paperback sales staff—all fans of yours—remains intact. They are already clamoring for volume 4 of The *Diary*.

For you there is nothing but good news. We are going back for new printings on both volumes 1 and 2, and our first printing on volume 3 will be 12,000, almost double previous first printings. The new volume is scheduled for publication on March 24th. I am enclosing a copy of the quotes I am planning to use on the back cover. Let me know what you think. I decided to deal with volume 3 only. The cover for volume 2 carried quotes for both 1 and 2 and proved confusing, since it might have led some readers into thinking they were getting both volumes in one book. You'll see what I'm doing with these quotes—trying to appeal to the young (*Free Press*), to the women's lib groups (*L.A. Times* and *Glamour*), and to the literary establishment (*N.Y. Times* and *Book World*). The Jean Garrigue quote is the only one I'm not sure of. We haven't decided yet what color you're to be for the next cover. Few people get the opportunity to see themselves in so many different skins.

I look forward to seeing you.

Love,

John

Letter from Rochelle Holt to Anaïs Nin:

Sioux City, Iowa, October 1, 1970

Dear unchanging Anaïs:

How beautiful your letter and your loan of two new poetry books. I have read them both; each is distinct from the other. I will write two book reviews and I have met a lady who works on the *Sioux City Journal*. She will help to get them published. Richard Centing sent me a picture of you with Jean Varda and said that you live in a one-room house. Someday, I would like to be invited.

Morningside Campus has begun a small group of writers, and I have the opportunity to spread my faith again. I'm to give a small talk on Anaïs Nin before I read part of one story which composed half of my MFA thesis at the University of

Iowa. What a sign of the times for writers and artists to colonize at institutions. My escape is my British sea captain, and his voyage this year may bring him beyond Singapore to New York.

I hope the television performances in Paris were not too taxing. How I await anxiously vol. 4 of your *Diary*. Your diaries are my life, which adds to the nth comment on that I'm sure you have received. At the meeting I will play a small selection of one of your records and, of course, lead students to Kosinski, Hutchins, Hauser, Breton, Hawkes. I am reading *Second Skin* by John Hawkes, and it reawakens my desire for involvement with sheer language.

A group here is to discuss *Soul on Ice* tonight. I think it a most superb documentary on the state of present-day society by Eldridge Cleaver (1968). I have finished three paintings and Al Wynne wants to paint my face. I am flattered. Ceramics is more difficult. My fingers tire too fast.

You are always a mysterious Gypsy, Anaïs. Will you never confide in me? Do write or call, early morning or late night; middles are taken up with quotidian tasks.

Love,
Rochelle

Letter from Sharon Spencer to Anaïs Nin:
New York, October 20, 1970

Dear Anaïs:

Forgive me, please, for not writing sooner. We enjoyed our evening with you and Hugo so much, and we are really hoping you'll come to have dinner with us when you're both back in New York. Perhaps late in November or early in December. I seem to recall that Hugo was to be away in November, or part of it.

No, the article I showed you is not part of the book. I just did it, thinking that you would know best where it would do the most good in correcting misconceptions and helping readers get the right orientation to the novelettes. Just let me know when the copy is needed, and I'll make the final (mostly minor) revisions.

I have been terribly busy with proofs of the book, checking the footnotes, and doing the index—a massive project. The press provides literally no editorial help. I've had to do everything, or risk its being a mess. This is especially true of the index. In any case, I'm nearly finished. If it weren't for this, I would have written to you much sooner.

I'm a bit low in spirits now due to all this tedious work and to my probably unnecessary involvement in some problems Serge has with his work and work plans. I should really like to phone your Dr. Bogner if you think she has free time. There's nothing urgent about it. I've been considering getting some professional help for several months, because I feel that I'm at one of those turning points when I need to disengage myself from some of my activities in order to bring energy and concentration to my writing. Self-exploration seems very attractive to me right now. I've begun to question some of the things I've always assumed about myself. I believe I experienced a breakthrough this summer in my writing, and I don't want to lose the direction that emerged by becoming immersed in all the trivia of daily life in New York.

Serge noticed your name on the cover of *Mademoiselle* and bought the magazine. What did you think of it? I'm always annoyed by the "cuteness" of women's magazine style. I was put off by the woman's description of your eyes, but in general I thought she did a good job of portraying your relaxed graciousness and your warmth and your views about men, women, and life.

I hope your work and your appearances and your relaxation are all gratifying and pleasant, and I look forward to hearing from you when you return.

Yours with love,
Sharon

NEW YORK, OCTOBER 30, 1970
Lectured at Pennsylvania University and the Art Alliance in Philadelphia.
Nursing Hugo after eye surgery again.

NEW YORK, NOVEMBER 14, 1970
Walk with Hugo.
Saw John Ferrone, Edmund Wilson, Hideo Aoki, Bogner, Gunther, Frances.

NOVEMBER 15, 1970
Return to Los Angeles.

Letter from Anaïs Nin to Wayne McEvilly:
Los Angeles, November 1970

Dear Wayne:
I did not distinguish the airmail letter from the special delivery letter because in my mind your book, notes and letters flow into one another and seem all part of a whole. Nothing disappointed me, but I am very glad you expressed this uneasiness because it is at the root of everything…you have faith discernment, confidence in others but less in yourself. And perhaps this is the Minotaur you have to face…your own lack of confidence. It is true that you are writing in a new way, free associating rather than a conscious construction. And one can get lost and one can discover treasures. I had rejoiced at your writing, but I have faith in its ultimate pattern. Blind faith.

I am not here to pass judgment, Wayne, never was. I was elated that all was flowing. The moments of arrest, which, believe me, I have known, might even have kept me imprisoned in the Diary forever. I once wrote in the Diary: *Audace…* So please just continue to flow. You are working from within. You are not bothering to discard now. Later. No thought now. No looking back. No looking… Later. Later one can cut, carve, refine, discard. Now, enjoy.

I was fascinated by your letter describing your first notations. The here and now. The license plates of passing cars… Everything. With people like Marguerite, yourself and me, the tendency for flights of imagination, contrary to those pedestrians who never fly, may produce the anxiety trapezists must feel at times if they look down. Two remedies: never look down; or else, anchor yourself in the earth, in daily life, the little things. Just as you said of the Diary.

I never asked you, and I don't know how you feel about Miller, but I sent him a copy of *20th Century Thought* because of Brodin's article on him. He wrote me: "I'm curious to know who Wayne McEvilly is. That was a most unusual piece of writing about you." And these days, when he is not happy and just out of surgery, he praises little...

Yesterday I was at UCLA talking to a small class of 15, intimately and freely. That I like. And today, feeding the birds and thinking that the poet, which you are, and the mystic, which you are, have more difficulty with fiction. We talked yesterday about the fiction, which is a disguise, a protection... I had great troubles fictionalizing, for I loved the truth as it was... Why was the first novel ever written? Not to reveal? To protect identities? I don't know the first novels, the first Spanish one *Celestina*, the first English one. A mask? A need to say it is not me, nor my loved ones? The near. You are also concerned with that. How to keep the things one has seen.

It may seem difficult to comment on a film in which one appears, but the truth is that the reason *why* I appeared in Renate Druks' film is *because* I admired her film of her own painting, as well as her painting of women. She portrays woman with an aesthetic skill, a penetrating vision. Woman is revealed in her many aspects. In her film on painting she reveals both technique and the organic growth of her vision culminating in a final assertion, the last encompassing painting. The harmony of technique and vision and their interdependence are subtly captured. She is, as an artist, bold, vivid, honest. As a filmmaker her work achieves the dynamic impulse, the physical incarnation of her vision. Her colors are intensely lively, she is always full of surprises, she is totally spontaneous, and above all she demonstrates a most unusual harmony of painter, woman, filmmaker, life and art, personality and medium, which we seek in this age of related arts and life.

Anaïs

Letter from Anaïs Nin to Richard Centing:
Los Angeles, November 21, 1970

Dear Richard:

I want to explain the matter of "executive." As Hugo asked to be left out of the *Diary*, the times I mention economic difficulties seem like falseness to those who discover the connection. I cannot explain how these came to pass (the ups and downs), but the legend of wealth started by bohemian friends in France for whom having a house, a car and a maid was "wealth" was such a falsehood that I never was able to extricate myself from its destructiveness. The house was rented, the maid cost ten dollars a month, the car was a small French car to go to work with, but in the eyes of Miller it was magnificence, and also, let us face it, a wish fulfillment.

For Marguerite Young's fantasy-making I am Lady Bountiful who will take care of her when she is old and sick. She dreamt up this situation. Because of the *Diary* this seems like a paradox. Thus I am trying to dissipate this destructive myth. I know you will help me in any way you can. You have been very thoughtful and tasteful and I do not want to make your editor's task difficult.

I mailed out fifty newsletters to new fans and hope for results. Your sending me the names and addresses of subscribers saves me from duplication. Do send me subscription lists.

I feel badly that you feel cut off from the warm, flowing human stream where you are. I was hoping the newsletter would bring you adventures and friendships.

Did you want me to write up the Paris visit? I am preparing a small article on liberated women. What is the deadline? I am immensely tired, overworked. Not working on the *Diary*, yet every day I put in eight hours of work.

Love,
Anaïs

Letter from Anaïs Nin to Sharon Spencer:
Los Angeles, November 24, 1970

Dear Sharon:

You are sensitive to my underlying moods! Yes, I seem to be going through a depression. It may be physical, fatigue, reaction to all that happened. Before I came to N.Y. I had been in the hospital for ten days with the flu. And then Hugo's eye surgery. I had a teaching engagement to fulfill. I turned in volume 4.

Yes, there are difficulties with Gunther; he quarreled with Swallow, and now they are withholding my royalties. I am sure he will handle your books. The irritations of being an agent in N.Y. are telling on him, but he is basically a fine person.

I am resting up now, catching up with correspondence. 1970 has been a difficult year.

About the anthology of my work—the disagreement with Swallow made that impossible (all on quoting rights), but Richard Centing, editor of the newsletter, wants to edit it, and it may be done by the university or he will interest a commercial publisher; he is very effective and a good editor. I have sent him your study of the novels.

I am so glad you are seeing Bogner. She is an island of wisdom in a maddening world.

I am glad you are teaching my books. *The Novel of the Future* is out in paperback already and volume 3 will be in paperback by March.

Hugo cannot read or write for several weeks, so I am taping entire books for him. If you have any tapes of interest for him, do lend them to him. Do you make tapes of your lectures?

That I am just winding up photographs of the architecture of Lloyd Wright for volume 4 is again prophetic. I run away from New York towards nature and meet two artists of stature, one giving beauty the other joy. And then Mexico.

Somehow, I have come to feel the city is poisonous to human beings. Not only physically, but in other more subtle ways.

Love,
Anaïs

Letter from Sharon Spencer to Anaïs Nin:
New York, December 11, 1970

Dear Anaïs,

Your last letter left me wondering—how long do you plan to remain in California? If the weather there is fine and your work on *Diary 4* is going well, why not stay on as long as you're in the mood? The weather here is grim; every day is grey, it seems, and though Christmas usually creates an exuberant, friendly mood in the city, it hasn't done so yet this year. I, too, feel that the city is poisonous in some very subtle ways, and I'm quite determined to find something around Princeton before summer. However, we'll keep this apartment as it's quite inexpensive and Serge will need a base of operations from which to make and sell photos in New York.

I would certainly have given Hugo any tapes I have, but I haven't got a single one. I've just never thought about taping anything, probably because I hate the sound of my own voice on tapes. You gave me his phone number once, but I scribbled it onto an envelope or something equally impermanent and now I can't find it. How long will it be before he will be back to normal again? Nothing is quite so bothersome or so much an inconvenience as health problems, especially for people who love to be active. I was very sorry to hear that you were hospitalized with the flu... but if the intuition of a friend carries any emotional credence, I have extremely positive feelings of assurance about your health, and they have been unvarying since last spring or late winter when you were feeling so bad and then regained your strength so quickly. I remember your superb horoscope, printed in *Diary 2*. I needn't suggest to you how great a power the mind is in mastering the body's illnesses (or in creating them).

Richard Centing, who seems like a lovely person, wrote me but didn't say anything about doing an anthology. He sent me a snapshot of you with Jean Varda, which was extremely sweet, I thought.

Last week I went into a shop called the Taj Mahal to buy some curly-toed slippers, and there were beautiful velvet dresses very much like yours in deep jewel colors—very lovely.

Anaïs, would you like to come to Jersey City State College in late winter or early spring? I know so many students who love your work. I have one who is writing on *House of Incest* for a course called "Literature and Psychology." Another, one of the brightest girls we have, is doing a comprehensive study of all your work; she, too, is interested in psychology as well as in literature. Could you tell me what your "lecture" fee would be so that I can see where the money might come from, who would sponsor you, and so on? That is, if you want to come and are not too busy with editing and making public appearances.

Stay well and be strong and keep your radiance glowing about you now and always...

Sharon

Letter from Anaïs Nin to Sharon Spencer:
Los Angeles, December 1970

Dear Sharon:

Yes, that is what we agreed on, for me to stay here until I picked up a vanished energy and finished vol. 4, but Hugo was already getting well when I left, able to read a little, to watch TV, go to the office, and has an assistant to read the paper and take care of correspondence. Best of all, he started a film with his cameraman, and that is a good sign. The doctor said he was healing very rapidly. I will be back on January 6. Hugo's films will be shown at the Museum of Modern Art January 5 and we agreed I would not be there as we are avoiding joint publicity. Hugo's telephone number is AL 4-4096.

A book I was asked to review for *The New York Times* by Henri Lartigue, 90 percent photographs and a little diary, very humorous and beautiful, made me think of Serge. Books of photographs seem to interest people with just a little text. Perhaps Serge might try that and make a book and we would get after some publishers. I am sure you could find text to go with the photos. Pearson's book with my quotes has gone so well he is now doing one of nature studies with Loren Eiseley.

Yes, I would like to come and speak at your college. My average fee this last year was $250, between $200 and $500. At Barnard they could only pay $100, but it was in New York, so I did it. See what you can do. Let me know.

Could you send me the address of the Taj Mahal shop, because so many friends want velvet dresses like mine. Were they expensive? I only paid $18 or $20, if I remember correctly.

Richard did not mention an anthology because they are also printing separate booklets of critiques, and I thought yours should be done that way. Next year should not be as heavy. I am giving myself a rest from editing.

Anaïs

Letter from Anaïs Nin to Nancy:

Los Angeles, December 14, 1970

Dear Nancy:

Thank you for all your activities on behalf of Hugo's films. I sent him your letter and he will call, or has called by now, Frances Steloff. I have not been as lucky with universities as they are all dismissing employees (Ronald Reagan's destructiveness).

In January I will be at two colleges, Maryland and Virginia, and will talk to them.

Until I can explain this to you, please, I must ask you, when you hear from Robert Haas of UCLA or any of the colleges, do not mention Hugo. I cannot explain this by letter. That is all I ask.

Love,
Anaïs

Letter from Anaïs Nin to Marguerite Young:

Los Angeles, December 15, 1970

Dear Marguerite:

I wish you had a refuge and a place to recharge your batteries as I have. I was so exhausted by bad health and work on vol. 4 that we agreed I would stay in Los Angeles and do nothing until January when the lectures begin.

I have been worried about Wayne McEvilly sending fragments of his book to Hiram and Goyen, which confused them; Goyen said the writing was sensitive but that it was diffuse. I read his notebook and was unable to understand it. He has derived this from you without the solid inner structure, which binds the unconscious flow together and makes a construction. He has no structure. I wrote him as gently as I could. He imitates your free association except for your "returns to shore," as

144

you once put it. It is not whimsical. He lets his free association run free, but has no core. I hate to discourage him. He has too much respect for you to send you anything to read. You discourage that, as you know. I had to discourage his long letters, which I can't answer.

I hope you feel better. We are all concerned. All the more so because I struggle to maintain my health, but you do not do anything about yours. You accept it. And extreme tiredness is a symptom.

Love,
Anaïs

LOS ANGELES, DECEMBER 1970

Perhaps because I do not have children I think of holidays as something to forget quickly because they only remind me of lost parents and scattered families.

Review of Henri Lartigue's photographs for *N.Y. Times*.

Liberation of Women for the newsletter.

Gerald Robitaille betrays all of us and writes a cruel book about Henry [*Le Père Miller*].

NEW YORK, JANUARY 1971

Harcourt volume 4 advance: $1,200; balance: $5888.26.

Letter from Anaïs Nin to William Young of Sans Souci Press:
New York, January 1971

Dear Bill:

If you have seen the new newsletter [Winter 1971], or will later, I feel I owe you an explanation. Richard Centing was absolutely in good faith when he responded to my request that *Nuances* be noted in the newsletter, which has 400 subscribers of people interested in my work. He sent it, with equal good faith, to a young professor of literature, Benjamin Franklin, who is writing a book about my work with Duane Schneider and is my official bibliographer. But here comes my request for your psychological understanding. Young professors and students resent expensive books and limited editions and are a completely different kind of person than the collector who is not in love with the writer he collects, but with the rarity of the book and its limited edition value. I do not control what goes into the newsletter—that would be dictatorship. Richard and I were disappointed, but as Benjamin is co-editor we could not turn the write-up down. Benjamin was not pleased with the book because his point of view is not a collector's point of view. He felt that $45, the price of *Nuances*, would buy a set of my books... But in any case, you have no need of newsletter approval; the book sold and will always interest collectors; I appreciate the aesthetic quality of it, and I can see the two points of view. The reader with little money, and the collector intent on a completely different aim. Both can be satisfied.

The *Diary* is out now in paperback, the three volumes... And *The Novel of the Future*.

I was shocked at the sale of the letters during my lifetime, by a friend who might have consulted me as to whether there was anything in the letters I did not want to be made public. But it is not the first time it has happened. I know they are valuable, because I hear this from libraries. I hope they were enough to cover his debt to you. But what a lack of ethics. All he needed to do was to ask my permission to see them. I was very good to him, wrote a preface for his poems or a story he had published.

We live in a strange world. Even the dead do not escape malice. The obituary of Rice-Pereira, a fine painter, in *The New York Times*, was shamefully hostile. I had the sorrow of losing Varda, who died last week; I loved him very much and I made a full-length portrait of him in the *Diary* to come, volume 4, which will be published in September, starring him too late.

I am in New York for two or three weeks. Will you call me up if you should be coming in? I want to show you the drawings for the childhood diary and the text I have and talk over how much of it you want, etc. Until now I was reluctant because I did not think it interesting unless you know the writer...

I have received many compliments on *Nuances*, from Dr. Weston, and from Sylvia Spencer who is a book lover of taste. I hope you are pleased with the reaction and response.

Anaïs

Jean Varda, Sausalito, 1970

Letter from Anaïs Nin to Elizabeth Cooney:
New York, January 16, 1971

Dear Elizabeth:

You must have been surprised not to hear from me. I only just returned from Los Angeles where I was ill with the flu and so only now found your beautiful gifts made by your hands. I love the scarf, which is perfect for this freezing weather, and I always love candles. If I had not been in bed I would have sent something for the lovely child. There are two Anaïses besides yours, and to my shock and surprise, the name turned up in a film called *Fools* with Jason Robards and the niece of Kathryn Hepburn. Her name is Anaïs, and when she told the man he said: "Are you kidding? How do you pronounce it?" And she says it slowly. I never heard the name spoken before and carried by another person! I wanted to hear about the Press, the magazine [*The Phoenix*], whether Jimmy had enough material (I get some every day), when it will be out. I am still mailing folders, especially to libraries. But I am glad 1970 is over. It was a year of illness and overwork, but I finished volume 4, which will be out in September.

The death of Varda recently was a heavy sorrow for me. He came to see me in the summer and Richard Centing has such a happy photograph of him with his white hair surrounded by the three graces who drove him down to Los Angeles. I wonder if Alan Watts will stay on the boat now. What added to my sadness was that I made a beautiful portrait of him in *Diary 4*, full length, with photographs, and he never saw it. I should have sent him a copy immediately; it would have pleased him.

I can imagine you in your snowbound place, a beautiful place.

Did your mother read *Sexual Politics*? She was interested in the feminist movement. Kate Millett is the author. She attacks Miller, Mailer and Lawrence.

In the newsletter from Ohio I wrote a little on the liberation of woman—my version.

Hugo's eye is healing. One of the dramas last year was his detached retina, just as he was getting his due as a filmmaker. But he is healing and has started another film. He had a showing at the Museum of Modern Art, which, of course, followed Edinburgh and Paris. They can only follow the leaders, never initiating anything.

Smith was the most unresponsive college I have visited in the last ten years. But it gave me a chance to see you and the Cooney family. The leisure to see my friends is what I miss since I became a known professional writer. You should see my mail. It is staggering, as is the series of lectures I have to give, as I am now self-supporting. I gave two in Philadelphia. I talk with Frances Field often by phone—she has a hectic life, too, assisting Michael in his tense career. But now she has the satisfaction of collaborating on his cookbooks, and she writes the description of the countries they visit and he writes the recipes. Thus she is traveling and seeing the rest of the world. She loved Morocco as much as I did.

Snow in N.Y.C. is not as beautiful as where you are. The wind sounds like Wuthering Heights.

Thank you for your warm glowing gifts, warm colors.

My love to you all,

Anaïs

FEBRUARY 4, 1971

Flight to Los Angeles 5:45 PM.

LOS ANGELES, FEBRUARY 9, 1971

Earthquake.

Letter from Sharon Spencer to Anaïs Nin:
New York, February 11, 1971

Dear Anaïs:

Forgive me for being so slow to get my book to you. The last few weeks have been terribly busy with my mother's visit, which was extended a second week, the beginning of the new semester, and so on. I just this second realized that you must have been near the earthquake! Good heavens! The disasters that are accumulating just now! (Obviously, the Indo-China war has been much extended by Nixon.) As I write I am worried about your having been affected by the earthquake. I have just phoned Hugo to see whether he has spoken to you since it occurred. But he isn't at home. Now I shall assume that you are perfectly well and that your house was not damaged and that you are getting a lot of work done on the next diary.

I was disappointed, of course, by Gunther's response to my novel. He said he "found much to admire" but called the novel "very difficult to launch." I wish that he had been more specific. As of now he is the only person besides myself who has read the novel, and I have quite thoroughly lost perspective on it. I wrote Gunther a note asking him, if he could, to be a bit more specific about the novel, as a more detailed view would be a help to me. That was a bit pushy, I believe, but I sincerely want to know why he considers it "very difficult to launch." In any case, I was glad that he read the manuscripts and that he returned them so quickly. That was a help...

Anaïs, the date we finally settled on for the college (Jersey City State) is March 29th at 5:00. If that is not all right for some reason, please let me know right away. I have arranged for you to get $125 (I wish it could be more) and for a woman who loves your work and has read everything including your book on Lawrence to pick you up and take you back to your apartment. I'll come with her, of course. There is a lot of enthusiasm about your visit already. I'll see that the bookstore is well supplied with your books.

Serge and I are going to have some announcements of *Space, Time and Structure* made up as soon as we can, but we aren't quite sure what to include. If you have any suggestions, let me know. Your help in suggesting mailing lists and reviewers is just marvelous, and I appreciate it very, very much!

I read Oliver Evans' book last week and I found it really quite good, though the developmental approach is conventional, as you said. I'm not certain what he means when he talks about unity and structure in your work, finding some books better constructed than others; and I disagree with his complaints about some of the repeated passages. What most interested me, however, was the virulent nature of some of the critics' remarks about your work. I was startled, in fact. I believe this astonishing nastiness is probably very revealing of the fact that your sensitivity and your approach to life and to the novel was simply profoundly threatening to people's unexamined assumptions. They saw that you *know* a lot about human nature, and they didn't like it at all and didn't welcome the presence in art of such a swift and deep intelligence that was not fearful of expressing what it knows. The clue to this is in the ugliness of the opposition. So it seems to me. It is wonderful how you have maintained your intellectual and artistic self-assurance in such an atmosphere.

Have I forgotten anything? I hope not. Good work and rest in the sunshine (I hope you have lots of sunshine).

Yours,
with love,
Sharon

Reading and Workshop at Pitzer College; interview with Judy Orenga for *Ramparts*.

February 1971
Expenses:
N.Y. Telephone Co. $93.10
Virginia Hage Secretarial work $100.00
Typewriter repair $58.57
Dr. Parks $20.00
Cedars of Lebanon Hospital $98.00
Dr. Weston $40.00
Mary Morris Half of lecture fee for secretarial work $125.00
Massage $10.00
Dr. Goldstein $65.00
Dr. Bogner $150.00
Millicent gift $50.00
Total $809.67

Letter from Anaïs Nin to Sharon Spencer:
Los Angeles, March 1, 1971

Dear Sharon:

Thank you for sending me your *Space, Time and Structure in the Modern Novel*. I am rereading it slowly, for enjoyment, and find it rich and nourishing and inspiring and illuminating. I am very proud of what I consider our first woman critic. Could your publisher send me two copies? There is no price on it, so I cannot send a check. Will they send it to me with a bill? I have to lend it to some people who cannot afford it.

I gave your name to a new, well-printed, intelligent edition, *Anon*, after they wrote me to recommend good women writers for a woman's anthology. I told them you wrote stories as well as criticism. They might run your article on me, or a short story, or anything you please to send.

Sharon, we have mutual friends, so I have to involve you against my will in my private life. They may mention my life here with Rupert, so please do not mention Hugo, and when I see you in New York I will explain. I cannot do it by letter.

Did I tell you that your book came too late for the next newsletter, but Centing's reaction was enthusiastic and it will be well represented. I am sorry that, being in it, I cannot review it, but I hope some of my professors will come through.

I have some more work to do here and will return around March 20. I hope all is going well with the book. I like its appearance, design and good printing. It is impressive.

Love,
Anaïs

Letter from Sharon Spencer to Anaïs Nin:
New York, March 8, 1971

Dear Anaïs:

I received your letter Friday, and of course will comply. I wish I could positively *assure* you that I did not mention Hugo to anyone last spring way before I could have known that it might have been indiscreet to do so. I just don't remember. In any case, I shall say absolutely nothing to anyone about your private life.

I taught *House of Incest* last night. It was a great success, revelatory for the students who had never read anything like it.

Anaïs, is there a subject to your March 29th talk? Do let me know on a postcard. People know you're coming to the college. Most are so eager to see and hear you, they don't care *what* you talk about, but some have asked.

Can you come, even for an hour, to a party a friend is giving for me to celebrate the appearance of my book? It's March 20 in the West Village in a wonderful loft. I sent separate invitations to you and Hugo in N.Y.C. and one to you in Los Angeles.

Much love,
Sharon

Money received:
Refund Medicare $172.00
Lecture Penn. University: $400.00
Books sold: $162.74
Lecture Occidental $400.00
Lecture City College $250.00
Lecture Cal Arts $250.00
Jersey City College lecture $125.00
Total: $1,759.74

APRIL 1, 1971
Lecture at Sarah Lawrence College.

APRIL 2, 1971
Reading for Committee of Responsibility, Inc.; Irving Penn makes the ugliest photograph of me ever made—a mummy.

Letter from James Cooney to Anaïs Nin:
Haydenville, Mass., April 2, 1971

Dear Anaïs:

It was foolish of me to write Eduardo's address on the back of a cigarette packet, for I thereby lost it and must ask you to send it to me again. Please do at your earliest convenience. And now I take this opportunity to share with you a letter that arrived in this morning's mail from Nidea Poller, whose essay "Paradise Lost to Good Riddance" is in our current issue of *The Phoenix*. Nidea writes:

"Anaïs was at Hopkins yesterday. She drew such a large crowd they had to move to a big room, which was unfortunate because something is lost in the move from seminar to lecture. A couple nearby me had brought their baby and it fussed a little, then a little more, then more. A man in front of me half turned and looked annoyed. Anaïs was getting ready to read from Djuna Barnes. The papa took the baby and started to leave, but Anaïs turned to him and said charmingly she didn't mind the baby. And she meant it. The man went back and sat down and within seconds the baby was asleep. So it was an example of what she was saying about the relationship between the imagination and reality. She spoke of the need for introspection, acquaintance with one's self, a reaction to our culture's exterior-ness—but where she left me is in her belief in psychology. She is not simple-minded about it, not at all. And her first loyalty is to art. But I thought she will have to consider why psychology, in general, is desensitizing and closing up spirits and bringing forth so many fake rationalists and madmen with sane armor. There was no chance for me to speak to her—I can't ask questions at a public meeting or wait in a crowd around a 'figure'—and, of course, one would not challenge her anyway. I found her very charming. But I have been waiting for such a long time on that bridge between day life and night life—no, I can't even accept the terms."

Thought you might like this glimpse into the thoughts and impressions of one of your silent listeners at Hopkins.

Love from us all,
Jimmy

Anaïs Nin with the women of *The Second Wave*, 1971

APRIL 6, 1971
Lecture at Philadelphia.

LOS ANGELES, APRIL 16, 1971
Reginald died in his sleep—unconscious. Sent his ashes to England, his family.

Interviewed by the women of *The Second Wave*, Female Liberation.

Letter from Anaïs Nin to Beatrice Wood:
Los Angeles, April 1971

Dear Beatrice:
Reginald died in his sleep, unconscious, Friday night, April 16. We went to see him but he was gone. I am writing to you for Rupert. Reginald's ashes will be buried in England near his mother. We did not want to phone you.
To turn away from death Rupert took me to your gallery, hoping your exhibit was still there, and it was, and I was able to appreciate your incredible talent and versatility, your wit and skill.
With our love and admiration,
Anaïs

Letter from Anaïs Nin to Irina Aleksander:
Los Angeles, April 1971

Dear Irina:
I'm delighted you are writing about the *Diaries* as you are quite unique in your point of view and vision and so adept at expressing yourself.
You ask about Millicent: She is retired, and celebrated her 79th birthday.
Poor Gonzalo died in Paris, of cancer of the throat. Helba is still alive.
I see Henry Miller occasionally, but we have nothing in common. I lost all respect for him. A film was made called *The Henry Miller Odyssey*—a two-hour documentary in which we all appeared. He was at his best as a raconteur. It is shown on television in France, Germany, etc.
I just received the Prix Sevigné for the *Diaries*. The American students have responded in an astonishing way. We think and feel alike.
Hugo is making beautiful films that have been shown at Cinématèque Française, the Edinburgh Festival, and the Museum of Modern Art.
April and May I will be in Los Angeles. After that in New York for June only.
Love to you and Bozedar,
Anaïs

APRIL 21, 1971
Lecture, Occidental College at 10:00 AM.

APRIL 22, 1971
Lecture on D. H. Lawrence, Claremont College at 3:00 PM.

APRIL 26, 1971
Lecture at City College; proofreading vol. 4.

APRIL 27, 1971
Lecture at Cal Arts.

APRIL 29, 1971
Lecture at California Polytechnic.

Letter from Carol Kort to Anaïs Nin:
New York, April 30, 1971

Dear Anaïs:

I have written to you before when I was in a softer mood—at that time I spoke of masks, the poet, the self. Now I write out of anger. Several weeks ago you spoke at the Old Cambridge Baptist Church. You were beautiful, strong, your face set like a cameo, you did not flounder. I knew how difficult it was for you. And then came the question period. How can you stand it? The inane, bitter, hostile, insipid remarks hurled at you were not even worthy of any response, yet you handled even that well. I was so furious with my sisters for being so blind. Why can't they see beyond the thin political veil? Why can't they sense beyond the immediate "women's move-ment" to the true revolution of liberation for us all, once we learn to like ourselves? I just had to write and tell you how frustrated I was. I wanted to speak to you of dreams and colors and visions, and more concretely of lying and being small and being true to oneself. But the words turned to tears when I heard the heated remarks, the circus that had nothing to do with you, or with them! I am growing, I am suffering, but often I am learning to be happy and free. Where are they leading themselves? Haven't they seen enough futile hostility wrought by men? Must they emulate the worst of men and ignore the best?

It is out now. I'm sorry to have troubled you. I would rather have spoken in my soft voice. But this was a time for screaming. You seemed to excuse them, under-stand them. I cannot. Maybe this is something I must grow into also.

Do not ever falter from the dream. Someday they will understand.

Carol Kort

Letter from Anaïs Nin to Carol Kort:
Spring 1971

Yes, Cambridge was difficult, but then the women's movement has in it the same element I disliked in the forties—the narrow, bigoted robots mouthing slo-gans. But even though they did not let me finish what I had to say and failed to see the bridge I was making, I felt I had more friends than enemies.

Anaïs Nin

Letter from Sharon Spencer to Anaïs Nin:
New York, Spring 1971

Dear Anaïs:

I am glad you wrote me after Cambridge. I could not measure the degree of hostility or misunderstanding as well as you did. I thought I could be useful to the liberation of women, but I wonder. Those who understood were those who knew the work. I must confess I am ashamed of some women's behavior. They will only add to the war, ugliness and despair; they bring only their psychotic angers. I don't know if my effort to mitigate hatred and war was effective.

Who has brainwashed so many women, programming them to follow the worst theories of man, not the best, and add more war and hatred to a war-filled world?

I've been envying your being in California. Since you left N.Y., the weather has been terrible, and everyone is impatiently awaiting warmth. Instead, dampness and cold. What are you working on now?

Anaïs, a man named Lou Kannenstine phoned me to ask whether he could have your address. Politely, I said "no," not until I had told you who he is and what he's involved in. He received my name from his dissertation adviser at New York University. Kannenstine is a doctoral student who is writing a dissertation on Djuna Barnes's work. He would like to write to you about the time when you and she were both in Paris. In any case, I didn't feel that it was right to hand over your address. Should I give it to him or not?

I'm looking forward to summer—to reading, writing, sitting in the sun. You'll be back in June—let me know if I remember correctly. I'm reading your study of Lawrence, and I think it's extremely good, filled with essential insights.

Much love,
Sharon

Anaïs Nin's London book promotion schedule:

Tuesday, May 26:
    Will be collected from Royal Court Hotel at 10:30 to come to Peter Owen's office.
    11:00 AM Mr. Grigs *Times*
    12:00 Lunch Peter Grosvener, *Daily Express*
    2:15 Janet Watts *Evening Standard* Londoner
    3:15 *Daily Mirror* Inside Page (arranged with Kenneth Hughes)
    6:00 PM At Peter Owen's home. Maurice Rosenbaum *Daily Telegraph* (will be sketched by admirer/artist Judith de Beer). Will be collected at 7:30 by Mr. & Mrs. Winks U.S. Cultural attaché at Embassy for dinner. He goes away next day so won't want to be out too late anyhow. But if you're too tired this is unimportant and could be cancelled.

Wednesday, May 27:
    10:00 AM at Royal Court Hotel. Mrs. Alix Coleman for *Times* Woman's Page
    12:00 at Royal Court Hotel Maxine Molyneux for *International Herald Tribune*
    12:45 Michael McNay lunch. Will pick you up at Royal Court Hotel
    2:45 Sue MacGregor radio interview
    6:00-8:00 PM Party and dinner after with Wendy and Peter Owen

Thursday, May 28:
   Peter Owen will fetch you at 10:15 to take you to Press Club
   10:45 at Press Club. Interview with Sue McHag for *Observer*
   11:30 Interview at Press Club with Allan Hall for *Sunday Times* People Column
   12:00-2:00 PM Party at Press Club
   8:15 Car will fetch you from Hotel to take you to TV studios for recording for *Late Night Lineup*, BBC TV

Friday, May 29:
   10:30 AM at Royal Court Hotel; interview William Foster for *Scotsman*
   11:00 Royal Court Hotel Jim Anderson or someone else from *Oz*, the underground magazine
   11:30 Stephen Bradshaw *Granta Cambridge*, student magazine
   1:00 PM Lunch with Clive Jordan who will interview you for *Nova*, big, important, sophisticated, intelligent woman's magazine
   3:30 Sue McKarl *Observer*
   4:30 At Hotel Court Hotel Judith Burnley, editor of Penguin Books, who is an admirer and wishes to do an interview which she expects to place in one of the good weekly or monthly magazines

Card from Sharon Spencer to Anaïs Nin:
New York, July 10, 1971

Dear Anaïs:
   I am rereading *Diaries* 1 and 2 in a search for the themes I will write about. I can detect so much growth in your artistic consciousness between vol. 1 and vol. 4. Everything you say about America is brilliantly to the point. In many ways my psychic life resembles yours. I too have a habit of wanting or buying *two* of anything I like or need very much. I'm incapable of cruelty, because I always imagine myself the receiver. I've always avoided heavily directive men, patriarchs, because I know I couldn't pursue my own development in a relationship with one. And more. Would like to do a book with Serge, but he isn't ready yet. See you soon.
   Much love,
   Sharon

Letter from Nona Balakian to Anaïs Nin:
New York, July 16, 1971

Dear Anaïs:
   Before answering your very sweet and welcome note, I must tell you how thrilled and proud I am to be previewing your volume 4 of the *Diary* for the *Book Review*. I am not quite midway through it but as usual with your books I want to pause over every sentence, absorbing all the fine nuances of your meanings and insights. It is fascinating to read your observations of writers like Wilson and Vidal, and what you have to say about yourself as a writer who resists being shaped into

an accepted mold is wonderful to read. How deeply and truly you have always managed to live—and how marvelous that you have not grown hardened by the realization that others are not as true and open and candid as you! Anna has been reading the *Diary* as well—Harcourt sent her a copy to comment on it—and she keeps telling me how much she is loving and admiring it. I think she is writing you a letter, so I will not say more here. She is very thrilled that you wrote such a fine review of *André Breton* and grateful that you (unlike most people) realized how wrong the *Times* review of her book was.

I will have to think of a worthy reviewer for your book. I would like it to be a poet if possible, or someone who understands what your essential quality as a writer is, what you have achieved for the novel as well as for the autobiographical form. Robert Zaller suggested that he might be that reviewer—he has such a true appreciation of you as an artist. But I wonder, first of all, whether he would stand a chance. The editor does not know his work, and I think he would prefer someone with a Name. I will be thinking hard and make some suggestions to you before we let the book go out. At the moment, I am concerned that the galleys they have sent us are somewhat defective—the later section's print is quite hazy and almost unreadable. So I have asked Harcourt for another copy.

Anaïs, I was *so* sorry that I couldn't get to see you before you left. I hadn't realized that you were going back to Los Angeles so soon, and in fact Anna and I had planned to take you to lunch in the vicinity of Washington Square. We were looking forward to it.

I heard from Lili Zaller about the great success you had on your lecture tour. You are at last reaping the rewards you so long deserved to have. I am delighted about *The Second Wave* and your interview in it. I will order a copy. Everywhere I see copies of your paperbacks. The young are especially interested in you right now. I know that nothing could please you more since the future is in their hands.

I do hope that all goes well with you there and you have had a good, restful time. Do come back soon. Anna and I look forward with great pleasure to a long, long talk with you.

Warmest greetings and love,

Nona

P.S. I find the Zallers a delightful, charming couple. Robert is a very gifted writer. I am reading his travel diary. I have to agree that Goyen would be a good editor to send it to.

Letter from Anaïs Nin to Joann Lawless:
Los Angeles, August 1, 1971

Dear Joann:

I sincerely feel you did a skillful job and accurate analysis of my work, an interesting comparison with other writers, and managed miraculously to interpret the work against standards I do not even recognize. A feat. It is an intelligent, acute, well-observed and deeply studied work. To weave together and give structure to such a fluid work is not easy. I found all of it interesting and well expressed. I have nothing to quarrel or disagree with. It seems a pity to give attention to the early negative criticisms when they have been so heavily outweighed by the new ones—

a book on my work coming out in October, an essay by a philosopher, etc., masses of positive acceptance now. But I suppose that is the academic necessity, to "make a case" and demonstrate the opposition. I did not find your style heavy. Footnotes are required by academic studies, I know. I really think you did a respectable work and I can understand your professor's praise.

For publication, I want to remind you of your promise to not mention what is not in the *Diary* (name of husband), and a reference to a talk we had about my supporting my husband with lectures, which I never could have said, or in any case is too personal and does not belong in a critical essay.

p. 13: I was a model in New York and of course not "coveted by Picasso."

p. 15: Perlès is the most unreliable source biographically of all. I would like it if you did not quote him. Miller did not understand me.

p. 29: My father did not beat my mother (she would not let him); he spanked us. They quarreled.

p. 44: It is the child diary these editors looked at (ages 11, 12, 13). Comment would not apply to mature diaries, which I did not show them.

p. 106: John Hawkes is a surrealist so I would not include him among Mailer, Burroughs, etc., and I wrote about loving the early Capote if not the later one.

p. 114: I would like to avoid a statement not made in the *Diary* (in love with H.M.).

p. 144, note 15: An indelicate reference to a private matter and allowance. Wish you would take that out. I do not think such details are to be considered in a critical work. They are too personal.

In other words, I have no criticism and only admiration for your examination and interpretation of the work.

I object to the invasion of privacy, which is intended to protect others, and the use of our private talks for publication, and I know you will keep your word about that, not only to keep faith with me, but because it gives a petty and personal journalistic air to a serious study. It is not in harmony with your historical, literary, psychological range of interest.

I do not have a copy of vol. 4 at the moment, but I will soon and can send it to you.

Your use of private and personal material makes me unhappy about seeing you as a friend. I have to be sure I can trust you, that you are not using our conversations to embarrass me and distress me publically. The work is good. Keep it on a level of writing, not gossip.

One more thing. I cannot find the paragraph where you discuss with your professor the attitude towards my marriage, my husband's attitude towards my life, which shocked me. I will have to wait before I see you while these things upset me. Would you discuss Virginia Woolf's or Simone de Beauvoir's income and married life in such a way?

Anaïs Nin

Letter from Anaïs Nin to Amy Mims:
Los Angeles, August 14, 1971

Dear Amy Mims:

It is true that I am overburdened and overworked and I cannot read manuscripts. I did look over your poems. They have great beauty and are truly expressive. But alas, nature turns things around; I have the wish to help others but not the energy anymore. Last year I had a bout with cancer, and though cured, I have less energy. So please do not be disappointed. As far as poetry goes, I have never been able to get any of my poet friends published. Years ago I showed editors the best poetry sent to me. The best poets are publishing their own work. The writer is not all-powerful in America as he is in other countries. But please go on writing as Miller did; in the end it pushed its way through like the plants. I wrote for 20 years in a void, and I learned patience. So did Miller. Just keep writing. You are definitely a poet, and you have a sense of meaning and richness.

Anaïs

Letter from Anaïs Nin to Hugh Guiler:
Los Angeles, August 29, 1971

Darling:

The dinner at Jennifer Jones's was very pleasant. Her husband is gentle and intelligent, tried to run for senator, is out for corruption, has a beautiful collection of paintings and art books. The house by the beach is big, of course. About twenty at the table, but informal and relaxed. Jennifer Jones's daughter came home from college and said to Jennifer: "There is a book I must get, you would not know anything about it, it is *The Diary of Anaïs Nin.*" So Jennifer was able to say: "I not only know about it, I have inscribed copies."

Richard Centing is going to England, but a week later than you, with his ex-nun girlfriend, very sweet. The public relations woman Harcourt engaged is a devoted reader of mine as well as her Berkeley college daughter, so she will do a good job. I will meet her this week as she says I must do L.A. interviews before I leave as they must be out simultaneously with publication of the book in October. She is sure of a Kirsch review. It is good that I am well supplied with photos.

I wanted to write you every day while you were away, but there is little to tell. Great heat. About 90, which makes it easy to be lazy. Even Piccolino is subdued. I wrote a piece on the volcano for a hand-set magazine by a friend. Just a page. The Evelyn Hinz book has been advertised already, as you can see. I bought 25 copies, but as they did not let me have them at cost (about $4.00) because it is a small edition, that is all I could buy. Most people will buy it. Hope you have a big success in Scotland.

Love,
Anaïs

Letter from Evelyn Hinz to Anaïs Nin:
Amherst, September 1, 1971

Dear Anaïs:

I hope you will not think me ungrateful. I received the invitation to the reception for vol. 4 of the *Diary* and am delighted.

But would it be possible for you to also have John Teunissen be invited? He has helped me so much with *The Mirror and the Garden*, and, as I told you, he was the person who first introduced me to your work. He admires your work so much, and would feel so honored.

If it is not possible, please don't mention when you write to me that I have made this request. Even knowing as little as I do about you "personally," I feel you will understand.

I'm doing this rather secretly, and so have to be brief. Right now we're both exhausted from reading the proofs of *The Mirror.*

All my love, in the way you use the word,

Evelyn

Letter from Evelyn Hinz to Anaïs Nin:
Amherst, September 8, 1971

Dear Anaïs:

If I tell you I have a habit of sending away for free samples and things just to have the thrill of coming home and finding something unusual in the mail, you'll have a small idea of how much I emotionally appreciate the magazines you have sent. Finding a brown envelope at work means some essay I've written has been rejected; getting one at home, with your handwriting, means another of your successes; thank you for letting me share your fortune in this way.

This afternoon, as I was working on a first draft of the *Diary 4* article, I suddenly forgot myself and started writing down impressions about your writing and methods, a hundred things I didn't say, couldn't say, and maybe never realized when I wrote *The Mirror and the Garden.* Nothing radically different, I realize as I reread what I've written, but things that still need to be said. But then, as I gather, that's your fatal charm for all your acquaintances. Maybe there's an ironic side to Pisces, or an inverted one.

We finished proofreading the last set of the first page-proofs before the long weekend. The printer spelled "Diary" "Dairy" so many times that we almost decided to retitle the book, "Anaïs Nin: The fair and happy milkmaid"!

Have you seen the flyer the Ohio State University Committee sent out? I liked everything except the blurb that I came to you via D. H. Lawrence, since, as I explained to you in New York—and to Richard Centing—it was the other way around. Obviously, they're trying to capitalize upon Lawrence. But for the record, I say again that I became interested in Lawrence because of your "study."

I bought a car last week, a very sporty and powerful type. Some moments I feel great driving it, but more often, at least right now, I feel like your description of facing trucks with monstrous wheels, even if I'm behind them. On a straight stretch of road, of course, it's different. But I can't bring myself to trust the highway lines and signs that predict what's around a curve.

Thank you especially for the invitation to the book reception. John has asked me to tell you he is most flattered to have received your personal invite. We will both be there, and delighted to visit you the next day.

Till then,

Evelyn

Letter from Sharon Spencer to Anaïs Nin:
New York, September 13, 1971

Dear Anaïs,

I have news for you about writing projects. A friend at the University of Delaware would love to have you come there and speak. I'm going to arrange for you to come to Montclair too. Meanwhile, I've been asked to interview you for a little magazine called *Shantih.* I'll show it to you when I next see you. I'm cutting the article I wrote on *Cities* and am sending it to *Twentieth Century Studies.* He wrote to me and is enthusiastic about seeing the article. All the envelopes for the flyers about *Space, Time,* etc. have been addressed and will be mailed in a week or ten days. There will be a second mailing with a coupon. I'm going to send for *The Mirror and the Garden.* My ideas for the book I'm going to write about your work have been developing, creating a pattern, and I expect to be able to start writing in November. My plan is to complete the first draft by early summer and to do revisions over the summer.

I'm terribly eager to see you—it seems such a long, long time since we talked. You are always in my thoughts; you are a bright and lovely presence, a beautiful inspiration.

Much love,
Sharon

Announcement:
Harcourt Brace Jovanovich and Gotham Book Mart cordially invite you to a reception in honor of Anaïs Nin on the publication of volume 4 of *The Diary of Anaïs Nin* on Thursday, September 30, 1971 from five to seven o'clock at the Gotham Book Mart, 41 West 47th Street, New York
Guests [in A.N.'s handwriting]:
Zaller, Boulogne, Bogner, Aldan, Amoia, Young, Jason, Schweiger, Suissa, Hanson, Dubrosky, Cohen, Sanders, Warner, Sedita, Hagenbuch, Nicolai, Attic, Stern, Britton, Claire, Centing, Cooper, Eblen, Freeman, Feminist Press, Williamson, Honickman, Harris, Hinz, Bettina Knapp, Kuntz, Malskovi, McVonathy, Wade, Zinnes, Krementz, Ruggles, Sherman, Stuhlmann, Newcomb, Goyen, Valerie Harms (writing on me), Belle Rosenblum, Claire Luce, David McDonnell, Sandra Hochman, Leon Edel, David McMountain, Frances Bolton, Cynthia Goude, Neal Ruram, Isabel Gardner, Mary Allen Bute, Halsbond, Dr. & Annette Baxter, Belle Kaufman, Kurt Wegener, Muriel Rukeyer, Gregory Corso, Brodins, Hiram Haydn

Money received October 1971
Royalties Germany & England $1,224.14
Royalties Swallow $3,592.91
Total $4,817.05

Letter from Gunther Stuhlmann to Anaïs Nin:
New York, February 24, 1972

Dear Anaïs:

Thanks for your card. Sorry to hear that there is such confusion over your invitation to the Nice Book Fair. I was under the impression that they had given you dates and details—but I gather they are confused—as I told you, they just sent me forms to fill out if I wanted to have an exhibit at the Fair. But that seems to be the way they arrange things.

Hope Bay can clear all this up and arrange things so you don't lose any lectures in May.

Enclosed is a small check for your contribution on Tokyo to *Marian* magazine in Hamburg.

Best, love,
Gunther

NEW YORK, SPRING 1972

Could not go to Festival International de Livre at Nice. Felt unequal to ceremonies, dinners, interviews.

Everyone wants to see me. The media has produced so many fakes—they need to know I am real—that I *am* my work. When I tell them it is all in the work they do not quite accept that.

Everyone wants me to lecture.

I refused to write a preface for the *Harvard Advocate* unless they include Marguerite Young, Marianne Hauser, Sharon Spencer, Anna Balakian, Bettina Knapp.

HARTFORD, SPRING 1972

Barry Jones was the only one who thought of giving the Diary back to me in the form of a tempting blank book. It reminded me I was losing the Diary, that I had not written in it for a long time, that this year everyone pulled me away from it. I gave it away, to the world. It was opened and shared. The response was love and friendship—friends come to see me, to be with me, answer my letters, ask me to their houseboats, please come and talk to us for commencement, come and visit, let us visit you—and I was imperceptibly drawn out, outward, flying to this or that college, on trains, planes, cars, talking, oh, talking from the moment I landed to the moment I left—my life's summation a bouquet of talk, talk in interviews, talk on the radio, on television, over breakfast in college cafeterias, over a formal lunch at the Psychoanalytical Institute, at dinner with Loren Eisley. And answering letters from Baghdad, India, Italy, Germany, France, and reading clippings, reviews, essays.

As I was criticized for once noting in volume 1 the praise or compliments friends expressed, considered narcissism, I felt I could not tell the story of this year because all of it was response, praise, thanks, not in the form of flattery, but in the form of love and friendship. I felt I could not tell the story because this time it was all "Thanks, Anaïs, you saved my life"; "Thanks, Anaïs, the diaries gave me strength, gave me faith, made me want to live and create." Even a painter in Switzerland, who intended to commit suicide, had bought sleeping pills and threw them away as soon as he read volume 2. All the feelings I had for human beings, all the love, all the friendships, were returned to me. How could I record that? I could only accept it because it was given by genuine feeling, sometimes with tears, sometimes with muteness, fumbling words, an embrace. I received countless kisses at times and no words. I received thousands of confessional, intimate letters.

I was invited by Hampshire College, and we had our commencement in the sun, on the lawn. I was the only woman among the tall, black-robed faculty. Timothy Landfield had invited me. "Thank you. And I look forward to dancing with you sometime." I was lecturing too much. I was tired. I felt myself growing empty because it was all given away in talk, but the invitation to dance I could not refuse! I said yes. And the spring decided to be festive. By a slender fruit tree in blossom, after commencement, stood three or four young women in long dresses, flower-like and in all colors of the palette, with their long hair floating, *les jeunes filles en fleur*, the modern romantics. I looked at them and felt all the elation I felt before Botticelli's graceful festive figures in green landscapes. Soon someone will awaken and make coffee. Soon Evelyn and John will come to drive me to the airport.

Soon I will be inside a completely transformed apartment at which I worked for a week with painters, carpenters, moving men, an apartment designed for Hugo's life and work. I took the large living room, used for visitors, and made a studio workshop out of it, with filmmaking equipment, shelves for film cases, a work table, cabinets, a barrel for strips of film being edited. All this had been in the bedroom, where there was no space to walk or breathe. My bedroom was transformed into an intimate sitting room, with two couches (I sleep on one), panels of copper plates covering one wall, and on the other a Varda collage and a painting by Frances Field.

My desk, as before, is the window sill, but I place two table tops over it, whose legs I had unscrewed and which conceals my stationery behind the curtains.

Hugo's bedroom, now spacious, has a desk, a bed and bookcase. As he sat there, it looked fitting for him. It was a plan I had first wanted, but Hugo wanted a formal salon to receive clients—a useless room—the biggest. When he began to earn less and to get an income from me, I thought we should move, but I realized he was attached to the place, that he loves his private apartment and the park he can walk in, and that I earned enough to give him what he wanted.

A week of chaos and hard work while he was in Europe.

With Rupert a telephone conversation every night at seven, which is four o'clock for him when he comes home from school. His love has deepened. Mine for him is the difference between life and death. I cannot imagine *life* without him.

This year we celebrated making two final payments for the house to free ourselves of the loan and monthly payments. It was Rupert's dream to own his house.

All the themes of my work were *talked* this year: relationships, creation, the creation of self, the creation of an inner world, and my only enemies were the militant women with ready-made slogans and a hatred of man—and the betrayal of Gore Vidal accepting his portrait in *Diary 4* and then seeking to destroy the *Diary* by lies and yellow journalism.

Small assassinations, which I survived. What predominated was the power to convert destruction into creation (I was only practicing with Gonzalo, Helba, etc.).

162

I was in training for this role, and when I found myself passive, I knew what to say, and I said it again yesterday, giving them the key to my secret for the refusal to despair—the key to my conquering of fear, timidity, helplessness, distrust, traumatic breaks, confusions and conflicts.

I can face an audience of 2,000 persons as if I were talking to one person, and each one feels I am addressing him directly. I have no notes. The talk springs from the deep well of feeling and conviction. I use the metaphor of integrated circuits and the image of the spirit house from Thailand.

So much richness offered me that ironically I cannot take time to enjoy—because the work makes its inexorable demands. When Stock invites me to France, pays my hotel and my trip, they meet me with a schedule, and for two weeks I am the prisoner of appointments, journalists, television documentaries, radio, and official dinners.

Anaïs Nin in Paris, 1971

But some of the events are ironic. I return to Louveciennes in the car of a German television crew, and I visit the owner of the house to seek permission to enter, a request that is refused, and the old lady who was told I was a famous writer and had once lived there said she would call the police. We had to stay on the street, in front of the rusty, corroded gate I once described while the old lady leered from her kitchen window next door. The house itself was closed and neglected.

Another day Georg Troller, the director of the documentary, brought Michel Simon and we embraced like old friends; he is effusive, full of love, and had asked Henry Miller many times to meet me. We stood on the quays, talking about the fate of *La Belle Aurore*. I told him how when I first returned to France I went searching for it in the cemetery of old houseboats up the Seine. He informed me that the Germans had shot at it until it sank. Just for the fun of it.

Michel has the same intense expression of the eyes as a mute criminal seeking to convey messages far beyond the power of words, the same pleading, intense look of a dog's eyes transmitting a love and distress or anxiety we cannot always understand.

Another day I spent in the Bois with Jeanne Moreau. But talk with her is peripheral and not deep, evasive and unfocused. She did identify with Sabina, too much—was frightened—but is now, years later, self-assured (analysis). I felt no contact with her. She is not as direct or open immediately as she is, perhaps, with her close friends.

In Los Angeles, when there was a possibility of her acting in *Spy*, she invited us to dinner with Miller and Hoki. During dinner I mentioned Jeanne having played a recording of Hoki's voice singing (Henry met her performing at a nightclub), and what a lovely voice she had, and Henry said spontaneously and devastatingly: "Yes, I thought she was like her voice..."

Knowing Hoki's hardboiled and calculating nature (she married Henry to get her permanent citizenship in America and for money, but for the money, Henry's lawyers were shrewd and she opened a dress shop when they separated), Henry's romantic statement amazed me.

Jeanne was vague about *Spy*. I never knew why—but the script made me physically nauseated.

The mirage vanished for good.

But—two powerful women are interested in getting my novels filmed. Everyone knows now that I have at least half of the feminist women behind me, and many more who are not feminists but consider me a pioneer in independence, a heroine, a legend, a model, etc.

At 7:00 AM Timothy Landfield came to say goodbye. He is a dancer with a fine-bred, sensitive face, Botticellian hair around his face. He will teach theatre and has been acting. When he received his graduation papers from Reed College, he turned to me and was about to kiss my hand, but I embraced him, a long, fraternal embrace as with the modern romantics. They set their own graduation ritual. No formal speeches. They wear Moroccan jellabas of various colors, they play electronic music, they read poems. The black-robed men were tolerant and natural. A conquest over formality and decorum.

I remember the anarchy of Reed College students (I was the first woman invited for commencement) the year before. Obliged to wear the black robes, they wore them with nothing underneath and, at a dramatic moment, took them off. So, the year I came they designed their own costumes.

Among the many struggles against the mania for classification and filing is the theme of chronological age, which Americans use to divide thought and creativity. Your birthdate determines where you belong, just as your race, religion or class does. A theme to explore. All of it is part of the divisional mania—the generation gap, the generalizations about parents or even birthplaces.

The most difficult task was to dissipate the taboo on introspection and the inner journey. To cast doubt on group psychology, group thinking, group rebellions. To point out the dangers of collective non-thinking—brainwashing—imitation and contagion.

Virginia Garlick wrote poetic letters and then appeared yesterday with pale, fair hair and a poetic face. Barry Jones appeared, a Black student studying my work, handing me this book, which, at first, I expected to be filled by him—I have received many diaries, from the beautiful Virginia Heffron who died recently at 40 of lung cancer, from young women in Berkeley who deposited them on Joaquín's birthday, or at the celebration itself in Berkeley.

I sit on the TWA airplane waiting for the right wing engine to be repaired. When we leave Hartford, in 25 minutes I will be in New York. Tomorrow in Los Angeles. Then work on vol. 5 in the small cell-like room I work in, all books and files. Rupert asked for an overdue sabbatical from school to help me. He sees me drowned in correspondence, some of it with colleges planning lecture dates and flights. He can also edit the Diary. He is meticulous and, though no writer, has a good ear for the English language inherited from his Cambridge-bred father and his mother's fine English delivery and the Wright family's respect for language—even when old-fashioned, certainly classical as one can see in Frank Lloyd Wright's book.

Reality: When Rupert asked for a sabbatical, he said he wanted to help me. But in part it was because he was disillusioned with teaching. The teachers' strike split the good rapport between the teachers. Then an earthquake caused the building he worked in to be condemned, and he disliked the new building. He has undertaken a double job, teaching and running the audio-visual department, and it is a heavy load. I was a little concerned about a year of idleness. When he is not upheld by external structures, he sleeps late, watches too much TV, reads only the papers. I was afraid this would clash with my overload of work. He has helped me edit 450 pages of vol. 5, but I have anxiety about the situation. I do not want to be put in the role of taskmaster. He asks for that.

It would be an adventure to visit all my correspondents, from Holland, Belgium, Switzerland.

Evolutions delight me—just as the destructive ones shock and hurt me, war, bombs of anarchists, holdup crimes, muggers, drug addicts, airplane hijackings, the "bitchy society" as it was baptized by others and prophesized by me in volume 3. The price is not, as they believe, social injustice, but the taboo on feeling and sensitivity, the taboo on art, on self-development and reflectiveness, analysis and all that would make each one responsible for the fate of every human being. By great collective abstractions, political theories, they achieved nothing but an incurable savagery of war and crime.

I was right to situate the source of both evil and creation from where it stems—within each of us, and the power to redress and create.

Anaïs, what have you become? Where are you? Have you become a teacher, a guru? Just speaking the accumulated experiences because so many needed an end to loneliness, a new faith, a rediscovery of human values. Lending my presence because so many wanted to ascertain if I had the voice of my words, the face of my words, and they have been so often cheated and betrayed by the media, by their heroes, that they fear to believe and want to confirm this belief in the words, and before I even speak, they give me standing ovations, at Harvard, at Berkeley, at this college, that college, so it is the work they respond to, and then I speak from the heart of the work—I, who felt always that the written word was more eloquent, more subtle, more meaningful than speech, and who said in Berkeley: "I hope you find everything in the work because there will come a day when I will not be present."

I never expected my love to be returned! I believed in personal love, but I never imagined or envisaged universal love. That is why this year I abandoned my solitary chant, and answered letters. "Yes," I respond, "I am happy you felt it was your diary."

In between the luminous moments, one student said: "You once wrote you wanted to live only for the marvelous moments. How does this talk with us fit into that?"

"It is also a marvelous moment. Our talk together was a marvelous moment."

In one instant I can detect a friend. A letter will confirm this.

Tragedies, too. Raella Weinstein wrote such inchoate letters. She burned herself alive. Lucie Parent, from Montreal, threatened suicide and sent a telegram to Harcourt Brace. All I could think to do was to call her up and say: "This is Anaïs Nin. Will you wait till I come to New York April 24?" She gasped and said: "I will wait." And she came to New York, talked with me and with Inge Bogner, and was strengthened and is afloat again.

Just as when Alfred Ryder asked me to telephone an alcoholic Kim Stanley and all I could think of was: "Do you wish to kill your children as Medea did, for if you kill yourself you are killing them too, remember that." And the image of Medea's murder did affect her.

And those who wish to come as disciples, to help me, type or cook or garden, live in my presence.

A symbol. So, Anaïs, you are a symbol. Even if I pointed the way, the struggle was accomplished, they do not seek the discipline of psychoanalysis to rescue themselves by a spiritual effort. They want to receive it with love and friendship, from me.

Evelyn Hinz persuaded me that a biography would supply a factual, objective completion of the *Diary*, which sometimes does not cover all the ground. If I do this, it will be for the *Diary* as well—to fill in.

MAGIC CIRCLE WEEKEND, APRIL 28-30, 1972

The drive to Rye, New York was with Beatrice Harris who has a deft sense of direction even while we talk of subtle subjects. We are redefining the much-distorted application of narcissism and ego. We talk about our lives, our friends, but it is always the meaning of our lives, our friends, our loves. If we had been born at the same time and if I had met her instead of June, I would have fallen in love with her, with that rare mixture of sensuous presence and intelligence and insight that adds humanity and vibrancy to all she does and says.

The house at Rye is a beautiful, vast mansion on Long Island Sound. It is a home, and though we arrive as guests with valises and are distributed into various bedrooms, Valerie Harms and Adele Aldridge are in the foyer and, like friends, welcome us to their home. The trees, gardens and the bay are present. I see the water from my window. I see a few strange faces, which will later become the faces of those I had corresponded with, whose inner face I knew, and it was my time to search for the face of letters—the bodily pressure of my letter writers.

Some were friends, Daisy Aldan, with her voice and laughter always youthful, and Lex Crocker, from Texas, studying philosophy, but in distress.

Bebe Herring is a tall and beautiful young woman who had written to me in distress, a failed marriage, a novel being written, and who had given me the word *furrawn*. There was Elaine Marks, a teacher of French at Amherst College and biographer of Colette; Trew Bennett, the potter who had written beautiful letters about her craft and her life; Jeffrey Mundy and his brother—Jeffery is an artist who also delights in juggling words, in mystifying and eluding finite meaning. He visited me in Los Angeles. I met his brother in Berkeley. They seem like twins, handsome, one more vaporous, one more grounded, completing each other. Nadine Daily is silent and seems strong and self-contained. The first evening they were all to introduce themselves.

The letters. A giant effort of memory. When they appear before me I try to fuse the living person with the letters. I do not know why I have a feeling that recognizing others, knowing others, hearing and seeing them is so important to life. I feel like a gardener concerned with the thirst of flowers, the leaf in danger of withering, the fruit torn off the tree by the wind. Human beings appear vulnerable. I read their eyes. I notice if one of them (Evelyn Hinz) sits alone. I want to hear every word and capture every message. And here I am, receiving a response to my attentiveness.

A vast dining hall. I sit at the head of one of the tables, and at each meal a different person can sit at my right and at my left. There are paintings on the walls, masks, sculptures. A locked glass cabinet contains the books hand-printed by Adele, Daisy and myself.

After the first dinner, we are gathered together in the library. They were to introduce themselves, but instead they described their first encounter with my work, its effect on their lives, and said little about themselves. I talked, and said they were proving my Diary was theirs and they were speaking through it; it was a revelation of them as they spoke of it.

The whole weekend was a ballet. Everyone brought their charm, skills, richness, and we moved about discovering each other. We discovered each other's struggles, evolutions, achievements. We touched, contacted. Mine was a difficult role because I was the catalyst, but with my passion for knowing others, I sought, in the few moments given us, to perceive a whole life, a whole person. I talked with Trew, with Lex, with Bebe, with William Claire and his friend whose mask was a smile and who later wrote a beautiful letter about her difficulties with unmasking.

167

Beatrice brought her insight and skill at balancing extremes on the subject of feminism. Frances Steloff sat in the library the next morning, holding a yellow daisy, and all the time she talked she held her eyes down, looking into the heart of the flower. She told her courageous life story, the birth of the Gotham Book Mart. She came away from the weekend convinced at last of the important role she played in our literary life, for every story she told always ended with "We took our books or magazines to the Gotham Book Mart." Her story was a story of courage and persistence. William Claire's story of *Voyages* was of a man who was occupied by a full-time job, persisted in editing a good magazine. Anna Balakian came later and read a dazzling study of my work. Everyone gasped, exclaimed.

Color and fantasy were given by Sas Colby. Her capes, skirts, masks were displayed in the foyer. She herself was a pixie, blonde, small, humorous. One of the loveliest moments was her little dance on the lawn Sunday afternoon wearing her own costumes and reciting brief, airy lines, humorous and in harmony with her fantasy letters. She was the playful one.

Saturday was an evening of film and slides. The evolutions of friendship, of exchange, or revelation, of communication by one's work, were vivid and continuous. Everyone was writing (diaries?). I found manuscripts at my door, poems and letters on my bed. The happenings were necessary, but we could have lived together for a longer time. I saw images. As I came out of my bedroom one morning, Bebe was sitting on the sun-drenched stairs, with her large, questioning eyes. I read parts of her novel. It was searching, not focused yet, tentative, oscillating between biography and fiction. On the curved stairway—was she dressed in yellow or green?—she seemed like a nymph. At 6:00 AM, while looking out my window, I saw Trew sitting by the bay, writing. Evelyn Hinz was more often sitting by herself, writing. She seemed more isolated—not as *liante* [connecting] as the French say. *Liante*, *liana*, a beautiful word. Lex was receptive, loving, absorbing. An atmosphere was created, of faith and appreciation and response. I felt strange, for I felt as if my work had made the links, and that I could lie back and watch the miracle. They were writing, they were talking together, they were taking walks, they were exchanging books, meditating—for me. I could rest, as after giving birth. I was being thanked. I received love notes, love poems. I did not rest. I wanted to talk at length with everyone, to read all the writing, but I couldn't. My body could not. At midnight I was asleep. The life current was strong. It belongs to them now. There was a wistful relinquish dictated by the body, but the receptivity never ceases, as if I were responsible for sustaining a life flame. I could sleep. At times I felt I was inside my Diaries and novels, and it was full of new people, new characters. The beautiful face of Trew. The perfect features and emotional sincerity. She bears the marks of suffering but not of any distortion—a noble pain, a courage. Her potter's bowl is heavy and strong.

Adele lays her book of illustrations of the *I Ching* on my bed. Frances Steloff tries on the capes, fairytale clothes. Daisy too. There is a blonde, lovely woman who had come to me at Green Bay in tears: "I love my husband and another man—what can I do?" And I, who cannot hold back from answering against the advice of Bogner, said: "Live out both loves until you find which is the deepest." And she is here, clear-eyed, graceful, out of torment.

I was reminded of the life of George Sand, when distances were so great by

168

carriage from Paris to country homes that friends visited for long periods, and I envied this life in a big country house surrounded by friends.

They wrote books, put on plays, and I thought how wonderful it is to have such deep, long days with others when modern life makes our meetings fleeting and travel disperses us. Here, we had just enough time to *begin* friendships, to open discoveries. How genuinely people talked the first evening. I have been the propeller, but the radiations of the circle extended far, and it was Jeffrey who shed his light charm and playful poems, and Nadine who read her novel-in-progress, and Beatrice, who came to bring her insight, came away confirmed in her desire to be a writer. I came away convinced I had found a way to sustain both creation and life, and this selection of people enacted it; the place was filled with beauty and talent and skills.

I wanted to share in all the prolongations of the weekend, its repercussions, the friendships born, and I could not. It is a difficult relinquishing for one who has that all-embracing greed and curiosity for life. Daisy says lightly: "I don't have time for new friends." It is Beatrice who will have Nadine build a studio. It is Nadine who does the horoscopes. I should be writing about the weekend for publication. What I write for the Diary is not for all to read. I see Evelyn, who has beautiful long hair but who wears it in a severe and prim bun, which reminds me of her academic stiffness that my friends dislike in her work. But I was grateful to be translated into academic terms so the academy would understand. It is the students of the two-year-old Hampshire College who came, not a politico or an academician.

Sunday afternoon we sat on the lawn in back of the house, by the bay. It was hot, but the writers did not tire of reading poems. I can't confess publicly that I am bored with poetry. It is like a miniature pond, and I want to hear the deep heaving of the ocean, the prose that sounds like the chant of the humpback whales, now recorded. You hear the cries, the purrs, the calls, light and young, deep and old, grunts and sighs, and you hear an echo, you hear the breathing of the ocean and you are aware of the vastness of the ocean, but poetry sounds like a pebble—yet I am the one who says the poet is the one who teaches us levitation. I mean the prose-poet.

Evelyn has large and emotional eyes, perfect features, is slender and graceful, but bound. She is writing in a corner of the library.

Evelyn Clark and Nancy Williamson, the feminist editors of *The Second Wave*, who made me come to Harvard—I feared their presence because I knew the weekend was focused on creation, not on politics. I even asked them not to come because I was traumatized by the destructive hostility of militant women. But they understood, they came, and both tuned into the mood of the weekend. Evelyn Clark, with soft eyes, read a passage demonstrating Trotsky's interest in literature, read timid and wistful pages from her diary on her discovery of lesbianism.

One woman read a poem called "Yes." She read it at dinner with impetus and emotion. Yes-yes-yes. So I planted all these seeds, and I now have to learn to say no occasionally, no to three days of television shows, no to two days of interviews, no to Antioch College, no to Viveca Lindfors for tea and woman's talk or a party at her lover's. But over the telephone I could dispel her anxieties, the kind I knew so well with Bill Pinckard, which strangle the lover—so she shared this with me, and her lover never knew. Later, I said, later if the love grows deep, you can explain to him the source of your anxieties, and what he does to awaken it.

169

Evelyn Hinz and Henry Miller, Pacific Palisades, 1970s

I like to think of Sas tripping gaily on the lawn, in her fairytale costumes, resembling Varda's collages, and her witty mask (one with a zippered mouth) and her little recitation.

The dinner gong was joyous—Adele has divinatory eyes; she was the first to read me to the feminist artist group who wanted the weekend. Valerie calls her essay on me "The Archetypal Heroine." Everyone will write about the weekend. I felt moved by the generosity of what was given me. Everything I shared was returned; I was enriched. We gave birth to each other.

Lex Crocker and Daisy Aldan told me the story of self-publication—told it with humor, but one detected the courage and persistence.

Rosalie Glein. She had written me a long and interesting letter long before. When I arrived I found a letter saying she could not come. But she did come after all and I failed to identify her. A missed encounter unless we talked and I did not know with whom I talked.

Note from Lex Crocker: "I do not want to bother you, but I only want to tell you that I have lived in pain and conflict most of my life and that you (the sweet, magic being that you are) have done much to give me hope and direction. It is hard for me to express my love for others, but your writings have revealed to me that this is all that is important in one's life, and I am trying on my own to become free of all my silent pains. So I only want to tell you now that I love you sincerely and tenderly even if it is difficult for me to emote these feelings in physical reality."

TWA 330. We will land in Los Angeles. Rupert will be waiting. Rupert, who for over 20 years immunized me against other men, enabling me to be kissed and embraced by countless young students with tenderness, feeling I possessed them all in Rupert. Passed the Mojave Desert in its lovely champagne color, passed the mountains enveloped in smog.

———

LOS ANGELES, SPRING 1972

As soon as I come home, I relax. The house gives me peace and beauty, the swimming restores me. I sit at my desk as soon as Rupert leaves, at 7:30. I work until lunch time. Volume 5. An article on my Press. A preface to an anthology of women's poetry. A preface to Judy Chicago's book. At four I go to the post office with Rupert. There I face an avalanche of letters, manuscripts, books from publishers (please comment), gifts. I have to return manuscripts unread. I answer letters with a card. There is correspondence with colleges—I have to send posters, photographs, announcements before lectures. And I must edit all the Diaries because no one else can do it. In volume 5 I stopped dating the passages! And as I lived so fast I often made notes that I now have to develop and expand. So much I want to do. The diary of Japan. I want many photographs in color. Little writing. I want to do a diary of letters received.

LOS ANGELES, JULY 25, 1972

The letters received are an important part of my life. Most of them are interesting, revealing, putting me in touch with many lives, all ages, all kinds of places and atmospheres. Teachers, students, mature readers, feminists, young men artists, poets, psychologists, novelists. They are all sincere, sometimes illiterate, but always emotional and genuine. An authentic current—revealing an America I did not know—each one escalated without the benefit of rich friendships.

I suffer from over-abundance!

Last night another lecture. I hated to tear myself away from Silver Lake, the house, pool, garden and Rupert's love so enveloping and attentive. It was at University of Northern Illinois, in DeKalb. It was difficult at first. Summer students are not prepared with knowledge of my work, but they warmed up towards the end. And faithful friends were there.

Because of the irrelevant questions, your wings can be clipped. You are made aware of the ones who cannot follow. They make no effort. They expect you to make the effort to translate yourself into mediocre terms.

I am weary of the public life even though I love the contact with the few. And talk, it always seems to me, falls below the writing.

On elitism: "There is no such thing," I said. "Every human being should push his development and skills and creativity as far as possible because only then does he become valuable to others, valuable to the community. It is wrong to hold people back to remain on a level with the herd. We need explorers, adventurers, pathfinders, models, inventors."

One day I found in my letter box a package of herbs that perfumed my mail. It was from the herb lady, whose painted psychedelic truck I see at the post office, thanking me for what I had given her. We embraced.

171

Every day a surprise. A painter brings her paintings all the way from Berkeley, one as a gift.

Joaquín came—read all the Diary, revised sections concerning Mother. (His second mother, Mary in Spain, is dying of cancer. His summer was sorrowful.) He asked for fair and just revisions. Mother was not *brutally* honest. She did not *endanger* my life. My father was 22 when he married, not 20.

Staff said in 1947: "Analysis is like a spiral. The crisis grows smaller, less violent."

Life heals you if you allow it to flow, if you do not allow it to trap you.

Freedom means that no one is able to destroy you, enslave you, paralyze you.

Anaïs Nin, Rupert Pole with Piccolino, early 1970s, Silver Lake

NEW YORK, AUGUST 15, 1972

When I arrived in New York I found that Hugo had made two beautiful new films and that he was longing to go to Edinburgh for the two-week film festival. What a joy to be able to say: "Of course you can go; I can afford to give you that." What a joy to be able to repay all the care and protection Hugo gave me.

My three weeks were filled with activity. Three days spent with Radio-Canada who came and recorded a one-hour documentary. France l'Abbé, my interviewer, was an interesting woman, steeped in my work, and we talked about her too. The *équipe* was wonderful, sensitive and individual. We enjoyed each other's company.

It was my work to prepare the diaries and books for display and talk. To walk in the park. To walk through the Village from ten to four! But the work was made enjoyable by their personalities, and we ended up becoming friends.

Two days of interviews and photographs for the French-Canadian magazine *Châtelaine*—from ten to four—with Hélène Fecteau, intelligent and cool, but also ending in friendship. I feel the most miraculous sense of contact with others. Perhaps knowledge of the *Diary* sets the level for intimate talks. I feel as if every cell in my body is alert and responsive.

Trips to the vault—to get all the diaries for vol. 5 because I found I need the originals to work from. They contain letters, programs, photographs not in the typed copies—clues to dates.

Dinner with John Ferrone. I feel great affection for him. Our friendship began the day the paperback of vol. 1 arrived with a hideous drawing on the cover of a hard, long-faced woman. I went to his office. As I entered, he said: "I can see why that drawing shocked you. It is not you." He made them change the cover. We work well together. He is intelligent, sensitive, well-read. A beautiful person, emotional and tender.

I received my first assignment for a commercial magazine, *Travel & Leisure*, to go to Fez. I will get $1,750 and all expenses paid! How late in life this has come. When Durrell's first book appeared he was asked to write for *Holiday* magazine immediately.

This dream is a warning: Rupert is in bed. There is something he has left undone that has weakened the resistance of the house to a storm.

LOS ANGELES, SEPTEMBER 12, 1972

From August 16 till today I worked on volume 5. Every day. Writing from 7:00 AM to 7:00 PM. At 10:00 AM Rupert wakes up. He works in the evening revising and correcting. He has taken a sabbatical after 16 years of teaching—to help me.

Writing. Swimming in the pool. Working for Robert Snyder's documentary on me.

LOS ANGELES, SEPTEMBER 23, 1972

Dreams:

Dr. Bogner wears glasses. She looks different.

I have to climb a strange mountain made of cement. One path is painted on in vivid colors. I choose that to follow.

I am walking over a bridge with the poet Alice Rahon. She falls between the planks—a bad fall.

I have nightmares every night. One night I was to lecture and had forgotten to bring a dress.

The underlying melancholy in my life is beautiful. Rupert is a passionate lover, a tender companion, helping me. Hundreds of loving letters. Interesting visitors. Work on the documentary. A pool, an enchanting, playful dog. The sun. Indian cotton dresses in my closet.

My age, yes, at last detectable—particularly in photographs. Inevitable now, a paradox because I do not feel as I look. I feel fresh and dewy and relaxed and not old! Freckles on the hands, wrinkles—how strange when nothing in my emotions corresponds to that. The feelings are crystal clear, perfect melodies, never strident or rough like voices of the old. A psychic youthfulness. When I swim in the morning, I thank the dawn. So strange, these hours of writing, so much like a spider web, but one in which people love to be caught and who start their own web of human connections. The letters I get stir me, touch me. I'm brokenhearted when I have to return huge piles of unread manuscripts.

I receive books of interest—Progoff, the Rank journal, *Dream Power* by Ann Faraday. Bad novels.

LOS ANGELES, NOVEMBER 11, 1972

Being famous is destructive if taken as narcissistic appraisal, but creative if taken as means of discovery and expansion. I discover *others* who come to me. More doors are opened. It is not a static pose to accept a tribe, but a means to explore and discover.

The praise is not the essential element of my visits to colleges—overflowing, standing ovations, stifling crowds surrounding me afterwards. I look for faces I can love—friends—daughters—a moment of contact, of intimacy, of revelation. That is what I love and seek.

I have resistance to lectures. In spite of constant success, constant effectiveness, my power to move people, I have a short moment of fear as if the gift of speech now acquired, spontaneous, inspirational, were to leave me.

I saw Barry Jones. His friends are intelligent and sensitive.

Dreams:
The son of Gonzalo comes and we are in a perfect sensual and emotional harmony. I feel joy and fulfillment. We are one. But when I mention Gonzalo he is hostile and says: "My father was a slob." I am shocked. I have the same feeling as when I defend the hippies—a social welfare woman called a guitar player a bum at a Rank Society meeting.

I dreamt of a leopard. I was reading Laurens Van der Post. The leopard suggests fear. I tease Piccolino when he barks too much. A bushman's dog does not bark. The leopard will get you. Then I dreamt that a beautiful, sleek leopard slept next to me— alongside me—just like a contented cat.

I dreamt I was helping someone with her manuscript. The pages were in disorder, and she was distracted and confused. I finally organized them. I gave them to her and said: "Now they are organized." There was a continuity. She took the manuscript and ran out into open country. She was playfully wrestling with someone (a man) and the pages were scattered. I felt that she was happy, that it did not matter, but when we began to look for the manuscript, we couldn't find it. I was on a bicycle. She and the man were waiting for a bus. I was afraid I wouldn't find my way back. The man gave me directions.

I dreamt I was about to teach school. I was nervous and unprepared. I finally decided I didn't want to be tied down. The principal was very well-equipped. The mood of the dream was of fogginess and effort to clarify.

I dreamt I was nursing someone (the same woman whose manuscript I worked on?)—everything was grey.

LOS ANGELES, NOVEMBER 1972

This year I had to reconcile the public and the personal—to make one as sincere as the other, not in conflict. Every year we have to make a new synthesis. Conflict in the public self is different—it is a role—there is no conflict if it is the same person.

Where is Anaïs? On a plane on the way to Chicago University, writing letters. In a car driving to Skidmore College with Frances Steloff, impressed by the flowering of her life, her life story. On my way to Dartmouth, where Barry Jones awaits me. Everywhere there are long, warm ovations. I speak well now. I improvise. The women and the men who come up to me truly reach me; there is a moment of intimacy in this vast sea of loneliness. I quote Baudelaire. In each one of us there is a man, a woman and a child. And the child is always an orphan!

I think I have drawn towards me all the orphans of the world. They weep when they come close. We embrace when they cannot find words. But after visiting so many colleges I found I was repeating myself and was in despair. It is not that it is insincere, but that I have become an actress performing a role.

On the road I am grateful for the love that I receive, but I cannot maintain the same feeling after a thousand exchanges. So Anaïs is now an actress (not insincere, says Bogner, not at all). I step on the stage of the Edison Theatre holding a metal mask before my face, sculpted by Suzanne Benton. I say to the audience: "For centuries woman has worn a mask and played many roles. Today she is unmasking herself and showing her true face." And I remove the mask. And read from the *Diaries*. I am uneasy about this new phase.

At home, or here at George Rousseau's apartment listening to the quartet music, I know how deeply I feel, how deeply I love Rupert, how deeply I feel the distress and the emotion on the faces I see.

I have unleashed a great force of love. I feel it flowing from me, and catching fire from others' responses. This is my sincerity—I do love these faces, these letters, these messages I receive, the poems, the paintings, the drawings, the student at Chicago who gave me a ring quoting from the *Diary*. I loved to give what it hurt me to give. The young woman at the teacher's conference who asked me to walk on the beach at 7:00 AM. The one who appeared at every lecture with flowers and whom I call my recurrent dream. So many lovely women. So many tender men. Why cannot I relive my life? Now it is full to the brim—overly rich! What if all this had entered the void of Louveciennes before Henry came?

The only time I feel power and enjoy my power is when I can praise a film, such as Henry Jaglom's *A Safe Place*, and my review brings a crowd. So, yes, Anaïs is performing the art of presence, but the feeling is there, intact. I have not changed, lost my responsiveness. "I have a million daughters," I once said in an interview.

I began these pages with a doubt. Can one multiply, share, expand without loss of substance? I answered my own question. Yes, if you can extend feeling into all you do, say, write. Yes, if you can spend one minute with a stranger and annihilate strangeness.

So I have emerged, but the blood is no thinner, the split did not take place. How could I have felt so weak and so passive at twenty and feel so strong now? I can take care of Hugo and understand he was half-alive and that is why I could not love him. I can take care of Rupert's family—a nurse for Helen Wright in her wheelchair and pay their taxes. It is so wonderful.

175

Frances and I talked about Hugo. She is now, at 59, a widow without income; Michael died of overwork. She is too intelligent to be fulfilled by most men and not very sensual. I suggest she marry Hugo—they would be good companions. She would be protected. He would be less lonely. It could be a gracious life for her… Frances and I have always lived with our eyes wide open. We talked with the sort of honesty I believe rare between women. I said, "I want to be unburdened, because Hugo to me now is only a burden and a duty. He was at first the father, and then he became a child. To me he only gives his dependence. We never became close. He is (naturally) resentful of my absences, and I am resentful that he has not freed me, loved someone else."

Frances was slightly taken aback. We went too fast in our fantasy. "Begin with a friendship…let it happen naturally. Enjoy his company." (She has no one to go out with.)

I gave her a Christmas present to dress herself in.

Hugh Guiler and Anaïs Nin, New York, 1970s

Yesterday when I called Hugo he said: "I feel terribly tired. This infection (following the prostate operation) has tired me. The drugs they give me spoil my appetite. Bogner suggested I go away for ten days to swim and lie in the sun. Frances wants to come and take care of me!"

I called up Frances.

"If you want to go, I will pay for your trip. Please do not feel guilty. I can earn enough at one lecture to give you ten days of sun and rest. I'm sending it to you anyway. Enjoy it. It makes me happy to feel that when I am happy with Rupert you and Hugo are enjoying an escape from New York."

176

Then I had this dream: I went to visit my father. He was not there. I met the woman he was living with. When he came we *talked French*. But it was Hugo. And I asked for a divorce. There was no emotion. Just a discussion of the problem. I wanted the divorce to be quick—no publicity. I felt relieved and free.

The last time I was in N.Y. I realized I am bad to Hugo because I feel imprisoned. I do not want to be there. Even when I most admire him as a filmmaker, I do not like to be there while he works. I do not feel connected to him. His presence depresses me.

When I see him dependent on Bogner or Roger Boulogne (his old friend from the bank days, a retired accountant who does all his accounting), to even discuss his problems with the maid, when I see him discuss with three persons his problem with a doctor's treatment of him during an operation, I cannot sympathize. When Dolores Holmes comes to tell us about her cave experiences in Spain, he is not interested in her adventures in speleology, but in what he can obtain for his next film.

We are bad for each other. Why won't he recognize it? Why won't he see?

I can only hope the alchemy between him and Frances is better. They are born under the same sign. They are both mentally inclined.

To Irene Liggett, whom I singled out in the crowd at Berkeley: "You made me painfully aware of what one loses when one tries to give to, respond to, and contact too many: you lose the precious individuals you discover by dispersion—the names are erased—the love is fragmented. I singled you out because your presence is beautiful and meaningful—yet I had lost you to pressure and dispersed energies. It was a lesson. I will act on it."

LOS ANGELES, DECEMBER 4, 1972

Hugo and Frances are going to an island in the sun—to rest—for Hugo's recovery.

I answer thousands of letters. I feel the public life dissolves the quality of my contacts. I'm in a conflict. But no lectures for two months. I'm preparing to revisit Fez for *Travel & Leisure*, with Rupert.

LOS ANGELES, DECEMBER 11, 1972

In a crowd at Reed College I singled out Claudia Cranston. She came to every lecture, always with flowers and large, intense, distressed eyes. She came to visit me yesterday—Saturday and Sunday. A tragic childhood. A tragic love life. Fully aware of dissolving power of public life by her visit, I recovered the concentration on one human being, which I value—it is not lost! We talked like very old friends—deeply—about her life, and I hope that mine, so lovely at the moment, will heal her.

Dr. Stone starts a course on the healing arts.

Dream: I am on a vacation with Hugo. He is angry. He walks away without waiting for me. I have not been able to communicate with Rupert, so I'm anxious.

In spite of everything good, I awaken depressed—but I am convinced it is physical because I have had constant digestive troubles since the radiation treatment—I have to watch my diet. One glass of wine can give me pain and insomnia. So all is not well with the body. But I throw it all off when I enter my work room at

177

7:00 AM, read letters, acknowledge gifts, revise volume 5, renew my friendship with Jim Herlihy, which is undamaged.

John Pearson introduced me to Laurens Van der Post, and I began to read all his books. I love the mixture of an adventurous life matched by philosophy and psychological awareness. He has wisdom and humanity. He writes well. He reminds me of St. Exupéry, but his life has been richer, fuller, and he has encompassed more experience.

LOS ANGELES, JANUARY 3, 1973
Meeting with Phyllis Deutsch, lawyer.

JANUARY 4, 1973
Return to New York.

JANUARY 26, 1973
Library of Congress visitors; evening with Chases, Daisy.

JANUARY 28, 1973
Lecture Drew University.

JANUARY 30, 1973
Return to Los Angeles.

LOS ANGELES, JANUARY 31, 1973
Womanspace KPFK.

Letter from Anaïs Nin to Hugh Guiler:
Los Angeles, February 3, 1973

Darling:

Tried to call you this evening but you were out. I stuttered over the telephone the other day because I wanted to say how badly I felt at leaving you alone. You still seem to mind that more than the pleasure of your intermittent freedom. And it is a short month.

I'm sending you one of your old letters you might want to destroy.

I am rereading some of your letters, one from Brazil, with a date. Would you rather I sent it to you in order to complete the 1948-1949 period? Do you have any time to recapture the sequence of these letters? I have the date of your Brazil trip: April 1949.

Let me know.

I'm overwhelmed with work—letters, lectures, etc. Next year I will have to give up the lectures. I can't finish vol. 5.

Love,
Anaïs

Letter from Hugh Guiler to Anaïs Nin:
New York, February 11, 1973

Darling:

I see that today you are going to be in San Francisco after Santa Clara, so I will not expect a call.

To answer yours of the 3rd, I think it best you return the letters of 1948-49 to complete that period and I will try to recapture the sequence.

I will leave for Washington by Metroline on Tuesday afternoon, will stay at the Ramada Inn there Tuesday night and return Thursday morning. I feel extra-ordinarily calm about my lecture, after working with Bogner, whom I will also see just before I leave.

Yass Hakoshima, the mime who has performed at Georgetown University, is writing to his friends there suggesting they see the films. At my suggestion, the library is notifying the *N.Y. Times* and also someone from the *Post*. Here is a copy of the press release, which is correct except that they refer to a "work in progress," which I am *not* showing.

I have to give *two* showings and lectures, but I will have several hours' rest in between. I saw Dr. Lehmann for my throat, and he thinks they must have put a tube down my throat when I was under anesthesia as the membrane (not the vocal cords) is rough. He has given me a cough medicine and will see me tomorrow but can't promise to clear it up in such a short time. Nevertheless, I tried not to talk yesterday and it seemed OK.

I am glad to hear you intend to give up the lectures next year. Boulogne says you are now at the point where, from a tax point of view, it is hardly worth your while, so long as the royalties continue.

The first trials of filming Frances's paintings came out well, with some extra-ordinary effects by superimposing on one of them (a bold one) with the X-ray films I got from Dr. Goldstein's former secretary.

The date of my departure to Paris is now confirmed as February 22, and it will be for a maximum of two weeks and perhaps less.

Love,
Hugo

P.S. When you call me on the telephone suddenly, I sometimes am just out of a siesta or otherwise find it difficult to collect my thoughts as quickly as you can, because you can choose your time to call. I have always said I would prefer you writing to me rather than telephoning, and the last two times have convinced me again because I could not immediately link the word "minotaur" with *Seduction of the Minotaur* and you got irritated at this. So I suggest no more telephone calls except in an emergency. I am sure you will also understand that I enjoy your wonderful letters, so perhaps I am trying to get more of them (but suggest printing the address and zip code as the postal computer handles only printing).

MARCH 6, 1973
Lecture at College of Marin.

MARCH 10, 1973
Lecture at UC Santa Clara.

MARCH 15, 1973
Lecture at University of New Mexico; Wayne McEvilly.

MARCH 20, 1973
Lecture at Roosevelt University, Chicago.

MARCH 21, 1973
Lecture at Central Michigan University.

MARCH 23, 1973
Lecture, Washington, D.C.

MARCH 24, 1973
Talk, Women's analytic group.

MARCH 27, 1973
Lecture at Ann Arbor; Benjamin Franklin; 1,000 students; from 3 to 5 signed books without stopping.

MARCH 28, 1973
Lecture at Fresno University.

Letter from Hugh Guiler to Anaïs Nin:
New York, March 31, 1973

Darling:
   Am concerned about your sudden feeling of tiredness, so do give me frequent news of yourself. Part of it, Frances says, and she may be right, is due to the let-down you felt about the taxes and consequent depression.
   I have just forwarded to you the envelope for Viveca Lindfors suggesting we invest in her play *I am a Woman* so that it can appear on Broadway (at $45,000). You have already, it seems to me, made your contribution of your material. But I suppose I should go on Monday night to the preview. If you put $100 into it, that would be all that could be expected, and it could eventually be a deductible loss.
   I'm having technical problems with the film, but I hope to finish next week and then get Dave Horowitz in. Joaquín does not like any electronic music, so he only admired (without too much enthusiasm) the last few films I showed him. But we had a friendly time together and he did help to arouse my admiration for Bach's music.
   Frances expects to be fired, but has feelers out for other work. I broke the news to her that I am not using any of her paintings in this film and she took it all right.
   I have my hearing aid, and while I can only wear it a few hours each day it does seem to help and it is quite inconspicuous.
   But, again, I am concerned about you over-straining, as you obviously have been (plus the letdown), so please keep me informed, and give me your revised schedule. You should cancel *all* lectures.
   Love, love,

H
P.S. I thought of a title for the film: *Intimate Safari.* What do you think?

APRIL 7, 1973
"Images of Women," Santa Cruz.

APRIL 28-29, 1973
Sonoma with Rupert.

NEW YORK, MAY 15, 1973
I start the oral medication with Dr. Parks and get my gynecological exami-
nation, which ends May 28th, and I get a test at Presbyterian Hospital the 29th. Dr.
Parks leaves on vacation or stops practicing May 30.

NEW YORK, MAY 16, 1973
I got photographed by the Rye weekend women who are putting out a book on
the weekend, and the photos were so bad I asked to have them done again.

NEW YORK, MAY 31, 1973
I leave for Philadelphia to sleep there as commencement exercises, at which I
am asked to speak, are on the morning of June 1. I stay for lunch and return to New
York.

JUNE 9, 1973
Fly back to Los Angeles.

Letter from Anaïs Nin to Hugh Guiler:
Los Angeles, July 1, 1973

Darling:
I am concerned that with the weekend and holidays you may get this letter very
late. I am enclosing articles on Jean Carteret that may interest you. Keep them well
as I want to enclose them in the Diary. The recurrences of people, themes, spotlights
and certain people always astonish me. Carteret is now publishing a book, which, I
suppose, his friends have taken by dictation. But how abstract it all is. I am not
attracted to all the occult mysteries as they describe them.
I wonder who you are seeing.
I work every morning on vol. 6, which begins in the fall of 1955. Then I swim.
Then I usually have visitors, the Masters and PhD candidates who turn up, hitch-
hiking here or driven by relatives, any way they can, for an hour or two with me.
But the essays are brilliant, quite amazing, equal to any intellectual critiques in
France at this point, and closer to the understanding of the subconscious than France
is. My last evening was with wives of doctors and psychologists studying my work
at Extension UCLA, a mature crowd, very warm and responsive. Swallow feels too
much emphasis has been placed on the response of the young and that I should
balance this by different kinds of appearances.

181

I sent Marie-Claire Van der Elst the new *Anaïs Nin Reader* with the Anna Balakian preface. I met Leslie Caron, the actress. Charming. She would be good in the *Diary* stage adaptation. Just foreign enough, but not too much.

Anaïs

JULY 1973

Trip to Mexico with Rupert.

Letter from Joaquín Nin-Culmell to Anaïs Nin:
Berkeley, July 27, 1973

Dear Anaïs:

Puerto Vallarta sounds like heaven and as yet unspoiled. The Mediterranean — for the most part—is completely spoiled. I went as far south as Tarragona this summer and was appalled at the high-rises and the elbow-to-elbow beaches. As for the beaches of Mallorca, you wouldn't even want to see them.

Terribly sorry Luis de Nin is giving you a hard time. Just don't bother answering. He is nice but a bit of a bore and his "poems" and writings in Catalan are mediocre stuff. I had dinner with them in Barcelona but was able to avoid a full meeting of the entire family in Montserrat. You should have a full-time secretary and send out different types of form letters. Otherwise, you will have no time for yourself and for your work. Send the diaries, if you will, but don't let people expect that this means a visa for further correspondence. Take, for example, Michael Taylor. He was delighted to receive the diary but why bother to write if in the end he really has nothing to say and you are wasting your precious time? In all cases I have said as follows: "Anaïs appreciates hearing from you but she simply cannot find the time to write and to write to you personally." The people who really love and understand you should understand this and if they don't, *tant pis pour eux. À propos*, Madame Madeleine Haas, Hotel Queen Mary, 9 Rue de Greffulhe, Paris, never did receive the first volume of the diary in French which you so very kindly sent her.

What are your plans for the next few months?

Love,
Joaquín

Letter from Hugh Guiler to Anaïs Nin:
New York, July 28, 1973

Darling:

I hope you got the letter I sent you to Post Restante, Puerto Vallarta. I received two from you telling me about the place and the two-day boat trip. Am glad you also had the time to rest. And it does sound like a good location for the film.

But if it is as hot as Acapulco was in the summer, it is not the place for me in this season, for I even suffered during the day in Paris, Ste. Maxime and Geneva, so I came back exhausted due also to the two quick changes of time zones.

You will be glad to know that I received a commission of $3,490 on the closing and distribution of Caresse's trust. Not the estate, which is still in a mess and may take much more time. I gave Roger $490 and kept $3,000, for he had helped me over the years with problems on the trust.

But I will have to wait until October for the film grant (from the American Film Institute) as applications can only be considered at that time. I have applied for $5,000, which can then go to finance some new films, like the idea of *rope* that I have had in the back of my mind for some time, as a symbol of attachment (like a ship docking) and parting—like the first rope—the umbilical cord that life starts with and the last with which it ends for some. But also the salvage rope for escape to safety; the endless miles of rope forming our intestines—the labyrinth; the analogy with the serpent and with fireworks; the invisible rope that unites male and female, as that may also shred through tension, pulling not in the same but in opposite directions; the sections of rope thrown from one generation to another, caught by some and grasped and strengthened by some, and slipping through the hands of others, or forming knots; the different ways of tying or weaving ropes or hair—hair rope, silken ropes for marriage tents and tassels. The whole film would be a tapestry of all these. A circus tent held up by ropes—and acrobats walking on tightropes. Walking in space holding on to a thin rope. You can actually think of more. Seems to me they are as endless as your words beginning with "trans."

Did I tell you Frances was crazy to see belly dancers, so I took her on Saturday night and, incidentally, found another belly dancer (Jemilia—that's her name) who ended her performance like a snake on the floor—only more sensuously. About 1½ minutes, but I felt like adding her on near the end of the film and am already making arrangements. A real Lilith. Will try to do this next week.

Also found another nightclub like the Egyptian Gardens where Jemilia's manager is the owner. He told me he knows Elia Kazan who has often come to him for dancers. Name is the Port Said Nite Club and Restaurant and he says he has the best shish kabob in town.

Love, love,

H

LOS ANGELES, AUGUST 1973

Nature was kind to me. First of all, sensual love can continue as long as emotional love is alive. I often desire Rupert because of something he has done or said that touches me. In my case my body was never distorted. My feet are unchanged, the ankles not swollen. I have no varicose veins. I have kept my 120 pounds weight, the same size dress I wore at sixteen years of age. I hold myself erect. I walk lithely, swiftly. The only sign of age that was ugly was the wrinkled throat, and I had surgery on the neck. I have no frown lines between my eyes. I have laughing wrinkles around my eyes, but no pouches. My forehead is smooth. My legs are slim. I can wear miniskirts. The flesh under my arms is a little loose. But my breasts are like a young girl's, the nipples pink. I have a slim, indented waistline.

When you love somebody for a long time, the expression of the body, its presence, takes on emotional attributes, and lovers do not lose desire because of the signs of age. Rupert is Rupert even if the love of beer has given him a stomach and his neck is wrinkled, and both our hands were always old. (My hands are the oldest part of me.) Other qualities appear. When Rupert lost his extreme slimness, he

183

acquired the radiant, expansive, generous appearance he has now, of a man who has flowered with all his being. He is so youthful when he body-surfs the highest waves. I am youthful when friends come and I talk with liveliness and am alert to what is said.

I am a tireless walker. I walk fast. They are not definable, age, desire and love. I still arouse desire and receive love letters. But the most beautiful of all truths is that Rupert and I maintained intensity. It does not come as often, but in the heat and sensuous beauty of Puerto Vallarta we made such absolute love that I cried out: "It is too much, it is too much!" It was almost unbearably keen. It comes out from our sharing an atmosphere, an emotion, from wanting to possess each other when I am leaving or returning home. We crossed the change of age successfully. Last winter Rupert had no desire. He worried about it. I made light of it. Said it was a phase that strikes every man, to leave it alone, to not force it. I was playful: "Get a new wife for a while; you need variety."

"I desire no one."

Only to Bogner did I confess my fears. Was it aging? Was he becoming aware of the changes in me? Was it my fault? But towards him I behaved well. He feared I would think he did not love me anymore. But nothing in his acts indicated that, and I decided to have faith. In a few months the crisis passed. A stupid doctor advised him to stop drinking beer. He did for a while. Then we broke the fast and took our usual martini, and after dinner we made love in the style we call "Acapulco" when our passion reached its heights. We have many games. The full moon is believed to influence us to full lovemaking, but occasionally a slender one will incite us as well. Where before I pressed the coltish, thin shoulders, today I find a more voluptuous man; his shoulders and neck have remained stylized, but the hair on his chest is white. My own distress is under my arms in spite of daily swimming, and I tend to wear short sleeves. Rupert had to live through the months when the radiation shriveled my vulva and uterus, and entrance was tight and difficult. Rupert said: "You are a virgin again." But after a while it softened.

It is a deep love that makes you accept the transformations in the lover. As if the body had to express new elements, maturity, highness. Naturally I was saddened by each symptom, first the throat where strain shows. Then the deepening laugh wrinkles, then the slight web of wrinkles around the mouth. Rupert, when he walks naked to the kitchen to fetch a drink, is unchanged. The silhouette of his body is still a Donatello. Has anyone described how we lie naked in bed with the sun shining on us? Either a talk about a movie on which we always agree, or a quote from a book, a recollection of an event in Japan, Malaysia, Cambodia, an impression of a person we both arrived at, plans for the future, future travels, make our thoughts and dreams run parallel until the proximity of his body and of mine, the touch of the skin, under which flow similar wishes, impressions and desires, becomes the touch of one's duplicate self, a twin, a lost half, another self, and one feels rising in the blood the need for a closer union, the need for fusion. Love nourishes this need of fusion, love enters it, and each time the embrace is different because we embrace different aspects of ourselves. The adventurer, the seeker of the unknown, the aesthete, the explorer, the new self, which like a new leaf has been born overnight and we want to possess it too.

Henry wanted very much to ask me how I felt now, but I would not answer, because I know for him sex was always a separate function from emotion, and he would not understand the continuity of love. He has admitted impotence. But he still looks at women as desirable or not desirable.

Much has been written about the durability of desire in older people. Much good could be written about the early impotence of homosexuals because they have rarely charged sex with the vitality of emotion.

What I have lost with time is sudden, wild and irrational desires for certain people. Perhaps because my eroticism has been concentrated on Rupert. I see him on the stage as the ballet dancer, as the *jeun premier*, as the young lover. For me he has everlasting youth. The quickness of his gestures, his wild swimming, his adventurous snorkeling through dark caves in Puerto Vallarta.

How lovely going to bed together, to read, or he watches TV with earphones so I don't have to endure most of the political trash. How lovely when I rise early and see him asleep, while Piccolino does all he can to awaken him. When I am working in my little room, he comes in, naked, to embrace me, and then we swim and have breakfast together.

When we saw the vulgarity and degeneracy of *Last Tango in Paris*, we both said we would never be able to make love again. But the next night we did as if to defy the ugliness of the movie. I feel Marlon Brando added his own brand of vulgarity to the language; they mentioned how often he improvised.

The sun shines on our bed. The moon shines on our bed. Piccolino sleeps with us.

And so love triumphs over age, maturity weaves an unpossessive love, dissolves jealousy, becomes generous; love when allied with sensuality is a potent aphrodisiac. The silk on Rupert's penis is softer than a woman's breast. The hair on his ear lobe is downy; the curls on his neck, though grey, are so lovely when tousled in the morning. His eyes are dazzling. I described them once as holding all the colors of Venice, gold and sea green and forest green, and so fiery.

Letter from Anaïs Nin to Philip Jason:
Los Angeles, September 4, 1973

Dear Philip:
Only terrible overwork kept me from writing you how angry I was at Benjamin Franklin's unjust review of the *Anaïs Nin Reader*. Your defense will appear, but I have asked Richard never to let him review again. The review from Marguerite Young will please you. Also watch for the *The New York Times*, September 8. The *Reader* will be reviewed by Wallace Fowlie in a positive way. All the fan mail I received referred to the *Reader* with pleasure and compliments, and I wish I had the time to pass all this on to you. I am drowned in mail every day and fighting for time to work. I have reduced the lectures drastically. How are you? Where are you teaching? I am editing volume 6. Volume 5 will be out April 1974.

I received the paperback of the *Reader* and many persons doing studies on me have used it and will quote from it. We have had little time to talk together and get to know each other, but at least I want you to know how pleased and proud I am of the *Reader* and what good selections you made. Sharon Spencer said only recently that *Hedja* was one of the main themes of my work and your choice to include it was very wise.

Love,
Anaïs

Letter from Hugh Guiler to Anaïs Nin:
New York, September 13, 1973

Darling:

I would have replied sooner to your beautiful, understanding letter that I got a few days ago, but I have had to be deeply involved with getting the film through its final stage. It left New York tonight and will be in Beverly Hills tomorrow by special air freight.

I am terribly sorry to have given you a miserable month after my return from Europe and the delayed emotional reaction to the trip. I am so glad to hear that you have also recovered physically and emotionally. Bogner says crises like this one strengthen us—or rather give us the ability to surmount them. Apart from some insomnia from stopping the sleeping pills for a few nights, as Dr. Duane suggested, I am feeling much better and the whole thing is assuming less and less importance. Bogner has arranged to see me twice a week for a few weeks, while we go into this more thoroughly. But she has already helped by saying that most of what happened was due to forces (some of them world forces) that were not under my control.

Certainly, it is now clear to me that I brought back from my work only the worries and the tensions, and that I could not expect you to understand that there were also many real satisfactions in the work itself. The truth is that I never really felt adequate in the business world, an inadequacy that was symbolized by my apparent difficulty with arithmetic. Great light has been thrown on this kind of problem by an article by a woman scientist [Maya Pines] in last Sunday's *N.Y. Times*. It is a long extract from a book, which Harcourt Brace is bringing out next month. I hope you will see they send you a copy. Essentially scientific experiments have proved that our brain is in two segments—the right side is inarticulate in language, mute, understanding only in images, and it is clearly related to our dream life. The left side is intellectual, analytical (like Virgo), and is something like a computer. Each of these two segments is locked under its own shell, and they are normally connected to each other by hundreds of fibers. But when these fibers are severed (as in the case of an operation for epilepsy) the result is two personalities in the same person, and the left, intellectual personality is always trying to provide rational explanations of apparent irrational (or strange) reactions in the other.

You helped me to keep these two personalities joined, rather than severed as they would have been with any other kind of wife. So I think that while my father had something to do with my actions, the whole thing is more mysterious than just that, and the woman scientist herself says that no one had been able to penetrate that area specifically.

What is remarkable is how you have been able to throw so much light on an area that was, as you say, alien to you, and in this sense you have achieved, for yourself, as well as for me, an extraordinary equilibrium, probably helped by your persistent efforts to be *articulate*, which, in someone less balanced, would have made a Virgo of you. In this sense, your writing did more than make you a great *artist*, but also kept the connection between the two shells in a state of *communication*, and your letter to me stands out as perhaps your greatest *human* triumph.

I received also a very warm letter from Joaquín thanking me for the present of coffee you made in my name as well as yours, and I have replied, saying how grateful I am for the regularity of his financial assistance particularly at this time and explaining something of what I have been going through; I now see the importance of my association with a family of artists, in which he was a very important element.

Above all, I ask your forgiveness for the pain I inflicted on you, but as you see there has been a positive side even to that.

Love,

Hugo

Letter from Hugh Guiler to Anaïs Nin:
New York, September 19, 1973

Darling:

I am very sorry I gave you a shock by telephoning. Please forgive me. I had assured you recently and often that I had turned the corner some time ago and have been improving ever since. So I could not imagine that you would jump to the conclusion that I was ill or something like that. But I now understand that that is what you felt had been the reason for my calling.

I do remember what you said about the plan to teach through the university, and I have to reread your letter of September 11. Indeed, it was the omission of the formal contract of your letter that gave me concern, especially since it is all to start in the next ten days.

In a case like this, any verbal agreement will be valueless unless it is incorporated into the contract and, in the same way, into the prospectus, which you did not send me. I am sure your lawyer friend will agree about this and will probably think of other features that should be officially covered.

I am also glad you said you would have Gunther go over the whole thing and that he may add further clauses for your protection. I know you said you know these people well and trust them, but you can never know who their successors might be who would take over if they should disappear or die.

You also said in your letter that the whole thing is very flexible and up to you, and this is of great importance so as to leave you free to do your own creative work, with enough energy left after all the extra things you do over and above what you undertake as your responsibilities. For all this, while it may be the equivalent of what you could make with 50 or 60 lectures around the country, Bogner remarked that the financial compensation does not, to her, seem adequate. Many high school teachers make as much and more.

I know you will probably feel all this is affected by the fact that you will be in great demand and could have more students than the contract calls for. But I also know how much you give to each person who comes to you, and if you want me to consider retiring before too long you must remember that on my part it is not a question, as you said (and which is not correct), that I have taken no pleasure in your making money. I am proud of everything you have done, and you have already made it possible for me to continue making films—but I just cannot think of retiring if I feel that it would add to the burden you have already been carrying—outside of the royalties, which I am confident will continue to come in without the extra push.

Above all, I have to feel that no such activities will interfere with your creative writing.

I am already discussing with Bogner this question of retiring and will tell you what I work out.

Meanwhile I am afraid the Ian Hugo account will need replenishing for (1) the final expenses of the film (have already paid $350 to Dave Horowitz today); (2) the cuts, negatives and prints for my London distributor, and the new one in Paris; (3) prints of all the films for the new French TV distributor; (4) and I don't know what equipment I will have to get in connection with video. Maybe they will supply it all except the tapes. Would it run you short to send a check to Ian Hugo for, say, $750?

Again, forgive me for the shock I gave you. I will just write the next time.

The increase in the rent, which I will be signing for in the next few days, is for a three-year period and will be 10% annually, bringing it to $475 a month, which seems a lot, but the landlords pointed out to me that they are just making up for the past three years, when the law did not allow them to raise the rents even under conditions of inflation. Roger still feels I should make it two years, with inflation roaring ahead, and it should not be difficult to find a new tenant.

Am taking my thousand steps in the park every night, but had some insomnia the last two nights—probably as a result of the mistake I made in telephoning you. I am sure I will come back to normal tonight after my attempt to sympathize with your feelings about this incident—and to explain what was in my mind.

All my love,
Hugo

Letter from Hugh Guiler to Anaïs Nin:
New York, September 20, 1973

Darling:

I received your envelope and letter of the 18th, and tomorrow you should receive the letter I airmailed you yesterday. The brochure you sent, as you say, obviously does not tell the whole story, just as the preliminary contract you sent did not, while I thought naturally it was the contract you were being expected to sign. You had just sent it to me without saying it was a rough draft, so as this is all I had to go on and what you had told me and written me was omitted, I think I was expressing a natural concern and did not deserve that burst of anger twice over the telephone, at home and at the office. If you did not mean that I should put my mind on it, why did you send it to me? Especially with no other comments as you now give me and which are reassuring as far as verbal agreements can be. Now, did you say you intended to get Gunther's comments on what will certainly be a different contract? So I was not at all acting as if I did not know you had handled your career well in the past. That is not a fair statement, for neither on this occasion nor any other have I expressed disapproval, and I think you mistake concern for disapproval or lack of confidence in your organizational ability, which I have told Bogner is extraordinary. Even when I am in ignorance of all the facts, I have always trusted you to get competent advice on something that, as you say, is not my specialty. So I am glad you are in this case also going over the situation with your lawyer friend, as well.

I really don't think that one telephone call, motivated by love, was enough to arouse your anger and give me guilt. It will certainly make me hesitate to put any more calls through for any occasion.

Love,

Hugo

P.S. The outline in your own words of what your attitude is going to be in the course you will be teaching is beautiful and inspiring.

Letter from Anaïs Nin to David Pepperell:
Los Angeles, September 23, 1973

Dear David:

I was so pleased to hear from you. When I gave up my [letter] writing because of overwork I always felt I was losing a friend. But no, here he is, quite changed. I don't really believe money needs to corrupt one—it is the guilt we have for possessing some that harms us. We all have dual wishes, dual selves. A flashy side that wants to be noticed and famous, and a quiet side that only wants to be left alone in peace to work. My resolution was always: do them all—they are all you; embrace them all. So now I do both, the public and the private. I must confess I prefer the quiet working life to the public life, but the public life gives me the means to be free, to move.

As a young man you wanted to be free, and Henry Miller's way was not freedom (debts!). So now you are free of concern over making a living. It is one kind of freedom.

The last two years were years of fame and discovery—a new segment of America, a new generation. Suddenly, we were in harmony. I just finished volume 5 of the *Diary*—September 29 I begin lectures at colleges. Someone made a film documentary of me (the same man who made *The Henry Miller Odyssey*, Robert Snyder). Did *Odyssey* ever come to Australia? It was on all the educational TV stations here. Henry has been watching over the new film because he thought his was not crazy enough…

From the tone of your letter I would say you have not lost anything of your sensitive and dreaming selves. They all have to live in peace with each other, all our selves! I notice once again, dear David, your focus is clearer on what you want, are, think, etc.

I sit writing you during the only evenings when I can write letters—when the musicians come and play quartets. One husband makes calculations for the satellite that photographed Mars, one wife knits, and I can write letters. But, like the sorcerer's apprentice, I now say I don't wish for fame. Henry, too, feels it deprived us of leisure! Tons of letters and books. Come to my exhibition. Come and see my film. Hear my concert, watch my play, come to France, come to Japan. Henry asked: "Where was all that time we had in Paris, to talk all night, walk about, read?"

I wrote a preface for Jacques Henri Lartigue's photographs. A preface for a book of women's poetry. I could not get to France for the Festival du Livre—too exhausted after 26 colleges!

About balancing analysis and action, and all the other balances that cause us pain: they will soon fuse into one harmonious whole. One becomes adept at balancing like a seal!

Love,
Anaïs

Letter from Anaïs Nin to Jean Fanchette:
Los Angeles, September 24, 1973

Two persons have told me the absurd and ridiculous lies you are telling about me: that I was in love with you and that I kneeled in the rain and offered to give up everything and stay in Paris with you. If you do not stop telling this I will divulge in the Diary how you treated the subscribers to your magazine, the libraries, collecting money for subscriptions and never delivering the magazine, borrowing from my friends, trying to exploit me, coming to New York for just that purpose, letting all the manuscripts and photographs accumulate unopened in a trunk at George Whitman's so that I had to come to Paris and pick them up and return them to my friends. Daisy Aldan will also tell the story of your dishonesty and using of people.

As to the story of the "obscene" letter: that was due, first of all, to your opening a letter you had no right to open; secondly it was a correspondence between two dogs, and the diary of my own dog, a purely amusing, comic diary and exchange of letters that will appear in future diaries. You have no sense of humor as well as no sense of the truth.

Even at that time I knew you were always lying. You boasted that all the women whose children you helped to deliver fell in love with you. Well, I never did, and you can now sell this letter as it is your usual way with letters, to a university for the record.

Anaïs Nin

Anaïs Nin with students, Silver Lake, 1973. Photo: Rupert Pole

LOS ANGELES, SEPTEMBER 24, 1973

It is 2:30 and I have been working quietly (except for a trip to the post office) since 7:30. I have already done 140 pages of volume 6, which John Ferrone will end dramatically with the publication of volume 1.

James Herlihy turned up, in very good form, seeking a new cycle. Emerging, I hope, from his corny period. I'm only interested in his diary writing. Reading a book on Frieda Lawrence with great interest. There are thousands of books on D. H. Lawrence and none until now about the woman who was, if anything, his collaborator in every way.

Mornings are foggy. Afternoons the sun comes out. As we all started so late no students yet. I have space; the lectures are once a month and only the well-paying ones.

Ferrone says vol. 5 will be out April 17 or thereabouts.

LOS ANGELES, SEPTEMBER 27, 1973

As soon as I am pried from obligation, I turn to the briefcase full of unanswered mail, volume 6 to edit, the phone, talks with Bob Snyder about *Anaïs Nin Observed* (he is in debt so I try to get him college rentals), talks with Tristine Rainer (because as soon as Henry Jaglom said he would film all the novels, he disappeared though he encourages Tristine to work on the script and calls to ask me what I think of Glenda Jackson as Lillian). Talks with Lynne Weston. Talk with Tracey Roberts. Talk with Hugo: "I am feeling better, finishing the film and seeing Bogner only once a week." I can write in the Diary.

Rupert had a difficult re-entry into teaching. His griefs were real enough; the room he loved is condemned as unsafe in an earthquake; the film class taken away from him when he took his sabbatical is not returned; he has a math class with a new abstruse, pedantic book—not what his students need. He misses the freedom. I felt sympathy, and in February for his 55th birthday we are planning for him to retire and to help me. He did help me all year, but only part time because he needs to sleep late, watch TV, and the newspapers are also indispensable.

I do *more* work alone, but there is much I can't do—Xerox, errands, photographs reprinted, copyediting lectures, articles, prefaces. And his slowing down my rhythm is perhaps good for me. Ruth Ross thinks it is bad for Rupert, psychologically. He must have his own thing. But Edith Gross is against the convention of working at a job if it is not necessary. I have to take care of Hugo next year. I am caught between my desire to free Rupert of rigid and shabby programming and responsibilities.

EN ROUTE TO L.A. FROM COLORADO, SATURDAY, SEPTEMBER 29, 1973

Great sorrow at confronting for the first time the limitations of my energy. The invitation to Boulder and Denver was tempting. Lee Potts wrote a remarkable study of my work. Linda Barnes revealed a personality in her letters.

But already I had to handle it with a plea to limit the activities—I was honest and refused a seminar in the morning, lunch with Brillig Bookshop owners, meeting a newspaper woman, doing a radio interview, having dinner with a large group before the lecture, etc. I dislike barriers—closing doors. But even with precaution I was swept irresistibly into a vortex. It was irresistible because all of them were so immensely lovable.

Lee met me at the airport. Lee's man, John, never read me, but I felt such warmth and quality of spirit in both. Long drive to Boulder. John loves his mountains and points to their beauty. They chose a motel among the pines. I had dinner in their home. No time to talk. We had to leave for the performance. This was planned in three weeks by Lee and Nancy Spanier. Dance, symbolic interpretations, electronic sounds, narration, a background of slides—some excellent moments. The best was the dramatic reading of the "Birth" story by a very young woman who fainted twice after rehearsals and wept when we met afterwards. There was a reading of the Varda passages, although not read with lightness or humor. The acting of the chess player was done by a skillful, good actor with a powerful presence. There was the reading of the bicycle passage in *Ladders to Fire* and the dancing of daughter and father in a *felt* passage from *Winter of Artifice*. Minor flaws—the last dance, which should have expressed lightness, ecstasy, liberation, was not light enough—the narration with electronic echo was not clear. But as a whole, it was a remarkable feat of interpretation and very moving. They are all so young. The dance of "Birth" was striking.

We went to the professor's home, and I met many people besides the performers and left only when a small group remained.

Before sleeping I read loving notes and letters given to me. They are all saying: "You have given me strength, you have freed me." They are all about the life currents. They speak of my radiance, and I myself wonder at the miraculous love that continues to be transmitted in spite of my physical handicaps. (The food has given me pains; I'm deeply tired.)

The next morning Lee came at nine, and we went to have breakfast at Nancy's house—a colorful table. Frederick Eversley, the sculptor at Rainbows, came from Venice, California to meet me. He is a childhood friend of Nancy's; he cooked an omelet. It was raining, a bitter, windy, wintry rain, and I was fearful of wet feet, of paying with a cold. In the rain we drove to the Grillig. The bookshop was utterly charming. It was created like a personal library, plants, couches, space. There is a series of rooms where people can sit and browse—a communal venture—personal and sensitive.

I signed books for 2½ hours, received flowers, homemade cookies, a gift of *The Life of Lewis Carrol* by Florence Becker Lennon—a very old lady with a scarred face, who dedicated it: "For Anaïs Nin, whom I have finally discovered just before closing time *avec éclat!*"

A wonderful, learned book, which I read from before sleep.

From the bookshop Linda Barnes drove me to Denver. The students had asked for a seminar, but I could not do that. I had barely an hour to bathe, rest and dress before the lecture.

I didn't give my best lecture—but perhaps because all they want is a confirmation of what I wrote by my presence (they gave me an ovation before I talked), I feel that my improvised talk was better than any prepared lecture. I also followed the contours of the questions, talked around them, beyond them.

We stayed until the lights were turned off. Went to Lee's house with a small group, where we talked easily.

Breakfast. Then the airport. Lee arrived from Boulder with the eyeglasses I had left behind. Photographs. Great affection between all of us.

When Linda first went to the faculty to ask for a lecture hall and collaboration, the faculty said: "Who?" All but Miss McIntosh, who filled my room with three bowls of flowers. They left Linda to worry about the tickets, doors, chairs. They could not supply a tape recorder except at a cost of $25. Linda was too immersed in the technicalities, and I finally discovered she had supplied $500 from her savings account so I wouldn't have to wait, while next week they are going on their vacation and need the money. So I have to remedy that immediately. Once again the rigid institution versus student needs and the influences that nourish them.

What is beautiful is that the American student has taken things into his own hands. The women set up their Women's Studies independently of the faculty. If they are not integrated with the faculty they go on just the same. I never realized before the *predominance* of men in all professions, nor did I realize fully the constant lowering of women's status. It is wonderful to see women struggling to get into filmmaking, into law, all professions. But I also find the radical feminists damaging, the man-haters, the artificial lesbians, the vociferous, bitter, violent women who achieve nothing. At last, the Institute for Women's Studies (sexuality) is honoring me as useful to women. But how detestable is the somber, bloodless woman who came up to me at the Gotham and said (hiding under a broad-brimmed hat): "How could you relate to a chauvinist pig like Henry Miller?"

LOS ANGELES, OCTOBER 15, 1973

Ever since the communion with the world has happened, I no longer suffer from loneliness. Even when Rupert is watching a reportage on Chile and I come to the little writing room and close the door, my briefcase, overflowing with letters, fills the space with entrancing figures.

There was a visit to Henry Miller just recovering from a very serious, near-death surgery—so frail and small in his bed, quickly tired, sinking into it, as he said, like a bird into a nest—blind in one eye, deaf—so fragile.

Henry Jaglom is in Israel (he is a fanatic Israelite—why?—he is no soldier). Jaglom does rotate in the Hollywood world, but his film is not tainted by any compromise. Françoise Ruddy, who loves my work and wants to film *Seduction*, speaks of appealing to the majority by having a stronger script. "You have to *grab* your audience."

On the video I see again the performance at Boulder, Colorado. I nearly sob at the reading of the "Birth" story.

Hugo plans his next film on the metaphor of the divided, dual brain.

I understood for the first time my impatience with Eastern religions, the *I Ching*, Buddhism, etc. It is because psychiatry (ideally, not always in practice) can give the sense of oneness with the universe, ecstasies and mystic visions. It can liberate both the human and the spiritual in us. It can stimulate our dreams, reveal the connection with life with insight to goodness and generosity. It *could* cure hatred, jealousy, envy, the misuse of power.

Will I be granted enough time to finish my work? I've done 275 pages of vol. 6. We prepared the new Miller letters for editing and dating this summer. Photographs come. Don Bachardy is appealing as he sits sketching. Young women PhDs, dazzlingly gifted, rebelling against the academic rigidities—*men's* thinking.

Meanwhile, our cathedral is the Palomar Observatory, with its noble, fabulous dimensions and mysterious mechanism—the opening of gigantic trap doors towards the sky, gazing with its giant glass eye at the life of the sun, the stars, the dark nests of clouds, while the Pope amasses wealth, invests in Wall Street and does not support the little Catholic school run by the Mexican colony of Silver Lake, where they have no dropouts and no drug problems as they have in other schools.

A blind black girl sends me cassettes on which she talks to me. She tried to shoot herself. She is writing (or dictating) her story.

While working on a volume of the original diary, I noted the tremendous changes in Rupert since then. He does read science books, but he absorbs what I read, its essence. He has assumed the responsibility of taking care of me. How and what I eat. We have to be home at five. The swim, martini and dinner are sacred. But why at five? We rush back from Miller's, and the Snyders'. When defending the timing, he says Piccolino will be hungry. And it is true that animals have a sense of time and that at five Piccolino demands his dinner!

So much work. A calendar of dates to find my way through undated letters or diaries. Work on the Miller correspondence. I wasted time on Mr. Cagle of the Bloomington Lilly Library. Took him to Brooklyn vault—corresponded—and he thought $100,000 was too much for 150,000 pages of the diaries. He also wanted it open to scholars. Yet he paid $3,000 for 100 letters to Roger Bloom, a minor correspondence. Where is the logic?

My faith in psychotherapy was revived by Rollo May's book on violence. He knows the cure for violence. He explains it. We won't follow it, but we could have integrated it. I long ago suspected violence grew out of powerlessness and humiliation. And America is the greatest humiliater in existence. It is always cultivating the power you get from humiliating others. It is the lowest form of power—and the power of Moloch. Rollo May is right. So I return to the only solution for humanizing the world. Why do people regress to Jesus, to the East, when a new solution was offered us? One compatible with science. (Duality of the brain. Abnormalities of the brain of the young man who shot 13 persons from a tower.) Prison has fostered crime. The media has carried the contagion. It does not perhaps create it, but it spreads it.

LOS ANGELES, OCTOBER 16, 1973

I have been at work since 7:30 AM. I have returned at last to the intimacy of the Diary, after letting the whole world walk through it. Some damage was done, but fortunately not the damage of consciousness.

Rollo May is illuminated on violence and its causes, but how do we train a culture not to humiliate minorities? He is illuminating on true innocence versus false innocence. He does understand our times. But the solution, psychotherapy, is far away. It is a luxury. Dr. Stone charges $40 an hour! It has to be free clinics, the early care of schoolchildren.

Last year, the year of 60 lectures, from September 1972 to June 1973, I had the feeling of living outside myself, or of coming entirely out of myself to meet the world. It was out of myself that I gave all I knew, and I responded to the love, but at times my constant appearance before the public created a mirror image, like an echo, which was not good for me. Too many images of Anaïs in a white dress, a pink dress, a purple dress, appearing on stage. Even if my *feelings* were strong, the repetitions deprived them of their spontaneity. I knew what they were going to ask, and I knew my answers.

We need to live on many levels, not writing alone, though I must confess the public life appeals less and less to me. And I love sitting at my desk at 7:30 and working on volume 6. I did read Kazantzakis, but I do not respond to religious preoccupations. I'm a pagan. Religion comes from within us and is expressed by our humanity.

I believe more than ever that psychology is going to cure hostilities and prejudices that prevent us from living at peace with each other. Religion, as you can see, causes war. I may be wrong, but I think war is pathological, never sacred. Read Michener's history of religions, all trying to annihilate each other. There must be another way to humanism.

John Ferrone came to Los Angeles for the Book Fair. Met Rupert. We made dinner for him. He is a superb cook, and gentle. He is an inexorable copyeditor, but *always right* and he suggests remedies. Perhaps because I was overworked, I found revisions arduous, endless—first Gunther's and then John's. But when the cover arrived I was delighted. It *glows*.

I like John so much. He is gentle and keen, human and yet firm in his judgments.

Marguerite Young said today: "I hope to become a capitalist by my socialist books." Poor thing—after surgery for tumors near her eyes, she has a scar from eye to temple.

Cutting down on the lectures has helped me regain my energy. In New York I have time to type 10 or 14 pages for volume 6. I see friends as well as interviewers. So much is happening I can't note it all. A book on self-publishing came out and was well received. It not only contains the history of my press, but of my friends' presses: Daisy Aldan, Valerie Sheehan, Adele Aldridge, Alan Swallow. The weekend at Rye produced another book. Lynne Honickman published her poems with my preface. The Capra Press published my *Paris Revisited*, a small book.

Rupert and I visited Henry Miller after his serious surgery—seven hours, then four hours on separate days. He was so weak and frail. He does not hear well. When he asked us to remove the pillows so he could slide into bed and rest I felt almost as if he was going to curl up and sleep forever.

The outrages of age—the cruelties—the slow corrosions. No wonder Auden asked to die swiftly and not as an invalid. He died of a heart attack recently before age could cripple him. I am glad Gonzalo died before being crippled. I hope the same will happen with me. I don't want to live as Miller has, limping, in pain, not able to travel, and now, for the second time, undergoing major surgery. Henry, once so healthy, jovial, lively, a tireless walker, a hearty eater.

And Hugo—*un coup de vieillesse* this summer, after his trip to Paris—he aged ten years. He walks, talks and moves like a man of 85.

This is the first time I take my Diary with me as I did in Louveciennes and in the '40s—I can't write being next to Rupert.

Tonight I feel the weight of time upon all of us.

NEW YORK, OCTOBER 26, 1973

But let the sun shine on a beautiful autumn day—let me have a morning free of engagements when I can work on vol. 6 and I am light again. Stay alive, Anaïs.

Father Monick of the hippie St. Clement's Church where I spoke—who invited the women to say mass with him, to become priestesses, to present poetry, films, jazz and theatre instead of sermons, or me instead of a sermon—speaks of the way I looked on the platform as if he were speaking of a miraculous apparition, luminous, and asks me to talk to his women whose hostilities and aggressions bewilder him. I steer him towards Hugo's films. Jean Stevo, the Belgian surrealist artist, sends me his daughter who teaches at Yale—I introduce her to Hugo's films. I'm told a private airplane was named after me. Whose? I am told that Pennsylvania College Book Store is filled with my books. Every day a college asks me to lecture. I only accept one a month. Japan will publish the *Diaries*.

Lauren Frost, who once came to me with flowers and tears, later went to see Bogner and now lives with Jules Frisch, is a talented stage-lighting expert who wants to adapt the *Diary* to the stage.

Every day a surprisingly beautiful, poetic letter arrives. Every day a surprise, a gift.

John Ferrone, to please me, obtains from the Harcourt art department a golden cover for vol. 5—a painting by Susan Boulet.

Jim Herlihy, who now calls himself Jamie as he was called originally, is moving to Los Angeles.

Michel, a French student, comes all the way from Paris to visit me.

In the sun, it does not bother me to be walking towards Dr. Parks' office for a weekly injection because I am bleeding lightly and afraid of a recurrence of cancer, but he says no, it is not that. I must increase the Delalutin.

I walk into an Indian shop where I buy cotton or velvet Indian dresses. The Tanagra style goes for 20 or 25 dollars, but I still look sumptuously dressed. The last dress I bought is from Pakistan, red and black.

Barbette Blockington, sturdy and vital, is the head of the Institute for Women's Studies. She has loved me from the day I hugged her after her brilliant lecture, a hug described as five-minute therapy (I gave her confidence). And she seemed so full of confidence that I wondered how I could talk after her—after her witty analysis of a novel, her historical and statistical knowledge, her animus-thrusting mind! She expressed her devotion to my work by honoring me in Washington, dedicating the first number of her *Journal* to me and fêting me at the inaugural cocktail.

For the first few days here I can type in the mornings, but after that the telephone rings every two minutes: Mr. Archie Bennett of World Publishing on the *A Casebook on Anaïs Nin* by Robert Zaller (anthology of original essays); Pasquale [Pat] Cool for an interview; Barbette Blockington arriving from Washington; or I call up those who will be invited to the Gotham Book Mart to see the one-hour documentary *Anaïs Nin Observed* by Robert Snyder.

NEW YORK, OCTOBER 29, 1973

Dream: All night long I was doing, or trying to do, mathematics. A sense of inadequacy and frustration—I could not do it. (When I took LSD I said I understood the infinite.)

I also dreamt that I kept someone from entering my house. I shut the door and windows. I knew it was a man in distress who wanted to enter.

Facts: I have been impatient with Hugo's depression, lethargy, clumsiness, self-undoing. When I returned from a five-hour drive and five hours of listening to talks and reports, while I was collapsing from fatigue and hunger (I could not eat the lunch they served), Hugo met me at the door lugubriously and said that he could not find the nose spray and he had a cold. Meanwhile, he let the rice burn. Eating with Frances and with me, he slumps over, not reacting. When I receive news of Henry Jaglom's generous contract—a $10,000 option for five books (twice as much as Mrs. Ruddy) and a 50% share in the films—there is no joy in Hugo. Rupert was delirious, because his trust in Jaglom, his impulsive acceptance of him, his unwavering admiration for *A Safe Place*, helped me to crystallize the decision to trust him. When I receive $4,000 from Harcourt and tell Hugo, "You can now make your new film, and your next year's income is ensured," he is expressionless. Sometimes he says nothing at all. I'm rebellious and angry.

NEW YORK, NOVEMBER 6, 1973

Poor Hugo finally arrives at the conclusion that he "flops" too easily, that he indulges in self-pity and tells Bogner that she and I are the women he most admires because of our spiritedness.

It was strange but explicable only by way of American concepts, by the collapse of his financial dreams and income. He took his only capital in Switzerland, borrowed on it to buy more stocks, and lost it all after he had promised me not to speculate with that as it was his inheritance from his mother, and half of it, he felt, belonged to me. I took it well, had no resentment or reproach —but only because it was consistent with Hugo's lifelong defeatism and because I had my own income to fall back on. But I don't take it well when we have an entire calm weekend to prepare for a film showing, and Hugo has two days to clean and organize his films, and then, when the 20 visitors arrive, he has left the film on the wrong reel—reversed! I don't take it well when we go out in 30-degree weather to vote and he walks three blocks in the wrong direction before checking for the address of the voting place. No matter how clever I am, I cannot forestall his errors.

A strange thing is that the armature of economic power having failed him, he has disintegrated in character: his writing has become smaller and more and more feminine, his voice weaker, his alertness and attention gone. His passivity is abnormal.

I have been distressed by my rebellion against Hugo, when under ordinary circumstances I wanted to be indulgent, compassionate, sympathetic. I have discussed it with Bogner. I have become towards Hugo that monstrous "nagging mother." I wonder if it isn't a belated effort at counteracting my earlier attitude of constant empathy, which weakened him, spoiled him. We weakened each other with sympathy.

I found a counteraction in sturdier relationships, toughening ones. I faced the world. Hugo, in spite of 20 years of help, never gained strength. He surrounds himself with advisors: in business or in film work, no decision is *made alone*. As I became stronger, his dependencies grew more obvious: on business partners, on his accountant, on Bogner. The traits that originally attracted me (gentleness, patience, kindness) have now become weaknesses. Women always react favorably: he is so sweet, he makes you feel good, he is so kind, he looks so distinguished.

So from the mutual sensitive treatment of each other (excessive sympathy for each other's troubles), one emerged weaker and in constant need of reinforcement, and the other emerged strong. And it gives me guilt…and anger.

John Ferrone, who imagined me the priestess of all spirits, was amazed to find me with family duties (towards Rupert's family). "No one is ever free," I said, "if one has a human sense of responsibility."

Fortunately, Rupert is objective about his family. We could have ruined ourselves supporting Lloyd's absolutely impossible dreams, or Eric's, which are just as impractical. They could become bottomless pits of failure to deal with reality. Rupert is practical. He refused Eric a loan of $10,000 that would have gone down the drain, knowing that Lloyd, out of work, still maintains an office and an assistant. Rupert has paid for the care of his mother ($300 a month) and taxes on Lloyd's property, now deeded to him and Eric. Any day we may be faced with Lloyd's destitution and inability to live economically, and with Helen's death, who will care for Lloyd; or with Lloyd's death, who will pay for Helen's stay in an expensive rest home? But Rupert's wisdom has not allowed me to be caught up in this. He is prudent. At the same time he wants us to enjoy the fruit of my work *now*. At one time he lived only in the future, but now he wants to live in the present. For all he has given me, the support of his love, he deserves this.

I cannot solve the contradiction between Eastern religion, which states that all evil comes from the ego, that one should get rid of the ego, and Western psycho-analysis, which says that all evil comes from the lack of knowledge of our un-conscious self, the self we do not know. They seem hopelessly contradictory, and I feel I have reached a oneness with nature and a oneness with humanity by the Western method of removing the obstacles. I have a complete repudiation of Bud-dhism and Zen, a deep and natural one. It is not my way. I have achieved *satori* [enlightenment] by other means.

There is some confusion between ego and self-creation. For Americans, all self-creation is termed an "ego trip," a disparaging judgment. That is wrong too. Then others warn us that a scientific and technological culture will destroy the individual. Television has already brainwashed millions of individuals. It carries the germ of not thinking, of passivity.

The feeling of oneness. How can one describe it?

Everyone who comes to the door I begin by *liking*, by being open to their invisible messages, by seeking links, correlations, affinities, by seeking to *know* them.

If later this is betrayed, as by the cold-blooded thesis of Nancy Zee, the most destructive and negative of all, I do suffer, being still vulnerable to disapproval, but I measure it against all I have achieved in giving inspiration and courage. Bogner stresses the great difference between defensiveness and self-protection. In defen-siveness, I would have written an angry letter defending myself, but by exposing my vulnerability publicly I would be giving her the satisfaction of having wounded me. In self-protection, I will write an objective letter for which I'm not yet ready. I have found I cannot trust my anger. When I became angry with Benjamin Franklin, I obtained nothing but silence and a break. I should have gone about it in a cool, studied way. I should have written to Richard Centing about my objection that Benjamin Franklin is a totally negative critic, that in the newsletter he constantly disparaged my friends, that the spirit of the newsletter was fraternal (A Café in Space), while his belongs to that of the Bitchy Society I am struggling against.

Nancy Zee offended me with her false premise that what I had left out of the edited *Diaries* was for the purpose of self-idealization. She thinks herself a genius at detection by putting together the *Diaries* and the novels as complementary to each other. The keys I gave myself, giving in another form what I couldn't give in the *Diary*. *Noblesse oblige!* She thinks to destroy me by her great discovery, never for a moment suspecting I might be protecting others or have human conflicts!

I awaken at 4:00 AM to write a defensive letter, but, feeling I am standing on irrational ground, I take Nancy's thesis to Bogner. She reads it and finds it brilliant and accurate and objective.

NEW YORK, NOVEMBER 8, 1973

Gunther comes at ten and we compare our two sets of galleys of vol. 5. At noon Hugo comes for lunch. At two a woman comes from Toronto for an interview for a book on woman artists.

Two days on tea and toast with my recurrent "crisis."

Dr. Martí Ibañez, now dead, explained Zen and I understand it for the first time.

Bogner talks eloquently about Nancy Zee's thesis. My vulnerability to criticism made me pick up only the negative vibrations. I misinterpreted the study. Bogner feels I should be proud of it. She herself believes an artist reveals more of himself in his art than in his autobiography. Bogner thinks I judged it with the *self destroyed by the father*. She read Nancy's letter and dissipated the old nightmare of being annihilated by criticism. I can be proud of this study. She wants me to read it again and become more objective.

EN ROUTE TO BUFFALO, NOVEMBER 14, 1973

I think I am withdrawing from public life because it focuses entirely on an idealized Anaïs. They have extracted from the *Diaries* only my faculty for giving hope, for inspiring, for changing lives, so that is what is expected of me again. What is heavily unbalanced is once again the practice of healing. If Colette Neville calls me up 20 minutes before I set out for Buffalo, it is to confide her distress: "In theatre work everything is intermittent. When I am working I give all to the work and cannot write. When I'm not working I don't write! I have a violent need for recognition!" If others call me, it is to praise how I appear in the documentary. I feel the Anaïs who is mirrored is an enhanced one I mistrust. I have work to do. I need an atmosphere that is more natural and better balanced. This is like too many flowers. I need severity, and I find in others a desperation to *become* me. An actress said: "I want to be you."

So I must return to this unflattering mirror—to my basic seriousness. Perhaps I feel this image of Anaïs on stage is too close to that of my father on his concert stage, to his telegrams that came regularly and were read by my mother: "*Succès fou!*"

199

Well, enough *succès fou.*

The positive beauty was the emotion of oneness with others—the miraculous communion with those who came up to me, the *sincerity* of the praise, which is more like gratitude.

At a certain point I started to carry the Diary around—to feel the need of it. Here there is no performance. An old friend disturbed me by speaking of my aura, which he traces back to the beginning of our friendship. The present Anaïs is a denial of that one, but he only notices the original me.

LOS ANGELES, NOVEMBER 19, 1973

I receive my first International University College student, a sensitive, talented woman, mature—Mrs. Shirley Osborne. She is an experienced writer who has already worked with Robert Kirsch at UCLA. I think all she needs is to be kept writing.

Letter from Anaïs Nin to Lawrence Durrell:
Los Angeles, November 19, 1973

Dear Larry:

So that we can enjoy each other's company let me catch you up on some necessary data. In 1947 Hugo and I separated amicably. In 1947 he resigned from the bank. Which means I am no longer a banker's wife. I have been living with Rupert Pole since then. Hugo also made the decision to be left out of the *Diary.* So those who are his friends make as little reference to the relationship as possible, which also enables me to continue my support of him as a filmmaker. Because I had to leave him out of the *Diary* at his specific wish, people tend to ask questions. I would be grateful if you sympathized with Hugo's wishes and did not answer that whenever possible.

I will certainly see you at Henry's, but as in the past you flatly contradicted my statements (that I was never wealthy, that someone who works for a bank at a salary is not a banker and that I never owned a Henry Moore [painting] but that Hugo's sister worked with him in London and that may have been where the wish to own one might have come from). I feel uneasy about giving you my home address and inviting you until I am sure you will not cause me embarrassment as in the past. ([Your essay on] Dylan Thomas.) You fictionalized my life (a child of palace hotels), and that is what made our friendship so difficult the past years. Please apply a little human consideration instead of your beautiful imagination to my life at the present.

Love,
Anaïs

Letter from Anaïs Nin to Hugh Guiler:
Los Angeles, November 19, 1973

Darling:

I am still under the painful impression that I cannot make you happy, no matter what I do. It may have been due to your depression. Your voice already sounded better and you did not have that "crushed" look I fought against, bending over, whispering, etc. I hope it was all a depression, but it left sad echoes in me. It took a few days to recover and rest. I had a big carton of mail awaiting me. Now I have until December 6 to work on vol. 6. I feel when I finish the editing I will be able to relax.

It is sunny but cold. No swimming yet. It is costly to keep the pool heated when it is very cold out.

Saw a frightening television show on the atom bomb by Alistair Cooke and was reminded that one man, the president, has all the power. What a democratic system! He can blow up the world. Why can't we do anything to change the dictatorship of a president as demonstrated this year?

Tell me you are well, in a better frame of mind. I thought it was all agreed that I could do more for you as an artist behind the stage.

Pat Cool is a young interviewer who wants to talk with you for *Interview* magazine.

Anaïs

LOS ANGELES, NOVEMBER 23, 1973

Dr. Weston: "The bleeding *may* or *may not* indicate recurrence of cancer." Dr. Parks had said definitely: "It is not a symptom of recurrence."

Depression.

LOS ANGELES, SATURDAY, DECEMBER 1, 1973

The musicians are playing—beautiful waterfalls of sound. At 7:00 AM I was finishing the 1958 volume, which is full of new themes: LSD, the Brussels World Fair trip, Jim's success, painful friendship with the Geismars, Durrell's unexpectedly inadequate preface to *Children of the Albatross.*

Rain. Post Office. Always interesting mail.

Work on a diary catalogue for libraries. I would like to settle the matter of the Diaries while I'm alive.

We buy a terrycloth robe for Helen Wright.

Someone sends me a fancy tea set, shocked that I should use Lipton's in the film!

Trouble getting Bob to polish and finish *Anaïs Nin Observed.*

Meditating on my lecture at Esalen. The necessity to *know* our unconscious has become more vital since women are studying programming. How can you separate the true self from the persona? So many elements have to be sorted out.

On the table lie the notebooks of Martha Graham, given to me by John Pearson, and a sketchbook of Sausalito houseboats.

Tristine Rainer taught diary writing and asked me to talk with her students once—which I did—and we became friends. She read her essay on my work at UCLA. She has big brown eyes, a nose with character, a vulnerable voice. I have watched her develop, from a suffering woman to an assertive one. Henry Jaglom is gambling on Tristine to write the script for the films, a young unknown writer. Jaglom is an intricate and many-sided person, which disturbs Tristine. But he demands total abdication because he is her age (35) and she is full of anxieties and spoiled the mood of the association by her need of a concrete, solid contract. In films, everything is a mirage, including contracts. This was the first time I didn't want the interference of business because I trust Jaglom as an artist, and he is my choice of filmmaker for my work.

In New York I was shattered by compassion for Hugo. All my rebellions and criticisms are a terrible defense against the compassion that threatens to annihilate, engulf me. When it reaches me, it is intolerably painful. I suppose I *have* to believe that he, in his self-undoing, destroyed my love. When I see him acting self-destructively, even masochistically, then I can say that is how my love was destroyed. Nevertheless I feel a terrifying compassion. When I'm happy, content, I think of him alone, though yesterday he had dinner with Barbette Blockington and took her to a Zen film by Ruth Stephan. Or he takes Frances to breakfast, or to a crêpe suzette place, or to the Greek belly dancers. From Frances I get a completely different image of Hugo: his jokes and his rather vulgar ways with women! He places dollar bills in the cleavage of the belly dancers. But when he saw the documentary film that portrays my life and atmosphere in L.A., he became *jealous* that another filmmaker captured my "aura." I told him he had caught it far more artistically in his films. He met me at the door (when I returned exhausted from six hours at the Gotham Book Mart), sulking. "You leave me out of your life."

I exploded: "You chose to be out of the *Diaries*. I have done everything humanly possible to include you. In fact, denying the marriage helped me push your films."

Later, he apologized. I had introduced his films to several persons while I was in New York. He was repentant but not ashamed of the jealousy. But I felt that this jealousy masked a greater one that he has not acknowledged to himself, of my other life. He recognized how gracious and harmonious it was, thought of his chaos and dispiriting chatter by comparison. I had dreaded his seeing the Snyder film because of the depiction of my other life.

Putting together his still "romantic" view of me and his vulgarity with other women, I also realized what went wrong with the marriage. *He idealized me.*

He retains this lack of maturity as if some part of him has not aged.

I asked Rupert if he could explain scientifically why the computer side of the brain should retain our childhood and yet everything else becomes blurred or even totally erased in old age. *Why* do we remember our childhood and lose our grip of the present as many old people do—why do we regress to childhood? Why should the first record be more vivid than the later one? I have been reading books about the brain, the two sides of the brain, the duality inherent in man's body.

Rupert's mother, after a stroke, is senile. She behaves like a bad child, won't go to the bathroom, won't dress, runs away down the stairs, and even lifts her cane to strike Leonora, her caretaker.

My only conflict now is that under incredible pressures (every day a visitor wants to come, every day I get ten letters or more, every day there is an interviewer or a photographer, every day a request for a preface). I had to learn to say NO. It goes against my nature, and I react with depression as I react after anger. It is easier to say yes, but my health, energy and work are in the balance. I have to say no. One interviewer from Toronto pressed the wrong button on her tape recorder and nothing was recorded. When she asked for a second interview, I said no. It is difficult. I have guilt, regrets, I feel ugly and hard! I say "Anaïs, you're changing." I fear hardness, defensiveness. I have always disapproved of these characteristics.

In 1958 I decided that Durrell is a brilliant cheat who does not have a deep knowledge of character. It showed in *Balthazar*, the *soi-disant* psychiatrist. He promised relativity of truth, but that lies in the acceptance of subjectivity, and that means introspection, going inward, and he has not done this.

The deepest disappointment was finding out Durrell does not understand me or my work. But why should he? I ask in 1973. He is superficial and lives in fiction. Like Henry, he invents. He does not *see*. Typical of his lack of art for relationship is the legend of my wealth, which he clings to, and all I can obtain from him is a courteous promise not to embarrass me when he comes to Los Angeles, but he never *hears* what I tell him.

Letter from Hugh Guiler to Anaïs Nin:
New York, December 2, 1973

Darling:

Derrick Knight, my European distributor, writes me that French TV is interested in seeing the film about you. This is a result of my having mentioned the film to Charlotte Poggioli, Pierre Nolot's friend who is in charge of the *IIIème Chaîne* (cultural). But Knight is assuming I was referring to Bob Snyder's film and has written him about it. This was a misunderstanding because the Snyder film was not ready then and I was referring to the film made by the Canadian group in Montreal. Seems to me it would be better for French TV to show the Canadian film, as it is in French and would not require dubbing. Let me know as soon as you can so I can inform Knight. I forgot to ask you about this when you called yesterday.

Too bad you are having rain in California. It has been pretty good weather here, and today was the first day when the house was cold even at 7:30-8:00 AM. They will, of course, blame it all now on the "energy crisis."

I see from the calendar that you are going to Esalen on the 6th so I don't know whether you will get this before that date.

Yass Hakoshima is coming back from Alaska on the 15th, so we will have our first meeting then about the new film.

Also before that date I have to get my last three films into the hands of the American Film Institute in Beverly Hills, and with the mess and delays in the postal service I may have to spend $8 to have them delivered by a private delivery organization.

Love,
Hugo

LOS ANGELES, DECEMBER 1973
Listened to Ira Progoff's cassette on counseling. He stresses that the method of the Intensive Journal unburdens the counselor. He discards "analysis," as if analysis were a purely intellectual, medical formula, when in the hands of Bogner it is the greatest stimulator of growth. She helped me understand the thesis of Nancy Zee, and now we can exchange opinions.

My student is literate and trained in psychology, yet she sees the two hours we spend together on Mondays as a duel—parrying—on her side she is wearing her armor, on mine I am probing, and yet she asked to be delivered of inhibition. She tries to convert me to Hemingway! She had 15 years of Christian Science and is now a Catholic convert!

But the tutoring is effortless because she is sensitive. She is already writing a whole yellow pad every morning. I suggested she show me only what she wants to. She reads certain pages and we analyze them. For example, her *Censor* is a formidable figure—an army and navy! Impossible to dislodge, I said. "Rules are necessary for our own protection!" How to free the writing without going too deep is an interesting challenge. "Examine your fears," I said. She wrote: "I fear becoming sloppy, loose, unstructured, chaotic."

I lectured at Esalen. I lectured at the Kabuki Theatre, stayed at Hotel Miyako in the Japan Center. I love even this pale echo of Japan. 1,100 persons. This time I am seeking the answer to how we deprogram ourselves and find our genuine self. Received poems, flowers, letters, kisses, tears.

I would like to carry this diary to Tahiti on Dec. 21, but it is too heavy a burden to hide! So I start a fresh one for the journey. It is our respite from the burden of Lloyd, Helen, and Leonora (who takes care of Helen), of Eric and his impossible dreams, of letters, lectures, students. My dreams have been heavy and active, but they vanish in the morning. I wrote a preface for Deena Metzger (an act of friendship; her writing is derivative), an article on women and erotica for *Playgirl* (to get Frances Field's drawings included), 400 pages of volume 6. I think when I reach volume 7 I will rest (it is a dialogue with the world).

Tristine was awakened, as I was, by *Lady Chatterley*. We talk openly. She is working on a script for *Cities of the Interior*. The script for *Minotaur* was a disaster. "I tried to modernize it, to make natural dialogue." I suffered so much for the false tones that I could barely read it. "The audience…" "The audience," I said, "one doesn't write for it. You do your work, as I did mine, and the audience comes to you. I did a timeless, poetic work, not a colloquial work. *Women in Love* was faithful to Lawrence. Why can't you be faithful to me?"

Joaquín is retired, traveling.

Hugo is starting a new film—he is interested in video. He is over his big dip into old age. His voice is normal. He is seeing people.

I love to say *no* to the colleges who ask me to lecture.

Letter from Anaïs Nin to Joaquín Nin-Culmell:
Los Angeles, December 14, 1973

Dear Cuchi:
I meant to send you my itinerary, but doing 20 pages a day on vol. 6 took all the writing out of me. Now I'm writing because you may call up when you return and won't find me in and may worry. On December 21 I leave for Tahiti on a magazine assignment of ten days in all. I will be back January 2 and will call you up then.

I do hope your trip made you happy. It was strange to go and speak at Esalen and to not stay at your home. I flew back the next morning. I did like staying at the Japan Center, because my lecture was next door at the Kabuki theatre, but I could not get into the restaurants, the movie house or the shops as they opened at 10:00 AM and I had to leave the hotel at 9:45. I have done fewer lectures, about one or two a month. 250,000 diaries were sold. Vol. 5 will be out in April 1974.

I hope you find Thor in good health.

Hugo is better. He went through a real low, a *coup de vieillesse*, which frightened me. But he seems to have recovered. He is starting a new film Dec. 15.

I wonder where we will meet next. January 6 I have to go to N.Y. by way of Kalamazoo, where, believe it or not, I have a godchild named Anaïs.

The country is in a worse mess than it was. It will be good to get away even for ten days.

A violinist came to play, who was once your student. She loved studying with you. She was there about four years ago, so you may not remember her. Six feet tall, plain but nice. We still have quartets once a week.

I was in Tahiti before, but stayed at Club Mediterranean, which meant staying in the island of Moorea and not seeing Tahiti itself. And it was winter there and not always as warm as I like it. In Moorea there was also a strong current that could carry you out to sea, which I feared, and I hope I won't find that. Also, if you boated and fell in, the coral was wounding and even poisonous. But it was utterly beautiful.

Your trip must have been hectic as I did not get my usual postcard. I miss hearing from you.

Much love and wishes for a free and successful New Year.

Anaïs

Letter from Anaïs Nin to Hugh Guiler:
Los Angeles, December 14, 1973

Darling:

I hope you find a way to get your films to Washington. I do feel Trew Bennett, as she should be coming for a pottery exhibit in N.Y., would be glad to help you. She admires your work and wanted a copper plate. She made the bowl you eat your cereal in. It would only be a matter of getting help to load and unload at the other end.

My one student is a delight—sensitive with a background in psychology so my method for healing her inhibitions, half-psychology, is working beautifully. Tomorrow I see my second one for an interview. She begins next year. I already have received $750.

Tahiti will be a rest. I will call you before leaving and as soon as I return as I have to visit several islands and will not know where I stay long enough for a letter. Trips are made by boat, so they won't be tiring.

I sent you my small massage pillow as I no longer get massages. The Belgian ladies are too old. I included the pillowcases they made for it.

I went to Snyder's sound studio to re-record the narration, which was ruined by bad background sound (the rain was too loud at the beginning, traffic noises that I couldn't hear but which the sound equipment picked up). It is hard to lip synch. I have to wear earphones and repeat my own words in the exact timing. Three hours of work.

I will ask you over the telephone if you want for Xmas a complete Sony set of a video camera, recorder, etc., which I saw carried about in a metal trunk by two girls. $1,500, I understand. Would you like that? (It may be more now. A Japanese diary book I once bought for $5 now costs me $10.) Would that fulfill your new experimental needs?

It made me sad that you said you wished you could get away for Xmas. But you never have. Could you do it now? Is it a matter of money? I am sending you this check because I know Xmas is a heavy expense for you. If you can get away, I will finance you.

On January 4th I do a video interview for cassette distributors and then I'll be returning Sunday the 6th. I'm reserving my seat now as you advised.

Keep well. Your voice sounds normal again.

Love,
Anaïs

Letter from Hugh Guiler to Anaïs Nin:
New York, December 17, 1973

Darling:

I don't know whether this will reach you before you leave for Tahiti, but just wanted to let you know that I will be thinking of you and imagining the lovely places and people you will be seeing. American Express is very smart to choose you to write about such places.

Hakoshima is coming day after tomorrow to discuss the new film with Bob Hanson and me. I have quite enough money to carry the Ian Hugo expenses at least until you return.

Bogner and [her husband] Martin are coming to dine with me at Alfredo's on Thursday and will come to see *Transmigration* afterwards.

We are having a real bad snowstorm here. Walking in the streets is difficult and I am glad you are escaping all this, as well as the horrible "spirit of Xmas."

I came across the enclosed review of a new biography of Colette, who I know has always fascinated you.

All my love goes with you,
Hugo

Letter from Anaïs Nin to Dolores Brandon:
Tahiti, December 26, 1973

Dear Dolores:

I brought your beautiful letter with me to Tahiti, hoping to have more space in which to answer, for you put your finger on a painful conflict—that when a work becomes universal, the love I have of intimacy, the time for my friendships, is threatened. It is ironic that this abundance is dangerous for deep living. I am struggling with the conflict. For example, I see you, hear you, become aware of someone I want to give time and attention to, and I am swept away by a tidal wave of activity! So I feel as cheated as you do, and unable to even be angry! The women have made me a symbol. I have cut down on the lectures. Friends put pressure on me: Ira Progoff teaches the Intensive Journal and wants me to talk with him at the New School. I'm to help women writers through NOW—I'm not by nature a public figure. I hope this never happens to you as an actress. I will be in New York Jan. 6 to the end of January. Send me your telephone number and we may find a quiet moment. I also feel I could help you with college bookings. We'll talk about that.

    Anaïs

LOS ANGELES, JANUARY 1974

Between Dec. 21 and 31 I wrote another small red diary on Tahiti. I couldn't carry this one around.

Tahiti and *satori*: Ecstasy and oneness with nature. I can add that to my life-giving adventures, along with Puerto Vallarta.

JANUARY 6, 1974

Flight to New York.

NEW YORK, JANUARY 6, 1974

A woman writes me: "How do you deal with aging?"

Answer: "I wish we could talk about aging. I was more concerned about aging at 30 and 40 than now at 70. Because I found that if you live deeply, remain emotionally alive, curious, explorative, open to change, to new experiences, aging recedes. It is not chronological, it is psychic. I was against the depressing acceptance of chronology by Simone de Beauvoir. Bow to age, she says. I say transcend it. I'm able to write all day, to swim, to lecture, to travel. Of course, I had to learn my energy was not infinite, but only this year. I think the youthful spirit wins over the face and body. You look beautiful and interesting in your photograph. Free yourself of the false mark of aging: it is merely a moment of tiredness."

NEW YORK, JANUARY 9, 1974

For months now I have been bleeding, like a light menstruation. It has worried me. The fear of recurrence of cancer is there. So today I am having an examination by Dr. Trotter and Dr. Parks in the same Presbyterian Hospital where I had the radiology treatment. Recurrence of bad weather—the same dismal rain and snow, the same long, ugly taxi ride. America has a gift for creating the ugliest environment; the speedway is lined with discarded cars, the hospital is unspeakably ugly, the cafeteria is a manger for animals, with cardboard trays, paper cups and the pile of discard next to where you eat. I wait in rooms which could be a set for *The Exit*.

I told students how I dealt with a grim situation by inventing an internal "film" during radiology—as an example of transcending experience.

Today I sit in transcendence, waiting. I have a cold. The days with Hugo are uniformly dismal. He always tells me the bad news. If I talk he tells me I am "analyzing" him. He eludes every subject by saying: "I will work it out with Bogner." He is a living symbol of the failure of psychoanalysis as I am of its effectiveness. He is childishly dependent on Bogner. He is obsessed and completely self-absorbed. When our accountant Boulogne tells us I can support Hugo but his films cannot, Hugo goes into a depression. Yet I cannot do more than I do. I had to slow down on the lectures.

Dr. Trotter and Dr. Parks are not alarmed. I asked if I had anything bad. They said no. Dr. Parks will make a test. Nothing for the eye to see. I came back in the slush, snow, rain, not entirely reassured. What does the bleeding mean?

NEW YORK, JANUARY 11, 1974

Dr. Trotter and Dr. Parks give me a test at Presbyterian Hospital.

NEW YORK, JANUARY 14, 1974

A happy dream at last! It took place in a room entirely decorated by a collage of bits of colored clothes, young women in colorful, happy dresses, and I was also in colorful Indian cottons—an atmosphere of color and warmth of texture. Nothing happened.

But this came after several grey days with a cold—the loss of my voice—pill-laden—coughing—sleeping badly, and Rupert ill too so that we telephoned each other two or three times a day—the same cold that hovered over us before leaving for Tahiti, left us at Tahiti, but pounced on us as soon as he went back to school and I to New York. Psychosomatic?

I don't earn enough to support Hugo at $20,000 or $25,000 a year, not including his filmmaking! Boulogne is there to give me what remains after taxes.

Hugo says saving money is a *negative* way of living! He now dreams of a trip to France (for speculation again) to retrieve his disappearing accounts. He trusted the wrong men. He mistrusted the best advisor in his own firm. He enslaved himself to two cynical men, John Chase and René de Chochor. They let him down. Because of them, he lost his best accounts. A change of apartment is impractical: he needs a movie studio and would have to rent one besides the apartment. He is rooted in his comforts—the best grocer, the best wines, massages, a maid three hours a day, his shirts ironed "by hand"!

I cannot work more than I do!

But the dream I had. What does it mean? It was all color—like Varda's life.

I don't need Bogner. I don't know how to say it. My loyalty to her is unmoved. But I despise Hugo's total dependency on her. She is the only one who knows him. How can you live with someone who is never open? And if he does open, it is only to say: "I am ashamed of all the mistakes I made." He has not gone very far in terms of growth. Just guilt. He has had continuous care. I can't talk with him. He turns it against himself. He is completely self-absorbed. *Nobody* exists warmly, except Bogner.

In the early stages of our marriage I joked about the lizard under the rock. Hugo was the lizard I had to lure out of his cave. I was patient with his inarticulateness, his indecisions about the most trivial things. Today I am appalled by his dependencies:

Noel as financial advisor (proved wrong).

Augula as legal advisor (brilliant father to a less brilliant son).

Boulogne who complains that he asks advice about everything.

Bogner. When she is away on vacation, he becomes unstable.

Me when I'm here.

But why should I not detach myself from him? There is no love. Only compassion. When he reads what I wrote about my mother's death, he sobs halfway through. He does not know why.

He says he has not expressed his love for me.

I never show him the new Diary anymore. We have nothing in common.

Anaïs Nin and Sharon Spencer, New York, 1970s

NEW YORK, JANUARY 15, 1974

The helplessness engendered in woman by the married state and the man providing may be the ruin of her life. I had no courage to leave Hugo when I should have because I felt helpless and frightened of life. This debt of protectiveness is what I am paying back. He never refused me anything, so I feel I cannot refuse him anything. When I wanted so badly that Jean-Gabriel Albicocco should film *A Spy in the House of Love*, Hugo gambled $2,000 or $3,000 for a script that had to be thrown away. His indulgence was infinite.

But now the conflict is different.

He was spoiled by his comfortable family, by his expense account, by his own *grand seigneur* needs of the best clothes and the best restaurants. So now I cannot support him, Boulogne tells me. My own expenses are half of his.

Talk with Sharon over the telephone: She looks 30, is youthful, laughs like a schoolgirl—almost exaggeratedly feminine before I sent her to Bogner—playing at being a schoolgirl rather than the brilliant scholar and teacher. Her book is dazzling. Now she tells me she finds it hard to accept her maturity (at 40).

She and I repudiated the homely role of liberated women. She dresses exquisitely. In fact, she is the only woman who wore a dress I hungered for. She loaned it to me. Because I know what it meant and because it was done to me so much, I knew they hoped to become me as I hoped to look like Sharon as she looked on the day of my doctorate at Philadelphia. Voodoo. The dress arrived from the cleaners with the elasticized waistline loosened, so I had to give it to a dressmaker who kept it for three months, and finally it hangs in my closet, never worn by me! Was it because I was ashamed of wanting to be Sharon the beauty? She has a delicate face, big eyes, finely designed features, a delicate, long neck, and her expression is seductive, lively, playful. She is slender. Her voice is light.

The whim passed. I'm back into acceptance of myself, of my age, which surprises everyone. Why should it have taken so long to gain in confidence, in decisiveness, in consolidation?

Pamela Fiori, a friend of Sharon. Immediate sympathy. She is now Senior Editor at *Travel & Leisure*. She sent me to Fez. She keeps recommending me. She likes the *Diaries*. She is a Piscean and twice we appeared with the same dress, hers the short version, mine the long—we laughed. We call her lover Scorpio. He is English. His *noli mi tangere*. His artificial talk. Insulation. I didn't like him. I didn't like Lauren Frost picking the English writers to adapt the *Diary* for the stage—a conventional play, when it should be impressionistic. For once Gunther and I agree. They are on the wrong track.

Mrs. Ruddy is also on the wrong track. "The book needs more action."

And Henry Jaglom is nowhere. Tristine can't work without his response, so she is ready to quit and accept a teaching job. I sent him a beautiful Japanese diary book. No answer. I put my faith in him.

Tristine identifies with my characters to the point of losing herself. She becomes each one as she writes. But she is apprehensive, suspicious. She *is* one of my characters. She has a lover who adores her, yet she is restless. She sees one of the best analysts, and she boasts of confusing him. Compared with Bogner, they all seen inadequate. Tristine's alternatives are not fatal. If she teaches, she can still work on scripts. Her lover is willing to support her.

In one day I received flowers from Sharon, from Barbette Blockington, from Beatrice Harris, from Dolores Brandon, from an anonymous girl.

Tomorrow I can have my discussion at the YMHA with Nancy Milford because Dr. Parks could not get a hospital room for my test. I'm in his office now.

Did I mention the letter from the Institute of Arts and Letters? A second honor.

Rupert is so loving—planning our trip to Bali this summer—and sends me a calendar for the hospital room. "Do you want me to come visit you?"

"No, I feel humiliated when I'm ill. I'd rather hide."

We talk every night—sometimes twice a day. It is my only luxury. I don't go to the movies, the theatre, and the only books I buy are at Marlborough's at $.40 or $1. So Rupert is my luxury. I can hear Piccolino tugging at his sock to draw his attention away from the phone.

I would like to write Hugo's history. Only one person knows Hugo well and that is Bogner. But she is so vigilant, so ethical in not sharing her knowledge—as if she knew *neither* of us.

NEW YORK, JANUARY 18, 1974

Test made. Yes, there is something brewing. I have to go to the hospital for four days for the painful insertion of a radium bullet.

A relaxed, trusting, tender friendship with John Ferrone. His is a firm editor, but also devoted and fair. He has a most difficult relationship with his partner Johan, who is super-neurotic, obsessed with his past in Africa, unadapted to America. He raves and rants as I once did on the subject of America and made both Hugo and Rupert unhappy. They suffer when I say I blame America because it *taught* other countries its materialism, but now that it has led to a total corruption. I don't say anything because Americans are unhappy, anxious, confused. The price they paid for the deification of money is very high. Now led by a gangster government, they are out of jobs, out of luxuries, gouged and exploited. I feel compassion even though the cause of it all was greed.

NEW YORK, JANUARY 19, 1974

Dr. Parks tells me I have recurrence of cancer; I see René de Chochor; dinner at John Ferrone's.

NEW YORK, JANUARY 23, 1974

Last night I talked with Nancy Milford at the YMHA. I admired her biography *Zelda* and had hoped for a deeper talk, but she was rather conventional, though pleasant.

I wanted to discuss the possibilities of Zelda having been able to publish her diary (Fitzgerald said no, he needed it for his work), to continue it, and that if she had not been suppressed as a writer she might not have gone mad. Fitzgerald used her letters, used her as a character, signed his name to her stories.

Also, we almost got into the "retaliation" I would have suffered if I had been explicit about sex. Many themes occurred to me, which Milford snuffed out. I asked her if she did not think we should eliminate *all* taboos. She hesitated. It was not an in-depth talk and not cohesive. Women always bring up children and husbands as obstacles to creation. I told about the thousands of people whose lives and work I watch over and still do my work. It is the equivalent of motherhood. I spoke of the need for continuity and for romantic intermittences.

Preparation for the hospital.

NEW YORK, JANUARY 24, 1974

Entered hospital at 2:00 PM.

New York, January 25, 1974
Implant of radium.

New York, January 26, 1974
Knocked out by anesthesia. Implant removed.

New York, January 27, 1974
Home.

February 2-3, 1974
Return to Los Angeles. Convalescence.

Los Angeles, February 4, 1974
Came home Friday.

I had planned all kinds of activities during the four days at the hospital, to read into the Sony cassette recorder, to write in John Ferrone's Japanese diary that he gave me, to read six books. But the anesthesia diffused and weakened me. For four days I was a more or less an inanimate object.

The hateful, harsh winter outside. The kindness of my friends. Flowers.

Several telephone calls a day to Rupert, who usually thinks of economy—but this time he wanted to hear my voice.

A doctor wrote me an anonymous note of admiration.

I had to cancel several lectures and an appearance at Town Hall for Viveca Lindfors' play.

On Friday I managed to pack, sent baggage by freight, arrived in L.A., turned up my nose at the wheelchair Rupert offered me! He took over the care of me, was tender and attentive. This morning at 5:30 AM we awakened. I hate to awaken at night because of the suspended living in the silence and dark. It is then I feel the *passage of time*, and only then I feel the course of time as a precipitation toward death.

Hugo broke my heart once more by confessing how much guilt, how many self-defeating self-lacerations he has—he is very ill. He wept at my description of my mother's death because he did not express his "love for me." I spent an evening reminding him of his gay and giving side—his Spanish dancing with me, his goodness to my mother, his generosity—but Bogner does not think that is a way to cure self-punishment. He considers himself a failure (money-making being his only standard—the films don't count). We are hopelessly estranged.

If he had been like Rupert would I have given him my *whole* love? But it was because he was not like Rupert that he lost my love. His broodings, his depressions, his worries afflict me. I cannot lighten his mood.

My student was afraid of my lucidity. I convinced her she had as much of that as I and that we were like two scientists working at the same problem: to free her writing. My insight had no other purpose.

Renate Druks asks my secret. I never accept being pinned down by a catastrophe. I think of the future. I *displace* myself. In the hospital I thought constantly of Bali, where Rupert and I want to go this summer. My imagination takes me away from the eye of the cyclone.

I found that Isak Dinesen said exactly the same thing about the power of the *tale* to deliver us from life.

People are amazed that I could talk at the YWHA Poetry Center the night before going to the hospital. But that is what saves me. I am not enslaved, possessed by what strikes me.

Letter from Gunther Stuhlmann to Anaïs Nin:
New York, February 11, 1974

Dear Anaïs:

Enclosed the Harcourt contract for *Diary 6*, with the payment schedule we had discussed, which should give us plenty of time. If it meets with your approval, would you please sign and return both copies to me? I'll then collect the first money due.

No word yet from Swallow. I sent them another friendly reminder the other day. Will keep you posted.

Was glad to hear you are gaining your strength back when I spoke to you. I was surprised that Marie-Claire Van der Elst had not acknowledged the receipt of the final corrected proofs, which went to her in early January by airmail. She would be making all the corrections!

Love,
Gunther

Letter from Hugh Guiler to Anaïs Nin:
New York, February 13, 1974

Darling:

Today got your letter of the 10th and am so glad you are recovering quickly. It was also nice to read Pat Cool's letter and I will try to have him see more of the films soon. I am trying to straighten out your Medicare and this is so far the result:

1. Dr. Parks has received your check and letter, and his secretary is mailing the Medicare form.

2. Columbia Presbyterian Medical Center—I called them and ascertained that the $27 was for Trotter's visit to you. But this will be included in the hospital's total bill, which you will receive later. The total is $1,685.06. Of this Medicare will pay $1,390 and Blue Cross $84. You signed the forms, and they have or will send them on directly. This leaves $295.06, which you should pay to the hospital when they bill you. So there is nothing to do yet. Roger also "gave up" on them (because of the confusion of banks, etc.) and asked me to take over, as I have done. There will still be something to collect from the Guardian Life Insurance Co. for Straten's Major Medical group policy, which also covers you. So be sure to send me copies of all receipted bills and any Medicare payments you receive; but that will take time.

I forgot to tell you that Olga has been away sick for the past ten days, so I have been taking care of the apartment and have a better idea of what the cooking involves—also prices. I am now convinced it could be a saving to shop for groceries and probably also meats, at Grand Union. The difference is at least 10%.

Hope you got the "biofeedback" book I sent you. Dr. Bogner may make it possible for me to experiment with it. I am intrigued by anything that is visual and

moves!
　　All my love,
　　Hugo

Letter from Gunther Stuhlmann to Anaïs Nin:
New York, February 18, 1974

Dear Anaïs:
　　As per my letter of Feb. 15, here is our check for $5,573.59 for the royalties from Swallow to July 1973, which finally came in. The total came to $4,624.21 on all titles plus $1,845 on the Nin *Reader*, from which 15% went to Phil Jason as per your agreement with him. The *Reader* sold over two thousand copies in the first period, which is not a bad start.
　　Two copies of the Dutch contract for *Diary 2* are on the way, and if they are agreeable to you—they did poorly so far with vol. 1 and want to pay $500 instead of the previous $750—would you sign initial both copies and return them to me.
　　Love,
　　Gunther
P.S. I am in for some six months of heavy dental work it seems...source of the neuralgia!

LOS ANGELES, FEBRUARY 18, 1974
　　Rupert's birthday.
　　Half awake, I practice the meditation Dr. Harold Stone came to teach me yesterday. I met him in Berkeley years ago for a few minutes, and I trusted him instantly. Sent him my troubled friends. Talked to his future therapists. Upbraided him for charging Tristine $40 for a 50-minute session, and he excused it by saying he was putting all his money and energy in the Center for Healing. When he heard I had a recurrence of cancer, and the way I spoke of the burdens I was trapped in, he came immediately.
　　My method of fighting negative happenings: to move my attention upon the positive; displace my attention (away from the hospital, the series of depressing scrutiny, to our project to see Bali this summer). He believes I must visualize the cancer. I will transcribe what we talked about and subject of meditation.

1st meditation
　　Vision of dark spot—burnt, dead.
　　Vision of white angel wings, or clouds.
　　Remembrance of wondering if illness was a punishment for being a pleasure-loving woman.
　　Vision of white spreading out over the black; gold light coming over whole scene; light box.
　　Impression that the black spot is dead, the cancer cells not active, halted by the radium.
　　White cells and cancer cells struggle between light and darkness.

Conscious:
1. Voice of responsibility as a child of nine who wanted to run an orphan

asylum.

2. I feel I have to give the gift of love of life to everyone.

3. Anyone in trouble has a claim on me.

Voice of pleasure-loving Anaïs:

1. I love travel; tropics; a real nature woman; wants to do nothing.

2. Always overruled by sense of responsibility (giving the family addresses when I travel).

3. Loved the assignment to travel because it gave me permission to enjoy.

2nd meditation

The cancer is the volcanic crater I saw in Hawaii—I hated it. Black and smoky, smelling of sulfur. I wanted all the beautiful young women who love me—Tristine Rainer, Lee Potts, Christie Logan, Sharon Spencer, and all the young men who embraced me—Danny Selznick and many others—to come. They filled the crater with water, and it was a beautiful crater lake; we all swam in it and the sulfur-smelling devil was drowned.

3rd meditation

The black is covered by a snowstorm in a crystal ball I played with—representing a castle. When you shook it, the snowstorm covered it.

Spent a long time dressing for my Spanish dance—half-rehearsing. Thought was that it was a *strong* dance. But at the last minute, as I take the first bold step, there is no music.

Awakened.

Los Angeles, February 19, 1974

Meditation: All the white subjects in the world: snow, sugar, flour, cream, white lilies, clouds, white cells, white rice, white tapioca, white crystals, white smoke, white mint candy, white cotton, all beckoned by me. They illuminate the dark, rotten spot in the peach. I take a knife and cut it out.

John Pearson came to choose photographs for a book. My student Mrs. Osborne came. I am tired, but not abnormally.

Dartmouth will give me a doctorate June 9. On the same day Scripps College wants me to speak at their commencement. Pleasure-loving Anaïs chose Dartmouth, and Scripps understood. "Of course, you have to go get your doctorate."

Dr. Stone admitted it would be a pity to *cut* off my correspondence completely. What he taught me was that it was not enough to combat the destructive forces by moving *into* a positive area (in one hospital the desire to see the Yucatan sustained me; in the last, images of Bali). The *killer* in one's self must be met. You have to confront the evil. I have never done that. My magic was to *move*. He insists on changing the way of life that harms you.

Rupert has been incredible. Giving of his energy. Taking care of me. I let him protect me.

Encounter with Durrell, who is here to teach a seminar: I had forgotten how he parries off with humor—how he talks to be amusing, not out of feeling. He has no sense of the reality of others. He lives in his intellectual Buckminster Fuller domes.

LOS ANGELES, FEBRUARY 21, 1974

Meditation: No more angel wings. Tennis balls with knives attacking cancer, which looks like caviar eggs!

Letter from Hugh Guiler to Anaïs Nin:
New York, February 22, 1974

Darling:

I had been hoping to get a call from you after the birthday message I asked Millicent to give you through her daughter, but I imagine you were planning to call me over the weekend.

Monday evening, a little after six, I had a bad nosebleed. After trying unsuccessfully to stop it myself I tried to call Dr. Lehmann but he was out. So I called Jennie and she came over at once (after she had just returned from a tiring trip to Maine). She also could not stop the bleeding and I had her call Dr. Duane's substitute, who recommended I go at once to the emergency ward of St. Vincent's Hospital, which I did with Jennie in a taxi. Here they succeeded, after some time, in plugging it up, and I was out in about 1½ hour. Since then Lehmann has been seeing me every day at his office and today pronounced me OK. But at his suggestion I have not been to the office all week. Frances reminded me that I had this when we were all seeing a Buñuel film. And I did have a slight nosebleed a couple weeks ago at the office, but I was able to take care of it quickly after calling Lehmann.

Anyhow, Bogner said I had handled the situation exactly as I should have.

The good thing is that I have had the time to finish reading the 5th volume of your *Diary* and I think it is the best of all. As I see it, it is the odyssey of one who steers her own course with courage and a determination that is greater than all obstacles, including her feeling that the rejection of the work is a rejection of herself. It is a kind of Road of the Cross but which gives the feeling from the beginning that the resurrection is inevitable—that you would, in the end, prevail, which you do. It is also a triumph of your use of analysis, and Bogner will be very pleased. I was also particularly impressed with how you worked out of LSD, showing how much more lasting a creation you could make as an artist, how you had already gone beyond the need for a drug, and the beautiful, poetic final paragraph, which is a plan for life and the living of experience rather than merely observing.

Actually, I think the U.S.A. is ready now, even in the world of politics and economics, to receive your message, and I can assure you that I see evidence of this every day in the questions that are arising in the minds of those whom you have considered most alien and remote to you, only they have to come to it in their own way, and the book on "biofeedback" I sent you is a sure sign that something like that is happening, helped by the approach to real suffering. I was also struck by your ability to transform so many people and things around you to reveal "faces behind the façades" of people like Jim Herlihy, the Barrons, the Ruggles.

I confess it was painful for me to read that you looked back on your life, up to a certain point, as hell, and I recognize that the tension of my business life contributed to that, but your recent letters helped me to understand how you have come to put even that in the kind of perspective that only love could attain. That was the side of me that was the most difficult for you to understand, because it was associated with all that was most alien to you.

I believe I have made a parallel effort, and my admiration for vol. 5, with its revelations of all *your* other sides and all your beautiful life apart from me, is something that I can only now express sincerely, with the help of your efforts to assure me that I have contributed, by liberating you, to the flowering of your human life, even more than of your art. The truth may be that we have created that *together.*

All my love,

Hugo

Letter from Hugh Guiler to Anaïs Nin:
New York, February 24, 1974

Darling:

I just want to give you the good news. I got a telephone call tonight from the American Film Institute that I have been awarded a grant I applied for—over $7,500. The first payment of $5,000 comes on March 15. Now I have to hear from Studio 46, which will determine whether I can use their equipment and technicians, but perhaps this news will help. If they don't come through then I have told Bob that we will have to make it on regular film using my present equipment. He was very pleased at the news and promised to think about how we would do it on regular film if we have to—perhaps by modifying the script a little.

I told John Ferrone I would like to have him to dinner sometime if he likes curried shrimp, which he said he does. I did not mention Johan but I suppose I should include him. Do you agree? Have also written to Myrna Greenfield to have a letter ready for Pat Cool. Also spoke, as I wrote you, to Lauren Frost and she wants also to see the films.

I am particularly glad to receive the grant because it means I will not have to drain your finances.

John said my interpretation of vol. 5 is very close to what he has in mind for the "blurb"—particularly what I said about the "odyssey" and the "Road of the Cross."

Love, love,

Hugo

P.S. I forgot to tell you I was very happy at the news that you have received $10,000 from the Swallow Press. Congratulations.

Los Angeles, February 27, 1974
I oil Rupert's skin cancer on his temple.

Letter from Gunther Stuhlmann to Anaïs Nin:
New York, March 1, 1974

Dear Anaïs:

André Bay has not answered any of my letters for the past three or four months. When I airmailed a set of final galleys to Marie-Claire I naturally assumed that after she had made the necessary corrections she would pass this set on to Stock. There was no sense in sending André a set of English-language galleys when he was getting the translation from Marie-Claire. Have you, by the way, heard from her? She did not acknowledge receipt to me.

I sent you a book under separate cover with a note about a possible introduction from you. Let me know.

I thought the offer from Harcourt for the photo book was rather niggardly— what is the use of doing the book unless you get a financial return on it? Maybe they will improve their offer. Let me have your thoughts.

Love,
Gunther

LOS ANGELES, MARCH 3, 1974

Meditation: I am Joan of Arc in a battle dress, on a horse, with a lance, attacking masses of locusts and bees (cancer?).

Dr. Stone stirred up my angers, which awakened me at 5:30 AM. He believed there must be a lot of hidden anger at the way people use me. Anger at Gore Vidal's vicious lies. At the lawyers who charged me an outrageous price for a copyright consultation: $700. Anger at demands: read my poetry, read my novel, read my essay, give us a comment on this book. Then, while working on the year 1959, I came upon such a masochistic episode that I was shocked: I had a terrible cold. Tana de Gamez called up and said: "I must come over. I have just divorced my husband and I'm leaving for Portugal." I protested *feebly.* She came. She talked to me for two hours. I finally went to bed. I awakened at 4:00 AM with earthquaky chills and a 104-degree fever. I could not get a doctor, only the answering service. Jacobson came at dawn and said I had pneumonia. When I got to the hospital I was told it was double pneumonia. The cold started from my giving Olympia Henderson my heavy winter coat. Suicidal? Olympia was a minor friend. She was a disturbed young woman who wanted to write and we exchanged my writing lessons for her typing the Diaries. Under the influence of LSD, she wanted a trip to New York. Everyone was appalled at my sponsoring her. She lost her nerve and became a frightened child. Wearing my ruby-red fake fur coat seemed to give her strength. And she kept it.

Worked on volume 6 from eight to ten. My secretary Mary Morris came and we worked at correspondence for three hours. Monday at ten my student comes. Other days my second student, Barbara Kraft.

Why did Varèse, who mocked psychology and all reference to the uncon-scious, turn to *House of Incest* for his last work? Why did Durrell at 28 believe me when I advised him against writing a diary? He thought it was a profound remark: "Life only became real when I wrote about it." Today that sounds like nonsense. The present is real. That is why I wrote less in the Diary. I talked to Rupert. I wrote letters. I confided to young women.

Letter from Anaïs Nin to Gunther Stuhlmann:
Los Angeles, March 5, 1974

Dear Gunther:

It is strange that Marie-Claire should not acknowledge galleys or tell André that she had them, but nothing from them surprises me. She wrote me only recently that she made all the corrections.

I have not yet received the book for which you want an introduction. If it was a translation from the French, I could not do it. It is not worth sponsoring.

If anything happens to me, you will receive by air freight a valise of diary manuscripts to be put back in the vault (the ones I am using for vol. 6). It has a lock, number 215. I left instructions. The same with my briefcase, lock number 254.

Now we have another ticklish subject. USC is presenting a performance of *Collages*. The same one done at Purdue by the same director, Christie Logan, who is getting her B.A. It will be done the 26th of March through the 29th. Students will pay one dollar for the hall and lights. No one is getting paid. You told me you just needed to know. We all hope it is good enough to be taken up by Vanguard Theatre here in L.A. If so, then it will be another matter of proper contracts. But we have not reached that point yet.

Do you remember the anthology of women's poems for which I wrote a preface, which they at first criticized and then accepted? Did they ever pay for that preface? The book is out and was received by Nona Balakian. Laura Chester was the editor. I sent an inquiry, but it was returned. If you do not remember do give a call to Nona. I can't lay my hands on her review. I should have received a copy of the book, no?

Can you lend me a copy of *Diary 1* in French? Durrell's wife is French and wants to read it. I have to order vol. 1 and I will order two copies for both of us.

Hope the teeth are not making you suffer too much.

Anaïs

Letter from Anaïs Nin to Hugh Guiler:
Los Angeles, March 6, 1974

Darling:

I keep getting this small bill from the hospital, and since they allowed me Medicare on the big one and I only paid something like $250 (I sent you the check or Boulogne, not sure), I feel I should pay it. Medicare is working smoothly. I received a $135 check on Bogner's bills, and was credited at the hospital, all in the name of Nin. With a push from you it seems to be working very smoothly. But I don't want you to take that on. Also, why, since I gave the postman money to forward mail, does so much of it come addressed by you? I want to unburden you, not burden you. I have had to take help for my correspondence, two mornings a week. But have been able to work all day. Very rarely in the evening.

If you have a chance, see *Don't Look Now*, a poor melodrama, but so wonderfully photographed and directed that one forgives the story, and it all happens in Venice, which is used to create fear and anxiety. Worth seeing only for photography and directing.

I am not pleased with the photo book. John won't use the photos in the *Diaries*, which are selected as the best, and he is using second choices just to be different, whereas I feel people want the *Diary* photos. Also, it is not a complete biography, and steals a little from future *Diaries*.

But it will be cheap, $1.75 in paperback.

I work every day at vol. 6. I have my two students (two hours a week), answer letters I have to answer. I hope you are feeling less tired after the loss of blood.

Anaïs

Letter from Anaïs Nin to Gunther Stuhlmann:
Los Angeles, March 8, 1974

Dear Gunther:

As you felt it necessary to remind John Ferrone of our contract on editing the *Diaries*, I would like to see a copy of it. I want to be sure it covers only *published* diaries, and not the ones in the vault, which I could not edit myself if not given time. It is the only contract I ever signed without reading it because it was yours. But I want to feel clear about everything. It includes a lot of things which later on I had cause to regret, even getting a percentage on every fragment reprinted; I need to have peace of mind about all that since I am flirting so often with death. You know, I still feel it was not quite right that, having edited the *Diary* in English, you should also have an editing fee on all translations. But I know that is in the contract. Please send me a copy. Also, did you give me a copy of the first Trust we made with expensive lawyers? I would like to know that no copies of that double-talk trust are extant. I paid the $500 very reluctantly, as I do not believe they spent all that time on copyright. In that case you did all the research, if I remember. But it's done. I just have to be more careful. Help me set all this in order. Rupert has to know our contracts too.

It worried me that you considered a book of photographs as part of the *Diaries*, as most of them are not even in them. We have to make everything clear.

Anaïs

Letter from Anaïs Nin to John Ferrone:
Los Angeles, March 8, 1974

Dear John:

Please consider this angle: When I talked to my devoted young readers who only own the paperbacks, they were extremely disappointed they were not going to be able to have the *same* photographs as in the hardbacks. Those who have seen them in libraries, or bookshops, would like to have them. Please remember this, as these are my devoted followers who will rush and buy the photograph book as they cannot afford the hardback diaries. I think having the photos from the original diaries is a selling point.

I read your letter yesterday with pleasure. You seemed so much in harmony with us here during your visit.

I asked Gunther for a copy of the contract I signed. I want to be sure it does not include the unpublished diaries I may not have time to edit.

I wonder why Gunther should consider the photographs as part of diary editing, don't you?

I love the new brochure. It is very well done. Only one mistake escaped us all, the usual one, of Frank Lloyd Wright instead of Lloyd Wright. It will upset Lloyd, but it is not inside *Diary 5*. Very important to see the book.

I'm up to page 450 of vol. 6. New themes. New characters.

Sunday we fly to listen to what George Barati composed to accompany my text for the 200th anniversary of the U.S.A.

Anaïs

Letter from Henry Miller to Anaïs Nin:
Pacific Palisades, Friday, March 8, 1974

Dear Anaïs:

I immediately wrote the UCLA library not to let Jay Martin have access to anything. I also wrote Martin *again*, telling him, or reminding him, that I never authorized him to do my biography, that I had in fact told him to his face and written him several times that I did not want him or anyone else to do my biography, at least while I'm alive. After I'm dead anyone can do as he pleases. I can't control from beyond.

If I discover what publisher he is writing for, I will write the publisher. But I'd rather let it be known that I want no biographer at all!

I *may* have a photo of Moricand—will ask my assistant to look. Save for "us." But I feel dubious. When and where, for example, would such photos have been taken? Most everything prior to last ten years has gone to the UCLA library. We'll see.

Cheers!
Henry

Letter from Anaïs Nin to Hugh Guiler:
Los Angeles, March 11, 1974

Darling:

I guess I did not make it clear that when I lectured at Santa Cruz I met a couple (she gave me the sun and moon copper necklace which you saw me wear); he is George Barati, a Hungarian composer and orchestra conductor. Ruth is devoted to my work. They decided right then and there to do a cantata or opera on a text of mine. I have heard his recordings. They are classical, not modern, but good. So after much postponing and waiting for me to feel well enough, I flew 50 minutes yesterday to their Montalvo Music Institute (which he directs) and listened to the first ten minutes of the opera. Unfortunately, as you know, I detest operatic women's voices. She was Italian and sang hard and tough enough for five opera houses. Not right for my text (mostly out of *House of Incest*). So I am disappointed. Also, one could not understand one word of the text. George thinks she can sing more quietly, but diction is another thing. They seem to be close friends so there is nothing I can do. Fortunately it will not be done in Washington, as I thought, for the bicentennial, but around here, and so it won't create much attention. They will have to print the text for people to read. That was one of the things I had to do here. On Wednesday I go to Cal Tech with Durrell to discuss D. H. Lawrence for an hour, as he is leaving March 23. The 26th I go to San Francisco to present Henry Jaglom's film and coax them to have a program of yours. Return the same day. Then the performance of *Collages* at University of Southern California on March 27. Next, on April 7, the big woman's festival at San Francisco for which I am paid $1,500 and a flight to New York. It has been a long time away, but you can see I had a lot to do, and in order not to get overtired I had to space it properly.

I worked on vol. 6 too.

I swim five laps every day, in the 80-degree pool.

I get help with correspondence twice a week.

I am so sorry you had the flu. That loss of blood must have weakened you. I am disappointed in your doctor. Was that the one recommended by Parks?

Take care of yourself, darling.

Anaïs

Letter from Hugh Guiler to Anaïs Nin:
New York, March 12, 1974

Darling:

Today I sent you a check for $27 for the hospital. I am holding on to the Medicare statement showing they cannot reimburse you for this, since you have not yet come up to the $60 deductible for 1974.

I got back to the office yesterday, but on Dr. Duane's advice (which comes back to the way I feel) only for a half-day this week.

The enforced rest gave me the chance to do two things I had been putting off. First, getting together and analyzing, with Roger's help over the telephone, all the Ian Hugo accounts for 1973 in case, as is possible, the tax people bring that up, in view of the fees from the Library of Congress. I spent much of the weekend on that but in the end was able to satisfy Roger that I had cancelled checks that added up to more than any income that I had received (not counting your loans), and he told me not to bother about it anymore.

I am so glad to hear you are getting some secretarial help twice a week. I don't know how you have been able to carry on without some help up to now.

You spoke of your writing being used by a composer for the U.S. Centennial. But that is for 1976, is it not? It would be very unfortunate if you are in any way mixed up with Nixon on that.

Love,

Hugo

P.S. This is a Japanese felt pen but I don't think it improves my handwriting.

LOS ANGELES, MARCH 16, 1974

While Henry Miller and Larry Durrell incensed each other, the women discovered me.

I can't do the meditation. I'm filled with vol. 6. What is missing, what to select. I don't like to describe the Durrell preface to *Children of the Albatross*. It was such a shock to me that he did not understand my work. But beside me I now have hundreds of studies by women who do!

John Ferrone walked quietly into our home, and for three days selected photographs. He is a skillful editor. Gunther now fights aggressively to maintain his editorship, which he jeopardized by over-tampering, cuts and changes in my meaning, which I fought.

John fought for the paperbacks of the *Diaries* to be done sooner (Harcourt was going to wait for two years). It became their best seller. I am sure this helped him to move into Hiram Haydn's place when Hiram died. I should always be grateful for Hiram, who came to Gunther's cocktail after Putnam rejected the *Diary* and said: "I love it. I'll do it." But, like André Bay, he thought it would only appeal to my contemporaries as a piece of nostalgia and had only 3,000 copies printed, which sold out the first week! I never enjoyed our lunches. Though he was ten years younger, it was a father-and-daughter affair. But with John, there was familiarity and ease and rapport. John said he was amazed that Jim Herlihy, so young, and so long ago, perceived what John only recently saw in my work.

John Ferrone and Anaïs Nin, Silver Lake, 1974. Photo: estate of John Ferrone

When I visited George Barati to hear his composition, Rupert didn't want me to go. He watches over my strength, doesn't let me waste it. "The opera isn't done —why should you go?" He was right, but it will be a long time before I can disregard the wishes of loving friends. And the struggle of musicians touches me particularly.

The difference between Rupert in 1959 and today is incredible, his thoughtfulness, identification with my work, his care of me. He said that I wrote about the "other" Rupert. I offered to tear up the pages. He said: "No. People should know what you went through."

I said, "You should say what *we* went through, for I didn't make you happy at the beginning. The relationship evolved, you expanded, we both yielded and finally became harmonized."

He explained: "In Sierra Madre, and until we began to build the house, I was afraid. I was afraid of failure, economic difficulties, no future, afraid to lose you, was unsure I could make a life for you." There was no future in forestry. He feared he would never attain his own house. He was afraid of my restlessness and my love for other ways of life. Fear made him tight and narrow—the specter of Reginald, the helpless, invalid wanderer. He was challenging his body to the utmost in the ordeal of firefighting, like going to war because he had been classified as suffering from bronchiolitis in the army and suffered occasionally from asthma. His mother, too, had weak lungs.

I did know all this, but I did not know how to expand our life. My work saved us both.

Meanwhile, I met a lively, charming Frenchwoman, Charlotte Hyde, through Hilda Lindley. She is a travel consultant. In exchange for an article, I can have a free trip—both Rupert and I—to Bali and Noomea. She represents Union des Transports Aériens. She would have sent us to Tahiti, but we have been there twice. She joined forces with Michael Shipman, our travel agent, and they are collaborating to get us to Noomea, which is Rupert's wish. We hear about the world-famous aquarium and the undersea life. I could hardly believe it! We had dreamt about Bali for years.

To think about Bali was my way of healing myself, but Dr. Stone insists I apply my energy *directly* against the cancer and unburden myself. Stress causes depletion. Cancer is a virus. He does not eliminate my way of healing myself but insists I have to face the *killer* in myself. Some of the killers are the loving, innocent people who want my presence, my answer to their letters. Such irony!

Letter from Gunther Stuhlmann to Anaïs Nin:
New York, March 18, 1974

Dear Anaïs:

Between struggles with the dentist, here are a few items:

I had the Harcourt check for *Diary 6* ready to go to your bank here as previously instructed, but in your last note you wanted me to send it to you in California. So I will follow that system rather than use the deposit slips you sent me.

I had to remind John Ferrone of our editing agreement since we had previously exchanged a letter with Hiram Haydn on this, and I just wanted to let John know that this was in the file and that we did not have to draw up any supplement for the contract for *Diary 6*. Naturally, I can only edit those volumes that are contracted for, and since under the Trust all mss. will be sealed for twenty years, I won't be around to edit any of the sealed volumes. As soon as I get to the vault I'll make a copy of our agreement and send you a copy. (By the way, all editing agreements usually cover the edited book everywhere, not just in one edition—that also goes for editors like Jason, for instance—and I never thought that this would be any question. It is standard operating procedure in all contracts that I have handled for various people.)

I did some checking on lawyers' fees here and in California and they all are outrageous—with hourly fees between $50 and $100—and if the lawyers put a few people on a job it really becomes astronomical. It makes it almost impossible to employ lawyers for spot jobs.

I don't understand your reference to my "considering a book of photographs as part of the *Diary*"—I never did anything of the sort and I can only assume that John Ferrone or someone else is informing you falsely. All I suggested to John a while ago was that we—you and I—had spoken about a picture book on your life, which had nothing to do directly with the *Diary*. When John and you decided to go ahead with a supplement picture book to accompany the paperback of the *Diary* volumes— rather than with the project we had envisioned a while back, and which I still think is a great idea—all I did was to wait for an offer for the rights for such a book and, when the offer came, I passed the suggested terms on to you and you said let's accept them, even though I thought the terms suggested would bring you very little in return.

Frankly, I am confused as to how to reconcile on the one hand Hugo's concern "that you earn enough from your work to ease his mind" with your note that you did not want to have a reasonable advance since you were already in a high tax bracket from the lectures, etc. As you know, I have already spread the advance on *Diary 6* over a three-year period (three $5,000 payments), and I am very much aware of the tax problem. At the same time, when we make a contract I think it is my duty to see that you get decent terms. You know I have always tried to earn you money from the excerpts, etc., and we have made some money from the *Literary Guild* magazine, from *Ms.*, but little or nothing from the "little magazines"—so I am a little surprised when your secretary asks me if we had gotten any money from the *Michigan Quarterly Review*, for instance, with whom you had dealt directly. But that has meanwhile been cleared up.

When will you be in N.Y.? The PEN wanted to have you as guest of honor at a party, but their only dates are April 1 and early May, which, I believe, are no good for you. But if you should plan to be here, let me know right away and I will set up something, for early May, maybe.

Hope you have recovered and are not taking on too much. I am involved in a long dental struggle—about six months, with bone grafts, surgery, so my head, at times, is a bit wobbly.

Love,
Gunther

LOS ANGELES, MARCH 21, 1974

I flew to Fresno with a sense of obligation because last year I cancelled my talk from the airport. I was ill. I have begun to hate the strain of the lectures. But I was able to talk, and the love, the tears, the fervor of the women and some men, touches me. Before leaving for Fresno, I was angry at my ambivalence about the desire to respond to the love I receive and the need to reduce my activities. I fell into the deepest depression. The man in charge, who was so eloquently admiring, stressed the fact that I transcended feminism and did not allow the questions to become the usual accusations. I challenge women's courage.

I passed by Henry Miller's to please Jill Krementz—she wanted photographs, and she has been friendly, and Kurt Vonnegut is one of those who voted for me for the Academy of Arts and Letters (he and Isherwood). Henry delights at being interviewed and photographed and I am withdrawing from it because it is not creative.

Letter from Anaïs Nin to John Ferrone:
Los Angeles, March 23, 1974

Dear John:

I wonder if your lawyer could help me with the following problem. I always understood that quotations or use of material by college theses or PhDs were not charged by publishing houses. That it was considered non-commercial use as they are rarely published—or, if they are, in a very limited way. How does this apply to readings, performances, etc.? Sometimes without my knowledge a college will dance, or mime or read from my work. Sometimes I hear about it and I am invited to the performance by students, as in Boulder, Colorado, which included a reading of the "Birth" story. Now a young woman I know, very clever, is getting a Bachelor of Arts at USC and has put on a performance of *Collages*, music, dance, mime. Gunther is raising a fuss, as he says it must be "contracted" even if no money is forthcoming, to avoid later problems with film or Broadway plays. I am enclosing his letter. I need advice. These events help the books enormously. They are definitely not commercial. Why should I make them so complicated, and what effect can they have on later (if any) professional performances?

Could your lawyer advise me, as it often concerns the *Diaries* too? I would need to know the general ruling about college use of material. Is that too much trouble?

Gunther has admitted that a book of photographs did not come under the category of diary editing, that he wanted to do a book of my whole life someday. He is having a very rough six months with dental surgery, so we must be easy on him. I would just like to know where I stand so as to deal with students who sometimes ask me, sometimes don't.

Anaïs

Letter from Anaïs Nin to Gunther Stuhlmann:
Los Angeles, March 23, 1974

Dear Gunther:

I do see your point about the magazines. I will watch for that from now on.

I am sorry you are having such a rough time with the dentist.

I was glad to have the $4,000 for taxes! Yes, there is an apparent contradiction between Hugo and what I say because he is full of anxiety about the future, and I am not. I am unable to cure him of that. So don't worry. I just did not want to get into the same bracket as 1972, but that was because I had so many lectures. This year I have taken far fewer lectures, and the best way, if I get stuck, will be for me to let you know, and I think Harcourt will be flexible. There is also a possibility of your needing money, which will concern me, and that will also be a factor to consider because I know what dentistry costs. So let us just be flexible and don't take Hugo too seriously.

I will get you a letter from Christie Logan to make everything clear. I gave her permission to do *Collages* in Purdue and she did it there once, then here at USC. But she is a very devoted friend and nothing will go wrong.

I often don't *know* what is happening in colleges. Evidently colleges don't know they have to ask permission.

I will clear up the copyright with *Travel & Leisure* and with *Playgirl.*

The pamphlet for the *Diary* pleases everybody. They have done it well this time. And the cover too. Did you get your copy? I got one by airmail.

Sorry you had to go through such an ordeal on top of all the work.

Anaïs

LOS ANGELES, MARCH 23, 1974

My dreams are heavy. There is a heaviness *au fond.* I can't analyze it. Is it because I have to give up the lectures? My physical state is marked periodically by digestive troubles. Is it that I feel the lessening of energy? Last year when I was asked by a teacher how I dealt with my diminishing strength, I answered flippantly: "Better ask Picasso"—and named my activities. But now I am defeated. The talks I give come out of spiritual energy, not my body. I went to Fresno on a two-day diet of tea and toast.

Charlotte Hyde phones me: The trip to Bali is all arranged.

So much to live for. The shining love of Rupert, Piccolino's clowning, the life-giving pool, the birds. Now coming in her truck to take me to the post office where there are always fascinating letters, Valerie Wade brings me beautiful photographs. John Ferrone is working on the book of photographs.

Joaquín is giving concerts in Europe.

Letter from Anaïs Nin to Hugh Guiler:
Los Angeles, March 24, 1974

Darling:

I received the letter from Boulogne. It is discouraging to get a $4,000 advance from Harcourt on vol. 6 and have to pay $3,500 for taxes!

I meant to write you as soon as I came back from Fresno. It had been a difficult conflict to accept that I can no longer give lectures. But I feel well enough to finish the ones I promised. Dr. Stone's effort has been to make me connect "stress" and "cancer." I don't know what Bogner will think about this. I remember long ago she gave us a book on cancer and duty-ridden people. Anyway, I am beginning to unload and unburden. The *Diaries* are being taught in hundreds of colleges and increasing in sales.

One disappointment I have to prepare you for. I had accepted a lecture in Michigan because it meant $1,500 at Grand Rapids on the 10th of April and suddenly find it is next door, one hour away from Kalamazoo, which I had to cancel when I got ill. I got a gently reproachful letter. I answered that I thought, according to usual procedure, that when money is allotted for a lecture and the lecture is cancelled this money goes back into funds for other lectures. They said no, they had especially kept that one for me and only for me. The $1,000 they generously offered me is for a seminar early in the afternoon, only 80 persons, and I can be home that evening, but it means I arrive in New York, the 8th, rest the 9th, and fly to Michigan for two days. Forgive me this *contretemps.* I did not know what to answer. It was a geographical error in tactics. But after that I have nothing to do until the talk with Ira Progoff.

Hilda said she would not ask me to do any publicity because I have had enough exposure.

I hope you asked John for a copy of the *Diary.*

I felt a little sad yesterday when a neighbor in Louveciennes, Jean-Yves Boulic, sent me photographs of the house under the snow because he said it was the only way to recapture the magic I described. The snow disguises the deterioration of the house. He also sent me a guide to visit Louveciennes in which 2bis, rue Montbuisson is listed as the home of Diarist Anaïs Nin. Funny? I don't remember snow in Louveciennes, do you?

You sounded well over the telephone.

Today I see the rehearsal of *Collages* at USC. Hope it will be good.

Tomorrow my student.

Tuesday I fly to College of Marin to show the Henry Jaglom film, *Safe Place* (I get paid for that and it will be easy), and return the same day.

The 27th I see the performance of *Collages*.

The 28th I see student no. 2 (both my students are interesting, good writers).

And so on.

Because of my article on Tahiti, I will get a free trip to Bali this summer in exchange for an article.

I hope you will soon start on your new film. You are always happier when you are filming.

Anaïs

LOS ANGELES, MARCH 24, 1974

If the *weight* on me is physical, I must try to relieve it. If it is psychological, I must examine it. Dr. Stone, after coming spontaneously as a friend one Sunday to teach me meditation, has made me come to his office for talks. I felt they might help me to accept these new restrictions on my expansive nature, these controls over the exchanges with the world. I have to distinguish between those who love me and those who use me. I am trying to do that. But I can't control the blow-up, which is part of fame. I accept a talk with Progoff at the New School because he teaches the Intensive Journal and it is a small group, but now the group has increased four times and there will be a videotaping. I accepted to talk to Durrell's 15 students, and the place was filled with photographers and tapers and video lights. The reception at Fresno was a crush—with five minutes only to give to each student.

Jim Herlihy is here and moving into a new house with a gentle, sweet, radiant hippie called Rainbow.

My calendar is full. Why the depression? I am helping women to live, to have courage, to feel, to believe in themselves. Evelyn Hinz is collecting my talks. I put down all the facts that give me pleasure.

Volume 5 is out—a golden, luminous cover chosen by me, painted by Susan Boulet, a young San Franciscan painter I met through John Pearson.

A grey morning. Preparations for tomorrow's trip. Tinting hair (Rupert does not want me to go grey), nails, notes, packing, telephone.

In May I have to begin giving Hugo $1,000 a month, not just sporadic help. His commissions have dwindled to nothing. I have been able to help his filmmaking, partly repaying his generosity to me, to my mother and Joaquín.

At 10:00 AM Mrs. Osborne will come—she is neurotic, but intelligent and responsive. She spent much energy on an hour of tape-recorded preaching against *The Exorcist*. For her, it is more important to moralize and fight corruption than to create. I try gently to guide her into affirmation and storytelling. She is at the moment more of a Catholic militant than an artist. It is true that whatever we fight in America is gigantic—David and Goliath—but the men at age 60, fired by the oil companies just before their retirements, believe in David's success. I admired them. Coming out and telling their story on television, getting a lawyer against Goliath.

We are now slaves of Big Companies, all of us. The Hitlers are replaced with men of power and wealth. I begin to see the need of Socialism and listen to Herbert Marcuse. Before I saw the tyranny of communism equal to the tyranny of money.

LOS ANGELES, MARCH 1974

In Harold Stone's office. The meditation against cancer stopped about two weeks ago. I rebelled against it, blocked it. It was invading my life. I didn't want to focus on it. I wanted to think about volume 6. I turned to my way of healing myself—to other places, other thoughts.

Now I am leaving for New York and I will visit Bogner to see how she deals with the feelings I have.

And every day, like a constant underlying theme, there is the painful thread of Hugo's life. I see him asleep in his armchair. I see him struggling with his contact lens (one night when I arrived I had to help him find it in the corner of his eye). I think of his hearing difficulties. The compassion I feel for his loneliness wounds me. A part of me would like to be there to take care of him—only that. The rest of me recognizes that I cannot live with him, that he has weighed heavily on my life, that I am alone and lonely in his presence, that I am stifled in his life.

All I can do until June 9 is fulfill the promises I made when I was threatened with having to support Hugo and Lloyd and Helen. Hugo will need $1,000 a month; Lloyd and Helen $800.

Rupert's economical nature has made us save $20,000 for emergencies.

KENTFIELD, CALIFORNIA, MARCH 27, 1974

Showing *A Safe Place*. A difficult evening at College of Marin, fighting for poetic concepts against the literalness of the political interpretation (I'm sick of women being portrayed as child-like). A part of the audience responds, a part clings to the moralistic and dictatorial feminism—the wrong kind.

I love to collect stationery from all over the world, but this is from a place I am not likely to see because Rupert and I are not attracted to India; it was sent to me by dreamer Wayne McEvilly. So I decided to write my Diary on it and then keep it. Wayne is the kind of dreamer I do not like. In fact, he angers me. He is like Marguerite, who does not hear what you say or read what you write. His words never answer yours or make sense. Marguerite reacted against him when he came to New York and the three of us met: "I can't stand wispy dreamers who never touch earth." She must have hated the exaggerated expression of her own cut-offness from human exchange. It is as if we talked a different language. His knowledge and love for Marguerite's work and mine was disastrous for his writing, because he imitated the flights, but not the strong patterns and links Marguerite makes. Wayne meanders, floats, has no contact with human beings. It is all abstract, I might say almost schizoid. It is strange how a certain kind of dreamer repulses me. Perhaps I see what I would have been if I had not struggled to contact others, the world. Now I cannot read his writing. Marguerite understands the "virtue of selfishness," as a French woman wrote me. She refused to read Wayne's 1,000 pages. She refuses to take time off her work. I tried. It is nonsense. When he went to India he scattered our correspondence left and right until I insisted on it being returned to me. I see how much I gave to that friendship. We never connect. I began to resent his dependency, as Stone wishes me to. It made me think of the friendships I did not make and regret.

LOS ANGELES, MARCH 28, 1974

What saddens me is that I have never recovered the same energy I had before January's recurrence and hospitalization. I can only swim six laps instead of ten. I have to help myself out of the bath by holding the handle. I have to make an effort to straighten up after crouching over my files. The martini I love, which breaks the tension between my day and evening, gives me pain. I dread crowds, standing up for hours, talking to admirers.

Collages was not a good performance, though no fault of Christie Logan. She did not have good dancers or mimes or readers to work with, but the *words* I was able to enjoy, the humor.

Came home that very night at 1:30. Poor Rupert would not let me take a taxi. Hearing the complaints of women about men resenting their careers, I see more and more how exceptional Rupert is. Hugo shows only anxiety and doubts and asks Gunther over and over again if my royalties will be sufficient if I stop lecturing.

Letter from Hugh Guiler to Anaïs Nin:
New York, March 1974

Darling:

I think I have at last found a felt-point pen that I feel comfortable with. It's a "Flair."

Got two envelopes from you today with the pamphlets, one on *Diary 5*, which I am glad to have as I gave my other to Bogner (she was delighted with it, and I wonder whether you intend to give her a copy of the diary itself—I leave that to you); the other envelope returning my "script." No letter, but you told me one is on the way.

I had about 12 people to the film party last night. The projection was fine and everyone was extremely enthusiastic, although I showed as many as eight films. Lauren Frost brought her friend Jules Fischer, who was most complimentary and offered me tickets to *Ulysses in Night Town*, the play for which he made the lighting. He is giving me two tickets so I plan to take Ms. Haag, the director of the American Film Institute, who is arriving today for a two-week stay in N.Y.

Pat Cool also came and wants to set up a film showing for one of the new administrators of the Whitney Museum. I accepted immediately because I have not been able to break into that place.

Victor Lipari brought a sculptor, Ian Duncan (Scotch) and his wife—both interesting and enthusiastic. I showed *The Gondola Eye* and those, like Marianne Hauser, who had seen an earlier version, felt that this is a great improvement and she called it my "masterpiece."

Unfortunately I had to take the projector back to have it checked again as the motor is giving a recurrent hum. I guess this is a point in its "life-cycle," as defined by Leo when he said: "It is the *nature* of any machine to break down."

I am indeed glad of the decision you have made to give up the lectures. I imagine what really encumbered you was the feeling that they did drain you, and also I remember you saying that you were tending to repeat yourself. So, at least, you need a vacation from public speaking, and also there is no doubt that the continuing success of the books is assured.

Love, love,

Hugo

Letter from Henry Miller to Anaïs Nin:
Pacific Palisades, April 18, 1974

I got *Diary 5* and started to read it last night. That description of Acapulco is simply glorious. Reminds me of your passages on Morocco.

I'm rereading, on the side, Nietzsche's *Birth of Tragedy* and Durrell's *Pope Joan*. By the way, I just finished a most unusual and delightful book by a woman called Erica Jong—title: *Fear of Flying*. It might interest you.

Best to Rupert! And hope to see you soon again.

Henry

Letter from Henry Miller to Anaïs Nin:
Pacific Palisades, April 23, 1974

Dear Anaïs:

I finished reading vol. 5 today. It's excellent. That "crazy" woman toward the end was a rare treat. What a find! I thought the bit on LSD was just marvelous. And I love what you said about Paris on revisiting it. Was also impressed with what you wrote about your mother's death. I fought with mine right to the end. I hope Joaquín is now doing well. You were so right to walk out and lead your own life. What a tragedy for Joaquín that he remained the loyal, obedient, self-sacrificing son. The very word "sacrifice" gives me the shivers.

I saw the ad for your book in the *L.A. Times* Sunday. What a surprise!

Good luck, all the best!

Love,

Henry

P.S. I wonder that you waste so much time on Max Geismar.

Letter from Hugh Guiler to Anaïs Nin:
New York, April 23, 1974

Darling:

Dr. Sterling is still working over Tiggy and unable to force the catheter through the urethra so he can urinate. Has to go on using a needle. I will be telephoning again tomorrow morning so will not have news until then. At least he has not suggested operating, as the other vet did. He is doing all he can, I suppose, to avoid that.

The apartment is very empty without you, and I even miss our oceanic tensions! Only Chico is left and he won't eat either.

The enclosed article appeared just today and I send it only because I had said there *is* an oil shortage, and this expert confirms this is a fact both for the U.S. and the whole world. Many of my own mistakes were made because of my assumption that there would be continuous growth in the future. Now, at this late date, I see that what is needed is the kind of economy the French peasant practices, rather than the wastefulness of Americans up to now.

No word from Leo yet about the TV but thank you for thinking of it. Roger says I should have had a color set long ago.

I see from the book *Biofeedback* that in Europe they have since long ago been experimenting successfully with a *combination* of biofeedback, psychoanalysis and hypnosis or self-hypnosis.

I am glad you are having two days of rest before your next lecture, and that your visits to Bogner relieved your anxiety about the cancer. I was also relieved.

Love, love,

Hugo

Letter from Gunther Stuhlmann to Anaïs Nin:
New York, April 26, 1974

Dear Anaïs:

Thank you for the various notes. André Bay is probably right that he can do more in trying to place *Collages* and *Seduction* with another French publisher than I could do from here, given the peculiar French publishing scene. But if he does not succeed with it, I can always step in at a later date. As you know, the whole publishing scene in Paris is a gossipy, incestuous family situation, and unfortunately there is nobody standing by to do anything that might upset the apple cart.

If André sticks to his plans, October of this year will not be bad for volume 5, and since volume 6 won't be available for another year or two, he would have no problem doing the novels early in 1975.

I will try to find out how the Spanish magazine published "The Labyrinth" without any permissions and will keep you posted.

Thanks for the letter from Beatrice Wood, which I am returning to you. I saw both of her books on India quite some time ago, and had to return them to her because there was nothing I could do with either of them, and I guess she has had no luck with them either for the past several years.

Last but not least I'm also sending you some money—the Harcourt royalties just came in, but they were, as you can see, substantially lower than last April. As for sales, they sold 13,370 copies of *Diary 1* in paper, 6,783 of *Diary 2*, 3,991 of *Diary 3*, and 3,302 of *Diary 4*. They also sold 1,490 copies of the boxed set.

I'm still flat on my back, but things are slowly improving thanks to Barbara.

Love,

Gunther

Letter from Anaïs Nin to Henry Miller:
Los Angeles, April 27, 1974

Dear Henry:

232

About Kerkhoven. Between the time I first read him and the rereading of him, I learned so much about psychological healing that I was disappointed to find how erroneous everything he said and did as a healer was. This does not mean he could not heal, because the *intent* to heal is often enough. I just felt that Wasserman as a novelist had not known how to reproduce a true analysis, an invented one, or even a composite one. I would say Kerkhoven may have been a healer, but he was no psychologist and his insights were not wise. It does not make him less of a saint, does it? I don't think the Zen philosophers are great psychologists either, as far as helping and healing troubles born of Western cultures go. But in the end, as long as people believe, it works.

I tried to call you today to find out if you wanted visitors. A girl with a funny name came to me at the New School, wanted to sketch me, and said you and Durrell sent her with the wrong phone number. Naturally, since I had only two weeks in New York and she didn't know where I was, I said no. Do you know who that might be?

I did not see the Jill Krementz photographs, but she said they were beautiful and she would give me one when I return to New York for the Academy of Arts and Letters ritual.

Love, good health, joy,
Anaïs

Letter from Hugh Guiler to Anaïs Nin:
New York, April 28, 1974

Darling:

Here is the ad in the *N.Y. Times.* Congratulations. A good photo and wonderful they were able to feature Anna Balakian's words. I did not know she had done a review.

I think Tiggy's death hit me so hard because of his beauty, and the association of beauty to you. I also felt, and perhaps this was good, that the flames that consumed his body were a symbol of the love with which I had surrounded him, and which he gave back to me.

I will have a difficult time to find a cat with that combination, but I must try.

Love, love,
Hugo

Letter from Gunther Stuhlmann to Anaïs Nin:
New York, April 29, 1974

Dear Anaïs:

The Mexican publisher—Era—that your friend Juliette Ocampo mentions in her letter is the same Mexican publisher to whom I sent copies of the four *Diaries* some time ago and with whom I have been in correspondence. They have expressed interest but have not offered any concrete terms so far.

Withholding volume 4 from André, I'm afraid, won't do any good as a pressure measure. We have no other possibility in France at this time and—as I find out in Germany—it is extremely difficult to switch from a publisher who has done several volumes to a new one who has only the recent one. You know I have been in France almost every year to work over the publishing scene, and it seems to be getting more difficult there every year. They just, by the way, cancelled the Nice Book Fair for this year and plans for next year are very uncertain.

Some money from England will follow in the next letter.

Love,

Gunther

Letter from Anaïs Nin to "Ms." magazine:
Los Angeles, April 29, 1974

Editor of *Ms.*:

I never expected a magazine devoted to women to print such a distorted photograph of me. And, believe me, it is not a matter of vanity, but a vital matter to other women. I have spent much of my time seeking to help women to overcome the fear of aging. I have made myself an example of how one could work, live, act and look at 70. I expect ordinary magazines to publish bad photographs, but not *Ms.* My agent sent you unretouched photographs by Margo Moore. Instead you chose some old photograph from 1967. Why? You returned the ones he sent you, recent, and done by a woman.

I expect some kind of retraction, or I feel you should print a decent, faithful photograph to make up for this in some way. When a homosexual like Irving Penn does a distorted photograph for *Vogue*, we all know it is because he hates women. But then *Ms.*?

Another thing that has prevented me from writing anything for *Ms.* is that several women have written good interviews and you have rejected all of them. Some came to me saying you had expressed interest and then turned the interviews down.

Anaïs Nin

P.S. If you mean well I expect you to call my agent and publish one of Margo Moore's recent photographs not washed in purple ink.

LOS ANGELES, MAY 1974

I dialogued with Ira Progoff at the New School. It was not successful. Ira is enclosed in his system, and we could not combine spontaneous diary writing with his planned, therapeutic way of using the diary. I could see a stimulating combination of the two, but Ira is convinced there is only one way. Our students shuttled between us because he can answer the questions I never could answer: how do you write a diary, how do you begin.

I was invited to become a member of the Academy of Arts and Letters. John Ferrone escorted me. Elizabeth Hardwick, the woman who denigrated my work, was receiving a cash prize for her critical work while I was being accepted as a member.

Where am I now, or, as the young say, where are you at? At 7:00 AM the alarm rings. If I'm well I make fresh coffee for Rupert. Occasionally, if I have a bad night from digestive troubles, I do not get up. But at 8:00 I'm in the writing room, with volume 6, enjoying new scenes, new characters. I write an article for *Playgirl* on "In

Favor of the Sensitive Man." I write a preface for John Ferrone's photograph supplement. Sometimes at ten I have a student. I have two, but I have refused more. I only accept very, very few lectures. I like both my students for different reasons. Barbara Kraft is young and involved with Lou Andréas Salomé. Shirley Osborne is older but struggling through her Catholicism, puritanism and her honesty. She is courageous. She needs psychoanalysis more than inspiration in writing.

Now and then at one I have a visitor because I know Rupert's arrival at three will deliver me. And then comes the best hour of the day (next to the hours of editing the Diary)—the swim, the martini and dinner. Relaxation. In the evening I write letters in bed while Rupert listens endlessly to every detail of what he calls *history*. I haven't enough respect for such low-grade history. I only want to know the barest essentials. I cannot understand his interest in every detail.

Letters. Even with Mary Morris's help, they inundate me. Most of them touch me and I respond. Poems from Mexicans, South Americans, books from France, poems and letters.

Ever since I talked with Bogner I do not *feel* ill. I have moments of depression because I would like more leisure, but I have to help Hugo financially (only fair) and Rupert's family. One night after Eric telephoned about Lloyd's problems, I dreamt that I was looking for Gonzalo, to give him his rent money. I was carrying it in my hand and seeking to avoid meeting Hugo.

I dislike lecturing. It is so uncreative. At first the dialogue with people inspired me, but after many lectures, the situations and questions became repetitive. I want a new lecture each time—but the same questions bring me down, deflate me.

I would rather have meetings, visits, fiestas—no lectures. But, naturally, I can't do that and get paid $1,000.

Los Angeles, May 4, 1974

Worked almost all day on vol. 6. Have to organize Roger Bloom's letters. I was tired out. But suddenly I remembered the light in Sweden in 1960. My anxiety. Did the earth stop turning?

Rupert tells me: At the summer solstice, the sun reaches its maximum height and starts descending; for one or two days the sun appears to have stopped in the sky.

At that time, I was living so fast I did not write much in the Diary. I have to fill in the blanks, jumps, holes.

Occasionally I wake up poisoned by anger. The destructiveness of Vidal trying to undermine people's love of the *Diaries*, the bitchiness of William Goyen when I was so generous to his work. These toxic poisons eclipse all the love and homages. I want to fight back. I want to wound them. What holds me back? In Vidal's case, his love of scandal would have injured Hugo. In Goyen's case, one can't fight an ambivalent critic.

Then I get up, have warm coffee, go to work. And soon the work, the letters, the house, pool, Rupert's love, heal me.

There is a fighter in me (Mars) who would like to annihilate her enemies. Bogner said: "Don't tangle with Vidal. He is irrational."

Los Angeles, May 6, 1974

The one constant pain I cannot eradicate is Hugo's loneliness. I call him up.

Tiggy, his beloved cat, had died. Hugo broke down, wept. I gave him a color TV to replace the small one that strained his eyes. He sends me a *Wall Street Journal* to prove the oil shortage is genuine, when I know it was rigged for profits. In politics we still find vestiges of his old positions.

If I had stayed there, I would have died.

How gaily Rupert and I drive to Burbank, fly to San Jose, give a lecture at the Santa Cruz Extension on the new woman. The young women teased me about Rupert being there to demonstrate the new man. He says: "*We* are giving a lecture." He spares me much fatigue and strain. It was a summer day. He photographed the redwood trees.

When we came home we found Piccolino petrified with fear at the thunder and lightning.

I was at my desk at eight this morning working on the trip to Sweden and Paris and Brussels.

A visit from Bill Lewis. He has written a charming profile of Marianne Greenwood. He was one of the nude beauties of *Playgirl*. His wife lovingly made a cover for the diary out of leather. He is a wanderer. He taught my work at Santa Barbara. He was amazed to find he had spent his childhood near where we lived in Sierra Madre. He was hiking in our mountains, taking his girlfriends to Chantry Flats.

Letter from Anaïs Nin to Hugh Guiler:
Los Angeles, May 7, 1974

Darling:

I have begun to pad your savings account at a rate of $500 a month, which I hope will increase.

I bought a book from Strand that I will bring back to you: *The Nature of Human Consciousness*, a book of readings edited by Robert Ornstein, the same one you read on the *Psychology of Consciousness*.

Have been working continuously. Diary editing in the morning. Articles and letters in the afternoon. Finished an article for *Playgirl*. Sending a Xerox.

I do not think it is cancer that is harming me, but the constant pain I feel at your loneliness, at having to leave you alone. What is the cure? You complained to Viveca and others. Barbette. At the same time I realize that this is something for you to solve, that your life could be full and rich, and it is up to you. That loneliness is self-created, isn't it?

How is the TV? Easier on your eyes?

Love,

Anaïs

Letter from Gunther Stuhlmann to Anaïs Nin:
New York, May 9, 1974

Dear Anaïs:

Finally heard from Morton Weisman of Swallow this morning—here is what he wants to do with *Cities*: A small cloth edition to sell at $15.00 or perhaps $18.00

a copy. The paperback edition would be priced, he says, "under $10.00, perhaps under $9.00." He also thought about a small, limited, signed, slip-covered, presentation type cloth edition of perhaps 300 copies to be priced around $25.00. Let me know your thoughts so we can proceed with agreements on this.

Have you heard anything further from Evelyn Hinz on *A Woman Speaks*? She is supposed to show you the completed manuscript before it goes to Swallow so you can make any changes and suggestions before it gets into type. There is no rush but I want to be sure that this time you see the material—unlike the *Reader*, which went to the printer without your seeing it. And I need to know if and when it is ready for Swallow since I keep an eye on the contract!

Love,
Gunther

LOS ANGELES, MAY 13, 1974

At 6:00 AM I awaken, feeling at the bottom of a well of depression. Cannot understand it. I read. Or I make coffee. As soon as the day begins, life begins, it lifts. I pack for New York. I work on my preface for the photograph book. At noon, Nan comes (the herb lady). She comes in independently by the garden gate. She changes clothes in the bathroom. She swims. It started when she had back trouble, but the effect on her health was so powerful I let her go in. She drives me to the post office. I get fifteen or twenty letters a day. A particularly beautiful one from Robert Zaller. A surprisingly emotional letter from Samson de Brier. Friends write me outraged by Goyen's review of *Diary 5* in *The New York Times*. Another betrayal.

Meanwhile Henry Jaglom tells *The New York Times* about his plans to film the novels.

At three Rupert comes home. We don't go to the movies as often, since they are so bad. We lie in bed and watch Cousteau films, animal films, science films.

I answer letters. I rarely get to the bottom of the briefcase.

Over the telephone I console Hugo for the loss of Tiggy. He talks about his new film for which he received a grant.

The trip to Bali delights me, and the letters are all love letters. Why the heaviness in the morning?

Read a *fantastic* biography of Romaine Brooks by Meryle Secrest.

The quiet evening, without restlessness. Rupert is beside me. We quarrel because he reads the newspaper from cover to cover—no books. We make up because he tells me he reads so much science in school he is mentally tired.

I work on our private photo album, on a scrapbook of Bali images.

Tristine is back from teaching. Jody Hoy is suffering the pangs of separation from her husband. Lloyd Wright is floundering in an impractical life. Eric is the same. They are dreamers. Awareness of this burden to come has driven me to work. But I'm deeply weary of the lectures. I would prefer an open house—to have time for friends.

After the two students I have, no more. They take too up much time. I need time to do volumes 6 and 7 and early Diaries, and then the ones to come afterwards.

LOS ANGELES, MAY 14, 1974

Shirley Osborne—my student whose life is all enclosed by the "censor" and *not feeling* for weeks—started to vibrate at the death of my mother in *Diary 5*—she began to confess and ended the day by giving me honesty. What she described was so much like Jung's second birth—the cry that *I have never been myself!* She told me the truth about her marriage and her love for a woman. The censor: hideous, monstrous, using every word in the dictionary to suffocate her. Her feeling of *being strangled* grows around her throat. Her husband's sarcasm and rigidities—he was older, a father. What really happened was a psychoanalytical birth of the self, from a most conventional, encapsulated woman. Again the *Diary* served to peel off the carapace. She wept (on tape) and I gave her full credit for courage. I stopped her when she intellectualized—I told her that her journey had been like a big circle beginning at the periphery and spiraling to the center, the heart of the journey. A tragic life. Her husband died of cancer a few years ago. They were separated. She took him in again and helped him. Her lover had a terminal case of heart disease, went berserk and tried to commit suicide.

I was proud of her courage, and proud that I did not let her swerve from the quest of the self because it is with this self that we understand others, relate to them.

The writing, which, technically, she always did well, became the reason for the emotional journey. *The writing stems from there.* If you close doors, you close up the writing too. When the self is there, you can choose between an objective or a subjective work. It will be *you* in either case.

The development of the teaching of someone stifled by the censor was so fascinating that I think we could do a book together, as I will not continue to teach. She has kept perfect notes.

When she first came she was so conventionally well dressed, so courteous and formal, I never thought I could get beyond the barrier of self-protective reserve. From the very first we hunted down the censor. Who was he? Parents, religion? He was, in part, her husband who was adept at sarcasm and at stifling impulses. In a photo album of the children she wrote joyous comments on them and he said: "You shouldn't be scribbling all over the photographs." When she took up studies (she has a fine mind for medicine, psychology, social science) she must have outdistanced him. But when he died, all her minor protests became crimes in her own mind.

EN ROUTE TO NEW YORK, MAY 19, 1974

I never make this trip joyously. I have a painful, compassionate concern for Hugo, but when I telephone it is always to hear of trouble. "I have been working ten hours on my new film. I'm tired out. And I have to take Ethel and George to dinner" (he does not have to). After losing Tiggy he gets another cat and the new cat has the same illness, which means the most expensive vet in town and a $6 taxi ride because he won't go to the Village vet. So I get ready for troubles.

Meanwhile, Rupert and I gave a dinner for the three people sending us to Australia and Bali—Charlotte Hyde (UTA), Christiane Emonin, Michael Seligman. I tell Rupert about the nasturtium salad from my childhood memories, so he collects nasturtiums from a field and makes a salad of sheer beauty and marvelous taste, which delights everyone. He grills the steak on the fire. He does it with such skill, smoothness, grace, ease. Our dinners work like magic.

I've worked hard. Signed books at the Women's Building for two hours. Gave two lectures. Wrote a preface for a biography of Lou Andréas Salomé. On the plane I read Judy Chicago's remarkable book—for a preface too.

I'm not excited about the Academy—it is only vanity, not a real sign of quality, just politics. I'm not overwhelmed by the Dartmouth Doctorate. Honors are a matter of chance. Many marvelous people never receive them.

I am very proud of Robert Kirsch's review of *Diary 5* in the *Los Angeles Times*. It is inspired, poetic and on the highest level of criticism. How can I say men did not help me?

Rupert looks so beautiful as he leaves me at the airport and goes on his way to the beach. He will retire from teaching soon.

"Next time we will travel together." Next time is Noomea, French Caledonia and Bali. Colin McFee's book on Balinese music is out of print—his life's work! I wanted to study it.

Judy Chicago suffered from the opinion of people and her psychotherapist that her husband became weak because she was too strong! This strikes me with particular irony since it was *because* of Hugo's weakness that I felt instinctively I must rely on myself—his passivity, masochism, inadequacies *drove* me into gaining strength. Dependence on him was hell, knowing that all his *bosses* dominated him, that he never stood up for his rights, never rebelled, was always the son and not the father.

Each return to New York is a return to an unresolved past, to a tyranny I cannot understand, a conflict rendered heavier each day as Hugo grows older. Why could I not leave him in 1947? No wonder I admire Salomé. With Hugo I want to die. With Rupert I want to live.

New York, May 21, 1974

Wrote a letter of thanks to Robert Kirsch, which made me realize that because I could not make a synthesis or see my work from the outside, situate it in time, that I was dependent on man doing that for me, or woman critics like Sharon Spencer. Robert Kirsch does that.

What I admire about Judy Chicago's book (as I wrote the preface this morning) is that she is able to make the link between her personal life and women painters in history. She did both the intuitive personal work and the historical. Her political training secured her in good stead. I may have influenced her to *include* the personal as she did not do this in her first version.

They are willing to follow me in this but get angry when I don't produce the link with history or social science. Nevertheless they learned to create themselves, to create life as their art.

American Academy of Arts and Letters

Aside from the presence of the artists themselves, a dull, pompous, graceless affair where obvious cliques and mutual admirers predominate—the Establishment in its dustiest form. To think these men can influence the life of an artist, decide on quality, dictate terms.

I was ambivalent about it. I am torn between having so long desired approval and knowing I should have refused membership. I was presented inadequately in what the feminists would call a chauvinist way. Obviously not one of the gang. It was the final revelation of the emptiness and falseness of honor. A *false* fraternity —worldly—and respected by the world. I remember Cocteau—the rebel, the unconventional, the playful, the chameleon, the drugged, the mischief-maker—was condemned by his followers for accepting admission to the Académie Française. Yet, at the end, he wanted acceptance. But Sharon is right, I have to work with the Establishment because it gives you the power to make changes.

Joseph Mitchell apologized for the inadequacy of the citation.

EN ROUTE TO DETROIT, MAY 24, 1974

On the way to Wayne State University. In the taxi I read 31 letters. I read Evelyn's editing of my talks—perfectly done. I reread my commencement talk at Hampshire College and was moved. I thought I had not talked well. Vol. 5 is selling briskly because no one wants to wait for the paperback. The wonderful discovery that I am free of the need of approval, that at last I believe in my work. My life is rich, I felt, as I received Evelyn's manuscript.

John Ferrone and I have an affectionate and relaxed friendship. We talk easily. He is sensitive and intelligent and trustworthy. I may leave what can be published after Hugo's death in his care. (I always assume I will die before Hugo.) John urges me to do this myself instead of sealing it all for 20 years.

Hugo's incapacity for pleasure. I persuade him to get a new projector. I call up from the airport to see if he has it. Instead, he tells me story of a taxi driver who went the long way and cheated him.

"But you have the projector?"

"Yes. Thank you."

His old projector was 15 years old and failed us at every important occasion.

Frances and I have a feminine visit: clothes, exercise, but also talk about her romantic life. She gives me a sumptuous, expensive dress she bought for the New Year. I question why she gives it to me. I feel she is always dressing me and downgrading herself, although this is often followed by an extreme contrast, her arrogance. She jumps from one to the other. The story is she bought the dress to go to the New Year's party with Hugo, and he flirted with an ordinary blonde. Is that why she won't wear the fabulous dress? She was in love with it; she described it minutely. Is she doing what I once did—making a sacrifice by dressing others? (I still do.)

For her sake, I am giving up the need to possess two dresses when I love one dress particularly.

DETROIT, MAY 25, 1974

Last night a dinner for ten and a lecture. A crowded reception. One person after another, emotional. "You changed my life." "I was born the day I read the diaries."

Questions:

"Do you ever lie to the diary?"

"You speak of the immersion we experience, but when I start to write I get distracted from the experience."

"How often did you use pseudonyms?"

"How much is edited out of the diary?"

"Do you still write in the diary? Does it not make you self-conscious?"

"A woman loses control of her emotions—can lose control."

Q: "Why are you optimistic?"

A: "I put my faith in you."

Mother and daughter find themselves reading the same books. I think of my mother. Oh, why was that joy denied me?

My playful remark about feeling obliged to lead a rich life so one's diary would be interesting, they took seriously. In total, they seem to be suspicious and mistrustful. Those who believe, believe deeply.

Detroit looks dismal to me. The Blacks are sullen. The buildings are heavy, stale. The atmosphere opaque. But the students were warm and sensitive.

They marvel at my energy, but I know deep down I can no longer respond for eight hours to these tidal waves. It drains me.

At nine a young woman will come with a tape recorder for an interview.

At noon Richard Centing will take me to the airport.

I read Evelyn's editing of the talks. So I have shown young women that a woman can flower, create, love, and I have reduced their fear about aging.

I am lumped in with Simone de Beauvoir and Doris Lessing. John Leonard (of *The New York Times*, who is, of course, only interested in politics, not literature) wonders why Beauvoir, Lessing and I are not close friends!

NEW YORK, JUNE 1, 1974

Irony. The English Department of UCLA, who would not let Tristine Rainer do her master's on my *Diaries* because I was "not important enough," after two years of frustrating attempts to do the *Diaries* in general, finally let her *because* I am now a member of the Academy of Arts and Letters!

NEW YORK, JUNE 4, 1974

The strangest mood overcame me yesterday at Sharon's and Velma's party. It was to be a garden party, but it rained so we stayed inside Velma's house. Velma is a vivid, intense concert pianist, very beautiful. It was a soft afternoon—all of them were artists. There was a beautiful mulatto girl teaching in Montclair. Sharon always looks fresh and delicate in her features and complexion.

Suddenly a great wistfulness overcame me. I was going to die soon without having completed my love of a woman. As Velma played Chopin with vigor and power, I wished that in my next life I might be a lover of women. I have now known so many, so fascinating, so intelligent.

It is too late now; nature denied me the sexual attraction for women, but thinking of my disappearance I regretted not having completely fused with them. So I imagined a second life would be given to me, as I listened to Velma's music.

She embraced me so vehemently that our breasts touched. She said, "You are *so* beautiful." The women surrounded me. They made my writing known. They gave me love and supported me. I always responded to their beauty and their lives and feelings.

NEW YORK, JUNE 7, 1974

Yes, I do enjoy the money coming in. $1,000 per lecture. I can give Hugo a new projector, a color TV. I can take Frances shopping. I enjoy being asked to preface Judy Chicago's book or a reprint of a biography on Lou Andréas Salomé by Heinz Frederick Peters. I enjoy the power to recommend others, to push good writers.

I do not enjoy being recognized in the streets, frequently, which makes me forever conscious of my work.

I am sad that when I wish for a carefree afternoon, so rare, perhaps five in a year, I have to play Dr. Nice for Frances, for a jealousy I can well understand, of her lover and her beloved woman friend Eleanor Friede getting together. Or for Eric Neville, who had a breakdown and screamed, "I hate my mother. I want to kill her." Never have I seen such a tragic conflict of a man seduced at 17 by his stepmother (she was young, perhaps 27), winning her from her father with Oedipal guilt ("I am going blind"), not able to see Bogner often enough to avert a breakdown. And I wanted to scream back: "Well, I want to leave Hugo, and I can't!" So the healing role continues, has to continue.

Anaïs Nin and Hugh Guiler, New York, 1974

But so many rewards.

I am invited to write about Paris and New Hebrides for *Travel & Leisure*, about Bali for *Westways*.

Rupert is correcting exams but thinking about Bali.

Hugo admits to seeing Bogner for nearly 30 years. I asked him not to say this to Sharon, or anyone. It reflects on either Hugo or analysis, and many people fear such dependency. Hugo is essentially a dependent man.

It is on my guilt that he plays shrewdly. He dropped his contact lens once at Dr. Goldstein's. I found it. So when I call from Los Angeles he says: "I lost my contact lens. If you had been here you would have found it." Frances cannot understand why I don't leave him. I think of all the gentle, good things he did. He went without lunch in Richmond Hill during the first weeks of our marriage to buy me a mirror, which he gave me with a poem about my beauty. Later in Paris he took care of my mother and Joaquín on his small salary. He excused me from the constant entertainment of people from the bank when he saw how painful it was for me to be with stupid or fussy wives, or to go nightclubbing with an endless stream of bank associates. Then he accepted the one night a week of going out by myself. He endured my more frequent absences—the trips to Los Angeles. He wept when I met Miller because he "felt he would interest me." In Paris he took some of his capital to pay for Jean-Gabriel Albicocco, who was going to make a treatment of *Spy*. He gave me money to offset the novels. At the hospital he was faultlessly attentive, thoughtful.

NEW YORK, JUNE 8, 1974

Last night, returning from our evening walk through the private park of the apartment, Hugo and I found our old neighbor sitting on the bench by the elevator. We asked if we could help. She could not find her keys. I don't know how old she is, but her vision is poor, she shakes, and she was mentally confused. We examined her belongings. No keys. I said to Hugo: "She is a caricature of what I am trying to prevent in you." His answer is always: "I am working on it with Bogner. Be patient." Patient! Twice in a week he went out without his wallet. Twice he lost his hearing aid and his night glasses.

Frances says: "When you talk about Hugo's goodness, you talk about the past. What of the present?"

The evening telephone call with Rupert is my high moment. We decided to reproduce an enchanting print of a Japanese woman at her desk holding a pen airily for my writing paper, and Rupert tells me he saw it and it came out beautifully.

His bad moment came when an article in the *L.A. Times* said that the week of covering Frank Lloyd Wright was only a way of advertising a new building.

I visit a shop for rubber shoes that prevent coral cuts.

I sit in the airport on my way to Dartmouth.

HANOVER, NEW HAMPSHIRE, SUNDAY, JUNE 11, 1974

At seven this morning I was at the coffee shop of the Hanover Inn. And there was Justice William O. Douglas sitting alone. He invited me to sit with him. He talked about the struggle of Vermont to defeat the developers. He also talked about his book, a mixture of memory and research among documents and checking with friends and relatives still alive. He has a gentle manner, candid blue eyes, rather wistful, careworn features. What he has stood for has always awed me. I respect him immensely. I left him to meet the professor who taught *Winter of Artifice*. I brought her a present of vol. 5.

Then in a building next door, we dressed in robes that remind one of the reign of Henry the Eighth, in sumptuous colors. They let me wear the white velvet capelet for the photographers. We all passed, in groups, in twos, threes, with Barry Jones (who really caused this to happen by distributing my books all over Dartmouth).

Then the procession with my partner, a professor, passing a row of graduate students. Bagpipes gave a note of gayety. I was sharing the Honorary Doctorate with

Justice Douglas; James Hubert "Eubie" Blake, composer; Agnes de Mille, choreographer.

We sat under a porch roof. It was a very long and sometimes tedious performance. A prayer. A song. 650 graduates. Many honors. A speech by a student—naïve and corny. The citations by the president were very well done. Douglas and Eubie Blake received an ovation.

It is still a man's college, strongly masculine.

At one we dispersed. I met Barry and his friends. We drove to Douglas Abdell's studio. He is an excellent sculptor, warm and charming. He lives in a vast house left over from the mining days—abandoned.

Of course, the honors please me. They heal all the neglect.

New Hampshire is all trees and lakes and smooth roads—no signboards. A small proportion of women and Blacks. Noticeable. They pamper Barry, who is brilliant. Everyone likes him. Many people came up to say they loved my work. Young women. The others say: "My daughter (or my son) wants a photograph of you," or "Will you sign a book for them?"

There is a heaviness over my heart. One of the faculty members said, when I mentioned playfully that all these honors should have come earlier, "But earlier we don't need them. It is later we need compensations for aging."

My diploma is beautiful—very impressive—in Latin.

EN ROUTE TO LOS ANGELES, JUNE 15, 1974

Finally, in desperation, I asked Hugo if he knew the meaning of his absent-mindedness. His evasive answer was "I am working on it with Bogner."

Yesterday I said: "After 30 years of analysis you must have an *inkling* of what causes this."

"My mind is constantly on the mistakes I made in the past."

I was stunned, unbelieving. "In the past?"

Over the telephone he says: "I have to adjust to the knowledge that I am not earning anything—not standing on my own feet."

"But that's ridiculous, because you worked for the income I have now. It is *your* income as much as mine! You supported me, invested in me, and it paid off. I am *your best investment.* How can I make you feel it is yours as well as mine? Will you work on that with Bogner?"

The knowledge I have refused to face is that Hugo is mentally unwell. He was struck by my *immediacy* in the video of my talk with Ira Progoff at the New School —the *presence in the present*—whether I am listening or answering questions.

Suddenly, of course, the inexplicable devotion to Hugo at the cost of my freedom and happiness became clear. He *is* as I was—after my father left, after coming to America, I experienced a break from reality—I was always elsewhere at our homes on 72nd and 75th St. (mostly inside books). Then, suddenly, in Richmond Hill I stopped dreaming and went to work.

My impression of no contact with Hugo was accurate (as I had no contact with my father).

The irritation I had to struggle against was that I blamed Hugo for the loss of contact. And that I felt it was another form of abandonment—a desertion. My last talk with Bogner was on my irritation at his zombie life. I see her now only for Hugo! Now it is all clear. I cannot expect from Hugo what he never gave me—but as the contact grows more and more wonderful with the world, the contrast becomes more extreme. Such irony.

It is as if all his reactions were belated.

When I leave, he realizes I have transformed the household. I found him a new maid. I had shelves put up in his studio for new material. I made him give his old projector to Arnold Eagle, who will never be paid for his filming the scene in the Brooklyn vault with the Diaries (for Robert Snyder); and Eagle helped Hugo get the new projector and has become a helpful, useful, devoted friend. Yesterday I repaired the panel of engraved prints. We took toasters to be repaired. I urged him to seek relief for the troubles the contact lenses give him—more trouble than anyone I know.

Yesterday I took the cats to the veterinary (the most expensive in town, Dr. Sterling). I fed the sick cat by hand.

We saw three exhibits—two were bad, but the witty Dadaist one was immensely funny—such as the "Lost Vagina" by a Swiss artist, which was abstractly sculptured blond wood vaguely suggesting the mount of Venus, with variation in size and details; such as the frigid one showing nails pointing out; a big one next to a small one called "Gertrude and Alice"; Marie Antoinette's had two spots of blood; a very old lady's showed wrinkles. The mood reminded me of the witty jokes of surrealists and Dadaists, but I feared the lack of humor in the feminists. The abstract sculpture was in good taste. I wonder what will happen.

The friendship with John Ferrone deepens. He wanted to be a writer. Right out of college he was offered a good job. Now William Jovanovich's irrationality is creating an anxious, unhappy atmosphere, so I urge him to work on his own diary and preserve and enhance his personal life to counteract a job that does not reward him, that is precarious. I was amazed to discover that I can't move away from Harcourt, that I am married to them and if John should leave, I can't.

Dutton asks if my early novels are in print. They would like to reprint *Ladders to Fire, Children of the Albatross*. They don't even know all the books are in print. This is the nephew of the same man who caused me such disappointments in the past.

Millie Johnstone comes to tell me of a young Japanese woman who has poisoned the last ten years of her life by insisting on being part of a household where she has the obsessed infatuation of Bill, her old husband and a homosexual, and now she goes to a Japanese man who is equally old. Millie cannot accept her, and the woman, who is infantile and confused, does not have the courage to make another life, to leave.

I buy books for the trip to Bali and books on Bali. I buy a dress or two. I found an African chieftain's robe for Rupert, from West Africa, Mali—all blue and white.

Rupert says: "From now on I will always travel with you." Hugo wants to go to Paris when I go.

John offers his help with all this.

Letter from Hugh Guiler to Anaïs Nin:
New York, June 16, 1974

Darling:

That was just like you to call me as you did yesterday. It's true the adjustment has been difficult for me, but I also now accept the facts of life, and among them, that I did make it possible for you to grow and that you are returning that to me (with interest!). So now I promise you I can begin to live more in the present. Thank you for the new maid, the color TV, the projector, and my new eyes (real and symbolic). Also for hand-feeding Chico, which I have been continuing to do successfully.

Would you or Joaquín object if I name the new kitten "Cuchi"?—which I like and seems to suit her.

Did some more work on the script today over the phone, with Hakoshima and Bob.

And again let me say how impressed I was with your "presence," your poise and your quick wit in the dialogue with Ira Progoff.

All my love,
Hugo

Letter from Anaïs Nin to Hugh Guiler:
Los Angeles, June 18, 1974

Darling:
For the first time I came away with a deep, real persistent pain. Is it your pain I took into myself? For the first time in years you told me where you were, and it caused me a big shock. I never knew the way you view your life. You take nothing good, joyous, fertile, successful into account. You only count financial failures, which were not even your own doing. I cannot understand this, a man of your talent and creativity, but I feel the pain you finally conveyed to me. Was it as deep as that, as abysmal? Or was it a passing crisis? How can you dwell on your mistakes and not on your achievements? There is something terribly wrong in this image you make. Anyway, I can't help you. It is all between you and Bogner. You never even bothered to tell me how you felt lately. It was always: I am working it out with Bogner.

I tried to call you. I will try tomorrow.

Do you like the print on this stationery? It came from a Japanese wallet. It makes me think of Lady Murasaki.

Good news. Some women in France have started a [publishing house] Éditions des Femmes. They want my books. It will enable me to get away from Bay the novels he does not want to publish (there is no paper, he says) after getting them translated and keeping me hanging for two years. The books they sent me look just as nice as Stock's. The women may become as supportive of me in France as they have here. It is an amazing solidarity.

You are starting your film. I am sure that will heal you.
Anaïs

Letter from Anaïs Nin to Gunther Stuhlmann:
Los Angeles, June 18, 1974

Dear Gunther:
I am so annoyed by Bay's waste of time—the two novels were translated two years ago—that I wrote him today that I want him to give the two novels to this new *maison d'édition* (Éditions des Femmes), and here is a copy of their letter. They sent me six very nice-looking books. I asked Bay not to make any difficulties. It is a

factor in our favor that they were both translated by women. What kind of contract does Bay have? Has he paid advances on them? Has he ever paid the poor translators?

Do help me get this going. They want the books. They have backing. I am enclosing their prospectus, but I would like it back.

I hope you are getting better.

Anaïs

Letter from Anaïs Nin to Hugh Guiler:
Los Angeles, June 19, 1974

Darling:

I am enclosing my Bali itinerary, and the reason I said it could not be trusted for mail is that since I am traveling at the courtesy of the airline who owns the hotels, if there is no room in one they may place me in another. My travel agent warned me about this, as well as occasional changes in flights. So letters will be precarious. I give you this so you won't feel you don't know where I am. When I am in a place for several days I will send you a night letter and you can answer me, just to know we are OK. If a plane is full, the same thing applies.

Today you must be working on your film. I will be thinking of you.

A Zen Buddhist priest came to see me, an American from Dallas, seven years in training. He came in a transparent black kimono overlaying another one, bare feet, shaved head. Bearing gifts, of course, like the Japanese do, green tea, prints, and a seal made around my name, a kimono. His wealthy family cannot understand his life: up at 3:30 AM chanting sutras, breakfast of rice and a plum, philosophy lesson, cleaning the monastery and gardening and then going out to beg for either rice or money. It is the monastery Ruth Stephan filmed, so you saw it, but the film was made six years ago, before my fan was ordained, so he is not in it. Big, gawky fellow, like a bigger Gilbert Chase.

Anaïs

LOS ANGELES, JUNE 20, 1974

It is almost frightening, always awesome, the lifeline that extends from readers of the *Diaries*, from Japan, Poland, France, Belgium, Spain, Italy, to wherever I am —the same message worded in many ways, poetic or plain, clumsy or subtle, but always "I feel less alone," "I feel I have a friend," "I feel I know how I want to live, to love, to be." A pianist in Brussels: "I live by the music of your words." Another is saved from suicide. They are not artists. They are housewives, welfare workers, nurses, teachers.

I feel obliged to answer, because after reading me they want to contact me, to visit if possible.

Letter from Gunther Stuhlmann to Anaïs Nin:
New York, June 22, 1974

Dear Anaïs:

As for the French situation: We control the French rights to the novels, and any contract for the books for France would have to be made between you and the women editors. Stock paid for and thereby owns the translations of both books, and the Éditions des Femmes would have a choice of either buying the existing translations from Stock or commissioning new ones.

Could you let me have the name and address of the woman publisher—I can't make out the signature on the letter you enclosed and there is no letterhead. I would be glad to write to them to work out something.

The only word of caution I have is that Tel Quel—with which they seem to be associated—is the same Dominique de Roux outfit with whom we had so much trouble in the past and who never paid their bills. Also it would be a question of what kind of distribution this new outfit has. As you know, Tel Quel did *House of Incest* and we had only bad troubles with them all along. They may be very enthusiastic and charming, but will they really do a good job selling books? That seems to be a serious question, especially in France, where I have had bad experiences with new publishers in a very staid publishing scene. Let me know and I will explore further.

Love,
Gunther

LOS ANGELES, JUNE 24, 1974
Restless. A desire to write, yet no specific aim. Am I letting others write for me? Barbara Kraft and her diary, and her life, which interests me. I spot the peripheral "notes" on stories she will write, the dance *around* the center. Portraits. Barbara makes portraits. And Shirley Osborne—so honest now—is working from the center.

I am learning to snorkel in the pool. Was afraid of a breathing impediment. Rupert is very patient. On the third day I snorkeled—breathed through a tube. Victory.

Yet there is something there—like the weeping willow leaves at the bottom of the pool—something floating, stirring in me. What troubles me? Is it that the overwhelming number of people prevents me from achieving intimacy? I see figures. A woman I never forgot, standing at the door of the Harvard auditorium. I saw her face for a moment. She is there. She writes me from Italy. The Brazilian pianist, one afternoon. I may never see her again. A woman who gave me a ring in Chicago, after the lecture. I am swept up in a current. Passing faces. They are the faces of women. Was my unlived love of June haunting me? I was denied the erotic response to woman, whereas Rupert's body constantly arouses me. An experience I missed. Is it because I may soon depart that I think of what I have not done? I wanted to be a musician, and the music of the quartet bothers me, makes me vibrate as under a waterfall.

Letter from Anaïs Nin to Hugh Guiler:
Los Angeles, June 28, 1974

Darling:
Big job revising the anthology of lectures by Evelyn Hinz. To keep the spon-

taneity but revise for meaning.

I hate to bother you, but among books and mss. received there must be one by Maryanne Raphael. Please forward it to me as I have to write a preface for it. She is worth the trouble.

And now for work on 1961 in vol. 6.

Fortunately it is summer so I can swim twice a day.

My documentary was shown for two nights by Grove Press. I didn't know. Was written up by the *N. Y. Times*, John Ferrone writes me.

Love,

A

Letter from Gunther Stuhlmann to Anaïs Nin:
New York, July 1, 1974

Dear Anaïs:

I heard from Norton and they offer a fee of $150 for the preface to H. F. Peters' Salomé biography. Is that agreeable to you? If so, let me know and I will confirm.

I wrote to Bay regarding the Éditions des Femmes and will also write to the woman directly.

I enclose a check for the advance on the Catalan edition of *The Novel of the Future*, which just came in. We also finally settled the contract for the Miller letters in Spain—Tierra de Nadie will publish them in a new paperback series.

I have had numerous discussions with the Spanish Consulate here regarding the unauthorized use of the "Labyrinth" story. So far, they have been unable even *to find* the magazine in Madrid. There is no listing in any phone book, publishing reference book, etc. We are now trying a way through the Spanish Publishing Council. The name of the magazine given to me was *El Urogallo*—but there seems to be no such beast. (Strange?)

Dear Anaïs, I have no intention whatsoever to "edit" the Evelyn Hinz mss.—I simply would like to read it and pass it on to Swallow, which I am supposed to do under the contract. As long as it meets with your approval, that is all we have asked for! I will have my hands full with the new Miller letters!

Slowly making some progress, it seems, and new tests are scheduled for July 10—so I will know a little more when the stuff comes back from the laboratory.

Love,
Gunther

LOS ANGELES, JULY 6, 1974

Reading the history of the Isle of Pines, Noomea, Bali.

Hugo did a brave thing, went into a new technology, made a film with computers, worked with a group. The grant he was given made it materially possible.

I do not understand the pain he causes me except as resembling the unfulfillment with my father. I even think my vulnerability to harsh and unfair criticism stems from that, because by now I should be immune to malice and obtuseness.

Tonight a strange mood. The string quartet is here—two cultured Germans, and two young designers, Richard Crawford and David Meckelburg, who make graphic designs around my words.

I feel a little strange, with three magazines waiting for my travel articles.

Letter from Anaïs Nin to Gunther Stuhlmann:
Los Angeles, July 8, 1974

Dear Gunther:
    The loss of the check from Peter Owen and your letter was a freak accident, but I prefer that to the idea of post office carelessness or a thief. I have a Japanese mailbox, built like a real miniature house. Being authentic, it has an attic. The regular postman knows this. But someone who did not know put two letters through an opening on the side, into the attic, where they stayed all this time. I happened to be cleaning away leaves and branches and found them. I am returning the check so you can confirm your stop payment. I was astonished when I saw the date. It was all covered with leaves.
    Still working on Evelyn's ms. A lot of work. And when I think I'm finished, she sends me a new batch. But you'll be pleased.
    I am glad you know all those women editors I mentioned. What is your opinion of college publishers? Lynn Sukenick is sending her study of Virginia Woolf, Doris Lessing (the *Golden Notebooks* author) and me, to Princeton. What do you think of trying the Rank publisher for the Lee Potts study?
    I am getting another honor Nov. 21. Faculty Distinguished Scholar Award, given last year to Joseph Campbell. Ironic?
    Did you see the *A.N. Observed* presented by Grove?
    Anaïs

Los Angeles, July 11, 1974
    Over the telephone Hugo tells me about his new film, how he mastered the new technology, his health, how when Bogner left, she gave him her itinerary and he promptly lost it, and found it again, misfiled. I cannot fathom the mystery of the immense distance grown between us. And yet I felt sharp, deep pain at leaving him on June 15. Away from him I regain my proper weightlessness. My depressions are, at the source, concern for him, not myself.
    It is 7:00 AM. The sun shines on my typewriter. I close the door so Rupert can sleep. His rhythm is different. He is not awake in the morning; he works well at night, while after dinner I can't accomplish anything but writing letters.
    Rupert had to fly to San Francisco for our Indonesian wear. He bought me three utterly beautiful Japanese diaries. Why can't our designs ever equal theirs? The sensuous cloth covers. I can't carry these on my trip, so I will write in an ordinary notebook and transfer the entries when I return.
    Without the Diary I feel like a balloon. The pressures come from the outside.
    The German publisher of Marianne Greenwood's book asks me to write a profile for a big German magazine to introduce her. Maryanne Raphael sends her manuscript *Runaways* for me to preface. My student Shirley goes through a crisis (the censor again). Barbara writes well, but I have to nourish her confidence. An art college in North Carolina wants me to come. Harcourt Brace sabotaged increased sales of vol. 5 by *not printing enough.* Mail is overwhelming. A Japanese artist sends me a beautiful graphic of my words on a "leaf." East-West publishes Jody Hoy's

interviews—and my photograph is on the cover. Sharon Spencer's book on my work is making the rounds. They say: "People who read a Nin diary do not want to read criticism..." Wrong again, for those who are *studying* me hunger for all information and interpretation. They are always wrong.

A new honor—a gold medal from Hofstra College, Jamaica. I ask if I can share it with Anna Balakian.

André Bay, because I am coming in November, suddenly decides to publish *Collages* and *Seduction of the Minotaur* with Anna's essay. Only because the Éditions des Femmes wanted to do them!

Letter from Gunther Stuhlmann to Anaïs Nin:
New York, July 16, 1974

Dear Anaïs:

Glad to hear about your Japanese postbox and that the check survived.

You ask of college publishers—they are all very slow and committee-ridden and move extremely cautiously, and they all claim they are broke and offer a writer who is not just dependent on his academic standing very little inducement. Rank, as you know, is published here by Knopf and reprint publishers who do not do any original work. So that makes it tough on the Potts ms.

Congratulations on the Distinguished Scholar Award—you will soon have a den full of parchments.

I did not see the film of *A.N. Observed* but sent you merely the *N.Y. Times* review. It only ran for two days. Someday we should at least get some accounting from Snyder, for the record, even if he has made no money.

Finally heard from the publisher in Italy who still has trouble finding a good translator for the *Diary*. They have been looking around for a whole year now.

Love,
Gunther

Letter from Hugh Guiler to Anaïs Nin:
New York, July 17, 1974

Darling:

Everything has gone well with Marie-Claire and she is delighted with the material I laid aside for her, after removing all but the files of clippings and the theses.

I took her to dinner in Chinatown the night she arrived and served her afternoon tea yesterday. She leaves tomorrow but will return in September for *six weeks*. She wants very much to see your film. It is no longer running here, but I hope you will have a copy of your own when you come. Otherwise she says she has the research money to rent it.

Maxine Holleff is coming for the video interview end of next week. I hope I will look better in it than in the photographs Bob and the TV crew took in Studio 46. The loss of weight plus the harshness of flash bulbs showed me quite haggard. This week I have been having trouble with my tonsils again and am going to Dr. Lehmann so as to have my voice at least in better shape. I suppose I am paying for the tensions of the past year.

I am sure much of it is psychological and I may be trying to work it out through an idea I have for another film or video. I mentioned to you about the Adelbert von Chamisso short story Bogner told me about [*Peter Schlemihls wundersame Geschichte*] and which inspired the film *The Student of Prague*, which you said was bad. But I am thinking about it in a different and more personal way and have already written part of a script I will send you. It is about how everyone *needs* a shadow in order to live and go on in the present, for it is the shadow that gives dimension, and it does not matter whether it is a benign or a menacing shadow. Anyhow, this seems to be my way of saying to myself that I accept *all* of myself, past and present, to build on it and to go forward and that above all no one can progress in the present without the *support* of his shadow. So it may be I can work out a kind of sequel to *Transcending*, with a different and perhaps more modern slant to the concept of the Double.

Please let me know if you want mail forwarded to L.A. or kept here while you are away. No sign of the Raphael manuscript.

I will miss your calls but I know you will send cables from time to time.

Anyhow, have a wonderful trip and enjoy it.

Love,

Hugo

Los Angeles, July 18, 1974

In the hammock. A summer day. Rupert is sleeping late as he loves to do.

Preparations for the trip. No address for five weeks.

Yes to the Smithsonian Institute. Yes to a big festival in San Francisco. No to a psychology group to talk for days. I would like to modify the lecture, to come just to talk with everyone. I am trying to make a change. The formal lecture is overdone. It induces passivity. Questions in public are not good. Private talks, yes.

I dreamt that there is danger and I have to pack *all* the Diaries (an old dream) and they don't fit in the valise. Conflict. The valise will be heavy. A dream tied to reality because I have to constantly plan for the originals not to fall in Rupert's hands. I have a big, strong valise with a safe lock I lock every day. It carries an order to be mailed to Gunther to put in the vault in Brooklyn. What has added to my anxieties is that I cannot trust Gunther to do as I wish. I once thought he could edit the Diaries after my death, but no longer. He is not faithful to my thoughts or my writing. It is too delicate a job. I trust Rupert, but the material would hurt him. So this will go into the trunk.

We have two very joyous white and red plastic valises. Indian cotton dresses. My clothes are over-clean, as my father's were.

John Ferrone dreams he climbs endless steps which crumble and he may fall into space. He likes to call me up.

A moment of peace.

I stopped working on vol. 6, now 550 pages.

I read Marquis de Sade's biography, and it confirms why I disliked de Sade so much. He was a hypocrite, a madman, pretending to lament over evil with such a naïve interpretation of good and evil. Even an objective biography, full of admiration for his writing, could not make me like him or his work. Pathologic.

I love my work, my correspondence, my friends. Rarely does someone come to the house whom I dislike. It is only the *too-muchness* of it that tires me. Mary Morris, while always rebelling at the "secretarial" position of woman, is nevertheless unable to take responsibility. As soon as I leave, she stops working! I need a better helper.

I do two hours of work before she turns up.

I read wonderful facts about Bali.

A fan with a sense of humor sent me a "LO/VE" stamp, recalling I had been upbraided for separating the word lo-ve in my *Winter of Artifice* handset edition. He said: "You were ahead of your time."

FINAL ITINERARY FOR MR. AND MRS. POLE
Unites States Travel Bureau, 11478 Burbank Blvd, No. Hollywood, Calif. 91603

Thu. July 25: Please check in with UTA by 11:00 PM. Leave Los Angeles at 11:55 PM on UTA #583.

Fri. July 26: Arrive Papeete at 5:10 AM. You will probably be met by someone, and taken to the UTA Maeva Beach Hotel, where a double-bedded room is reserved for two nights.

Sat. July 27: If you are not too busy, try to meet a Swedish professor (I think named Danielson) who lives part time in Papeete and is the curator of the Stockholm Museum of Ethnology. Everyone knows him, and we think you would greatly enjoy speaking with him.

Sun. July 28: Leave Papeete at 6:40 AM on UTA #565A.

Mon. July 29: Arrive Noomea (after crossing the international dateline) at 11:20 AM. Again, you should be met by someone from the hotel or the tourist board, but in any event, a limousine goes directly from the airport to the Chateau Royal, where you are expected for a two-night stay.

Tues. July 30: In Noomea.

Wed. July 31: Leave Noomea at 3:10 PM on UTA #563. Arrive Jakarta at 7:25 PM. The UTA Hotel Ambassador, has been reserved for one night.

Thu. August 1: Leave Jakarta at 12:00 noon on Garuda Indonesian Air #680. Arrive Denpasar at 1:45 PM. Here the Hotel Bali Beach is confirmed, as a protection, through the evening of Aug. 12, because the Hotel Tandjung Sari never replied. You might try to call them from the airport, and if they can accommodate you, cancel the Hotel Bali Beach. Other beach hotels are: the Wisma Samudera and the Sindhu Beach; and fifteen miles away in Ubud are the hotels Tjapuan and Puri.

Fri. August 2 through Mon. August 12: In Denpasar, Bali.

Tue. August 13: Leave Denpasar at 2:30 PM on Garudo Indonesia Air #681. Arrive Jakarta at 4:05 PM. Leave at 10:00 PM on UTA #564.

Wed. August 14: Arrive Noomea at 9:45 AM. Return to hotel Chateau Royal, for a stay of two nights.

Thu. August 15: In Noomea.

Fri. August 16: Leave Noomea at 9:15 AM on UTA #608. Arrive Port Vila,

New Hebrides at 10:15 PM, where you will be met, and are expected at the Hotel Lagoon, for a stay of five nights.

Sat. August 17 through Tues. August 20: In Port Vila. You will undoubtedly meet Michukin, a very colorful promoter of oceanic and primitive art, and his charming protégé. We suggest trying some of the local flights to volcanoes, and/or more primitive islands.

Wed. August 21: Leave Port Vila at 4:40 PM on UTA #605. Arrive Noomea at 5:50 PM. Return, once again, to hotel Chateau Royal, where you are expected for a stay of three nights.

Thu. August 22 and Fri. August 23: In Noomea.

Sat. August 24: Leave Noomea at 8:00 AM on Air Caladonie #401. Arrive Ile des Pins at 8:30 AM. The hotel Relais du Kanumera is reserved for three nights, but the fourth night (Aug. 27-28) is sold out, so you will have to either get an extension for the extra night there, or come back to Noomea a day earlier, the afternoon of Aug. 27.

Sun. August 25 to Tues./Wed. Aug. 27/28: In Ile des Pins.

Tues. August 28: Leave Ile des Pins at 4:45 PM on Air Caladonie #404. Arrive Noomea 5:15 PM. Return to the Chateau Royal for one night (two, if you choose to arrive the previous day).

Thu. August 29: Leave Noomea at 9:50 PM on UTA #562A.

Thu. August 29: Arrive Papeete at 7:35 AM, after crossing the International Dateline. You have a little over an hour stopover in Papeete and we suggest you take soap and towels and take showers in the excellent restroom showers before getting back on the plane. Leave Papeete at 9:00 AM on UTA #562B. Arrive Los Angeles at 7:55 AM.

NOTES ON BALI, AUGUST 1974

As I descended from the small plane, the first impression was a soft, caressing climate, the smell of sandalwood and the overwhelming beauty of the Balinese. With their long, glossy black hair, honey-colored skin, sinuous walk, soft contours with no bones showing, their small but perfect proportions, it was difficult not to believe that they had been selected as prize beauties for the pleasure of tourists. This beauty, a soft blend of Polynesian and Oriental, is at first unbelievable to almost everyone. Even the old women walked so voluptuously that men followed them. The Balinese wear sarongs, tied with colorful sashes, in vivid designs of flowers, foliage, land-scapes. The women's sarongs touch the ground, the men's end at the knees.

The people of Bali were kept in isolation for centuries, thanks to treacherous reefs and currents surrounding the island. They had time to create a high form of life in which religion, art and nature harmonized, in which self and society were one.

There are no ugly houses. They are designed in the same way, a stone wall covered with ivy, lianas, bougainvillea or moss. There is always a small bridge of either stone of bamboo to cross the stream in which the Balinese bathe themselves and the beautiful, sleek cattle. The gate may be elaborately carved sandstone, divided to symbolize Yin and Yang, with a center of red bricks.

Anaïs Nin in Bali, 1974

Life, religion and art all converge in Bali. They have no word in their language for "artist" or "art." Everyone is an artist. Creativity is natural and widespread. It is a means of honoring the gods and serving the community.

The Balinese sleep with the heads pointed towards the east. A person who does not know where north is, they consider crazy. They have a great need of orientation. They judge reasonableness by the way they see the sun coming up.

Wealth is immaterial for the Balinese. They hold it in contempt. For the practical side of life is intrinsically imperfect and they prefer to dwell on its spiritual meaning. Margaret Mead noticed what she called "a vacancy": that is, the absence of anger, of strong emotions, except for laughter. They feel emotion leaves one off balance and open to invasion by the spirits. The Balinese are serene and delightful, never out of sorts. They seem superficial, but this is because they are in harmony with nature, with everything around them.

Cremations are joyous events because the Balinese believe that death is a freeing of the soul—free to float away, join its forefathers and merge in the ancestral soul. Musicians gather in front of the house where the body lies in state, while special craftsmen complete the bamboo tower on which it is to be carried to the cremation grounds. The height and richness of the tower depends on the distinction of the dead. The tower rises high above the people (thirty to forty feet for important persons), pagoda-shaped, covered with tinsel ornaments, mirrors, festoons of gold lace, scarves, flowers, tassels, fringes, pennants, fantastic umbrellas. It is sprinkled with holy water, and incense sticks are lighted. At the very top a white dove is tied; it will be allowed to fly away when the body is burned and the soul freed.

The crowd, in its most colorful dress, waits patiently and listens to the two gamelan orchestras, sometimes playing different pieces at the same time. Finally the body is brought out of the house on the shoulders of friends. The women of the household place themselves in front of the glittering tower and unfold a bolt of white silk, which they hold over their heads. The body has been carried to the top of the tower along a specially designed ramp. Hundreds of men now line up on the four sides of the tower base and lift it onto their shoulders. It sways like a ship on a stormy sea. To foil the evil spirits it must be turned around several times on the way to the cremation grounds. The crowd follows quietly but without sadness. The musicians manage to play as they walk without missing a note. All the children are there, including babes in arms. We all walk along the road to the fields encircling the cremation grounds.

The red-orange bull (or cow, for women) has arrived, in which the body is to be deposited and burned to signify the last journey back into the womb, the end of a cycle. It is a mythological animal, hollowed out of a great tree trunk, with an unbelievable tail and head, partly unicorn, partly a creature out of Egyptian frescoes. More holy water is sprinkled before lighting the fire. When the fire is fully started, the bird is freed to fly.

All this happens with a natural dignity. Dignity and a deep joyousness transcend their daily life. They have parlayed with the gods, contemplated eternity, eaten the food of festivities. They have considered death as mere transmigration. They are bathed in golden sounds; their eyes have feasted on shocking pinks, aquamarine, indigo, parrot green, sun yellows and oranges and all the colors of tropical birds and flowers worn by the men and women. Every house they passed on the way is beautiful with its stone walls, its gates of lacy sculptures around a heart of red bricks. They have flown kites and bought birds at the market for the purpose of freeing them. They have orchestrated simple human life with art and religion, painted their hardworking peasant life with all the colors that great painters restrict to a canvas. They have asserted, by a million small mirrors on one of their superb gods, the Barong, that life is reflection. They have learned to enhance, transform, elevate the life given to us.

The one who travels like a lover searching for a new passion is suddenly blessed with new eyes, new ears, new senses.

I made a wish: let me think of death as the Balinese do, as a flight to another life, a joyous transformation, a release of our spirit so it might visit all other lives.

———

NEW YORK, SEPTEMBER 4, 1974

I feel like writing as I did as a child: *Cher Journal*, forgive me for neglecting you!

For five weeks I traveled with Rupert to New Caledonia, New Hebrides, and Bali. All my energy went into the notes and reading for the five articles expected of me in payment for the trip. When I have written the articles I will include them in the Diary, as well as my notes and postcards and reading list.

As I experienced all the beauty and felt all the music of Bali, I will speak only of the shadow for the moment. Sitting in Dr. Parks' office because the bleeding and staining continues and gives me anxiety. That anxiety lay constantly at the bottom of my life.

The day before leaving Bali, sitting on the beach while Rupert snorkeled, I wished I could one day return to Bali. Did I doubt it?

After another night of bleeding I asked Rupert: "Am I doomed?" I talked with Bogner. In reality I look and feel well except for a heaviness resembling pains before menstruation. Bogner's intuition is that the medication I get stirs up uterine bleeding—that it is not a cancerous bleeding.

The trip to Bali had the sun-drenched quality of a dream—I want to dwell on its deep beauty. But I have to rid myself of the fear of recurrence, which means treatment, hospital and months of weakness. It is like getting ill in the middle of a fiesta. People want articles—I want to write joyously about Bali—when free.

I read Daniel Stern's new book on Hollywood and was distressed by its repulsive subject. He is so loyal to me, so discerning—what can I say? That he saw it with a *new* sharpness such as we now have about Watergate? Open cesspools—I regret he wasted his talent on that theme.

Marie-Claire is here. She wants to meet the writers I admire. She delighted Marguerite by quoting *Miss MacIntosh My Darling* and displaying a knowledge of America Marguerite did not expect.

I saw Anna Balakian—Barry Jones is on his way home from Oxford to Virginia. Talked with Gunther. Sweden is translating the *Diaries*, as is Poland and Holland. Stock wants me to come to Paris. I feel this strong current pulling me outward when I should sit still and write.

John Ferrone wants me to prepare the Diary so that it *can* be published after Hugo's death.

Sharon is launched. Went alone to Mexico, had a love affair, while poor Marguerite has trouble with her eyes and ears and had a tumor removed, but the ear still buzzes. "Nobody loves me." I scold her for spreading the old legend of my wealth. "You lament having to teach; I hate having to lecture. If I could, I would stop."

The book of photographs chosen by John Ferrone is out. It is printed on good paper and is delightful.

Anna's son, given a car, refuses a two-seater as a "selfish" car and wants to be able to drive family or friends. Anna writes a brilliant essay on Breton and drugs—"Surrealism is intoxication."

The mystery of intoxication. Rupert and I did it on Balinese music, on the scenery, on the dance.

Rupert and I were so close on the trip. The same rhythm, the same reactions. He is a good traveler. Explorative and curious. I'm more contemplative, but I yield to his active curiosity as it is enriching. We were befriended by the tourist office, treated with special privileges and courtesies.

Symbolically, the green bag with wheels I have used for many years fell apart, and now my "invention" is obtainable anywhere with ball-bearing wheels. I bought a new bag for Paris and somehow have an adequate wardrobe.

If I could pray I would ask for time to finish volumes 6 and 7—and the childhood diary, time to edit what has not been released, time to enjoy the love I am receiving.

This yes to life and activity must cease. I am turning down lectures.

Results of the tests: Negative.

NEW YORK, SEPTEMBER 16, 1974

Wrote a citation for Marguerite Young for the American Academy. Phoned for Sharon's manuscript. Phoned to request a copy of *A Casebook on Anaïs Nin*, edited by Robert Zaller. Phoned to request an Avon *Spy* and a paperback of the *Anaïs Nin*

Reader. Wrote the preface for John Pearson. Wrote a comment for Daniel Stern. Answered 59 letters with cards. Saw Beatrice Harris.

Spent Sunday with the Balakians at Westbury, Long Island. Such a loving family, a sun-filled house, space, plenty of land, brilliant talk. Haige drove us to a new causeway linking with the tip of Fire Island. Uncrowded beach, wild land. We visited the little cottage in Babylon, which was their weekend refuge when the children were small. Nona uses it. Haige keeps his boat there. Suzanne is so beautiful, with large, soft, black eyes, gentleness of manner. We laughed, talked at length.

NEW YORK, SEPTEMBER 17, 1974

Bogner, once more, put her finger on why I could not resist or control the impulse of activity. Its deeper source was the fear of waning energy. When I was asked by teachers in an audience how I coped with my waning energy, I was very defensive, asserting I had given 60 lectures, etc. That was not the answer. But it was *my* answer. An anxiety about withdrawing. That was why I felt activity as an *irresistible* current. With this confrontation of anxiety about aging came relaxation. My tempo slowed down. I allowed myself a rest after lunch today (I started work at 7:00 AM).

John Ferrone is as tender as always—cooked a special dinner. We achieved harmony with Johan and the talk *à quatre* works gently. John is angry, hurt, negative. But with us he is warm.

Sharon looks luminous. Valerie Harms is soft-toned, working on a study of an early version of *House of Incest.* Marie-Claire van der Elst was given a grant to study my mss. and critical articles on my books.

Talks with Rupert every night at seven.

Progoff and June Gordon came. He wants to do more talks with me, but I don't want to—I want just to write now.

Velma came last night. Hugo took them all into the studio and showed films for an hour. He was so self-engrossed he forgot to be a host.

Velma disturbs me emotionally, more than other women. Perhaps because she is *all* emotion, just one burning flame, and was rushing towards self-destruction (like June Miller). She is Austrian and Portuguese—two warring factors. Sharon brought her, and even though she had stayed in my memory I refused the burden of a suicidal Velma until I heard she was going to Bogner.

Because of Bogner in the background, all of us are escaping the despairs of our times, the monstrous knowledge of the Banks and Big Business ruling our lives, the Big Business I always instinctively hated, knowing some of the men behind it.

Ugly times. Crimes and fear. Shocked when people speak of "primitive" people, when the Balinese culture is infinitely more refined and more humanistic than ours.

8:30 AM. Dr. Parks had two reports made to reassure me. But I'm bleeding and sometimes in pain and have to take pain killers.

Now my aim is to sit still and write to stem this public life, which has devoured me.

NEW YORK, SEPTEMBER 22, 1974

We make a joke of my waning energies and I allow myself a rest when I need it. *I do not have to work* all the time.

I write hundreds of cards to answer the letters.

Barbette comes, bubbling, effervescent, witty, earthy.

Progoff and June Gordon. He has fallen into the habit of teaching. He cannot talk, only teach. He is always talking to his students. And June echoes him. The use of a zoom lens in our New School video creates such distortion that we look like two witches!

Sunday. My best moment is when I talk to Rupert.

Hugo is passive before the women who are interested in him. Velma says: "He is an attractive man but he does not believe me when I tell him so." He weighs on my spirit. He makes statements such as: "If I don't get a second grant I will have to stop making films." This refers to the *expensive* way of making films (video). He never contemplates a technique that only cost $2,000 or $3,000 and is artistically superior. He has succumbed to the inferior color and texture of video. Absurd. He can make his own films as he did before video, and I will give him the money.

For this he torments me with his gloom. All he needed to say was: "Do you have enough money to make the next film?" When I say I have the money he does not believe me. He has no faith, no sense of security about my income.

When we quarrel, I feel it is irrational and leads nowhere. We are always in hell together.

I stay away longer. But I have contempt for his lack of courage, of spirit, and his incurable neurosis.

NEW YORK, SEPTEMBER 23, 1974

Very vital things were solved by Bogner. She cornered Dr. Parks and found out facts that cured my anxiety. I feared the bleeding was the first symptom of tumors and later of cancer. I associated bleeding with recurrence. Not so. It is a seepage from an unhealed incision made when the radium implant was used in January. Also, vitamin K will help, and stopping Delalutin, which caused too much hormonal stimulation. The tumor is encapsulated, has not shown signs of life, cannot spread, is quiescent. So that fear is removed.

Next, Hugo's deep depression can be immediately cured with a $3,000 check to start a new film. His old-fashioned sense of failure and inability to enjoy or consider my income as his (as Rupert does) is something I can't remedy.

The concept that I *must* work all day from seven to four (when Rupert comes home), and often all evening, the uncontrollable activity, is broken.

So Hugo is functioning again. I refused to give a *statement* of my income as I now demand trust and faith in my ability to handle it. Figures would not give him security. He is convinced of my inability. What a strange reversal. In the early days of our marriage I believed in Hugo's ability. After the stock market crash and his gambling with our capital, I lost my faith. But my loss of faith was justified. He has continued to speculate and to lose, and now he has lost it all.

So I will go back to Los Angeles, write every day, swim, enjoy my blessed house—so warm, so passionate. I want to edit volumes 6 and 7 and the childhood Diaries, *erotica*, and propose non-edited Diaries to be done after Hugo's death.

NEW YORK, SEPTEMBER 24, 1974

Max Frisch's *Sketch Book 1966-1971.* Absolutely dull, lifeless, like Beauvoir's autobiography, and Paul Bowles'. Surely they have more to say.

First chilly day, but sunny. In New York I like having errands to do, walking around the Village, but now I have lost my privacy. I was stopped four times yesterday by young women, and today when I was enjoying a moment's leisure in an Italian coffee shop a young poet spoke to me the entire the time when I had wanted to enjoy the illusion of Paris café life.

It doesn't make me happy.

Met Hede Von Nagel—an interesting artist. She spoke to me in the streets. I promised to see her work. Her childhood is the most gruesome I ever heard of, almost impossible to believe. She sculpts it, writes it, is obsessed with it like a mouse in a trap. She practiced Primal Scream alone.

Frances has become a screamer. She screams her difficulties, problems, in detail, on the verge of hysteria. She does not recognize her anxieties as well as she did in the '40s. She is unaware. I cannot make her aware of anything except of the fact that screaming (I hate my job, I can't find my date book, my accountant is on vacation, I have no feedback, I am alone) in itself does not help because she is ashamed of it later and apologizes.

Many of my errands are for Rupert (books he wants) or for Hugo and the apartment. I have to get new dishes, new glasses. Fix the curtains. Tidy up. *To scream is not enough.*

In two visits I solved crucial problems, but poor Frances can't afford Bogner. I resent analysis being a luxury. The feminists do too, the socialists and the Maoists. It is absolutely *essential* to everyone. Without it I might have killed myself with overwork as so many people do, as Michael Field did.

Here I am at 5:00 PM resting…with the Diary. The neglected Diary!

Pamela Fiori: a warm, expressive face. Pisces affinities, tormented by a Scorpio (Rango/Gonzalo?). She gave me the assignment to write on Morocco, and now on Port Vila. She brings a "feminine" personal note: not to write just about the city, but also about the people who live in it.

Rebecca West, now over 80, weeps at Henry Jaglom's *A Safe Place* and writes him a letter: "It was the way I felt at 17." It is the warm Rebecca I knew in London and Louveciennes, who later refused to be in the *Diary*.

Rupert reads me a letter from Henry Jaglom—a self-confession, a conflict between serving politically and artistically—feels guilty about enjoying Paris—my Paris—as he is deep in vol. 2. An intimate letter. Not a word about our film.

WBAI plans a reading of Marguerite's work—the readers are all coming tomorrow night.

Hugo's new film, on the split brain, the labyrinth, painful journeys, is remarkable, but I ask him: "Is it a picture of how you feel today?" The split head came together at the end. I feel the most painful compassion and rebellion as well. He talks politics at 7:00 AM and when he sits in my room before going to sleep.

I say to Bogner: "If he has gradually become aware of my life and has a justified resentment, why does he not choose another woman?" He is courted by Viveca and Barbette. Viveca is intensely interesting, and Barbette is buoyant and gay. Of course, Bogner has to look like a sphinx about Hugo. And, of course, he says nothing.

This time I carry with me James Herlihy's diary, my best winter wardrobe for Paris, boots, etc.

October will be a writing month. I'm eager for it.

After reading about Mishima's life I lost all interest in him. Closeups are fatal. He repulses me. His obsession with death and blood, his vanity and incapacity to love. His mental illness. His death, even. Such confusion of values!

NEW YORK, SEPTEMBER 29, 1974

This Diary will stay in N.Y. while I am in Paris at Bay's invitation. A new green valise with ball-bearing rollers is awaiting the Paris wardrobe. Frances gave me her best dress, grey wool, *robe de style*. I gave her my clinging sweater dresses I can no longer wear because of occasional swelling of the stomach.

Sharon's eyes are magnetic. She is my most aesthetic daughter.

Nancy Zee and I became friends. I had been defensive when she questioned me, thinking it was for her thesis, but it was for her personal use, her own life, and when she wrote me a personal letter I responded. I have watched many young women turn their backs on pure intellect and assert the personal life.

The next newsletter will be dedicated to Marguerite Young.

Gunther and I will read proofs of *Cities of the Interior* this afternoon.

I tint my own hair, read Valerie Harms' study of *House of Incest*. Now people go to the Evanston collection and get facts left out of the *Diary*. I did not foresee this when I sold the collection for a pittance because I had no room for it—and felt detached from it.

A minute after I wrote about Sharon's "magnetic" eyes, she phoned and told me that all her other studies of *Cities of the Interior* had converged into a marvelous preface. An interpretation based on alchemy. She had just finished it when I was writing about her. Alchemy. The quest for gold as illumination (Golconda). Symbols of flight. The journey on the surface and underground. Lillian on the airplane. I *had* synthesized the novels. While proofreading *Cities*, because of my daughters' interpretations, I began to believe I had done something deep and worthwhile.

Another talk with Hugo. After much red wine, Hugo admits he needs "contact with business and politics," and for this he wastes the last years of his life from nine to three sitting in an office where he has *nothing to do*. He is 76. I suggest if he gave care and attention to the distribution of his films, he would have an income. In one evening I obtained three engagements for him. I asked forgiveness for my scolding, explaining I could only achieve the enormous work I am doing by extreme efficiency. Hugo said he understood and that he realized this was the basis of the richness of my life and that he actually envied that quality in me. If anyone had the opposite of efficiency it is Hugo. His entire life is a slow, hazy, formless, sabotaged activity with constant backtracking and additional burdens. Anyway, we expressed tolerance, compassion. I am the one who rebels against the unwieldy life patterns. I tried to give him a sense of security in my work to return the protection he gave me for so many years.

Returning to Los Angeles.

LOS ANGELES, OCTOBER 2, 1974

Disappointment with the questions following my lecture at the Smithsonian Institute. I will no longer try to talk with audiences. The sensitive ones say nothing. The aggressive ones take over. One woman talked too long about the incompatibility of creation and marriage. Imagine the quality of creation that cannot allow space or time for relationship. The questions are what make me want to give up the lectures.

After the lecture, we had a dinner with the Smithsonian members and Eugene McCarthy. He is a man of great charm, a poet. But it was a dinner with too many martinis, political gossip and unsavory stories. I was grateful for Stanley Kurnick, who sat on my left and was not drunk, so we talked about writers and writing. It lasted until 2:00 AM. I was exhausted. Kurnick told me he voted for me at the Academy. He does not recognize the genius of Marguerite Young. He is poet in residence at the Library of Congress.

One story about the Kennedys saddened me. When they wanted to drink a toast to the two dead brothers and break the glasses according to tradition, they turned out to be plastic.

Letter from James Herilihy to Anaïs Nin:
October 6, 1974

Dear Anaïs:
Leaving Thursday for Puerto Vallarta and then on to Guatemala and ??? Don't know when I'll get back. Perhaps a few weeks.

A few months ago we had a conversation about a snowstorm in a glass ball. Rainbow alerted several friends to be on the lookout for one to give you. Yesterday Dran Hamilton (of the Seitz twins—*great* fans of yours!) found one at a flea market sale at 20th Century Fox; another was found at an Arizona gift shop when we were at the Grand Canyon last month. I'm sending them to you. The Arizona one is pretty awful, but the other is nice, a ski scene made in Austria, and Dran was delighted with herself for having found it. She has a lot of feeling for your work and is glad to have a chance to present this token.

I hope, Dr. Nin, that your trip to the East was fun—not too exhausting. Give my warmest and best to Rupert.
Love,
Jamie

Letter from Anaïs Nin to Lina Rydin:
Los Angeles, October 8, 1974

Dear Lina Rydin:
What a coincidence, I signed a contract for volume 1 of the *Diaries* to appear in Sweden just a few days ago! What can I tell you? I am intensely active, have remained open and curious and interested in so many things, went to Bali this summer for UTA airlines, a free trip in exchange for travel articles.

I am 71, alert, able to travel, writing when at home, all day from 7:00 AM. I am overworked, that is my only complaint. I lecture, I write prefaces for women's books, for friends' books, and I have just finished working for a documentary film on my life, my work, my house, my students, my friends. I am sending you some informative material.

For a long time I wondered what happened to Sweden; they were the first to translate me. I visited Stockholm in 1960. Were the books badly translated? The rest of the world discovered me, but Sweden was silent. I am still writing in my Diary (working now on volume 6). Right now I am deeply involved in helping women, in directing the women towards development. I am asked to talk at every college with Women's Studies programs. I will be in Paris November 1 to 15 for volume 5 and two novels appearing. Artur Lundqvist once interviewed me on the radio. My description of Sweden will appear in volume 6.

Your friend,
Anaïs Nin

Letter from Hugh Guiler to Anaïs Nin:
New York, October 13, 1974

Darling:

Last night I saw *The Henry Miller Odyssey,* which I liked very much. He is a wonderful human being. And you looked more beautiful in this film than even in your own. Afterward several people had seen you in the Miller film on TV and remarked how beautiful you looked. Congratulations!

Saw Howard Wise today at the suggestion of WWET/13 and showed him the video tape transfer for film. He distributes video tapes, or is about to, and liked *Transcending* very much. He is inserting it at once in his catalog that goes to schools, colleges and museums.

I have now shown the film transfer to a significant number of people to be sure it is going to be a great success, even with the frustration I had in making it. Wise will also show *Levitation* and *Aphrodisiac II* on tape to make a half-hour program.

Tomorrow, another long session with Maxine Holleff to shoot excerpts of my films and the video in black and white for the video documentary of me and the work. I bought some nice African beads in a necklace of leather yesterday, but afterwards thought the leather string will not do. So I may just buy her some perfume at the tax-free shop at the London Airport.

I see I am going to be rushed to have everything ready, and several more people want to see the tape so I will have to arrange an evening.

Love,
Hugo

Letter from Henry Miller to Anaïs Nin:
Pacific Palisades, October 19, 1974

Dear Anaïs,

Thank you for the wonderful collection of photos you sent me. I have looked at them several times. There are some unforgettable ones among them.

As I said on that watercolor you reproduced, "You yourself are a masterpiece."

That one Rupert took of you with arms akimbo [in Puerto Vallarta] is one of the best. The surprising one (to me) was you wading in the water at the place where Burton and Taylor stayed. It's incredible.

I ordered only a half dozen copies. I should get at least 20 more to send around. Thank you again.

Best to you both.
Henry

Letter from Robert Zaller to Anaïs Nin:
October 20, 1974

Dear Anaïs:

I was deeply distressed by your phone call on Thursday and I still am. I immediately went to dig Tristine Rainier's essay out of my files and see just what I had done to it. I enclose it with this letter, just as I found it. I may have made errors in editing the manuscript, and I certainly made an error in not submitting the changes for the author's approval. I thought at the time that I was supposed to exercise my discretion on minor points, that it was part of my job. Certainly, I was never advised to the contrary, nor did I ever receive the least criticism or assistance from my "editors" at World or New American Library. I worked in the dark, with no prior experience and no guidelines. I agonized over every change I made, and some of them tied me up in moral knots for days. I worked under a tight deadline that made consultation all but impossible in any case, as well as under other conditions of extreme tension and uncertainty. I did the best job I could. Afterwards, I never received separate proof sheets, and, as you may know, the manuscript itself was several times actually lost. There is no need to go into all that. You know what a fight was needed to bring this book into existence.

I take responsibility for the book, with all its faults, because I was made responsible, willy-nilly, for every word in it. If I had to do it over again, and I wish I did, I would not change a comma without expressed approval, and if I am ever thrust into the unholy position of judging another writer's work, I never will. I have learned that lesson with bitter remorse. I was wounded and amazed at the suggestion that I had betrayed your trust. I don't think I could live with the thought that I had. I would never knowingly harm anyone. If I have hurt Tristine Rainier or anyone else, I am desperately sorry.

I never regretted the tribulations of the *Casebook*. I intended it purely as a gift to you, just as Lili's translation of *Spy* was her gift. That it should cause you to doubt my integrity is something that, whatever mistakes I have made, I do not deserve. I would rather the book be destroyed utterly than that it be something that came between us.

I can't say anything more about this. I am heartsick over it, and I judge myself, I think, as severely as anyone else could. I made a mistake, an ethical misjudgment. But I am not a hack or a cynic who chops up people's work for newspapers or magazines. Whatever I did was only in what I thought were the best interests of the book. That, at least, Anaïs, you must believe.

I have written to Tristine Rainier.

I spoke to New American Library on Friday. I am still trying to get books sent to all contributors. There is no editor at all at the moment.

Lili sends her love.

And I send mine, as always.

Robert

LOS ANGELES, OCTOBER 28, 1974

After the five articles on travel, Rupert and I settled down to revising vol. 6. It was peaceful, and we had so much enjoyment of certain passages that I would like to continue, working, swimming together, and this morning when I washed my hair for Paris, tinted my nails for Paris, packed for Paris I wondered at the impulse that projects me outward when I would rather live quietly. We have everything: a deep love, the ability to travel (Charlotte Hyde is so pleased with my article of Bali she will show it to the Indonesian Tourist Bureau perhaps for a deluxe book), and interesting friends come to us.

PARIS DIARY

PARIS, NOVEMBER 3, 1974

This time Paris is a science fiction airport, all glass, metal, plastic and mechanical. It is the old smell of roasted chestnuts, of rain. It is the clean subway. No feeling, as in New York, of the presence of a morbid underworld painting of the trains. The old houses contrast with the new.

The old houses somehow have not lost their colorful ghosts, evocation of history without which one cannot love Paris in depth. I see so many figures on the balconies, George Sand and Chopin, Zola and Balzac, Rimbaud in the darker cafés, and shadowy figures in the rain could be Leon Paul Fargue, Breton, Picasso. The artist Mechtilt has a studio on Quai D'Anjou, and out of her window I see the same view of the river, bridges and trees I saw from the apartment of Stuart Gilbert, translator of Joyce and Malraux. It could be Proust's window I look at, or Colette's. It could be Cendrars behind the clouded window of a closed café. It was Marguerite Duras who sat in that small café facing St. Germain-des-Prés.

In the windows there are always designs of individual taste, always a note of inventiveness in every detail. Always the indefinable taste, the posters of art exhibits in bookshops, a hand-painted dress, a single antique *meuble* in a window, small restaurants, small, intimate cafés. Always the possibility of intimacy—the covered lights, soup in a terrine as in a farmhouse, bread in a basket.

If you are careful you never bump into gigantism, the abode of giants in America, except at the airport, which belongs in New York. When I arrive, it is a brand new hotel in an old house, so it still has its intimate proportions. The *toile de Jouy* is joyous pink. There are flowers on the desk from Stock, from those who love and admire me, a note from André Bay and Jean Chalon and a message from Hugo, who is staying at the Madison Hotel.

As a cure for a deep depression, Bogner and I encouraged Hugo to come and collect money due for the showing of his films and to show his new film. The sight of him depresses me. We have a good dinner together, but he is full of small preoccupations—joyless. His contact lens, which he loses, chips. The unsatisfactory maid. The cats. The imperfections of his hotel. I help him through the ordeal of visiting his old clients. When they became disappointed with John Chase, they withdrew their business. Hugo was crushed with his passive, ineffectual role, and blamed himself. Bogner had difficulty prying him out of a *mea culpa* bog. He answered he was out of it. But he has insomnia, etc.

I reread Romaine Brooks. The failure to live fully always frightens me. It could have happened to me. I escaped. I think my impatience with Hugo is that with more help than any other human being—advisors in business, accountants, doctors, psychoanalysts, me—he has not been cured.

265

I only sleep five hours—jet lag. I reread *Seduction* in French (*Seduction* and *Collages* have appeared in one volume). It reads well. I can't tell if it has the magic of the English lyricism or not.

There is a postal and telegraph strike, so I telephone Rupert. You can hear the sea intervening—the voices waver. But at least the communication is immediate; it once took hours.

Marie-Claire came to the airport. Expressionless. I cannot reach her. (Before I left Los Angeles, I felt a complete exchange with Jody Hoy and Tristine, openness, contact. We are working together to share the teaching. My life has over-expanded, and now I must concentrate on the *work*.)

With the Science Fiction airport, I expected the disappearance of the handmade croissant, that it would be made by a computer, wrapped in plastic and tasting of paper. The croissant was still there, not only made of genuine butter and flour, but, like Venetian glass, hand-blown with an airy lightness that made it melt in my mouth, and breakfast promised a buoyant day with air and oxygen between the layers. And still, there is the immense luxury of breakfast in bed granted only to the rich in America, which gives the psyche time to prepare for the day.

Seeing the ex-clients as if symbolic of Hugo's world, was to see the ultimate in aging—true decrepitude in contrast to Varda's and Henry's aging. But in the French, the *grande bourgeoisie* is cultured and the connection with arts and letters is visible, which makes them more tolerable. One of them wears his Legion of Honour medal and could write a treatise on the lungs as well as read *House of Incest*. It saddened me, his fragility—so extreme.

It was good, by contrast, to visit Mechtilt, once a prisoner of her neurosis, now free, working well, interestingly. Her lover is a filmmaker—not there during the visit. She was frozen and heavy when we first met, she as an interviewer. Marcel Moreau was once her lover, a tormented love *au fond de gouffre* [at the bottom of an abyss]. He left her, inexplicably. They were matched in self-destruction. When I first met her, she was suffering from his disappearance. Two infernos burning at once.

I am now fearful of Jean Chalon who calls himself the *hermanito* [little brother] but who writes so cruelly of Louise de Vilmorin in *Une jeune femme de 60 ans*. He was her last love. André Malraux was the childhood friend, the marriage of convenience, familiarity. Louise died of pneumonia. I never knew how she felt about my portrait of her, or about my work. We met at an autograph party accidently, tried to meet again, failed.

It was a mistake for me to come before publicity activities—it allowed me to wander into the past. I could not reach anyone because of the holiday. I even remembered Henry's lovemaking in small hotel rooms, the wildest and most absolutely jungle lovemaking, the most orgiastic.

But with Rupert there is total fusion, total merging, which completes the lovemaking. How perfectly we oscillate. In the morning he is lazy, has difficulty in emerging from sleep, so then I make fresh coffee and bring it to him. At night I am tired, and he brings me toast and beer before sleeping. We were given a box of beautiful persimmons from a ranch. We looked up the word and found it was not an exotic fruit, but native to America. We also found, looking up the spelling of "sumptuous" in the American Heritage Dictionary, that they quoted me ("He likes big meals, so I cook sumptuous ones" from *Ladders to Fire*)!

The post office strike made my letters to friends I wanted to see undeliverable—and this compounds the difficulties.

A renewal of friendship with Jean Fanchette, now a doctor of psychiatry— mature, compassionate. We cleared up the distortions created by second-hand gossip. He endured much poverty, finished his studies, has three children. We talked about Durrell's "madness"—his flippancy towards psychiatry and analysis. Fanchette did not sell my letters—Richard Centing's claim was false. His book on psychodrama is excellent.

Saw André Bay and realized he is not the boss of Stock; I liked him as I did at first, and I understood his problems.

PARIS, MONDAY, NOVEMBER 4, 1974

Dinner at the Van der Elsts'. Marie-Claire talks about India, and her aunt who is the director of *Musique du Costume*, which is about the psychology of costume. Her mother cooks a simple dinner with black mushrooms like I never had before.

Hugo clings to life temporarily. This morning over the telephone we talked about his *lack of spirit*. I told him how I am most of the time in pain and bleeding, and yet I am not depressed or at least not to the eyes of others. Why has he no courage? (I *didn't* ask this.)

Now, at 10:00 AM I see public relations people of Stock—Betty Duhamel, André Bay and Jean Chalon. Bay gives me good advice, talks about the books. Journalists always try to make the talk about the person. I made notes: during the eight years of volume 5, 1947-1955, I wrote five books in the hostile silence of America.

Lunch with André, with Betty Duhamel, Ducourt (*Elle*). Interview with Jean Chalon. Lively talk: American literature, French literature, Kate Millett, Wilson, Mary McCarthy. *Talk* in France is an act of artistic creation. Apt expressions, descriptions, also sharp perceptions on target always. This does not change. Talk is heady, intoxicating, intelligent. My proudest achievement is to have touched and pleased them—they are discriminating, incisive and have unerring taste for quality. Their communication is lucid, and they can distinguish between what sells and what they admire.

A grey, cold day, but a sparkling lunch.

This quarter of Paris is fascinating: modern, bookshops, antique shops, art shops, exotic shops, small restaurants. But Betty Duhamel tells me now it is fashionable to move to the Marais. No more room in St. Germain-de-Près, my favorite quarter.

PARIS, NOVEMBER 5, 1974

Dream: Rupert and I live on an island, a plain island. We feel that places like Bali, Fez, Mexico were too tempting if you have *work to do*. They invite you to live, not work.

Jean Chalon speaks of my *passion* for human beings. Yes, but I do not have it for public life. I have no desire to meet the interviewers, the critics, the admirers. I

267

desire the island…a plain one like Port Vila—just green and sea. I see temptation as color, exoticism, the spectacles of Bali. I want to work.

In Paris there are the designs of Geneviève Doering. Batik technique on silky hand-woven textiles. The beauty of shop windows, narrow streets, small, intimate restaurants six feet wide.

Betty Duhamel is the granddaughter of Georges Duhamel, whose series on Salavin, a mournful, withdrawn character in a sufficatingly narrow life, I once read. I remember tiring of the grey tone. No one reads him anymore.

Jean Chalon tells me what lies behind the novel *Une Jeune Femme de 60 ans*, which distressed me by its cruelty. But I see now the cause for the cruelty was when Louise, always a snob, desperately in debt, needing protection, in a *mariage de convenance*, became the mistress and future wife of Malraux, who moved into the Château de Verrières. So Jean was estranged and left her (he was her constant companion) and wrote cruelly, I felt, a humiliating image of her pursuing him insanely when he did not love her anymore. How writers avenge themselves! "*He killed her.* The day before she died of pulmonary congestion she had a 104-degree fever and he made her come down to dinner!" The last image of her extravagance, her unreality, her need of millions; nothing was enough, though Leigh Hunt helped her. As if having premonitions of her death, she visited Leigh Hunt and reassured him her three daughters were his, not those of her great one true love. Because she never gave up her artificial *grand monde* (I knew her in Louveciennes), she remained a superficial writer, a failed artist. (Hugo explains he cannot surrender his business world because it is *half* of him. In college he took up economics *and* literature. He does not love the artist in his films *wholly*, even now when business has failed him, almost destroyed him.)

The interview with Françoise Ducout was no interview, but rather a lively, bright exchange; her insight was so sparkling. It ended with a hug and a sense of understanding. She has read me so well and so thoroughly. Keeps a diary. Loves America.

A deep evening with Claude Combet and Mireille Gerschwiler—she is a great beauty who was willingly chosen to be his mistress within reach at any hour. She lives aesthetically; she spends all day waiting for his visits and does housework at night to not feel alone. He was her philosophy professor. She gave up the theatre just to live for love. With these seven years of an extraordinary love that would fulfill any man, he writes nightmares! He is killing his mother over and over. Literary murders do not seem as effective as the final ones.

Press cocktail—I already knew most of the guests, and there was great warmth.

Marcel Marceau came—Claude Combet, Françoise Wegener, Françoise Ducout, Diane de Margerie, Josanne Duranteau…

Durrell was having an opening the same day, same hour!

Dinner with the Bays and Christian de Bartillat. Bartillat is full of charm as always, saying wonderful things, that the combination of art and life I had made was the greatest of all. But he printed fewer photographs in *Diary 5* and neglects the novels. He always captivated my interest, but through Bay's eyes appears capricious and often unreliable (he promised Daniel Stern to publish him in January, and Bay says it won't happen). They make nothing with paperbacks, so they are not interested, which prevents dissemination—this is short-sighted.

Bartillat, homosexual and aristocratic, *adores* Miller. He visited him. Henry tells him it was I who influenced him to write autobiographically and inspired *Black Spring* and *Capricorn*, his best books. If we had stayed together, could I have fought the false stances in *Sexus* and *Plexus*? Durrell killed his father, Miller. The cable at the end of their correspondence nearly put an end to the sequel to *Sexus* and *Plexus*: "When are you going to stop writing history?" Durrell, however, did lose his high status with the books following the *Quartet*.

What an amazingly high level of talk here—not comparable even with the most brilliant of my friends, who *write* brilliantly, but their talk is inferior—Sharon, Nancy Zee, Tristine, Judy Hoy, Zaller. Yet Bay says the French can no longer write.

The evening with Claude Combet was the deepest. This living, pulsating contact with others is like passion. I do not want to die yet—I am not ready. But was anyone ready? Only those who died in life like Reginald.

PARIS, NOVEMBER 8, 1974

An evening with Eric Neville, who is desperately seeking independence, a second birth, away from Colette. She will not set him free. He tried to escape through madness. Bogner saved him. He is a child seeking to become a man.

Durrell's new book [*Monsieur*] is distressing: top-heavy with *ideas*; impossible human beings; intellectual games; superb descriptive writing; depiction of neurosis without the slightest insight; empty words; Edgar Allan Poe situations; lack of unity; obsession with death unresolved; handled with sensational exoticism; he can only describe Alexandria; no feeling for the metaphysical... Summation: *Trompe d'oeil.* I was bored. Fell asleep reading it.

I waste the entire morning on difficulties with the telephone. But my Hotel de l'Abbaye is warm, cheerful, charming, comfortable. I look forward to breakfast— hot coffee, an evanescent croissant. There are always flowers on the desk, books to read.

I called Rupert twice. Because of the postal strike, there can be no letters, no cables. I miss our life. Perhaps I feel I have garnered enough riches and must return to work. But I do respond fully to new friends, new experiences. I love Paris with a passion. The walk yesterday through the Marais was a walk through history—so alive—Ninon de l'Enclos, all the historic families, down to Edith Piaf singing in the streets. The ghosts are still glowing, still shedding light. Americans fear death because they try to live without the past. The past is comforting as it is not *ashes* at all, but an eternal flame whose light illumines our spirit and defers death, incites us to live.

I refuse a television program in association with Simone de Beauvoir on aging. Dwelling on age *is* aging. All I concede is health problems. Pain. Discomfort. Not age.

How many personages walked with me yesterday through the Marais? From all the books I read sprang these lives—George Sand, Mozart, Chopin, Zola, Balzac, later Gide, Julien Green, Proust. What is immortality? When the spirit has a voice in words or color or stone or garden, which is transferable.

Those who had no voice? Those we never knew, who dissolved—does not even science say their voices are still in the air? Who knows what we are breathing from the past? Why is my past here and not in Spain or America? Away from America, I think of friends I love deeply, but not of a country I love.

Who lives in Paris? asks *Travel & Leisure*. Millions. The colorful present denotes the accretion of a colorful past. More and more faintly, the art of writing and speaking may be inherited—but it is there.

The small, intimate restaurant in a small square that would make everyone a painter. Trees the opposite of sumptuous, tropical trees, and therefore more abstract as are all ideological trees not nourished enough by the senses. Intelligent trees.

Impression de la vie.

No museums, no dust.

Wearing my long black sweater dress, white wool coat and white wool beret, I felt the stirring of many lives at their moments of luminescence, not decay.

It is in us that decay is formed when we cease to feel the *lives* of others.

So Paris may be old stones like the high wall facing my window and covered with sturdy brown-armed ivy, mossy, but it is as if I had written these lines for Docteur Marthe Lamy, in her 80s, an extraordinary woman, lively, bright, sparkling, the doctor of Gide, François Mauriac, Georges Duhamel, Romaine Brooks, Edith Wharton, Colette and more. She is named in their books. She is still practicing. She keeps her "professional" secrets. She reads. She is discerning, keen, open, frank. We took to each other. She told me about the Society of Women Doctors that was created to help American women doctors fight *prejudice*. She has never known prejudice. She loves my work. She knew my father. She began her studies in 1919— against her family's wishes. I want time with her. Today, in her, this past is vivid, and her present is still reaching out as she reached out and wrote to me. Life has nothing to do with age.

Barry Jones came to Paris from Oxford, by boat and by train. We had lunch. He met Dr. Lamy.

(I love this diary book. You can hide letters in its fold.)

Evening at Jean Chalon's. A nest. All books, pictures, red walls, a tea cozy feeling. A Spanish friend. He knew Natalie Barney for ten years and is writing a book about her. He knows Bertha, her maid, who still receives letters from Djuna Barnes. He has photographs she gave him, a list of her liaisons and a list of her adventures. She was faithful to women all her life. I encouraged him to explain the role of Djuna Barnes, who is mentioned in Romaine Brooks' biography. Thus the life of everyone becomes unfolded after their death. An artist who disguised his life in his work, made a confession on the radio with a promise it would not be disseminated until after his death. A need of truth, like the Catholic confession. We all have it. Jean Chalon has to explain why he had to write a novel and change the facts about Louise de Vilmorin. (Not enough—he *is* a journalist; invention is not his forte.) He delights in the freedom he has in writing about Natalie Barney. She must have trusted him. Over 80 years old, she asked his help in tidying her papers. She had time to burn letters. Love letters. Why? It did not matter to anyone. She had no children, no husband. She once seduced a woman away from her husband.

Then I hear about another side of Dr. Lamy. She is wealthy. She is possessive. She fell in love with Jean Chalon and also Carlos de Angulo. She wanted to give them one of her apartments. She is quixotic, capricious, an image in a Coney Island fun house mirror.

Natalie Barney. Her house on Rue Jacob was sold. How or why, I don't know. It was a scandal. She had to move to a hotel.

Jean has a storage memory. Carlos says he is the soul of generosity and goodness, who does not see evil, whereas I found flashes of malice in the Vilmorin book, which was actually an act of revenge as Louise turned towards her protector, Malraux.

Hugo is not well. Not actually ill—but not well. His mind wanders. I cannot control my impatience. He is malingering, I feel, for me.

Combet sends flowers, which almost touch the ceiling! Pussywillows among them. It is 10:00 AM. I have to get dressed.

It is easier to write about the dead—do we always have to wait for that? To live the life of others when they are gone? We spent an evening with Natalie Barney, Bertha the maid, Djuna Barnes; their lives belong to us.

I read Chalon's *Ouvrir Une Maison de Rendez-Vous.*

I can no longer hear those who say Paris is dead, Jean-Michel Forsey—I cannot hear the negators. "I cannot hear Barcelona. I can only hear the Blacks, Harlem, South America. *Paris est fini.*"

Marcel Marceau has a beautiful mistress—intuitive, interesting. I like her. She has been to China, Japan. She is a specialist of Oriental art. Marcel vituperates against surrealism (he gives the work a narrow definition); he speaks of the *visceral* origin of his work. One descends to the "gut" level. That is true. Hugo looks like a ghost of himself—he is not there. Barry Jones enjoys everything. Mechtilt is a stranger to the fireworks of words. Gisele is soft, permeable. I find the word I had lost in French: politics are rigged: *truquée.*

My fictional characters are composites: amalgams. I suddenly found the last one myself as if I were recovering a deep knowledge of French.

I go to see Marta Weber's "dolls"—modern witchcraft—Mechtilt describes them as "murdered." All the trappings are there, so much like voodoo dolls, though they are named "Marilyn" or "Sylvia." Weber looks like one herself, appearing in an Indian mirror dress trembling from the alcohol flowing in her veins in place of blood. Almost unconsciously I am writing my article for *Travel & Leisure.*

The French abstract intellect—I can't follow it.

I dream that Piccolino has run away; I search for him, and when I finally find him I spank him.

I dream that a *turtle* is bisexual but what the turtle has to do with us, I don't know.

Telephone calls. Militant revolutionary women. A woman working on Rank's *Le Double* asks: "Did Rank know the Bible? How could he omit the biblical case of the double?" Others love the *Diary* and just want to see me.

Gisele kisses me emphatically as if to complete our understanding.

I open the door of Françoise Wegener's apartment while I wait for her: It is Julio Cortázar. Big, rough-hewn, but with tender, big blue eyes—familiar. But unlike his work, which is full of games, he is direct and human, his talk genuine. Françoise describes her terror of flying, Julio's of submarines (a slow death). Her childhood memories of war were so that *peace* was not believable and that Hiroshima was natural and expected. She was seven years old when she saw a child of three shot in a Vienna ghetto. Julio envies musicians, as I do, who are eloquent and unrevealing. Françoise talks too much and nervously. Julio admits there is total freedom in his novels and no need of a diary. I explain why there are no inhibitions in mine, a vice begun at 11—the assurance of secrecy. He says anyone who separated the novels and diaries is mad. They interlock.

A *rez de chaussez*—old beams—old courtyard—a *colimaçon* [spiral staircase].

Julio was at ease, not Françoise. She never was. I met her five years ago—I liked her, but she had washed her dark hair and wore a blond wig. "It is not me." She is unsure.

Cortázar said one of the natural activities of love is to know all about a person. He wants to know everything about a friend or a lover. He is amazed that there are no blocks in the *Diary*.

It is only two o'clock in L.A. I miss my love. I miss my love. My love, my heart, my vital center.

At Marie-Claire Van der Elst's there is a lovely atmosphere. Her aunt dressed in a hand-painted dress, made by an artist friend. Marie-Claire's mother, mischievous and lively, tells me she knows the homely governess my father made love to charitably (otherwise, according to him, she would have never known love); Martine Laroche, whose young husband died in a ski accident, is now a translator; Susan Reznick, a waif, more French than American, has been teaching here for a year.

Eric and Colette Neville are experiencing the tragedy of separation. He dreams that his great-grandmother, grandmother and mother stood one behind the other as in a family portrait, and one *unknown woman* was in the foreground. To escape them, he breaks the glass window *with his feet*. Yet Colette does not let him go. He always looks down, like someone at confession, looks away, not full-faced.

At midnight I am inside *La Surréalisme et les Rêves*—at last at home. Every word is familiar to me, except for the farce and jokes. My roots are here, my writer's roots.

At one o'clock I could not sleep, so I called Rupert. His voice! He is worried about me overworking, eating the wrong food. He is working on editing vol. 6. "How beautiful! Your best writing. That description of Venice! I went to the beach. Take care, darling, I want you back soon. I love you more than ever."

PARIS, NOVEMBER 11, 1974

Jean-Yves Boulic wrote to me after reading the *Diaries*. He was living in Louveciennes. He wrote rather formally, and because he was working on politics and economics, I imagined him stuffy and fat, square… Oh! Monsieur Boulic is young, slender, with a Spanish face—a Breton—very interesting! He chose to serve in the military as a teacher in Algeria—near the sea. He became one with the life there—loved it. He is 31, married, with three small children. We discovered a mutual love of Ninon de l'Enclos. He has read her letters.

He had invited me in the name of the mayor to a reception, which I could not accept as it was too heavy a schedule, but now I regret not visiting him, for there is nothing I enjoy more than the fusion of the past and present. He was too modest. He called himself a "classicist," rather startled by the *Diary*, but it was a false image. He brings me a handsome history of Louveciennes written by his father-in-law.

Now I await the TV evening. Hugo came to have tea. I finally analyzed my anger and irritation. I had lived in expectation that his absentmindedness was a neurotic symptom that would disappear with time. Instead it has become alarmingly worse. At first I combatted it with "systems" that he promptly defeated. Then anger. The other night, after carefully writing everything down, he invited a friend to the wrong place and had to wait for her, intercept her. He lost not one, but two umbrellas. He leaves me saying, "I'll see you at Shakespeare and Company"—when we were going to the Van der Elsts'.

Television program: not satisfied. I was surprised by their moral judgment of *Story of a Marriage*, so I assert that *no judgment* should be made upon love. Not happy—the moderator was very kind to "ideas" and potential books, but not to books concerning life.

The program was just as superficial as American TV. Some writers came with a prepared speech—orderly and clear—I was subjected to Jean Chalon vagaries. I was unhappy, but Fortune, a devoted young man, and Betty Duhamel were pleased. At least my naturalness and sincerity came through.

The visit to Geneviève Duchâteau was ruined by her political ventriloquism. I never realized how terrible thinking that follows a political formula is. I was ready to like her as a human being, but you can't love a propaganda leaflet. And her combativeness reminded me of my mother's. I left in the middle of an argument. I refuse to meet the militant feminists, to join them, to speak in general terms about entirely personal and subjective griefs against man. Jean was tactless. He presented me as the "Simone de Beauvoir of America, but not boring and full of charm." I should have defended Beauvoir, but it meant hurting him, and he is known for his devotion to me. Fortune says the *Diary* was therapeutic. He thought that I put the TV moderator in his place. The reaction to the show was favorable. A telephone call from Durrell. Larry asks: "How do you maintain your energy? At 60 I feel like fainting away." I can't tell him: don't drink.

Jeanne Moreau: the smile of a playful, young woman, a mischievous child, radiant, new. Wistful face, deep eyes, depth. Lovely, soft hands. A soft outline to the body—feminine, her life self-created, loved by the new wave directors because she did not smile artificially, because she showed her moods, because she was natural. She is so intelligent as an actress. In the hands of a director, she is malleable with so many aspects; she can be the prostitute, the moll, the sadist, the neurotic, the obsessed woman—always suggesting depths beyond the role. Yet she felt emptied, depressed. Why? Her self has been stolen, used, fragmented. She saw herself in *A Spy in the House of Love*, the *voyageuse* always prepared to leave. It was easier not to love. Five years ago she underwent a transition. She wanted *receuillement*—to consolidate herself, to *be*, to write, to speak for herself.

She was asked by a man in Berkeley: "Who are *you*? Does anyone know *you*?" The identity crisis in the supremely talented artist is far more complex than in others. But Jeanne never acted in life. Her house, her cooking, her care of others, her tasteful dreaming are all real. She *was* a *natural* actress. But that makes it all the more difficult to make distinctions—obsessed, indifferent, tantalizing—the choices are vast.

And there she is. She spreads herself over the armchair. She cooks. She offers me a shawl. She has sacrificed many roles in the quest of fusion. Integrity. She has gone through extreme difficulties in the quest for her own life.

I hope these men will never write about me, because they do not know me at all: Henry Miller, Gore Vidal, Lawrence Durrell.

300 or more persons came to Shakespeare & Company. George Whitman is lean, older, partly toothless, but picky as always. I signed books for hours. Half the customers were French, half American; there were students from Santa Cruz and Santa Barbara, from Madison, Wisconsin.

We had dinner at the Algerian restaurant Couscous.

Dr. Lamy's books—she remembers all I said about my desk. Her *cabinet de consultation.* Her extraordinary memory. *La mémoire ça se travaille.* The memory of Natalie Barney has not been good for the last ten years. She is translating one of her books written in English. At 60 she could have been operated on for a broken hip (a pin). She refused. At 70 she gave up her love life. She was unnecessarily bedridden for the last ten years. Her house is on the same street as Gide's house, Julien Green's.

Françoise Wegener's house is a mansion. She has a small apartment, but her friends have a big one, opened for parties—a big garden—contact with the aristocracy. She tells me of her last lover. It was a man of 50, who weighed on her, was jealous and possessive. She put an end to the relationship. A big gate. A court-yard. She loves the past.

Chez Fanchette: "What alienated you?" he asks. He is a taker, not a giver. He is a successful psychiatrist. He and his wife loved Claude Durrell. He repeats: "What happened?" I don't know. I think I reminded him of Claude.

Bay says my passage through Paris was absolutely sensational. Reactions wonderful. On the bitchy television I was cool, collected, serene. Fortune, a beautiful, dark young man, loves me. My phone rings. Fans, fans, fans. Interviews.

But Bay is not the man of ultimate decisions.

I was so weary I asked for no more phone calls. I went to bed. My valise is three-quarters full of books. Jeanne Moreau invited me to stay with her.

Telephone call from a fan: "I was looking for a clinic for my wife, who has cancer of the brain. I thought of Louveciennes because you were there. She is perfectly happy there, and I owe it to you. I am sorry I cannot see you."

It is 9:00 PM and I am exhausted. I have finished packing and I am in bed.

"There is someone downstairs who wants to see you." I can't. They bring up a recording and a letter. Her father was a pianist. She feels numerous affinities with the *Diaries.* She telephones me.

At Shakespeare & Company, I promise hundreds of people I will see them when I come back. Will I come back? I have a constant pain in the lower abdomen. I live on painkillers. People come to say goodbye. If I had been younger, I would have fallen in love with Fortune.

The militant and revolutionary women wanted me to inaugurate a woman's building at Les Halls.

Grey, cold days. Strikes: post office, garbage in the streets, hardships. Such misery caused by the greedy, the rich, the politicians. Is China happier?

I am asked about the meaning of our nostalgic return to the past. It is because we are unhappy in the present. We can idealize the past. Who remembers the sorrow of the '20s or '30s? The bad is erased with time. People who read the *Diary* will see Acapulco as it *was*, and only what I thought worthy of noting.

Flowers. A happy doll. The lovely, intimate restaurants. The *small* bookshops.

The negative: the French sharpness of manner—they talk too much, too fast, a nervous habit saved only by apt expressions. At the airport I pick up, by chance, a biography of Coco Chanel, which completed my image of Paris again, this time unembellished, sordid at times: her avarice, her selfishness in times of strikes, her collaboration with the Germans, her incapacity to love. Yet in spite of it all, she led a romantic life, associated with all the creative activities, was loving.

————

NOVEMBER 16, 1974
Return to New York.

Letter from Daisy Aldan to Anaïs Nin:
New York, November 20, 1974

Dearest Anaïs:

I want to say this to you for whatever it may be worth to you. I have thought of our conversation yesterday. According to my beliefs and philosophy, nothing is to be gained by cutting life short before it comes to an end naturally. Since I believe in life after death—that is, the continuation of the individuality beyond the threshold of death, such an act, even if one is senile, etc., solves nothing and may actually prolong suffering. I know you don't believe this, but I'm telling you anyway. I mean, life should not be prolonged artificially as they do these days, but also it should not be ended artificially.

Secondly, I say the following to you from my deepest heart: If you are ever in a state where you need care, and I am not in that state before you, I would, if you called on me, take it upon myself to care for you. You talked about being a burden, not wishing this ever. I would never consider this a burden. Should such an eventuality arise, and it may never, you now know that I am there for you, if I am healthy.

When my mother needed me in this way, I was incapable of such an act, but I have grown more compassionate and capable.

Your loving friend always,
Daisy

THE BOOK OF PAIN—MON JOURNAL

This book was given to me by Rob Noah Wynne, painter, collagist and beautiful young man engaged in making Marguerite Young known to the public by readings at WBAI.

LOS ANGELES, NOVEMBER 29, 1974
Home at last—to love, warmth, rest. I slept—slept. I love this diary with its shadowy ships on every page. Where are they going? Plants, birds, fish…

Music last night.

How strange it was in Paris to see my documentary film, to hear Rupert playing, to see Piccolino—in Hofstra College, Jamaica, where I received a medal, to Columbus, Ohio where the film was shown—to see an image of the life.

Pisces—where am I? In Los Angeles?

LOS ANGELES, NOVEMBER 30, 1974
At the post office—a carton full of mail.

LOS ANGELES, DECEMBER 4, 1974
Since January 1974 I have lived with pain and diminished energy. The implant did not stop the bleeding. Dr. Parks explained that the bleeding is not a symptom of cancer, but it is seepage from an incision that did not heal. It was humiliating. I have to wear Kotex as if I were having a period. Pain was caused by the medication Megace, the infections by Delalutin, which cause a pain similar to a bad period. During the trip to Bali, if I wanted to feel well I had to take Darvon. Now I have to take Darvon every four hours. I feel dragged down.

And today I lived one of the happiest days of my life: Rupert said he was *completely, fully happy* to work at something I love—and wished to be free of the slavery of teaching to travel. We have a rich and wonderful life. While I was in Paris he revised vol. 6. He met me with two different sections, different because *I* wrote two sections, one for the Diary and one for the magazine *Eve*.

I began to work only yesterday—before that I was too tired. Paris had been too heavy a charge—even its memory was too rich, and my body is weighed down by pain.

6:25 PM: Rupert's words made me happy. We made a beautiful life. He was sad to read in the Diary about my discontent with Sierra Madre. "Why didn't you tell me? Why didn't you share your loneliness, the stark poverty of the life?" "I couldn't burden you. What could you do? You were young and faced a new life, one which suited your belief in nature, in conservation. My restlessness would have made you uselessly unhappy." Oh, I remember the drabness of Sierra Madre and the violent contrast with the week at the Brussels Fair with the Baroness Lambert. It is an unfair comparison, between the elite of Europe and the desert of Forest Service life.

LOS ANGELES, DECEMBER 7, 1974
Dream: There is a gentle, understanding woman doctor (Bogner?). She had to become a balance between the pessimism and psychological brutalities of Dr. Weston and the casual, relaxed attitude of Dr. Parks, who never explains or clarifies. So I discussed the whole subject with Bogner (who is an M.D.). She obtained clarification from Dr. Parks (the unhealed incision, seepage, medications as sources of menstrual pain, that because of pain I live on Darvon). Weston's threats did frighten me. This morning I could not get up until Rupert brought me coffee (and Darvon). I worked all day, but not well. There is a lack of energy. I have no desire to answer letters. Rupert's love sustains me.

Letter from Anaïs Nin to Hugh Guiler:
Los Angeles, December 7, 1974

Darling:
I do acutely regret leaving you alone, yet I know I cannot carry the burden of both our lives, only one at a time. I only began to work three days ago. I was more deeply tired than I knew. Now it is going smoothly.

I am returning the "honor" you sent me, which sounds fake. They say nothing about you as a filmmaker. If you want to make sure, ask Gunther. It sounds like a money-making scheme.

I had a dream last night: that you carried *all your film equipment* in the shopping cart, very heavy stuff, on your way to Bogner, and I was pleading with you to leave it in the baggage room. Don't know what it means.

I have very special gifts for your very special friends, which I am mailing you. Japanese wallets. They can be mailed. They last a long time and are very beautiful.

I am working on a description in vol. 6 of the week spent with Baroness Lambert, a beautiful week, and now about Paris.

I had to turn down a lecture that would have meant three lectures in one week in the north.

If you see Barry, tell him I can deliver some original diaries in February, that I will get Gunther to prepare a contract, and a letter from them would be required confirming their wish to buy the original diary collection at so much a year. I said $20,000 a year if possible, but I would prefer $25,000, which would assure your income and taxes. But Gunther cannot make a contract until Dartmouth makes an offer. In February I may have to come myself with the first batch of deliveries.

A

Letter from Hugh Guiler to Anaïs Nin:
New York, December 9, 1974

Darling:

Just got your letter of the 7th, and I am glad you got rested after your deep fatigue. You must not allow yourself to go so far ever again, and I am glad you turned down the lectures in the north.

I myself am slowly recovering, but on Bogner's advice, I am stopping the sleeping pills, which, she says, often give me that hung-over feeling and she does not recommend that for me.

I also had a dream about you—that you were wading through the water dragging a log, like a dugout. The log, of course, I associate with your diary, so here is a curious *parallel* between our dreams, which crossed in time.

Thanks for the idea, the Japanese wallet.

Last night Barry Jones called me from Times Square, and I invited him to dinner. We had a wonderful evening. He is certainly an exceptional young man. He has made a special printed folder, one page with fine Chinese rice paper for the material I had given him in Paris on the films, and he has gotten Oxford interested in them. He told me more about the details of his effort to get Dartmouth to buy your diary manuscript, and he says he is going there to be present when the Executive Board needs to make a final decision. He is very optimistic, but it was clear that he only will be able to give you definite news after next Sunday, the 15th. He will probably call me, and I can then pass what he says to Gunther, but obviously the letter Gunther needs will not be forthcoming until after the 15th. As he is unlikely to call me before then, it may be too late to bring up some suggestions for $25,000 a year instead of $20,000. I will also ask him if you should bring the first batch in February.

Love,
Hugo

P.S. Have just got the news that Harcourt Brace has announced they expect 1974 net earnings to be $3.05 against $2.81 in 1973, and they expect 1975 net earnings to be 11% greater than 1973.

Letter from Anaïs Nin to Gunther Stuhlmann:
Los Angeles, December 15, 1974

Dear Gunther:
    Working hard on volume 6. I have a project. If you are in touch with New American Library, and if the *Casebook* has gone as well as I think it has (based on the fact that all my readers seem to have bought it—they printed 5,000), and if they are convinced that people do read criticism, do you think you might edit an anthology of all the good theses we now have (by Sharon Spencer, Nancy Zee, Lee Potts, Lynne Sukenick, Tristine Rainer, etc.), for which I can't find a publisher? I think it might go as everything else concerning me has gone this year. In each case, I think women would erase the academic flavor. Students read critics particularly when they are about to engage in a study, and every day I get a letter from someone starting a thesis or study.
    Le Monde was very favorable towards me. *Le Figaro* was positive even though shallow (Jean Chalon). Now I wait for *Elle* and *L'Observateur.*
    The documentary showing was packed today, at 11:00 AM. Reviews are excellent.
    Think about the anthology. It is good timing, I feel. Hope you are progressing.
    Love,
    Anaïs

Letter from Hugh Guiler to Anaïs Nin:
New York, December 15, 1974

Darling:
    Thank you for the two Japanese purses. They are lovely and will come in handy.
    I am still thinking about the introduction to my lecture at Columbia on Feb. 20th, in which I mention both Anna Balakian's and Sarah Alexandrian's writing on dream and reality. It seems to me that I should add, if you have no objection—"and of course, Anaïs Nin, who has written so much over the years about living from the dream outward." What do you think about that?
    I had a conference with Roger on the Ian Hugo accounts and spent several hours yesterday preparing a statement from him, showing that I made no profit this year. He is satisfied, therefore, that it means I don't have to make a tax return for this year, which was a relief for us both. But it would be nice if you could send me a receipt for $705 to Ian Hugo, which is the amount you paid for my trip to Europe, and which I was supposed to have reimbursed to you in Paris. You might date it November 1, 1974. Just say "Received from Ian Hugo the sum of $705 in reimbursement of that amount paid by me for his return airline tickets to Europe October 24-November 16, 1974, including deposits for hotel reservations."
    You began a recent letter saying you "will not any longer bear the burden of two lives." You are already bearing the financial burden, after Roger says the $1,000

a month is sufficient for the Hugh P. Guiler account, together with what I get from Social Security and Joaquín. So it's really not necessary to think in terms of $25,000 a year. As for the moral and psychological burden, I do not wish to pass that on to you, as I feel quite capable with Bogner's help to pay it myself. She has advised me not to be in any hurry about taking a decision regarding the office, and this fits in with my present feelings, with a few exceptions. I am now at my desk only in the mornings and even then occupy myself with the papers and administrative work connected with my files, telephone calls and letters. I have about five or six contacts here and in London, and also problems with them and the videos.

So all this sort of thing is taking up most of my time and is likely to increase next year. The little time I need at the office, until business picks up, at least, and even then, plus the time on the phones in the office, has changed my feelings about the latter, and I am not any longer experiencing any conflict. Also, John Chase called me out of his own accord the other day, saying he just wanted to keep in touch with me, and from what he said about his plan, I gathered there is a good chance of some orders before the end of June 1975, and I would not feel good about losing that opportunity to make my own contribution and lighten your financial burden.

But during this season I have much more to do to occupy myself. I think Anna Balakian is going to invite me for a Christmas meal, and probably there will be another invitation. Then there are Christmas cards, presents, etc.

I hope you will understand that my decision to make no move at this time is based on the absence of any conflict or tension between my two occupations.

I imagine you will try to call me today, but I don't want to take too much of your telephone time, so I think it's better to write.

Love,
Hugo

LOS ANGELES, DECEMBER 16, 1974

Able to work on vol. 6 again. A few pages a day.

1,000 persons went to see my *Anaïs Nin Observed* this morning. It received beautiful reviews. Every night I write a few letters.

My comments about the Jill Krementz Henry Miller photo collection:

We often fear that the qualities we love in a young writer will vanish over time, that they will change, freeze, cease to give out warmth and inspiration. This is not so with Henry Miller. When Lawrence Durrell and I visited him, on the occasion of our birthdays, there was no change from the old meetings in Paris. Henry continues to be a colorful storyteller, his handicaps never intrude in the conversation, and he is rich and abundant with memories of encounters, with what Bachelard calls "the feasts of friendship." He is still inspiring, alive, and humorous. No time or handicap can fade his love of life, his memory, his love of portraying his life and friends as great adventures.

We had come to entertain him, and the evening ended with his entertaining us. No story, no description, no encounter could surpass his. We were not visiting a man made heavier with time, but illumined by the riches he amassed. Every name brings up an anecdote, every anecdote inspires another. I was reminded of the storytellers of Morocco, where most people cannot read. If you could not read Miller you would still be allowed to hear the abundant richness and color of his experiences.

Note from Henry Miller to Anaïs Nin:
Pacific Palisades, December 16, 1974

Dear Anaïs,
　　Thank you for that page. Too bad it's wasted on Jill Krementz's photos. I don't think she's so hot as a photographer.
　　In Durrell's book *Monsieur* there is a chapter ("Macabru," I think) describing a jaunt into the desert, a feast, and some magic—*marvelous writing.* But I agree [with you]—the whole makes a crossword puzzle!
　　Henry
P.S. Was I to return what you wrote about me or what?

Letter from Anaïs Nin to André Bay:
Los Angeles, December 18, 1974

Dear André:
　　So relieved to find the strike is over and we can get letters again.
　　I have a delicate mission for you that I know you can fulfill with your tact and gentleness. As you know, I wrote about Lesley Blanch and Romain Gary in *Collages.* I have no way of knowing whether she ever read the book. I am working on her portrait now in volume 6. I wrote her a loving, charming letter showing her how I had caused thousands of women to read her with my list of women writers printed by all the colleges. I told her I wanted to be in touch with her because it was my custom to show my major portraits to the person concerned and obtain their permission and opinion. I have to do this for Harcourt. They will not publish without a release. The "changes" were always minimal and unimportant. She has not answered me. Did she mind what I wrote in *Collages*? I admire her keenly. During her painful separation from Romain Gary she came to me, and I helped her in every way possible. We have not been in touch since she left Los Angeles. She lives in Menton, France. If any business takes you there I think you will find her fascinating (her book on Russia, her *Wilder Shores of Love*). If nothing takes you there before I finish volume 6, then we may have to resort to telephoning, but I would rather rely on your personal charm with women; let me know. I could send you the pages concerning her, and you might show them to her and obtain her consent, or, if necessary, let her cross out anything she doesn't like. It has to be done. I never had any trouble with the *Diary*, because I did proceed this way. Sometimes even a minor statement can do harm when you do not wish it to. She was written up in *Vogue*, with photos of her villa. She could be traveling. She is a great traveler.
　　I am glad you are pleased with my stay in Paris.
　　I am still reading the book I was given, that strange, sad diary of Mauriac Fils, *Le Temps Immobile*. Almost the opposite of mine.
　　Anaïs

Los Angeles, December 20, 1974
　　Doctor examinations.

280

Letter from Anaïs Nin to Shirley Osborne:
Los Angeles, December 21, 1974

Dear Shirley:

I was naturally disappointed at your therapist's not understanding me. But I do understand your feeling that I "opened a Pandora's Box," and I made the mistake of thinking that this would not be difficult since you had a therapist to help you. However, now I feel it was a fortunate period for you, *not* to be further disturbed by a way of teaching writing that requires psychological in-depth explorations.

You say that you want to *close the lid* on what we opened, that you believe this freedom, as I call it, is described by your therapist as unstructured. I have always had the collaboration of the therapist: you can't have two *kinds* of teachers. At this moment I feel it is more important for you to believe in *her*—she can do more for you. She is necessary to you.

The daring experiment of saying that deep writing can only come from a deep knowledge of one's unconscious was too great a stress on you (according to her). I think it best for the present that you give yourself to the therapist and believe in her. Later you can make a re-entry into the writing world. You see, I have no faith in someone who makes the statement there was nothing *new* on your tape. We were not seeking the new, but *your* discovery of yourself, and *that* was new, and the two visions are in conflict, which I would not like to work with. I have not changed my feeling that you are talented and courageous, but I don't want you caught between two *contrasting* ways of teaching. Psychological help is more important at this point for you than achieving a writing creation. So let us wait for a while—I feel opposite theories are working in you and we can't achieve anything without total faith and a solving of our dualities.

It is interesting that you *enjoyed* the difference, but as I told you once, I feel it is not the *differences* that are important, but it is important to find the harmonies that make the creation positive and single-minded. I personally want you to get well and avoid all conflicts. Take your dream to your therapist. I am not one. I believe there is no freedom in writing unless there is psychological freedom. Please get well.
    Anaïs

Letter from Joaquín Nin-Culmell to Anaïs Nin:
Berkeley, December 22, 1974

Dear Anaïs:

Here is my letter as promised to you and to me. So sorry to hear that you are not feeling well and have undergone some new tests. *Please take care of yourself* and don't let yourself be used for other purposes than your primary one, which is your writing. In some ways, success is a great impediment. Thank God you have the guts, the drive, and the talent! So many gifts remain at the seedling stage. Not so with you. You have grown and grown and grown. Blessings on you for that!

So pleased with the comment on Father's book. It did turn out well in spite of the many, too many, errata. On the other hand, the young publishers did a real labor of love and have taken tremendous interest in the whole project. If all goes well— numerically speaking (Maria Rosés used to say: *en la vida todo son números* [in life everything is numbers])—I may go ahead with volume 2 and eventually with volume 3. It will be devoted to Spanish music and musicians. I'll be devoted to other topics and some significant letters. Wish me luck!

I'm afraid that you are right about the energy business. You must have surmised that I was at the very end of my rope a few weeks ago. Exactly why, I do not know, but perhaps the delayed reaction to the operation had something to do with it. So sorry about the misplaced comments. Am learning little by little that I don't have endless energy and hence I must make a list of priorities. I hate the selectiveness, and yet it is a must. You must feel the same way.

Let me know if you want to make my place your headquarters if and when you come to San Francisco for your lecture in January. My only obligation that month is a concert in Stanislaus on January 17th.

Am alone in the house (Ted has gone to Santa Barbara to spend Christmas with his family) and am rather enjoying the peace and quiet and work.

Deepest love always,

J

Card from Masako Karatani to Anaïs Nin:
Japan, December 1974

Dear Miss Nin:

I hope this card will find you enjoying the merry season of the year.

Your *Diary* came out in Japan at last early this month, and I'm sending you a copy. Please let me know if you need some more.

I called on Catherine Broderick at Kobe College the other day, where I had a nice talk with her students about your diary. People are beginning to be interested in the diary, and before long I will find out how it has been received by the Japanese readers. To help them with a direct approach to your diary, I wrote, as an introduction, my own interpretation of it, which I am translating now both for you and for Catherine. I hope to complete it before the New Year and send a copy to you.

May I ask a favor of you? I'd like you to send me a copy of vol. 5 of your diary, for it takes almost four months to order one through a bookstore in Tokyo.

I hope to see you sometime next year, probably on my way to England next summer. I'll write soon.

Sincerely yours,

Masako

Letter from Anaïs Nin to Masako Karatani:
Los Angeles, December 1974

Dear Masako:

I was very glad to hear from you, and that the *Diary* is out. Let me know the reactions, not full reviews, but summaries; I don't want to add to your burden. I am deeply grateful for your work. And glad you wrote a special preface to introduce the *Diary*. It needed that, as there are subjects that are inexplicable to Japan: not being attached to any one country, feminism, creation of the self, etc.

I am mailing you today an anthology of criticism, mostly by women. Also a supplement of photographs that were not in the *Diaries*, as well as volume 5. I was out of copies before I left for my big summer trip, and when I returned I had forgot-

282

ten who I wanted to them for.

I am working hard on volume 6. It is difficult, with the avalanche of mail, demands for lectures, visitors, friends who have a right to my time (especially when in trouble). This summer I was given a free trip to Bali in exchange for five articles that will appear in different travel magazines. The same airline goes to Japan, so someday I am sure I can make the arrangement and visit you.

Please remind me when there is something you want. Sometimes I cannot keep track of my notes.

I wonder if Japanese women are becoming the majority of readers as they are in America; because of the wave of feminism, every college now has women's studies. They read everything by or about women. They form a strong majority.

I know Japan always had wonderful women writers.

Greetings and wishes for the New Year. Give me news of your work and life and health (you had tired eyes, you wrote me).

Anaïs

Letter from James Herlihy to Anaïs Nin:
December 1974

Dear Anaïs:

When you mentioned on the phone that you were always short of reading matter, especially biography, a button was pushed in my head: Do you think it might be good for you to read my journal of the past few seasons? Or samples thereof? Notice how I ask the question, and might it be good for *you*? That matters to me. I know it would be good for me. Because I know that you would approve of my life—no—you would not be interested in *dis*approving. Reading some of our old letters recently made me so nostalgic, made me yearn so intensely for understanding companionship of the secret self—we had it in such a vital, serene, *totally* spirited way!

You spawned the creature in me who learned to honor his unconscious life. I think that's why you referred to me as your "spiritual son" (even though we had experienced one another humanly as brother and sister). This "son" has gone through serious changes and feels the need to re-establish deeply the psychic ties. This is the spirit in which I offer the journals.

But I realize there are *two* of us—and what you need might well be reading matter that is far more *diverting* than *involving*. And this is why I phrase the question as I do: could it be good for *you*?

Your light shines even over the telephone, and with such a unique brilliance and tonality. I will be meditating on that splendor a very great deal in the days and weeks ahead. I feel your essential health and well-being in my soul, dear Anaïs. Humanly, I'm *concerned* about discomforts in your experiences (and I know there's not a damn thing I can do about it), but I cannot *worry* about someone I know is filled with light, creativity, love, and wisdom.

Accidentally, I found a letter from you written in May '58, about what you experienced in Paris. It's thrillingly exuberant in pictures and images. Let me know if you'd like to see it (you might like to include it in vol. 6).

Love,
Jamie/Jim

LOS ANGELES, DECEMBER 24, 1974
Visit to Dr. Weston.

LOS ANGELES, DECEMBER 27, 1974
Xmas dinner at Wrights'; hospital.

LOS ANGELES, JANUARY 5, 1975
The pains increased, became intolerable. So Dr. Weston made me take the tests —two days in the hospital—then home again to await the results. On New Year's Eve I was told the cancer is threatening the urethra or the intestines. I cannot have any more radiation. There is no alternative to surgery. If there is no invasion of the bladder or intestines, all is well, but if there is, I will be mutilated with a hole in my stomach and a bag for evacuation. I have courage for the surgery, but none for the mutilation.

Rupert's love flared into passion, passionate care and sensual passion, saying plainly: "Don't leave me; you are the love of my life," making me feel wanted, loved, desired.

I try to think it might be good, it might deliver me of the cancer, prolong my life—I keep thinking of that.

We stopped working on the Diary. The painkillers dulled me—I couldn't work.

So here I am tonight, in Cedars of Lebanon, and it is nearly seven o'clock. Rupert will come.

Tomorrow anesthesia—and a cystoscopy?

Usually I have been able to surmount pains and to work. Not this time. I read, read, read. I write a few letters. Can the love given to me by so many this past year keep me alive?

The night before last, when Rupert made love passionately, and we drank champagne, I felt I should be grateful, grateful, to have attained a great love, to have been given love for my work.

LOS ANGELES, JANUARY 8, 1975
My life is now in the hands of Dr. Raymond Weston, Dr. Maclyn Wade, Dr. Leon Morgenstern, Dr. Edward Stadler. I have confidence in them. I want to live, for Rupert and my work.

LOS ANGELES, FEBRUARY 7, 1975
I survived the surgery. But what followed was a season in hell I do not want to describe—a pit of pain, complications I never want to describe. I was so weak that I even lost the desire to live—all I was aware of was pain because the drugs could only diminish it but not control it.

Western medicine has not controlled pain.

Rupert is calling me back to life. "I can't live without you!" Radiant, devoted. "Hold on, Anaïs." In one sense I did. Nothing has reached me except Rupert.

Jaglom has 133 pages of the script of *Cities*. Love messages from far away. Honors. Everything I care about. The United Nations invited me to come and talk about the Year of the Woman with Germaine Greer and Françoise Gilot.

284

LOS ANGELES, FEBRUARY 1975
Hospital.
Visitors: Ruth Ross, Edith Gross, Jody Hoy, Jim Herlihy, Pamela Fiori, Mary Morris, Barbara Kraft, John Boyce, Renate Druks; Catherine Broderick from Japan.

Letter from Binnie Bernstein to Anaïs Nin:
Studio City, California, March 3, 1975

My dear Anaïs:
Recently, I heard of a cancellation of appearances by you because of ill health. I have been concerned. In your letters to me you spoke so often of being overbooked, many college appearances, lecture dates, a busy, crowded schedule, all that could lead to exhaustion and fatigue. I was alarmed and so I write to tell you of my concern for your health and well-being. You are so important to me and to others. Are you truly aware of your impact? Everywhere I go, I meet others who have found fresh courage because of your writings and encouragement.
I hope you can continue to reach out to the many who need you.
Sincerely,
Binnie Bernstein

LOS ANGELES, MARCH 7, 1975
Home from hospital.

Note from James Herlihy to Anaïs Nin:
March 17, 1975

Dear Anaïs:
A young friend of mine in Maui, building a new life in the jungles there with his friends, apparently read *Diary 5*; his recent letter contained this paragraph:
"Blows my mind Anaïs Nin is an old good friend of yours. Held in such high esteem by many of my people. Give her some hugs from us Maui people. Thank you, Anaïs, for being such an inspiration. Om. Love you."
That's the message; I'll deliver the hugs in person.
Jamie

LOS ANGELES, MARCH 1975
I had three radiations. Two in New York, one here. The flesh around the ruptured appendix of childhood was probably already weakened (I was three months draining the abscess). After surgery here the stomach wall burst in the same place. It is a hole about a half inch while, enough to let out a lot of liquid. As it is placed between stomach and small intestine and ilium, where intestine meets the large one, a great part of my food spills out through [a fistula], a bag has to collect the material. The bag leaks often because bile, stomach acids, etc., sneak out. When they operate they make a bypass so the food will go the right route but this means an artificial drain, a planned hole, with a bag in another place. That is why I was not eager to have it nor were the doctors. We all hope it will heal as the first one finally did after

two months. I have been back from hospital only three weeks. So there is hope for healing.

I wouldn't write a word until I felt the updraft again. I couldn't write while I was a prisoner of pain, of my body's disturbances, unbalances, chaos, distress. I lost my spirit, my freedom, my faith in my own strength and wanted to erase these five months from my life. What I most believed in, I lost. I felt weak, helpless, unable to transcend my body.

The first help came from Dr. George Falcon, who is of French and Spanish descent—dynamic, young. A curious blend of psychological acuteness and sug- gestion. Jody Hoy heard him speak on alpha waves and universal energy. She *felt* his energy. He came today. I told him I had lost something I had long ago found— my source of energy. That for the first time I was a prisoner of my body. That I even felt I could not write anymore. He asked me how I felt just now. I said weak, unable to lift myself.

Soon after we talked, because when he asked me when I have felt that way *before*, I brought up the analogy I had not made before: At age nine I had a ruptured appendix. I stayed in the hospital for three months while the abscess drained and came out a skeleton. The fistula I now have, which began to drain after this surgery and went on for 2½ months, is *in the same place*—where the scar of the other abscess was. The two events were linked in my unconscious. He said: "You were nine years old. How did you feel?" Helpless—hopeless—it seemed timeless, those three months to a child. And, having heard the neighbor say that "Nin's daughter will not live the night," it is now the same long wait for a draining fistula—still draining.

"But you are not nine years old. You survived another ordeal. You are not helpless or hopeless." Then he made me close my eyes and turn my vision upward towards the center of my forehead. When my eyelids fluttered he said: "You have contacted the penial glands—the third eye."

He obtained complete relaxation. Then he asked me to remember myself inside my mother, and I kept remembering what I had been told about, the circumstances of my birth. He did not want that; he wanted what I *felt*. Asphyxiation. Not enough oxygen (my birth was much delayed, and I was born in a coma—a blue baby).

I breathed deeply. It didn't help. I went through moments of struggling for air and moments when I felt it was best to breathe shallowly, to be as quiet as possible. The birth produced a sensation of cold and *death*.

Then he asked me to visualize my body surrounded by an intense white light— and then to open my eyes and feel peace, joy, as we should feel naturally.

I did feel better. We had talked about Sister Teresa performing a miracle, "saving" my life at age nine. Joaquín reminded me of this playfully and said he had reproached Sister Teresa for not completing her job. This reminded me that at one time I ceased to believe in miracles performed by saints as gods and took this power into myself. Dr. Falcon approved of this totally. "That is where it belongs. It is all in you, and yours to draw from. It is universal energy. You did this only when *you wanted to*." He spoke of two children with leukemia. The little girl wanted to live. The little boy's attitude was: "What is the use of eating? I'm going to die anyway."

I know there was a flow in my life transcending age and health and my unusual energy. I thought I was tapping a universal energy, but Dr. Falcon discovered that I had not taken my body with me. I addressed my body severely: "You didn't serve me very well, you're always hanging behind, I do it all with my spirit"—it is a spiritual energy.

I once felt my body had punished me for treating it so arrogantly, like an ill-used servant. So my reaching such great energies was achieved only partially—and nature protected me.

"We can solve the *present* situation—but often we mix the present situation with a past one, and we get confused. The *past* one is not salvable. Any pressure? Any tightness? Contemporary situations are not a problem to us—we are intelligent and educated. I'm going to help you separate the two situations. The natural state of the mind is calm, serene, relaxed."

If I don't feel that way I am not here, *I am back there*. Falcon works until the person feels serene, blissful. The other situation took place when I was very young.

Falcon: "I want to search for pure emotion, not abstractions like: 'I have a sense of responsibility'—that is not a pure emotion. I seek emotions of fear, helplessness, pain."

I remember the episode when I was nine years old. The same abscess, three months draining in the *same place*—the fistula just where the scar is.

We are now nine years old.

LOS ANGELES, MAY 2, 1975

The irrational feeling that I could no longer write, that the peak I reached just before illness was a magic, smooth flow—this was neurotic. True, I had no energy; true, I could not type because my stomach ached—but the writing comes from somewhere else. There were holes in the 1960-1966 Diaries that had to be filled. They were the over-active years. I began very slowly, for several days, but only today did I feel the old inspiration. It pleased Rupert.

Dr. Falcon thought the flow was not taking my body with me—I reached energy only with spirit.

Letter from Anaïs Nin to Inge Bogner:
Los Angeles, May 4, 1975

Dear Inge:

I suffered a real block in writing until this week. I thought I had lost my power. This is overcome now and I am at work again. But as for writing you I realize it was because I had *too much* to tell you. I will try. The surgery predictions were so solemn, the concern of the surgeons so obvious, the pain so great, that I felt I was facing the possibility of death. At the same time, Rupert's love and determination that I should live, the wholeness of his love, and my need to unburden myself, my need of his support and taking over (small things like the key to my post office box), brought on a total confession.

Rupert's attitude was perfect. He understood the motivation for the double life. I never realized the weight of this burden until I suddenly shed it. He accepted the responsibilities. Finally, I did not have to conceal my mailing of Hugo's income; I

287

could telephone Hugo openly.

In millions of ways Rupert was there. Under the influence of Demerol, great pain and great weakness, I told Rupert everything, but what frightened me was my open rebellion against Hugo, my feeling I no longer want to return to him, that the dual life was the cause of stress, that to tell Rupert the truth suddenly made me feel whole and at peace, able to concentrate all my strength on getting well. I was never in so much danger.

As the doctor may have told you, I went from one complication to another: jaundice, evacuation of the lung, diabetes, the fistula, an infection of the urinary tract. There was a time when Dr. Weston admitted defeat. During that entire period, Rupert threw all his energy and faith into the fight. He came four times a day. But what a relief to be able to lean, to confide, to trust.

So much of my strength went into forcing myself to return to Hugo. I was shocked by the total break in myself, an admission I could never make. I did not want to see Hugo. I felt him merely as a burden. I felt we were bad for each other. Of course, the relief, the absence of tension, helped in the struggle for health. When I came home March 7, the fight was not over. Rupert became a nurse; he cooked to tempt me to eat, was full of positive thinking.

I realized the problem had not gone away. For the moment I have to stay here for chemotherapy—a new drug called Adriamycin from Italy. I call Hugo up and I write, but the break continues. That is what I could not tell you over the telephone. I feel completely detached from Hugo. I miss my talks with you. I want to know how Hugo feels. The last time we spent together, in Paris, he dragged along his depression, his total absence of livingness and made my task heavier. He was like a dead weight. I was already in pain and getting through my interviews with pain-killers. When someone complimented him on the humor in his films he wrote to me: "And I see myself as a sad sack."

For the moment I am applying my efforts in regaining my health. The fistula has dried up at last after a doctor friend who deals in alpha waves pointed out it was in the same place as my ruptured appendix at age nine, which put me in the hospital for three months while it drained. For the first time in my life I lost my faith, my energy, my inner strength. The symptom that startled me was I could not write anymore. But this week I recaptured all that. Even the shock of suddenly losing my hair and having to resort to wigs I didn't take too badly. Rupert takes it playfully, like a change in personality.

Please tell me if Hugo is taking the long time lapse well. I wish he would admit he is happier without me. Friends tell me he is better when I am not there. I feel he is, towards me, in a perpetual sulk, resenting the past. I don't blame him. I don't think in terms of blame for either one of us. We were unsuited for each other. Because he was not alive, I sought life elsewhere. Because of my behavior, he was depressed. I have to wait until the end of my treatment. Then I will come to New York and face the situation. While Rupert has accepted all I had done and interpreted it as wanting to protect him and Hugo, he also expects me to put an end to the situation. I am not physically ready to face the results of ending the dual life.

For the first time in my life, living one life, one love, reveals a peace I never knew, an absence of strain I never knew.

My love and gratitude,

A

LOS ANGELES, MAY 5, 1975

Mount Sinai. Waiting for a cardiogram. The chemotherapy and the blood count have been an ordeal for 2½ months because the veins are exhausted.

Dr. Falcon is my source of energy now. The negative information that the doctor is obliged to give (you may lose all your hair; your blood and heart have to be watched) has to be combatted by Dr. Falcon saying: "About medicine, chemotherapy, all I will say is that if you believe it will do you good, it will. If you can achieve by your own energy a reversal of the cancer process, all the better. You won't need the medicine."

Anaïs Nin with her diaries, Silver Lake, 1975

LOS ANGELES, MAY 13, 1975

I will not describe all the aches, pains, difficulties of recovery—only the few moments of near-normalcy when I received my seven students, twice now—when I typed three, four and today seven pages for volume 6, when I finally reached the bottom of my briefcase, which was full of unanswered letters, when I swam for the first time, when I bought a wig and took the loss of hair playfully.

I receive beautiful letters. I am sure the love I received helped to cure me.

Rupert has been an extraordinary nurse, determined to feed me, walk me, care for me.

Today was my first good day. Seven pages. Swim. Three walks. No unbearable gastritis. I put on an orange dress. I look forward to Dr. Falcon's visit. Luckily, my face does not reveal pain or even a loss of weight. 107 pounds now.

Weston keeps calling. "You are *my* patient. Dr. Wade is just a mechanic—I should be seeing you, checking on you."

I did not go. He is puzzled and tries gentleness. Dr. Wade explains there are rules we cannot ignore. When a doctor brings a patient to a hospital, the staff cannot appropriate him. Weston lost me—a bully, egomaniac, although a brilliant doctor. I asked Wade to take care of me. I feel better when I see him. Weston is the worst psychologist in the world.

Renate came. She is strained and not well. In vol. 6 I wrote about Peter and was overwhelmed by the material. But most of it is composed of letters, mine, friends'. So I had to reconstruct the Diary from letters. At one point I named it *Journal des Autres* and I almost stopped writing altogether in 1963. Occasionally I covered my activities briefly.

Dr. Falcon, as Bogner would have done, detected an emotional overtone in my digestive problems—the past hurts me. He asks me to look at all the events that hurt me in a different way—to learn from the past. From the earliest recollection: Typhoid fever in Havana when we went because Grandfather was dying. I may have been four years old or more. I lost all my hair. The little boys, cousins, ran away from me.

Hurt
Father leaves
Hurt
Thorvald leaves us in Paris
Hurt
Betrayals
Oliver Evans, disappointment
Marguerite Duras, disappointment
Jean-Gabriel Albicocco, disappointment
Tracey Roberts, disappointment

Falcon asks me to look at *why* my father left. He could not bear life with my mother. She was tyrannical. Thorvald hated the "artist," his father, and Paris was Father's city. Joaquín was happy to study music; my mother loved Paris; I did. For an ambitious businessman Paris was just a grimy old city with bad plumbing and no money-making place.

Oliver Evans, who said "The poet in me is dead," could not write a poetic interpretation of my work.

Marguerite Duras is too much an individual and too neurotic to enter another world.

Even Gore has a reason for his hatred. I abandoned him. I went off with Rupert.

And today? asked Falcon. No betrayals today. The irresponsibility of Robert Snyder, always in debt and who made a contract with Swallow, leaving me out after he told Gunther I was to get 50% of the royalties—even his agent worried about that. But I am not *hurt*. So I react differently today. I know Bob is irresponsible. I do not expect money from the film. So I have learned to accept the "treacherous" Tracey who plotted to sue the producers of the *Spy in the House of Love* film because they portrayed Sabina, who appears in *Seduction*, her own brother told me. They would wait till the film was done and then hold it up for money. It would be her one chance to get money, as my *Spy* producer was wealthy. So I have to look at this past exposed in the Diary with new eyes because the hurts are making me more

290

ill than I need to be, allowing for bad reactions to chemotherapy.

The child's vision: I am homely. I am left alone. My lusty Cuban cousins laugh at our city ways. We are afraid of cows, the ranch life. My father abandons me when I look like a concentration camp victim after three months in the hospital. Cruelty? Thorvald leaves us when, at least, we were always a "clan"—leaves us all in the care of Hugo. He could not bear the life of Paris and what it meant. He was Americanized in one sense. Didn't Hugo's brother write us when we had to come to America because of the war that "At least you will enjoy good plumbing"? So Thorvald went to South America to seek his fortune. But before that, was it not clear that Joaquín was the favorite of my mother and me?

Gore's love turned to hate when I deserted him. I am to blame for my poor choices of friends, the ones who threatened my life when I cut short our affairs.

Walter Lowenfels, who taped our phone conversations—a parasite.

I wasted so much care and affection on the wrong people. And I judge Henry for that!

Today no betrayals? I don't see them as such. The anger I did not want or believe in was there—toxic. So today I spent the day reversing the events that spring at me from letters and renew the pain.

Los Angeles, June 1, 1975

I love my seven students, and Tristine and Jody. They bring flowers, their work. Suzanne Smith fills a Japanese sketch book with love poems to me. I love the older woman, Jill Henley, who tells of raising five children, following her husband's military life, constantly moving for 40 years, and ends her story of a good wife and mother with these words: "But I drowned." She writes well, a family history. They all write poetry. They work with Tristine and Jody and meet me once a month (but I let them come every three weeks to catch up for time lost during my illness).

Dr. Wade, a Dartmouth graduate, collector of prints, offers to add a few valuable prints to my collection of papers if Dartmouth decides to buy them.

I finally reach the end of vol. 6. It ends with the triumph of the *Diary* and enough acceptance, love and praise to erase the past.

Rupert's devotion is absolute. He fights for my health, makes me walk, eat, swim. He works at the Diary, improves it. Revises. He has become a writer in the process. He expanded my description of the oldest trees in the world. His voice over the telephone sounds more assertive and confident. He recognizes his identity as an artist. He gives his attention now to the artist. He is proud of his work. He has changed his mind and regrets not being in the Diary. How can I solve this? He expands and affirms himself better when I am not there. I must remember that.

Los Angeles, June 7, 1975

Finished vol. 6. Now polishing and revising. Rupert took on the heaviest burden. He has retired from teaching and has given his life to me. He works on the Diary, he shops, he cooks, and he gets my mail. I have bad moments of pain and anxieties.

Dr. Falcon comes once a week. The last time I complained about my memory lapses. He discovered I was trying to erase the hospital experience. Suppressing a memory affects the whole of memory. He made me remember it all, all but the pain.

I was to look at it as a scene on a screen. I tried, not altogether successfully.

I work on the Diary in the morning. Lunch. A walk. More work, or a visitor. Frances Ring takes my article on Noomea for *Westways*.

Pamela Fiori asks me for my Paris diary for *Travel & Leisure*.

I write letters at night.

LOS ANGELES, JUNE 23, 1975

Barbara Kraft came as a private student. I liked her immediately for her loveliness and sensitivity. We worked well together. She is writing well, with passion and poetry. There were many affinities. When I became ill, she gave blood for me. She received a card notifying her of her blood type—rare: A negative, which is mine. It seemed like a mystical bond. Our friendship deepened. She responds to all I tell her. She stimulates me. Yesterday she came with flowers and a white Mexican dress. I had told her that Dr. Falcon wants me to see myself in a white light—white, the color of energy.

So many good things—my life so rich—with only that constant background of pain. At times I lose courage.

Rupert's unflagging devotion and care. Greater and greater estrangement from Hugo—and sadness.

So many loving friends—so much creativity. Sharon writes brilliantly on Rank for the Rank Association. Tristine writes a beautiful short story. Falcon keeps reminding me that we have sources of energy within ourselves. I was in a dependent mood. I wanted to weep before Dr. Wade and say: "Help me. I'm tired of pain." I wanted just to weep.

Barbara comes and her face is vivid, her hair so naturally and softly waved around her face, brilliant dark eyes, and a dazzling smile.

LOS ANGELES, JUNE 30, 1975

On Thursday Rupert and I finished the revisions of volume 6. Rupert took it to Xerox. Friday it was mailed. I coaxed Rupert to rest, to go to the beach. I am finally defending my energy. I eluded a visit from Eric Neville and the heavy tragedy of his life. I wrote an explicit letter to an Indian poet, Hoshang Merchant, who writes daily letters after being told of my illness and plans a visit. I tell him doctors have forbidden visitors and correspondence. If I write one letter, I get ten in answer, and a plea to visit. It is unbearable to close the door. These are love letters, but a love that devours me, that will kill me.

So today we started work on the Child Diary, because the problems of vol. 7 (permission for every letter quoted) seemed too arduous. I could give work to any of my brilliant daughters: Tristine Rainer, Sharon Spencer, Barbara Kraft.

At the bottom of my life is an undertow of almost constant pain, the side effects of chemotherapy. Painful stomach, painful digestion, gas. Undercurrent of depression. Will I ever be well? The response of the world has become a danger. The friendships that touch me, tempt me, are a danger. Those I do see are lovable.

Rupert has to be severe—I have to refuse prefaces, visitors, long letters. I weaken. My defenses are not very strong. Paula Peper, stuck by an illness that will ultimately paralyze her, decides to live in nature in the Forest Service, a natural life as long as possible. I answer her letters. I admire her courage. Cayle Chernin has done the *Collages* script Henry Jaglom wanted, but Jaglom does not pay her, and they quarrel—so the work may not result in the filming of *Cities*. When we talk together, Jaglom and I, there is perfect accord. He can edit his film *Tracks* and dream over *Cities*. He says they nourish each other.

Los Angeles, July 5, 1975

Hugo accepted Bogner's warning that I should not return to New York too soon, that is, immediately after chemotherapy on July 15. After chemotherapy, I will have two or three more weeks of side effects. Hopefully, August will be easier, and I may recover the weight and hair. This gives me a respite from my painful sense of responsibility because his deafness is increasing and he has trouble with his contact lens. I write frequently and telephone once a week.

Rupert is more passionate than ever—the threat of losing me seems to have intensified his love. He kisses and embraces me in the pool. He makes love. It is as if he wanted his love to heal me.

Richard Centing visits me and takes note of the incredible activity around my work. Publications, theses, interviews. The Corey Critics Prize went to Harcourt for publishing the *Diaries*.

Summer days. How I love them.

Now I have to write a review of Progoff's book on the Intensive Journal. Nancy Scholar (Zee) repudiates her thesis as being written by the academic intellectually trained critic, as not what she felt. It was her thesis that caused me so much pain. Today it is Nancy herself who disparages it. Such ironies. Now she writes a brilliant essay on Bergman's *Persona* and *House of Incest.*

Los Angeles, July 21, 1975

Last chemotherapy.

Los Angeles, July 23, 1975

One Sunday afternoon Dr. Wade and his family came to visit. All that I admired in him was confirmed, his sensitivity, brilliance of mind, and multifaceted personality. He married young: his wife studied dancing and literature. She read my early works. They had first lived in Connecticut. He gardens, builds, makes frames for his prints. His children are self-confident and artistic. They spent part of the afternoon drawing. He responded to the house. We spent a serene, harmonious afternoon together. He became very essential to me because he neutralized Weston's rough manner and bungling psychology. Weston created fear. Wade healed the fear. He was civilized and soft-spoken. A man of many gifts, at the top of his profession, cancer surgery, though not yet fifty. Weston became the tyrannical and insensitive doctor. I had dreams of firing him! But I owed him a great deal. He is famous for his discoveries in intravenous feeding. For three months he kept me alive with his bottles. It was only psychologically that he harmed me. I asked Wade to take care of the chemotherapy. Weston wanted to. Fortunately, doctors were warned not to do it—only specialists.

Just as I was rejoicing at the last treatment July 21, I discovered my right eye is clouding. New anxiety, after nine months of almost constant pain. I weigh 104 pounds.

It takes me great efforts to write a review of Progoff's book, which I admire.

So much accomplished thanks to Rupert. Today I receive $1,700 from *Travel & Leisure* for my Paris Diary. Rupert worked on it often, while I lay in the grips of stomach or bladder pains (chemical) or under the influence of painkillers, which prevent me from thinking clearly.

The saddest thing of all is that Rupert's beautiful, unflagging passion causes me pain, so I do not even have the joy of lovemaking—only the pain. Yet I desire him, hunger for him. And I can hardly believe in the magnitude of his all-encompassing love, which mysteriously has grown immense in me. I love him more deeply than ever.

LOS ANGELES, JULY 25, 1975

Rupert is xeroxing the child diaries in case Dartmouth takes them. We went down to the vault. I had sent for them when I realized I would be in Los Angeles for many months. They were flown from the Brooklyn bank to a bank downtown, and here I was given a little cell-like room of my own, where Rupert and I can work peacefully. We started with 1914. Volumes 1, 2, 3, 4...

One diary, which looked like the others, was labeled as a 1921 diary book. We did not notice it was number 56 and was actually misfiled. Rupert saw the names of Gonzalo and Henry and waited till I was asleep to read it. I had always dreaded this moment, not knowing what his reaction would be. Yesterday, with great emotion, he confessed having read it. He embraced me passionately and said: "I love you more than ever. How strong and passionate you were, and what beautiful writing!" No jealousy, no withdrawals. He was deeply moved, lamented the reasons that made me leave out so much. "After the child diary and vol. 7, you have to work at the full diary." It was a new hurdle in our love. I couldn't believe his reaction, generous and selfless. He read me a few pages to demonstrate the beauty of the writing. "How strong, how passionate you were."

We reminded ourselves of how passionate we were, especially on trips. On trips we always have honeymoons. Rupert makes love to me every day, in Tahiti, Morocco, Bali, Mexico. We had orgies in Acapulco. We became sensually stimulated by the beauty, by exoticism, by being free of duties. In Japan it was the same. What can I do about the Diary? My protection of Hugo was not altogether successful. He knows a part of the truth. He would not react as Rupert did because Rupert feels loved—and Hugo was not loved with passion.

Hugo and I have lamentable telephone calls. He cannot hear me. I do all in my power to encourage the artist. I persuaded him to make a new printing of the engravings, to attend to his film shows. I introduced him to a young group who is devoted to the art of the book. He always creates obstacles. I dread returning to New York. I also have a new difficulty—if I cover my left eye I cannot see with my right eye. Wednesday I will know what it means. I am slowly getting better, but the side effects of Adriamycin are still with me.

My fan mail, while demanding, delights me. A genuine Spanish Gypsy writes me from San Diego. All kinds of new healers write me. Some are dangerous, repudiating doctors as the Christian Scientists do. Others, masseurs, herb dealers, or Dr. Falcon, do me good. He now gives me intensive massage, and suggestion. "Close your eyes. Visualize your body surrounded by a white light. This white light penetrates your whole body. You are now healthy. The chemical is doing its work.

Keep your spirit separate from it, healthy and in no need of side effects. We will take the good of the chemical, but not the side effects."

I work at the review of Progoff's *At a Journal Workshop*. A beautiful book. Perhaps too complex for the majority. I do not like his separation of memory, dreams, dialogues with figures of wisdom, inventing the future, twilight imagery, stepping stones. I wonder why they had to be separated. In my Diary they happen simultaneously and they fuse, past, present, future.

What will my future be if I am not healthy? This should have been the happiest year of my life. Rupert is retired. We could travel anywhere we wish in exchange for articles. I receive love, honors, wonderful critiques, beautiful fan letters.

Rupert is dedicated to getting me well. He cooks to tempt me (I would rather not eat; I am never hungry). He has nursed me back to health with infinite patience.

Los Angeles, July 27, 1975

A passionate Rupert. "It is like Acapulco." Acapulco signifies our best love-making.

It is so harrowing, the symbolic telephone. Hugo cannot hear me. We cannot talk.

These are the last weeks of side effects after my last chemotherapy treatment.

I had an eye examination. Yes, it was a cataract, but one that did not require surgery immediately. It was a blow. My eyes. Just at this moment I have to read and write less when I need both to sustain me.

I felt the deepest depression at the timing. A cursed year.

I type five pages in the morning in the best light (the Japan diary). I try to keep busy. I read very little at night. And I try not to think of surgery and the horrors of contact lenses acquired from watching Hugo in perpetual trouble. They irritate his eyes. He forgets to remove them before going to sleep. He drops them, scratches them. But other people tell me it need not be so.

I enjoy the Japan diary—the Orient. It seems even more beautiful as our barbaric culture worsens. Incredible crimes, greed. Everything is greed. The bill-boards uglify Los Angeles, but they will not pass a law against them for "economic" reasons. The oil companies have not only swindled us, but have bought up all the television stations to glorify themselves.

Los Angeles, August 4, 1975

I am expecting Sharon who has been in Mexico and is on her way to New York.

Rupert xeroxes all the French diaries—up to 1920. But I refuse to waste my eyes on translating them. I don't like them. Too religious and goody-goody.

Sharon came, bringing her delicate beauty and radiance. She and Tristine met and had much to talk about. It was a summer day. They swam in the pool. It was a joy to see them—lightly tanned, slender. But that night I wept as my tremendous loss of weight has made me ashamed of my body. For the first time I wanted to hide.

The mood passed. Rupert's love gives me courage. The eye doctor said I could read and write all I wanted in spite of the cataract and that it was impossible to tell when surgery would be needed—so meanwhile I try other remedies: vitamin C, massage, more swimming, more walking.

I work on the 1966 Japan diary. In the morning when I awaken, I rejoice that I will relive that beautiful trip. It is my longest travel description.

Today I await a phone call from my Japanese translator Masako Karatani.

LOS ANGELES, AUGUST 13, 1975

Masako came, but we could not talk. Her four-year-old son was mischievous, destructive, tired, impossible. We spent all our time preventing catastrophes. He threw everything in the pool, including food; he drank and spilled wine; he hit the older brothers. Masako's husband will teach at Yale for a year. He was reticent and could not speak much English. They left for New York the next day. A failed visit. The 20-hour plane trip must have tired the children.

Back to work on the Japan diary. My scrapbook is a delight.

Blood test yesterday. Dr. Falcon speaks of the discipline of the mind (positive thinking). He wants me to avoid surgery—take vitamins, eat raw food, exercise. So I swim three times a day—walk. "Pay attention to your body." The metaphysical approach, belief in mental healing, in miracles. I can't digest raw food, nor vitamins. But I try. Meanwhile, he gives me a deep pressure-point massage, makes me meditate on the "white light" and health.

LOS ANGELES, AUGUST 25, 1975

Donna Ippolito came to work on Bob Snyder's documentary book. When I first met her, I loved her, but she was hidden and closed—a little impersonal. She wore jeans and blouses. Today she arrived in full blossom, soft and feminine in a long dress, her beautiful black hair shining. She went through harrowing experiences, a difficult love (he complained she did not love enough), a bad trip on LSD (all anxiety and death-like feelings, a breakdown, therapy). She is writing. She wrote a book of erotica, which Adele Aldridge illustrated and Moira Collins calligraphed.

Moira came to the celebration at Rye and made friends with Valerie Harms and Adele Aldridge. Donna made friends with them too. She is publishing Sharon's book on me. It is a universe of brilliant and lovely women. Sharon said my unorganized Diaries were a far deeper influence than Progoff's organized theories. She severely criticized him, whereas I have just written a good review of him. But as I said to Sharon, I felt he was elevating the status of diary writing, destroying the concept of narcissism or neurotic introspection, restoring its value and, above all, *teaching* it. Barbara's diary is accepted by a small publisher I discovered. Life, oh, life-giving, yes.

Bert Mathieu says: "You *must* get well because we need you." He wrote the best book on Henry. He will write one on me. A young 24 years old. Jeffrey Bailey writes a beautiful interpretation of my work.

Rupert is so loving, patient—feeding me, weighing me. "You have gained two pounds." In the pool he always clasps me. I am rewarded for all I gave. It is miraculous.

My letters from John Ferrone are full of poetry and feeling. Jean-Yves Boulic's letters touch me so much that I like to fantasize. He is in his thirties. If I were thirty, living in Louveciennes, I would have loved him. But with Rupert I cannot love anyone else. Our closeness is a miracle. He is working with me, has taken charge of everything, acts as husband, father, young son, lover, collaborator.

Los Angeles, August 26, 1975

All the good things that happen to me come out of love. Barry Jones' devotion to my work ignited the interest of Dartmouth and they are trying to raise money to buy the original diaries. He has worked indefatigably on this. It was because of him that I received the Dartmouth Doctorate. We just talked over the telephone. Oxford was too severe and demanding, and he will study law at Stanford.

Los Angeles, August 29, 1975

My correspondence is a delight. Full of surprises, gifts. I hear from Pamela Fiori, who has been such a good friend, that she was made Editor of *Travel & Leisure*, one of the few woman editors in America. Toni Barron brings me a woven hanging. I hear from Nicolai Michoutouchkine, the king of Port Vila. The Port Vila article will come out in November. The Noomea article will come out in *Westways*. Rupert's photographs are admired.

He works at the volume 6 changes required by Lesley Blanch and Romaine Gary, and by Daisy, over trivialities.

We moved the diaries from bank to bank by Air Cargo, and Rupert and I can go downtown and we have our own little room to work in, not as in Brooklyn where I shared a large room and had to be watched while I filed. I felt sorry for the woman who had to unlock the iron door for people coming to work on their safety boxes, answer the telephone, open the safety boxes, unlock the communal room, watch me (a law). Now here we are alone. The room is 15 feet by 10 feet.

I asked Rupert: "Do you really love this work?" "Yes, I do," he answered. "I am fascinated, I am proud to be able to help you, and I think I do the job better than anyone." He does enjoy it. He laughs at the child diary, at the teenage diaries, as he Xeroxes them.

Because Barry Jones is sure Dartmouth will raise the money I asked for the originals, John Ferrone now tells me he estimates the value at $250,000, and I asked for $100,000.

We have saved money. I am able to take care of Hugo—$1,000 a month. Rupert and I worked at editing the book of articles that John cleverly called *In Favor of the Sensitive Man* (one of the essays). When Donna came, soft and flowering, and we told her about reading from *Miss MacIntosh My Darling* together for the Free College, she exclaimed: "What a team!"

In the last year, Rupert's gifts have blossomed, as critic, editor, advisor, manager. The love is always there. Great celebration when I begin to gain weight, to be free of painful gastritis, to feel increase of energy. A week ago I weighed 104. Now I weigh 107. Moments of deep depression are occasional, mostly due to the cataract. Moments of pleasure are when I work on the Asian diary, now over 100 pages. I want to make a separate book of that with Rupert's photographs.

Barbara Kraft makes me a custard, and we exchange dresses to lift our moods because she is going through the agony of a divorce. Her husband found and read her diary. Did she want him to? To open the truth he would not face?

My friend in Australia, a photographer, sends me beautiful photographs and introduced me to Hunderwasser, my second love after Varda.

I met Nick Dunnes from the days we stayed at Gore Vidal's home in Guatemala, where it was the rainy season and we had to entertain ourselves with talk and storytelling. He confirmed that Gore has become incredibly venomous, bitter. Nick heads the future video cassette industry and will buy *Anaïs Nin Observed*. It was my first day out, this meeting at his office, and he promptly introduced me to his beautiful son—an actor, devoted to me.

Bob Snyder continues his self-destructive maneuvers. He advertises that I will speak at UCLA to sustain his film showings when I was not consulted and then pleads that I should do it for friendship's sake. Rupert refused. But I have to learn to say "no" myself. This year the illness helped me refuse all lectures and shorten correspondence, but what will happen when I get well? I told Dr. Falcon about the danger of becoming well and fearing the demands of the world. They come to the door. But no more.

The beautiful letters, the love, the outpourings. Barbara does not know how I liberated her, made her writing flow.

Letters from Japan. Susie Sugisaki writes me as if nothing happened to estrange us (her brief affair with Rupert). I answer the same way. She is translating me.

My German publisher names his new child Anaïs, asks for information about the name. Jeanne Moreau did film her script and directed it. But she does not answer letters. Valerie Harms will publish my early stories. They possess the traits my later writing lost: humor, irony, and feminism.

Letter from Anaïs Nin to Lawrence Durrell:
Los Angeles, September 10, 1975

Dear Larry:

Your letter to Swallow pleased me deeply. If you could write all this about two lectures you must have wanted to praise me. I was very touched.

It all came like a bouquet of flowers after nine months of fighting cancer. I am recovering but energy is very low. I managed to finish vol. 6 with help—remembered your generous cable: "Carte Blanche" when I asked if you wanted to see what I wrote about you. *Pas contre* Lesley Blanch, whose portrait was done with love, refused to allow any of it except my praise of her work!

Your (and Ghislaine's) visit last year was such a joy. I wish we had had more time to talk. It was too frustrating not seeing you in Paris and our parties one block away from each other.

The writing in *Monsieur* was as magical as ever. You appear again in vol. 6.

Love,
Anaïs

Los Angeles, September 18, 1975

I expected to be free of the pain and problems a few weeks after the end of chemotherapy, but it has not happened. I still suffer from incontinence, occasional stomach and bladder pains. My half-clouded eye with a cataract I seek to arrest with vitamins, eye exercises, nutrition.

Rupert is miraculously good. Cooking for me. Answering letters. Defending me from visitors.

Dr. George Falcon comes once a week, with a little psychology: "Don't you feel you deserve all that you have received this year? Are you atoning for all the love received?" This is a lesson in relaxation: Cancer is due to stress, they say. Doctors are not sure. To forget the discomforts of my body I once more turned to the solace of work. I became interested in vol. 7—the last. I look forward to working on it. It makes me forget.

Rupert is meanwhile xeroxing the child diary and teenage diary in preparation for editing. I did not want to move backward, but forward.

We bathed Piccolino for Charlotte Hyde and Christiane Emonin, who were responsible for our trip to Bali. Charlotte is so lively, so witty, such a storyteller.

LOS ANGELES, OCTOBER 1, 1975

Such strange days. If I thought I had given myself to Rupert at the time of my illness, I was to learn it was not total. The total giving came with confession, truth, trust, wholeness. He took possession of me—to heal me, to take up my burdens, to share my work. He says he loves me more than ever. I feel the same. We start the day at his rhythm, which is to sleep late (and my rhythm of early work was changed by the illness). He makes breakfast for me after we swim. He goes to the post office. He opens, answers correspondence with John Ferrone. It has to do with permissions. Lesley Blanch became hysterical and bitchy. Karl Shapiro was curt. Tom Payne cut out so much, regretfully, but he said confronting his portrait did more than any therapy could.

I work on vol. 7. Swim and lunch. I grieve over how much energy I have wasted, mostly to help friends. Enormous expenditure. My body has paid for it. I am appalled at the demands made of me—the pressures.

Occasionally a visitor. Deena needs a preface. Miggy massages my feet. George Falcon massages my body, talks metaphysics, teaches meditation. I have pains. He tells me to close my eyes, place the pain in a little box, place the little box in a big cement box, close the lid tightly and push it into the sea.

Tracey, so self-destructive, does not have one good photograph of herself—all artificial and Hollywood style.

Rupert reads me the child diaries in the evening. They sadden and bore me. At 18 I wrote for my mother and I ignored what was really happening. Eduardo played a major role. We were reading about him, and after years of silence he writes to ask if he can come and see me. Synchronicity. Joaquín came twice. We talk about the past. He took the child diary and wrote me a beautiful letter. I don't want to journey backwards. I work on vol. 7—on and on.

I have moments of deep discouragement. Will I ever be what I was in 1974— vital, radiant, not looking my age, making women feel hopeful and lose their fear of aging?

Barbara Kraft is my favorite student. We have innumerable affinities. Music, painting, books. Today she supplied me with a key word to organize the lectures in vol. 7: "montage." I can't name them all. Tedious, but I have to give the impression of quantity and character.

LOS ANGELES, OCTOBER 12, 1975

I found I had written all about the lectures in the diary Barry Jones gave me at New Hampshire—a summing up. So it is already done.

Visits from Barbara Kraft, William Lewis.

Much work on vol. 7, preparation for editing.

Back on painkillers—not allowing myself to be discouraged.

Bogner calls me. It cheers me to hear her voice. Clarity and musicality. Reminded me of the feeling I had whenever I entered her room: a clear atmosphere. Order. Harmony.

LOS ANGELES, OCTOBER 16, 1975

Preparing vol. 7 for editing meant reading thousands of fan letters. They gave some chronological sense of events.

Daisy tells me Rudolf Steiner followers believe creativity helps heal cancer and advises me to paint when I'm doing my best writing! Or she preaches to me how she will make me like Shakespeare. She has regressed into the past after spending her life with junior high school students, who are the future.

Gunther has surgery—and advises changes in vol. 6, which I refuse to make. I have worked enough.

Barry visits rich men to raise money for the diary originals—$38,000 so far. Barry. I remember our first meeting. He exudes warmth, liveliness and is always high. He is now my favorite son—sensitive, loving. We had good moments together in Paris—a dinner alone, book talk, but illumined by his enthusiasm and fervor. The Van der Elst family likes him. Everybody likes him. His handwriting is feminine, but he is not effeminate. He is roguish, saucy, bright. His family lives in Virginia. I gather they are successful farmers. All the children went to college. He was so well liked in Dartmouth that they paid for his trip back from England to be at my doctorate—for which I owe him.

Return of pain. Need of painkillers.

The happiest year of my life besides the illness. Rupert's love is a constant fire that makes me want to live, to be well. He is caught up in the drama of the Diary. He reads to me about the period before Louveciennes. He is not jealous. I decided to entrust him with the Diaries as I have less and less faith in Gunther, who has become autocratic and has a strong ego. This way Rupert can decide on everything, and I can trust him.

I am not sure what Gunther would do with the Diaries now that he has convinced himself that he is their editor. He makes several errors, including heavy editing that changes my meaning. When Evelyn Hinz sold her book to Swallow, he insisted on "protecting my interests" by making a contract and then told Evelyn he would make the final editorial decisions. Same with John Ferrone editing a book of photographs—Gunther said it was his idea, that he wanted to do a deluxe book, that I had appointed John as editor over his head. In other words, he is possessive.

LOS ANGELES, OCTOBER 18, 1975

Something happened that means far more to me than the membership to the Academy. Frank Alberti writes me from Paris: "Maurice Paz was very moved by your letter and has written a complete rendering of an article about you: 'Anaïs Nin et son édifice Proustien,' which just happened in the *Bulletin de la Societé Nurlandaise de la Societé des Amis de Proust*. The article is by Ronald de Leeuv. Paz, who is an enthusiastic admirer of yours, wrote of the Proustian affinities in the Journal and of Anaïs '*prolongerant l'œuvre de Proust tout en restant elle-même*' [continuing Proust's work while remaining herself]." He had already written me that les Amis de Proust spent more time talking about my work at this meeting than any other subject.

After I joined the International Community College they were besieged with requests for studying with me. We gathered some brilliant students. Tristine Rainer and Jody Hoy shared the teaching with me. The results were wonderful. Barbara Kraft wrote 800 pages in her journal, and it was accepted for publication. Another student is having her poetry published. The combination of psychological exploration with writing continued to produce rich, flowing, spontaneous work.

Letter from Anaïs Nin to Inge Bogner:
Los Angeles, October 20, 1975

Dear Inge:
I had to simplify the [Anaïs Nin] Trust because Gunther has become more and more autocratic and possessive about the Diaries. As I had to bring them here to work on them (I am now doing vol. 7, the last one), and Rupert is retired and able to collaborate and work with me, I made Rupert sole Trustee so he could make decisions. He has my complete trust. He knows what I want sealed and not sealed. I found Gunther more and more overbearing. This is simple. The original diaries are all here. We have hopes of selling them to Dartmouth (they are trying to raise the money). It looks as if most of the time I will be here.

I am getting a second treatment, Uracil, small injections for five days as a followup, and something else I will tell you about orally. I don't know the name yet. When this treatment is over Dr. Wade will call you. He is civilized and clear and has a better effect on me than Weston.

I am working well in spite of the aches and pains and digestive troubles. I forgot to ask you if you found Hugo well; as long as he keeps on an even keel I do not worry about him.

I will phone you this week. I am sorry to give you the trouble of signing before a notary. You would have had to sign every operation, one more chore for you.
With all my love,
Anaïs

Letter from Anaïs Nin to Gunther Stuhlmann:
Los Angeles, October 20, 1975

Dear Gunther:
You will receive a notice of the old Trust being changed. It was much too complicated, as because of my health I will be here in Los Angeles most of the time. I had to bring all the original diaries from Brooklyn to be able to work on them. Rupert Pole has been my common-law husband since 1947, and so he is working with me on editing. He knows best what I want sealed, not sealed, etc. There were too many differences of opinion, and this will simplify the work. The diaries are in a vault here and I made a living Trust. We have some hope of selling them to a university. Decisions can be made by someone who is devoting his whole life to the work, which does not mean I will not honor the contract saying you will be editor of all published Diaries.
Anaïs

301

LOS ANGELES, OCTOBER 29, 1975, 3:00 AM

I tried meditation to stop the activity of my mind to rest, to heal myself, but it was ineffective. I was thinking of too many things. And, of course, there was the physical cause, the terrible gas from the chemotherapy.

I was stimulated by an article in *Bulletin des Amis de Proust*, and by a letter from Jean-Yves Boulic, who wants to write about Louveciennes and my stay there, who wants to rectify erroneous biographies on me, who sends me the registration of my birth.

Tout passe, tout continue.

This year was my acquaintance with death, my familiarity with it, and we talk about it because of the Trust and its problems, my need to escape Gunther's domination, to entrust all decisions to Rupert.

Probably the greatest sense of the passage of time was Rupert's reading the Diaries from the time I started to write in English till the publication of volume 1 of the *Diary*. At first it was entertaining, then painful when it traced where the marriage eroded: Hugo's absence, the possession by the bank and my need of multiple lives.

But more painful than this was Eduardo's visit. He regrets his first reaction to the Diary and blames his dependency on his family. Now he has been freed by their deaths and he regrets having bowed out. He is proud of me. But he has aged badly; all his beauty is gone, he is heavier and flabby. He lives alone. He does research on Machiavelli, a seed planted during his life in Florence.

Eduardo today is not the one I remembered, not the one Rupert was reading about, who came to Louveciennes and helped me paint the house. We had struggled with attraction and non-attraction. Joaquín was tired of Eduardo's visit. Eduardo came because he felt he should come while he was able to.

John Ferrone wants me to include the hospital stay in vol. 7. I don't want to. I want the *Diary* to end at the peak of my life. I do not want to register the slow journey towards death. I had premonitions in Puerto Vallarta, in Bali.

A woman writes me beautiful letters and does my horoscope. I asked her how it was possible for me to live such contrasts in 1975—fulfillment on every aspect of love and work, and such a devastating illness. Boulic is sad that the Louveciennes house is deteriorating. He too imagines time receding and us meeting in Louveciennes when I was 30.

In 1974 I believed I had triumphed over time and age. This time I feel I am not getting well. But I wrote two prefaces today, one for Deena Metzger and one for Bert Mathieu's translation of Rimbaud. There is so much life to be lived.

Aside from spasms of compassion, Hugo does not exist for me.

George Falcon will come tomorrow and work on suggestion. "The white light will heal you." When he says I am healthy, I obey for a moment—I have intimations of health.

All I ask for is a little more time with Rupert, but well, so he won't be sacrificed to his nursing. He lives now to get me well. He shops, cooks specially, reads to me so I will fall asleep.

LOS ANGELES, OCTOBER 30, 1975

Dream: By the ocean. One woman is about to deep-sea dive for something she has lost when I notice a huge hippopotamus emerging from the water. A small dog is swimming nearby. He begins to swim backwards, keeping his eye on the hippopotamus, but the hippopotamus catches up with him and swallows him. I am still concerned about the woman who is swimming in the depths. (We saw a film of hippopotamuses by Ionesco.)

THE BOOK OF MUSIC—MON JOURNAL

LOS ANGELES, NOVEMBER 1, 1975

In the old days, when I had a new diary book to write in, I would hurriedly fill the last pages. Now I have the most beautiful one of all that Rupert had made for me, the finest paper, leather bound, and in gold, in my handwriting: *Mon Journal, Anaïs Nin*. He spent days getting the right paper, the right cover (deep red), and I would like to imagine a healthy Anaïs writing in it, as Falcon wants me to imagine her in my meditations. In it, Rupert wrote: "May this diary give life and love to the love of my life."

Anaïs Nin observing Rupert Pole and his string quartet, Silver Lake, 1970s

I have to abandon the hope of being well. I have to accept this half-healed self. It is now almost a year. I had pains in Paris and was taking painkillers. A year ago, I was ill but keenly alive. Now I often feel I'm walking in the shadows. I have bad nights. Heavy dreams. But there are a few great joys: Rupert's extraordinary love and passion, work on vol. 7, and my daughters. The world will hear about Lynne Sukenick, Jody Hoy, Tristine Rainer, Nancy Scholar, Sharon Spencer, Deena Metzger, Barbara Kraft, Lee Potts.

I receive pleasure from the groups who meditate for my health. Pleasure from my students writing well, including the new one, Jessie Baker, who had a breakdown and is so sensitive and lovely. I nourish them with books—Anna Kavan, Sharon Spencer, Progoff, Judy Chicago's book, *Story of a Marriage*.

LOS ANGELES, NOVEMBER 10, 1975

The most continuous, unbroken, life-giving thread of my life has been love and music, and Rupert has been the source of both. Over the years there was always the deep, rich tones of his viola; there were always the waves of music to lift our ship away from dangerous reefs, icebergs, to keep our nerves vibrating, our being resonating, never lulled, but pierced with arrows of gold. Our love's blood transfusion was music.

His body sways, his foot gently beats the time, and all sorrows and tensions are transposed. Love and music make of dissonant fragments a symphonic whole.

Music: It is as if the strings strained away the dross. Sharp ends soften. Dreams float to the surface. Memories pulsate, each note is a color, each note is a voice, a new cell awakened. It stills other sounds, drowns the harsh ones, it erects spirals and new planets. When the heart acquires rough edges, there is the muting effect. When the heart freezes, music liquefies it. When it is lonely, secret notes will escape and find their way to the pulse, restore its universal rhythms. It is remote and gentle. It sobs for you. It laments, it rejoices, it explodes with vigor and life. It never allows our body to die because every wish, every fantasy breathes and moves as if we were in the place of our first birth, the ocean. The notes fly so much farther than words. There is no other way to reach the infinite.

Monday night the pain began—excruciating. Painkillers did not work. I sobbed with pain. Tuesday I went to the hospital, but Dr. Wade was away. Yesterday he examined me. "It is either radiation damage or the tumor." Monday I go in for 24 hours for tests. The acupuncture relieved me from 10:00 AM to 6:00 PM. Yesterday Percodan every 3 hours. At 6:00 AM pain.

I go about my business, answering letters, but I cannot work.

LOS ANGELES, NOVEMBER 14, 1975

Almost a year later: Relapse. Pain, at times excruciating. A week in the hospital for tests. Yes, the tumor is active, and I need radiation treatments. Fortunately the hospital is five minutes away.

That week I reached the ultimate in pain. I also reached a control of pain. I had pain during the night, called the nurse, called the doctor. They did not come. I began to meditate and by the time they came I was asleep.

My first day in the hospital I was sent a print by Hunderwasser. Also a book by Laurens Van der Post on Jung. Are all these riches going to be dissipated by my disappearance? Rupert had a diary book made for me. I said I would not write in it until I was well. Rupert asked me to write in it. Then I decided it would be the book of music—music only. And I wrote about music the night the quartet came, Sunday night before going to the hospital.

LOS ANGELES, NOVEMBER 17, 1975

At two o'clock the first treatment: three minutes under a linear accelerator.

But I can come home to Rupert's burning love, Piccolino's antics, books, music, paintings, the garden. Who was ever as spoiled or had more reason for living?

Henry Jaglom talks at length—his eloquence is subtle. I try to calm his fear of betraying my work. I said, "You can't, because our vision is the same."

"But that is just it. I want it to be your work, not mine. I reread the whole *Cities*. You plumb such depths, interior depths. Cayle Chernin's script is too skeletal. It left out the poetry. So far, people who have read it said: 'It is a play.'" He is going to France to be fêted. *A Safe Place* becomes *Souviens-toi*. His backing comes from there.

I want to live. Life is rich and fascinating. Every day I receive an understanding of the work, a response to the work. Royalties are pouring in. Love, above all; a group is meditating for me. French television will come in the summer, a famous painter and Dumayet as interviewer.

LOS ANGELES, DECEMBER 1975

Dick Stoltzman, clarinetist, and Bill Douglas, pianist and composer, come to play for me. The most tender, lyrical music. Incredible people—unspoilt. Not ambitious—and the music undulates tenderly the waves of feeling, ebbing and flowing like gentle tides. No harshness, no dissonance, no savagery of rock and roll. The sweetness of a tropical climate, an outburst of joy—playful, wistfulness without diffusion. Penelope Singer on her guitar forever weaving her tapestry, waiting—so many of us waiting, but creating nothing.

The pool is steaming as those pools in the mountains of Japan; everything seen through glass, through amethyst water, acquires a different dimension. It enlarges itself, its colors; it is so beautiful.

LOS ANGELES, DECEMBER 3, 1975

New Yorkers in essence are cynical, and their attitude is always that the West is crackpot. That is why it is so hated. It happens that the West, being near Asia, has been influenced by it. Not having any religion, or at least rebelling against dogma, a gangster government, a big-business dictatorship, Californians turned towards the East for metaphysics and medicine. After my relapse, I began to lose faith in Western medicine. The sum of Eastern teaching is exactly what Bogner would have done during this period: to summon up one's energy and courage (as when she said you don't have to be depressed because you have a cold), to remove the energy leaks (demands of people for prefaces, letters, visits), to find out causes for stress, worry. These people do that, only with a difference of style. They are healers. They try to summon your own energy to eliminate negative thoughts, discouragement. They come with a love and tenderness that is unbelievable. They are the new America, as spiritual as the other was criminally greedy. One group came (no charge, they are trained to "minister"). A young woman sang with such a pure, lovely voice that I cried and remembered the time I sang hymns and believed in miracles. Because God did not grant me my wish to bring my father back, I broke off all communications with religion. I didn't even like people who used the word God.

Here, it means something. It is not Christian Science. They do not say illness does not exist. They say it is there, tell you to continue doing all your surgeon tells you, but we will work on giving you energy. They meditate from seven to eight o'clock all over the world for me to get well.

Some people do not understand that California is Eastern, part of the Orient.

I feel infinitely better, helped in every way. Their philosophy is like psychology. Neurosis is negativity, lack of courage. This reconciliation with God, this sharing of energy, this effort to form communes in which one shares, gives. The gentleness of Asia; the sense of universal unconscious (Jung) is immensely deep and a source of strength.

LOS ANGELES, DECEMBER 15, 1975

In the hospital. The fistula was opened and drained as before. I was tied to an intravenous feeding bottle.

Dr. Brugh Joy came. He investigated the possibility of martyrdom, taking illness and pain from the world, but that was not what I want. But martyrdom brought up the consciousness of sacrifice, atonement, guilt. And I was back in a well of guilt. Hugo, of course. Dr. Joy said I would not get well until I lived truthfully—and was free of Hugo. This is the most difficult thing I have ever had to do, but I need to save my life. I will otherwise die of guilt. I wrote to Bogner. I can't bring myself to write to Hugo.

Sad days again, with one problem after another, too much sugar, retention of fluid, breathlessness, weak legs.

I appeal to the healers: meditate, call on the White Light, imagine Brugh Joy healing me.

A year of pain and difficulties. I feel, at times, like surrendering.

So much love and energy has been given to me, but I am so tired of the struggle.

Dr. Wade just came in. The test will determine whether there will be surgery or not. "I want you around for a few years."

Brugh says I am a beautiful soul.

LOS ANGELES, DECEMBER 20, 1975

No surgery.

But writing to Bogner, discussing Hugo with her, was the hardest thing I ever had to do—to save my health? For Rupert?

A bad night. Pains. Caught between a fighting spirit and extreme weakness. The healers incite you to struggle.

Weight going up, but I am out of breath.

No loss of interest in the outside world. Communicating with Barry Jones, Sharon, Evelyn, Frances Field, who has moved to Carmel.

In America the young loved me. In Europe the mature. Here my peers don't care: Karl Shapiro, William Goyen, William Carlos Williams, Christopher Isherwood, Elia Kazan. All but Robert Kirsch and Anna Balakian.

Letter from Anaïs Nin to Inge Bogner:
Los Angeles, December 1975

Dear Inge:

What I have to write you about is not new for you but it has become critical. You know how many years you worked to eradicate my sense of guilt towards Hugo. Once I said to you: "What would happen if I stayed away completely?" You answered: "Knowing you, you could not live with your guilt."

The subject came up again when I met a Dr. Joy. A year and a half ago, he quit a promising doctor's practice. He went to the East. He returned a mystic who had cured himself of an illness and discovered he had strong healing powers. He came to see me. He read the *Diaries* before coming and had the instant intuition: too much giving, a tendency to sacrifice, guilt. Yesterday he brought the [recording of his] talk on the meaning of cancer, which is possibly an obstacle to growth and freedom, a growth gone wrong. Martyrdom? No, I said, not martyrdom, but sacrifice and guilt. Why should the cancer have come at the best moment in my life? When I had love, honors, enough royalties to not have to lecture?

But I had guilt for being happy when Hugo was handicapped and felt a sense of failure. As you know, instinctively, when I was very ill, I wrote you I could not return to Hugo. You suggested I wait until I could come to N.Y.

But now I am lying here with the same fistula draining, and while it is draining I have to be fed intravenously. When I was ill I felt Hugo was the source of my illness, that it was like a lifelong stress, effort, deception and unhappiness. We are never at peace or happy together. I wrote many times: he is my burden—he is a thorn in my side. There is a conflict between compassion and the need to be free.

Dr. Joy feels I may not get well until I let go of this, that I weaken and over-protect Hugo, that I don't let him go. Will he let me go? Should I ask him to come and see me? Should I let you tell him?

It is now a matter of my survival. I don't want a divorce. I don't want people to know. I want nothing injurious to him. I want no recriminations—I want a loving, warm separation, and when I'm well I will visit him.

I thought making the separation in my mind was enough, but not if guilt hurts me, not if there is any doubt that I may use illness to stay here.

If the illness is an expression of guilt, then I need your help too. How sorry I am not able to see you.

Do you agree with Dr. Joy? He says when we deprive others of all experience we interfere with their growth.

Do I see Hugo as much weaker than he is? Am I projecting?

Perhaps he felt peaceful this year. We always quarreled.

Please help me.

Whatever he has become conscious of, can he release me?

I will phone you too, but I can explain things better by letter.

Needless to say, I will always take care of him.

With the best will in the world we are not good for each other.

Please tell me where Hugo is now, how much he is aware of. Whether I should see him. Write him. Could he see this letter? He always said he would never stand in the way of my growth. Now will he not stand in the way of my recovery?

Anaïs

Letter from Anaïs Nin to Hugh Guiler (not sent):
Los Angeles, December 1975

Darling:
    With all the love and all the good will, we could not manage to live together. It is my fault because when you, long ago, promised not to thwart my growth you did not know I would accumulate a well of guilt towards you for my liberated life. Inge worked on this guilt for years. Every trip, every success, every adventure made me feel guilty. It is true you chose the "other woman." In this case, the other woman was the bank and business, which sucked your life blood. I needed more life, more love than you could give me. This guilt has grown. It lies now at the bottom of my illness.
    Whoever investigated the possible psychological cause of cancer came upon this guilt, even for earning more money than you.
    I ask you for a loving release. We will always be there for each other. There is no blame. One neurosis played into the other.
    I feel I could die of guilt if you do not let me go. Nothing will be changed. No divorce, no telling anyone. I will come back and visit when I'm well.
    But darling, I have to get well and my health depends on utter truthfulness between us, which we never had—and all these secrets estranged us. I could not bear the secrets anymore. Please write me. I hope this year without quarrels gave you peace. The love is there, darling, and I think highly of you, and I know you were acting for my own good. Try to understand this: if I did not feel committed to you and your happiness, I would not feel guilt for everything I do. Release me from this. I do not mean never to see you again. I want to take care of you, as you did of me.
    All your intentions were good, darling. I wish we had been born later. Young couples take things so much more lightly than we did.
    We always were each other's best friend. But we each sought different lives. We tried and could not harmonize them. This may be hard for you to understand as you have no guilt towards me. But I, every time I examined my life, found a well of guilt I can no longer bear.
    Anaïs

Letter from Gunther Stuhlmann to Phyllis Deutsch (lawyer):
New York, December 21, 1975
Re: Anaïs Nin Guiler Trust

Dear Ms. Deutsch:
    As per your instructions, we have cancelled the trust's account maintained for the above at the First National City Bank, and I enclose the cancelled account book as well as a cashier's check, made out to "Anaïs Nin" and dated December 9, 1975, for the amount of $110.31, which represents the balance of the account.
    Yours sincerely,
    Gunther Stuhlmann

LOS ANGELES, DECEMBER 21, 1975
    Having written to Bogner and talked with her, I could not do any more. She

could not speak to Hugo because she was going on vacation until January 8.

Jim Herlihy tells me of the superhuman sacrifice I made for Hugo. He observed me during the period on 9th Street when Hugo would not go to the hospital for traction but stayed home and Jim came to help me.

Los Angeles, December 26, 1975

I recoiled in horror when people asked me to describe the illness. Oh, no—I don't want to live that hell again nor make others live it. But they reminded me: they need to know how I dealt with illness, what I learned from it.

First I learned from George Falcon, but meditation and relaxation were ruined by his proselytizing for Eastern religions—quoting Buddha, Chinese sages, by disregarding the meaning of creativity: an energy leak, so I was fearful of delaying my healing and of me stopping writing.

When Tristine questioned me, we both arrived at the conclusion that I had been with people who did not consider what I had accomplished.

"I have to realign your thinking," said George.

Brugh Joy's attitude was a shock: "The moment I read the *Diary*, I recognized your uniqueness. You spent your life transforming matter into spirit. Illness does not come from creation, but from an obstacle to creation—from some thwarted creation. Creation is your life-flow, it gives you energy. No, the illness lay elsewhere, in guilt, perhaps, in sacrifice."

Tristine's probing was good for me. She was giving back to me the source of creation and energy. I have grown to love her more and more. She helped me.

Los Angeles, December 28, 1975

Hospital. Corita Kent, once Sister Corita, phoned me. She experienced the same illness this year and is in chemotherapy. Does sharing give strength? I was touched by her call. She is alone. "By the time I have finished shopping, I am unable to do anything else." No, I have not been able to work inspirationally.

Wade comes in. He does not approve of Weston's methods. They are at odds. It creates a conflict between them and within me.

Brugh came. When he is there, I feel strong. Other times I feel weak. I can't rise above my body, harassed by one problem after another. The fistula creates such excoriation of the skin that changing the bag makes me weep with pain. Diarrhea. Incontinence.

Los Angeles, December 30, 1975

Home again. Dilapidated, but home. Fistula behaving diabolically, leaking unexpectedly.

After a meticulous, skillful and painful job by Mrs. Morrison of applying the bag, I became obsessed with going home. Rupert, nurse Mary Maxwell and I were awaiting Dr. Weston. He came. He was very proud of his job. I weigh 110 pounds —I escaped surgery—I walked down the hall. When I returned to the room, I was covered with the filthy, smelly, putrid flow from a leak.

Back to bed—to the same ritual. I was truly depressed. This has been repeated every day—at night there was nothing I could do but lie in it—sleep in it.

Finally I made it home with elaborate plans to have either Mary or Mrs. Morrison come, or poor Rupert, who had to learn. The only hope is that my skin will heal and then the bag will hold. There are people who live like this. And again, as usual, the doctor is too proud to learn from the nurses' personal experiences.

Last night, because of the joy at being home, I wanted to make projects: write a portrait of Rupert. It has to be in vol. 7. But the bag leaked and the evening was spent fixing it with Mrs. Morrison.

The goodness of the hospital nurse, the kindness, is worth recovering. They all took care of me, night and day. Two young ones, Sue and Cathy, would come unbidden, to talk, and the attendants were natural. Mrs. Korst, with her pixie face and Russian accent. The black nurses, soft-spoken. And, of course, Mary who was my nurse in January. She has a way of saying good morning that makes all the wetness and miseries of the night disappear. She cleaned the room, me, measured me, weighed me, made me comfortable, would not allow negative thoughts or moods. Loyal, wonderful.

LOS ANGELES, NEW YEAR'S DAY, 1976

Rupert prefers to have me home even if he has to nurse me. He makes a big fire with the Yule log. He shows me the film of firefighting he did in the Forest Service. We were finally able to afford it.

In the hospital he shows me slides of our trip.

LOS ANGELES, JANUARY 2, 1976

If only I could tell what I learned from the illness—but I don't think I learned anything. I did not die during the illness, or grow indifferent, withdraw. It is not my nature. I went on feeling, feeling for Rupert, for the doctors, for the nurses; I was never indifferent. Is that a contribution? Mary Maxwell says I spoiled her so much she can't be content with any patient now.

Today was a better day. The bag leaked once.

George came. I told him how I felt. He is Jesuitical. He turns words around.

Frances Field calls me up. She is happy to be in Carmel and out of New York.

Jody reports on the seminar on my work in San Francisco. All the young women were beautiful, alive, non-competitive. I seem to have created a world in which they shine radiantly. They feel united. The other seminars were deadly. My women are drawn to each other, magnetized. Lynn Sukenick, Tristine (Jody said her paper was brilliant), Evelyn, Sharon.

They never treat me as someone of a different age—they scold me, criticize my being overly generous to Progoff.

LOS ANGELES, JANUARY 1976

Flowers from Corita, who has suffered as I have.

Brugh started me working again—to dream.

Twice I dreamt I lay in an Egyptian marble sarcophagus. The first time I levitated about 12 inches. The second time Varda was not dead and painted my whole body in all his favorite colors, especially gold. Then I levitated again. (I wonder if this has to do with his saying to me after his first stroke: "I am no longer afraid of death. I saw the most beautiful colors.")

Association: The Egyptian sarcophagus was prepared for a journey to the sun and the moon. I have been fascinated by the legend of the solar and lunar barques ever since I read the legend.

Jim will talk about me at Bob Snyder's film showing.

Tristine has the pearl eyes of Orpheus. She has crystalline laughter. She is full of depths. She became my friend, not my daughter, when she warned me against George.

Barbara Kraft loves Sharon Spencer. "She is a golden creation." Barbara is going through a powerful experience of change, but Sharon is more courageous. Barbara had the best help—George was her therapist and I for a whole year. But she lacks courage—she is awaiting the break. She wants everything. She won't find passion until she learns to give, not to demand. We are magnetically close—with affinities of all kinds. Rochelle Holt is a problem child. Jody is intuitive, intelligent, intellectual.

Women are creating a new criticism. The seminar at San Francisco was the loveliest.

LOS ANGELES, JANUARY 1976

The quartet played Debussy. It unleashed a flood of tears. I did not want to die. This music was a parting from the world. Music was always the music of exile. There existed another world I had been exiled from. The core of it was from Debussy to Erik Satie. Sonata for viola and piano. The Persian flute, the conch shell of the Tahitians.

I never tried to explain the feeling of exile. I accepted the weeping. But today I spoke to Dr. Joy—and I asked him. He feels the same way. Yes, music indicates a better place, another place. One should think of it. If it follows death, then it is a beautiful place. I assumed he knew music. He knows everything in depth.

I am suffering because my writing through the dramas has distorted me. Like now. I want to write about music and I write like a nine-year-old child. I'm frightened. Tristine helps me by writing my evaluation of my students' work.

Yesterday I thought of painting Rupert as the Phantom Lover who stands as an obstacle between each lover, and woman for him is the dream. So Rupert is the dream, but he becomes real at the end of seven. Seven is a magic number.

Dream: I order all the servants to light all the lights of the chateau—there is to be a surprise.

LOS ANGELES, JANUARY 15, 1976

Talk with Joaquín about his music. Yes, he knew about this new world lost to us, about exile and lost lands. Yes, he knew the longing. But, said Brugh, it is a lovely thing to look forward to—a promised land. So I will die in music, into music, with music.

After so many years with music as a part of our lives we never discussed the effort of it.

So, music. An undiscovered realm. Yes, it enters the body, fills the body.

LOS ANGELES, FEBRUARY 2, 1976

Celestial.

311

LOS ANGELES, FEBRUARY 22, 1976

Hospital. Yesterday I woke up too early, so, so weak that I thought I was going to *die*. Weston sent me to the hospital. Blood was down to 73.

Friends brought flowers, gifts. Inge Bogner came to see me, Barry Jones, Tristine, Jamie Herlihy. Meanwhile, my friends and Rupert fought for my life. They heard of a Japanese vaccine and wanted to take me to Japan. After surmounting unbelievable obstacles, Jamie arrived from the airport with the vaccine, and the nurse Jo Harrington was there. We formed a circle of love and I had my first injection. Jo explains not to be alarmed by lapses of memory, or misspelling of words, a well-known symptom of drugs.

Sunday, Monday, and Wednesday Brugh came and sat in the corner of the room, silent. I worked two mornings with Jamie answering mail in a light mood. I receive so many gifts with loving messages.

Of course, I never acted upon my letter to Bogner, or to Hugo. I cannot. In spite of Brugh's words: "You must live truthfully."

Dream: The third night Brugh appeared. I awakened trying to eat my thumb, thinking it was a fig. (Jim had told me the story of Christ's death, not on the cross, but walking to an island where a woman restored his health with *figs*.)

Sue Merrill, the nurse, a heroic figure—completely dedicated to her work but also sensitive.

Great love between me and my students, friendships.

I had an important meeting with Tom O'Horgan, who is interested staging the Diaries. A sensitive, gentle, imaginative person. Oh, lucky day. I must get well— get well.

He asks, "What made you guess at Artaud's greatness?"

"There was no guess. There was affinity and common vibrations. Yes, I felt their other dimensions and potentials."

I knew Tom O'Horgan when he was a 17-year-old actor living in a cold-water flat in SoHo. He always favored my work. He has become a very successful director. He wants to stage the Diaries poetically in essence. I love him. Irish eyes, warmth, sensitivity. Immediate connection. I offered him absolute freedom as every poor artist deserves. It was a short visit. I must get well. He is returning here on his way back from South America. I was elated. A horrendous night, incapacity to walk, but nothing could drown my joy. If only I could get well. Rupert, with incredible devotion, makes me walk, even though he has to carry me.

A nun came, held my hand, intended to talk about God, but we talked of other things. The Church seeks me back, but I do not believe in dogma.

All my friendships are flowering to their maximum worth. Deena and I became closer. Tristine and I are very close.

Brugh says: "Do not dwell on the aches and pains—try to live above and beyond them."

Jean Sherman is translating the child diary. Rupert finished correcting the galleys of vol. 6. He keeps me alive by his care and love. Brugh visits me every night at nine.

Dreams. They sustain me. Every evening I see Dr. Joy. Everyone sends me strength, presents, energy, a deluge of love. I am free of George's endless preaching—an hour and a half of theology. But sisters, priests, come to see me.

312

Los Angeles, February 1976

Another day at the hospital.
Last night Rupert and I could not separate. We clung to each other.
Today a small improvement. I can walk around.
I talk with Renate, who has to be operated on. I feel inert and passive.

Los Angeles, March 1976

Home. I wake up to the green trees and the pool. Sometimes I have the energy to work, but most of the time I am too weak. One morning I awakened to see the bag had leaked, a disaster. So I wait for the maid or Rupert. That is my only consolation. Telephone. It is Jo Harrington, the nurse. She will come in an hour.

THE PHANTOM LOVER

There was a party at the Chelsea Hotel, the old-fashioned hotel writers loved. I wore a long black taffeta skirt and a blouse. I entered the elevator. A very tall, very slender young man lowered his head to see the other passengers. I suddenly became aware of large eyes, brown, green, gold, eyes the color of Venice. His eyelashes were dark and very thick. His eyebrows very hairy. He had a long, slender neck. This whole design of his neck and shoulders was of extreme stylization and yet he looked sturdy. We happened to sit on a couch. And then we noticed each other's hands: ink-stained only as printers get stained. We talked about printing. He was an actor, and between jobs he helped his friend Eyvind Earle to print Xmas cards. And I was printing my own books. He appeared to me the ideal figure for Paul in *Children of the Albatross*. I told him how Irene Selznick had asked me to write it as a play. We found much to talk about. He accepted my invitation to visit me to discuss the play.

Hugo was away. I had bought a leg of lamb. In that small kitchen about two by four he took over the seasoning and acted so at ease that I enjoyed his taking over. We had a delicious dinner. Then we sat on the couch and put on some recording. In the middle of *Tristan and Isolde* he kissed me. And we made love.

I had never responded fully to the first lovemaking. With him I did. We seemed incredibly well matched.

Another strange detail. In most casual love affairs the men and women withdraw from each other. They have no need to continue the embrace. He quietly lit his pipe and lay very close to me like a very contented lover, for the sensual embrace was not complete without a tender nearness.

Then he stepped into his Ford Model A and disappeared for several days. I did not know he had poisoned one of his fingers with lead and so I assumed that for him it was a one-night stand—and proceeded to try to forget him. I didn't.

When his finger was cured he telephoned me.

He came to dinner and we had another delirious evening. He had brought his guitar and sang.

There are a million ways of making love, but there is only one which happens miraculously, one of such intense merging that body and soul seem to fuse.

313

We hardly knew each other, yet I gave him all of myself. Again he rested gently, smoking at my side—tender—relaxed.

The next meeting was at the printing press. I watched him work. It was snowing heavily. I was due at an important dinner. But when he asked me if I could not stay with him I took up the telephone and broke the dinner engagement. He took me to the little bare room he lived in. Such fiery lovemaking. He read to me from Gillibrand at the end.

Next meeting was at the Spanish restaurant on 14th St. I told him how my visitor's visa had expired and I had to leave the country while my papers were being revised. I planned to go to Mexico. He had joined the Forest Service. He found the actor's life intolerable. He hated the desperate seeking of jobs, etc. At the end of the dinner he said: "I have to drive to California. Why don't you come with me and go to Mexico from there?"

I said yes.

I prepared myself for the trip. Millicent, who is a severe, religious person, seemed to accept my life and blessed this trip as she blessed other trips I made. She liked Rupert. She suffered at Hugo's fussiness. She helped to prepare a picnic lunch. And off we went. Both of us looked back with anxiety as if we feared to be swallowed by New York again. We did not feel safe until we had crossed the tunnel.

While we stopped at a gasoline station I watched Rupert getting the car serviced. I thought to myself: I am running away with a most beautiful man.

We ate our picnic lunch somewhere on the grass.

Rupert had always driven with the top down. So we drove with the top down not thinking of the condition of my skin. Already, on the drive to Washington, my skin was burning.

Our other mistake was too much baggage. Rupert had his guitar and I had a big valise. It troubled me to see him carrying all that baggage. We could not leave it in the car.

The real journey began from Washington. Rupert had wanted to do publicity for the Forest Service, radio talks, but they were not interested. He had another job possibility in Denver. By now the landscape dominated our life. We drove into the dawn, we drove into a burst of sun, we saw more sky, more forests, more rivers. The little Model A seemed like a scarab on the road.

To entertain ourselves we told each other about our lives. He was born in Palm Springs and played with Indian children. He hinted at Indian blood, which interested me keenly.

He wanted me to see everything. He had been so shocked when we first met that I spoke of not have seen anything but New York. The idea that I might return to France knowing only New York appalled him. So he made sure I did not miss anything.

On the flat plains it seemed as if we only traveled through the sky. Changes of scenery and climate were amazing. By this time my face was severely sunburned. I had to cover it with oil and wrap my purple transparent scarf around it. It startled people so they must have believed I was Mati Hari.

We both had very little money. We started keeping a small account book so we could share the expenses. After a few days we threw away the account book, pooled our resources and no longer counted.

We covered 18 states. A discovery of an astonishing country. He knew the best places, the best views. He dragged me out of bed early enough to see the dawn over the Grand Canyon. I heard the wind whistling from canyon to canyon. It vibrated like a multitude of stringed instruments. The Canyon was incredible. It reminded me of the Great Wall of China.

On flat land the sky gives you the same feeling you have on the ocean. That you will never reach the end—that it is illimitable. It was a surprise to reach a town. One night I asked if we could make love on the sand, in the desert. We stretched out the blanket and it was only later that Rupert told me we had risked meeting a snake.

We ate where the truck drivers ate—French potatoes and hamburgers.

We almost lost Rupert's dog, Tavi, who went for a walk by himself and we did not notice he was not in the car. But he was waiting at the gas station where we had stopped.

At six o'clock, after a day of hard driving, Rupert would show tiredness and irritability. It was the frustrations of the day, looking for a restaurant or a room for the night. We fell asleep instantly after so much fresh air. Rupert spent some time studying maps. We were unbelievably harmonious, sensually—the same rhythms, the same pulsations.

To entertain ourselves we talked about our past lives. Rupert talked about the history of Palm Springs and Nevada. I told him the story of Monte Carlo. Novels, biographies, history. Even Romain Gary's *Colors of the Day*. He told me stories of mountain climbing and skiing. I told him stories of Switzerland. We had plenty of stories to tell.

We read Dane Rudyar's astrology book. Rupert drove with him from Harvard to Hollywood. He was a man just distinguished enough, just charming enough, to keep a harem of American women studying astrology. They had spoiled him. Rupert found him a finicky, difficult traveler. I once thought he was a clever astrologer, but since Moricand I have lost interest.

———

Projects:
An anthology of essays
Lynne Selznick
Nancy Zee
Lee Potts
Jody Hoy
Bebe Weber on *House of Incest*
Anthology of *Diaries*
Trip with Rupert in next Diary—a separate one

LOS ANGELES, APRIL 13, 1976

When I first woke up, I experienced the very opposite of what I did in my twenties. Awakening was always preceded by a thrusting forward of the arms in the dance. Life is a dance. Today I do not wish to wake up. If I do not move exceedingly slowly, I may discover a pain. To be fully awake is to be in pain. So I reach for the painkiller.

Rupert prepares the breakfast with gayety. He bought a sumptuous breakfast tray from the chichi department store in Beverly Hills. At least today, April 13, I do not have to go to the hospital.

The fate of the day depends on Jo Harrington's bag. If it leaks we have to lie and wait for her because the fistula's material is so corrosive it wrecks the skin. So Jo comes running from where she is, and in half an hour I have a new bag. It may or not may leak. Sometimes at 4:00 AM we find ourselves bending over the ugliest object in the world. A fistula.

Jo and I are fond of each other—she is the ideal figure for Pietà—and she has the Catholic desire to serve. She was going to be a missionary nurse. She has the purest features I have ever seen, an easy laugh. She took to our life as the most natural in the world. She heard Rupert sing with his guitar for Xmas at the hospital.

I try to work. I may work for a few hours. Or have visitors. Joaquín comes and answers my travel letters. Jamie answers my American mail. Sometimes he adopts some of my orphans.

LOS ANGELES, APRIL 1976

If you took a submarine and searched the depths of my ocean, you would find a mournful landscape. On one corner lies a damaged body, pierced near the right hip with a hole unrelentingly pouring out an evil-smelling liquid, acid, burning the skin. A bag has to cover it, but it does not stay on. When it leaks we have to call the nurse. An hour or two wasted. I have to lie in the bed with the wound uncovered. I cannot move or write. In this landscape there is no light. I listen in amazement when people speak of my radiance. Down there, there is no light. The heavy sorrow I feel, which is partly hidden from the world, takes light and oxygen away.

I once spoke of illness not having reduced my responsiveness, but lately it is not true. I do not care. Things happen and they do not touch me—Tom O'Horgan's interest in dramatizing the *Diary* and its failure because of some scenes I asked to be cut.

UCLA wants the original diary.

I was chosen Woman of the Year by the *L.A. Times*.

I get beautiful reviews of *A Woman Speaks*. My friends are generous and loving.

It is most hurtful when I put on my favorite dress, put on my wig, prepare myself for visitors. I am aware of the façade, the dress that covers the bulge of the bag.

Last night we okayed *Anaïs Nin Observed*, the book, for final editing. I lay on a chaise longue. I risked staining my dress. Only at the end of the evening did the bag leak. So everyone hurried home. And I went through the usual ritual. Lying in bed, waiting for Jo, wiping the drainage with washcloths. This weighs down my spirit. I cannot transcend it.

Flowers keep coming. Julieta Campos came. We did not have much chance to talk because she came with a friend.

I'm losing weight.

Brugh's words do not comfort or strengthen me: "You can will it not to leak. Don't let the fistula rule you." But I know that my mind is concerned with the fistula, that I weep at the sordid slavery to it. I have learned nothing from the illness. Every happening is tormented by basic pain—gifts, flowers, love letters. The brightness has dulled.

The room looks beautiful—sun, dancing shadows from the pool.

Yours, confessedly despairing—A

LOS ANGELES, APRIL 24, 1976

Digby Diehl's article about the Diary roused much attention. UCLA had a conference and decided they must have the manuscript I catalogued. Digby called Joan Palevsky and asked her to help him raise enough money for UCLA to buy the diaries. Her answer was: "Oh, we have no time to waste, we are too busy, both of us. I will give you the full amount."

She came to see me. I liked her immediately. Simple and direct. She was a teacher of French and Italian, married a fellow student. Her husband invented a new computer and became rich. She read me well. She is a Pisces. I gave her the first vol. 6 to come out of the oven, and a small accordion diary I wrote in Bangkok. She wrote me a sweet note saying that she had enjoyed herself, that she was usually tense with new people but felt at ease with me and wanted to come again.

The lawyers are consorting. Rupert is bringing back the diaries from the vault. We work most of the time on vol. 7.

I have many problems. The continuous torment of the leaking bag, the over-active fistula, hours spent lying flat in bed waiting for the nurse, the hours spent with Jo, of whom I am very fond—the anxiety when a visitor comes that the leak should happen, awakening at night to find it has burst, wearing a dress I love and the fistula staining it—getting up two or three times at night to empty the bag, the feeling of an impure body.

All this gives a sad undercurrent, casts a shadow over pleasant events: the arrival of vol. 6; winning a prize for best travel article I wrote on Bali; good reviews on the lecture book and essays; French Television asking Durrell to adapt *House of Incest*; Joan Palevsky who will give UCLA $100,000 to buy the diaries.

I cannot levitate. I should be working on vol. 7.

The saddest hours are those spent waiting for Jo. When the bag leaks, I have to take it off and lie flat in bed with wash rags to sponge off the horrible content of the fistula. The hole is deep, the discharge ugly, green, yellow; I often weep. No illness could have been a greater trial to my sense of aesthetics. Jo is struggling to find a contraption that stays on for at least a week.

Yesterday Joaquín was here, Joan Palevsky, Jean Sherman who is translating the child diary—and suddenly I felt the warmth oozing along my leg, and everyone had to leave while I pulled the bag off.

LOS ANGELES, MAY 1, 1976

Visit from Corita Kent. Beautiful, narrow face, very pure and emotional eyes, very aristocratic, arched nose, a sweet smile, a sweet voice. We both have cancer and have exchanged confidences. She has talked with Dr. Joy. We both find it difficult to meditate. I suggested it might be because we were accustomed to use meditation for our work, I to see images for my writing, she perhaps for seeing colors for her work, not accustomed to meditating for our own bodies. When I close my eyes I see the images that haunt my writing. I follow labyrinths that lead to new perceptions…a scene from the past that I interpret differently. Or I recreate a person who has written to me, Boulic, or Maurice Paz, or Chalon, or the life of Josephine Bonaparte, whom I dislike intensely, or the life of Mishima, which is terrifying, or the flower arrangement by Val equal to a Japanese flower arrangement, or the parts of the Diary that are too brief and need expanding. I imagine myself in Tahiti, in Bali again. I see visions of travel, or that of friendship, or a memory, of a fantasy about the future.

At first, concentration on the white light would relax me and put me to sleep. It may be I lost faith in Falcon because it did not deliver me from the pain. I was shocked when Dr. Joy the healer talked about surgery. Did he lose faith in the healing of the fistula?

One of the worst days of all: the bag leaked and Jo was at the hospital. Then Rupert's two temporary bags gave out. So I have to lie in bed, and with paper towels or wet rags stem the flow of the horrible matter. I weep. So much precious time wasted. I have nightmares.

But I was determined to work. I put my typewriter on a tray, sat in bed, and typed all that was missing from volume 7. I was too active then and could not write much in the Diary. I wrote about Dartmouth, meeting with Judge Douglas, teaching Shirley Osborne, and have yet to write about the films Hugo made between 1966 and 1974. I want to introduce the women who wrote to me. My role in the feminist movement. The extraordinary quality and beauty of the women around me. Connection with the world. Must write about Japanese food and *satori*.

How I fail in meditations.

Joaquín comes almost every week. He is working on his opera *La Celestina*, which, I believe, is about the old Spanish novel. He enjoyed reading the childhood diaries.

LOS ANGELES, MAY 18, 1976

Hugo is sick and I got concerned. I called up twice.

I worked on four pages today.

The fistula is bleeding.

I had the joyous visit of John Pearson, Suzanne Goulet, Dick Stoltzman. John says he believes he could reform the world if someone would publish the Diaries and place them in every hotel room instead of the Bible! (And he used to be a minister.) He saw Van der Post. Van der Post told him how much he likes my books.

I wrote an expanded version of the two days spent with German television in Paris directed by Georg Troller. In 1970 I wrote every letter in the Diary. My activities were unbelievable. I am preparing to write the "chorus" of women's letters when they invaded my life.

The quartet is playing as they do every Sunday night.

Letter from Anaïs Nin to Lawrence Durrell:
Los Angeles, May 18, 1976

Dear Larry and Ghislaine:

A specialist-selected television *équipe* are coming in July to do a series of interviews for each *Diary*. I wish Ghislaine could join them.

318

Henry and I talk over the telephone as I can't leave the house. Too much radiation damaged me and caused a fistula which prevents me from going anywhere. Otherwise I feel well enough to work on the last Diary, volume 7.

I am sending you *Diary 6*, which has photographs of you and your family and the story of my visit to you.

The diaries and letters have been bought by UCLA. Some will be sealed, the early ones open. It will help with all the medical expenses.

Typing four or five pages a day and interesting visitors make the days short. And of course in this house one does not mind being shut in.

It sounds as if you were entering a new cycle.

The translation of *Under a Glass Bell* is even better.

Everyone asks about you and hopes you will come again.

My love to you both,

Anaïs

LOS ANGELES, MAY 1976

I had a visit from Mr. and Mrs. L. Levitt who offer me a doctorate from International Community College. They feel I was the most exciting of all the tutors and brought the college glamor. In the evening Digby Diehl. Very human and sincere. Good talk. Praise of Kirsch. Dr. Wade maintains his offer of Alber prints to go with the original diaries. Dr. Wade himself came Saturday morning while Jo was changing the bag.

If it were not for the cursed fistula I would feel normal. But I have to empty the bag every hour at least. It burst just before Digby's visit. We had to talk behind the panel that separates the bedroom from the living room.

Music: The long sweetness, tender accents, the wistful lingering plaint and burst of joy. Joy wins out. Every note is set dancing, starting gently, ending vigorously. Then the plaint again, the repetitions of the longing, the tenderness, the heartbeat, and a burst of ecstasy. The mingling of lyrical tones with soft, shadowy secrets—feelings are suspended—then burst open—step, step, step towards intensity. Always a reverie, gentle and in unison and then a tempestuous meeting of all the instruments. Peace, serenity, storm, and undercurrent of intensity. The intensity wins in harmony and in moments of repose, reverie. The lullaby sets you dreaming; you float on tenderness but a storm awakens you.

Gently now, the violins, the viola, the cello lull you, repeating your most secret wish, lulling, caressing, swinging on a hammock of silk—then the inner fires of the world burst and burn and spill, and all the reveries are forced to hide—one does not hear them anymore. Then the instruments seem to mourn the early reverie and seek it again. Drops of water from the trees, golden sparkles on the sea, words of passion, caressing notes all light and sorrow.

LOS ANGELES, JUNE 25, 1976

Unalterable sadness. Because beautiful Rupert kisses and desires me in the pool, because he takes infinite care of me, because everything around me is beautiful, because visitors bring me news of the world, Michoutouchkine and Pioloco from Port Vila, because I am surrounded by love and praise, because I am in Paradise, but with an aching body so weak and out of breath, I felt I was dying. I saw myself in a coffin and all the writings praising my work became flowers for the dead.

Then I dreamed that I was in a huge masquerade, all my friends in disguise, many people. Suddenly I felt I must see Brugh—I began to ask for him, to seek him in the crowd, and could not find him. I had lost him. The pain awakened me.

This dream came after his sudden visit when Michoutouchkine and Pioloco were there. Brugh stood a moment to greet everyone. The sun illumined him. His beauty at that moment overwhelmed me. Ever since then I visualize him, those startling, firm, blue eyes, the perfect profile, the curly blond hair, his white clothes. And I fear that this time his beauty struck a chord it had not touched before.

He will come Friday. Sharon arrives Friday too. Brugh must not touch this personal cord because I have never loved Rupert more deeply and more passionately. He has immunized me against other men.

Joyce Carol Oates writes the review I expected. Petty and old-fashioned, full of clichés. Nona loves me but does not have perception. Her choice of Goyen as a reviewer could have turned out well, but didn't. However, I no longer suffer from these narrow judgments. I am content with Kirsch and Millett, and Henry's extraordinary preface to a book of photos.

Rupert asks me to write about the music.

LOS ANGELES, AUGUST 1, 1976

I have not experienced for many years the split in my nature between how I live and how I feel. I wake up in pain. Rupert jumps up and gets me the painkiller. When it quietens me, it is nine or ten o'clock. We get up. In the morning I feel the worst. Rupert gives me my breakfast. I fall asleep while he goes to the post office. The post office always cheers me. A letter from Sharon. A letter from Durrell, who will adapt *House of Incest* for TV and Mai Zetterberg will direct. I sent a cassette of Dick Stoltzman for the music. I get a letter from a ballet company saying they wish to make a ballet of *House of Incest*. I say yes. They add lyrics of their own.

Letter from Maurice Paz, a scholar of 80 whose letters are full of charm. Then a friend arrives—Frank Alberti; tender, thoughtful and generous. He is the one who informed me of the *Amis de Marcel Proust* article.

A letter from Frances who is in the hospital. Rochelle Holt, Nancy Scholar. The sun shines on gifts I receive, perfume, costume jewelry. Rupert is busy running the household and working on vol. 7. Outwardly, it all looks beautiful. I wear my Indian dresses. Barbara and I enjoy the same things.

Tuesday when we packed the car and drove to Sky High Ranch, and met Brugh all in white, and his disciples who effused their energy and love—the faces, Brugh's beauty, all around me like a dream—I was not inside my body. When Brugh held my feet and worked on them I felt as if I danced for an hour, perfectly, gracefully. But as I look at the desert, the faces, I am still not there. Why? I had these feelings when I was younger. Why now?

Return home. Rupert's faith is shining brightly. He sings on the way. He is outdoors. He has learned to be a complete nurse, learned to put on the new bag so we do not have to wait for the nurse. He makes love to me in the pool, on the outside because it hurts me when he enters me.

I am not there. My body has slipped away. I exchange love, letters, presents with my friends. What is it? What has happened to me? A sorrow of enormous depth lies at the bottom. Oh, so heavy. I cannot resume my joy. It is not the concept of death, it is the parting from all I love. It is a profound sorrow at the loss of my energy, my fire. There is a veil—a veil. Rupert is moving away—or I, perhaps. Everything from waking, which was a joy (the lover of dawn), the coffee, the dressing, the work. Before my illness I was physically and emotionally close to everyone. Now that is at a distance.

The dream of the masquerade in which I am desperately looking for Brugh. Does he represent the core I cannot re-enter?

The disciples told Brugh they had never felt so strong a charge of energy, and I had come for *their* energy.

I have taken no notes about my concern over Hugo. Tuesday he had surgery for a hernia—alone. I am a prisoner. I can't obey the rule of my life: compassion. Rupert fights my compassion, but he was generous and helped me to telephone Hugo. I gave Hugo a beautiful private room and a nurse. I called him every day, twice a day. The surgery was successful. He was surrounded by friends and will be cared for.

Rupert's generosity is superhuman. He even showed me Hugo's last film. We commented on it together. But I have no desire to see Hugo or be near him. Rupert's love envelops me like a refuge—a source of life.

LOS ANGELES, AUGUST 6, 1976

I spoke to Brugh about the sense of distance. He said it was due to the painkillers and other drugs. I want to believe that. I spent four days without taking painkillers. But then a new pain attacked me, an abscess. Rupert spent hours putting hot rags on it to bring it to a head. We succeeded.

LOS ANGELES, AUGUST 9, 1976

One day without pain. I put on the Mexican wedding dress and received the quartet and Barbara.

Then Jean Bradford came to visit—a beautiful woman, exuding warmth. She told me the story of her two years with R. D. Laing. He has several houses. He does not practice psychiatry. He is cold, out of contact with everyone. Jean was desperate. One day he came to her and said: "Will you help me? I am in trouble." Jean said hesitatingly: "I don't think I am equipped to help you."

She teaches in Maryland. She came to study with Laing. Another time he said to her: "There is something wrong here, isn't there?"

"Yes," said Jean, "it is the absence of love."

Was he drugged? Schizophrenia. I remembered his behavior at the Santa Monica auditorium. (A Zen Buddhist came to talk. He observed their depressive attitude. He asked them why they looked like people from an insane asylum.)

Jean finally gathered all my books, formed a group of women, and they began to study as if it was a psychology course. She tells me they derived comfort, love, nourishment from these studies. She wrote me a letter. She came with delicate gifts, a Chinese embroidered box, perfume, a sand sculpture bottle. I loved her warm presence.

I began to dictate into my Sony tape recorder as I cannot sit and type very long. Had to rewrite about Bali because the formal article did not harmonize with the journal.

Anaïs Nin with Brugh Joy, 1976

On Proust

The eternal dimensional mobile that can be read a thousand times for different meanings. I read him all over again each year, and each year I saw a new aspect, discerned a new meaning. It is as if he had struck an infinite chord that never ceases to vibrate on different levels. It is the quality of infinite depth that makes each reading a new experience. The work does not stop vibrating; the soundings come from deeper and deeper depths. As one returns, one discovers a new perspective. No other writer has ever achieved this continuum. Is it because he explored every aspect, every mood in a state of perpetual movement, that the change is achieved each time as if each word had a thousand meanings? Proust's words do have a thousand meanings.

Is it that the flux of change of mobility was finally cornered or captured at the moment of its evolution so that the evolution never ceases? He has never described states, fixities, metamorphoses as stone, as petrified hearts or bodies. The life current was never interrupted, and so whenever you catch it you are drawn into its vortex and life offers you a new vision.

I never understood why Proust was the only writer I read each year and felt desolate whenever I came to the end.

I was very disturbed by George Painter's biography because I knew Proust would not have wished his beautiful transposition reduced to literal facts. Proust wanted to live and leave us the legacy of a transposed life.

Because he penetrated the unconscious of his characters, they did not age and die in our imagination since the unconscious is a stream of revelation, which is never touched by time, fashions, history. Proust's universality made his writing on music applicable to any music; his writing on jealousy fit jealousy at any time. He never fixed a date upon anything. A painting could apply to all painting. Very few novelists escaped the stamp of time so that the experience could only take place once.

Joaquín Nin-Culmell (l) and Robert Kirsch with Anaïs Nin, Silver Lake, 1976

LOS ANGELES, AUGUST 10, 1976

Trying a new pen, which is clearer.

Joaquín came. We spent an afternoon together. Recalling the past, telling amusing stories. He has finished his opera *La Celestina*. Frank Alberti came last night and interviewed me on a cassette.

Rupert works on vol. 7. I still feel sadness when I lie naked on the bed, the fistula exposed. It seems like precious time lost—slipping away. I'm getting better, but Rupert is irritable. And this makes me feel guilty. I don't know how to relieve him of too many duties. He does not wish for this. What I dreaded has come to pass. My illness has overburdened him. He does not let me tidy up, make the bed, wash dishes—all of which I can do. I feel entrapped. He rebels: "I made the bed three times today." Yet he is the one who insists I stay in bed between visitors.

Talk with Joan Palevsky over the telephone. I have an offer from TV to serialize the Diaries. I have to find out who will do it, how—no money will mean anything if the Diary is vulgarized and cheapened. Conflict.

One day without pain. Brugh cannot come today—I tell him not to be disturbed as I have no pain. "But I want to see you for my own pleasure," he said. He said it first. I find his presence dynamic, inspiring.

LOS ANGELES, AUGUST 1976

Pain. Visit to Dr. Wade. Excess radiation condemns me to digestive troubles, blocks, pain. But at least I can stay home. Barbara can come and tell me her sad divorce story, but as it once happened with Frances, it becomes lighter. But Frances has lung cancer and I can't bear to imagine her going through the tortures of chemotherapy and radiation.

Brugh came between planes. I was depressed. We talked about how I had succeeded in maintaining a life rhythm in the house but that I missed attending Les Amis de Marcel Proust, and Durrell's adaptation of *House of Incest.* Brugh said simply: "Well, go. You're independent from the nurse now that Rupert can repair you. You must not let your body enslave or reduce your life." I know I can't go. At home I spend half my day in bed because the warmth of the electric blanket quietens the pain. Brugh cheered me, but we had only 20 minutes to talk and I was suffering from a digestive obstruction.

LOS ANGELES, AUGUST 1976

Brugh left his seminar, his ranch, and drove four hours just to see me. He drove the pain away. I really love him, always so white and radiant. But the pain has a concrete cause and tomorrow I go to the hospital to have the abscess lanced.

My pleasures are beautiful love letters: one from Cortázar recommending me for the Nobel Prize, which Nona copies for me. Henry Jaglom is spending hours to study the contract for the TV diary to help me.

The interview with me in French is very interesting, and I received a beautiful letter from Bert Mathieu who has nearly finished his book on me and defends me from a shabby attack in *The Village Voice.*

I have never received so much love. Frank Alberti came for *mise au point* of an article for Les Amis de Marcel Proust. He and Maurice Paz are constantly preoccupied with me. Henry writes me generously, rejoicing over Kate Millett's praise of me. Barry telephones.

Rupert discourages visitors as I would have several a day.

I wrote three pages for vol. 7.

The painkillers reduce the clarity of my thinking. I have difficulty in sequence and coordination. Nurse Jo loves me and gives me all the care she can.

I can write several letters in the evening.

Rupert has returned to his obsession with TV. He listens by the hour to commentary, which has no substance. I sometimes tell Rupert that I can't bear how much trouble I give him—that I feel I am giving him nothing but unhappiness. His answer is that I gave him life, that he considers taking care of me his most important achievement. It is amazing and beautiful how we work together. We read the mail and divide the work. He edits my writing on Tahiti, which Charlotte Hyde sold to *Holiday* magazine.

Barbara came—she is always beautiful and so alive that her troubles seem like adventures.

On Thursday we drove to Brugh Joy's place. The road is not crowded and the landscape of the desert is beautiful with its strange plants and blue mountains. Brugh greets us, in white, as always. I am wearing a white caftan of a heavy textile, which Ardith Gibbons made me. The hood has a little bell.

The group is made up of people who believe in holistic medicine. We sit in a circle on huge pillows. We hold hands. Brugh places me on a high table and passes his hands over my body. Then each member of the group lays their hands on me one by one. I felt such energy entering me that I felt compelled to leave the table and dance. But for the dizziness I would have danced, but as it was I made just a few gestures. But the effect of the healing was startling.

We had a merry lunch, and before lunch we sat on the porch and talked. I lay on a chaise longue. The group sat all around me. They were all interesting. We left at about three.

In the car the pain began—excruciating, and not responding to the painkiller. It was agony.

Came home and took Demerol, two doses. The pain flared up in spite of that. Nothing but exhaustion enabled me to sleep. The next evening Frank Alberti came to read me his transcript of our interview and Maurice Paz's translation of my one-page comment on Proust. The pain was so intense I had to send him away. I asked to see Dr. Wade. He planned a blockage of the sciatic nerve for Tuesday. That day the pain ceased. We cancelled the hospital.

Brugh cannot explain what happened. No one can. But today was my first almost normal day. Usually in the morning I am at my worst. Today I got up at nine to receive Val who is building a tea house. I sat at the typewriter and worked. I telephoned Hugo, my daily phone call, because leaping out of the bus he cracked his heel and had to have surgery, and his leg is in a plaster cast.

Now I lie in bed. Rereading my mail, answering letters. Maurice sends me the *Letters of Marcel Proust.*

We had a Sunday afternoon at Jamie's. A friend had painted a mural that looked like the island of Moorea. René Charlip gave a dance and presented an actress who teaches the deaf, having herself overcome her handicap. She was full of humor and is an amazing mime. It broke my heart to see her struggle for communication. Jamie is surrounded by gifted homosexuals, tender and mystical. It was a magical atmosphere. He has fixed up his house with fantasy and beauty. There is a touch of the East in the curtains. Jamie seems happy.

LOS ANGELES, OCTOBER 27, 1976

I was afraid to write my thoughts for the first time. First came the pain—then painkillers, Demerol. Rupert learned how to inject it, which made it stronger. Weeks? I can't remember. Then they put the catheter in—for bladder trouble—and I was confined to bed and uncomfortable. Then the withdrawal symptoms overwhelmed me as if I were an old drug user. The shaking, the blurry eyes, insomnia and the worst depression I ever suffered. I awakened at 3:00 AM and wanted to drown in the pool, to run away from Rupert (to free him), to hide in any old hospital. Or I had thoughts of death, until Brugh Joy telephoned me early this morning to explain my condition I so I could objectify it. My spirits rose again. I also talked to Bogner who helped me by telling me Hugo was ready for separate lives—lightening my guilt.

So today I lie in bed encumbered; walking is difficult, everything complicated with the two bags—no, three.

I'm still depressed, but able to dominate it. I have to wear the catheter for ten days.

Meanwhile, Rupert will read to me until I fall asleep—he watched over the tea house built by Val after I made a casual wish for one—beautiful workmanship—a view over the lake, the forest, the pool. I just caught glimpses of it. It was strangely comforting when I heard Val hammering and sawing wood.

Rupert keeps the fire going, he shops, he cooks special food, he is always there, patient and with faith that I will get well. Two years of this! Unrelenting pain and difficulties.

"Too much. Too much," I cried out. The sciatic nerve made me scream out with pain. They stopped that at the hospital with a nerve block.

So I refused to go to the desert to a cold house—Brugh had wanted us for three days to work on me. His call this morning did save me. Cool, collected Dr. Joy calling, explaining what neither Dr. Wade nor Dr. Weston did.

So today I sat up and wrote to Hugo and John Ferrone.

And here, I dared to face my ultimate fear—I am not prepared to die. Rupert's love is burning as always, the beauty of the house, garden, the closeness of Piccolino. Phone calls to Hugo when I could not sleep through his surgery for a broken heel.

Uncomplaining Hugo—but a heavy burden financially—$3,000 for a new film, nurses, home aides, etc. I encourage him to get the best care. I encouraged him to make his new film, but it was a heavy, heavy burden, even though my books are selling—three new volumes this year: *Diary 6*, the essays and lectures edited by Evelyn Hinz, and *Aphrodisiac*—selections from my love writing with erotic drawings by John Boyce.

The nurse comes every day, a brave and clever woman, but suffering with an alcoholic lover.

Letter from Hugh Guiler to Anaïs Nin:
New York, December 3, 1976

Inge has told me that you called her, as I suggested, and that you are receiving some new treatment which is temporarily upsetting, but which the doctors believe will help in the longer run.

Inge also said you asked if I could do something to give you "emotional freedom" at this time. I thought I had tried to do just that in my last letter, replying to yours in which you wrote that while suffering depressions, you feel guilty that you had been only a "half-wife" to me. I want to relieve you completely from any such guilt. My every conviction is that we have each in his and her own way adjusted to the realities. You have your independent life and I have mine. And on my part I can say that I have been accepting this peacefully and even creatively, and I hope you can feel the same way. I am living and expanding with that awareness and sensitivity that you planted in me and helped me to cultivate. I am infinitely grateful for what I received from you, and for achieving in yourself your own goals, as I predicted you would. All this more than compensates for whatever I gave you. I am convinced that we gave generously to each other what we could, within our respective limitations.

If I thought you had failed me in any way I would not feel as devoted to you today, as I do. On the contrary, I feel that to have lived with you for so many years, in spite of all the ups and downs, was a privilege any man would be proud of. I, for one, will continue always to think of you as the ideal woman in my life.

Once, speaking of the liberation of woman, you said that in your case you had been liberated by your husband. I want to liberate you emotionally, so please let me know if there is any further assurance you need from me.

Love,

Hugo

LOS ANGELES, DECEMBER 6, 1976

[A.N.'s handwriting] On Nov. 26 I went to the hospital—and died. Died among the clean sheets, medicines, finish like an insect.

[Rupert's handwriting—the rest of the diary entries are in his hand] I died—among clean sheets—finished like an insect. Injections here, there, everywhere. Painkillers, sleeping pills—fast, endless dreams. No self, no ego, nothing to cling to. All my energy taken away. The usual ceremony, cleaning uncovered big sheets, emptying bags. Back painful; lying on back painful. Unable to walk. Full of strings and claptrap.

Barbara brought a little candle shaped like a tiny round house. The little candle seemed to be all that was left of me. I hated to see my body uncovered—bags, tape, everything like a robot—not my body anymore. So ugly.

The only happy moments are when Rupert arrives—then everything seems all right. He takes charge.

I asked Deena, "Am I dying?" Brutally truthful, Deena answered, "No, you're not, but you must prepare for death."

Dream: Found my bed at the top of a waterfall with D. H. Lawrence. We wonder whether to throw ourselves in or not. We look down and see Lady Chatterley swim by in the ocean. We watch terrified while she swims from one ocean to another.

Dream: My bed finds itself in a Florentine room—shaped like a regular room but surrounded by sandalwood. I opened the door of a huge armoire to get big, generous sheets, the best quality. I thought the Jewish tradition had everything of the best quality—biggest—best. So I made up my bed. People came in in little Florentine caps—there were little Jewish cakes to eat for breakfast. I thought it was wonderful not to have heavy Jewish pastry. Nurses wore little Jewish caps on their heads. My bed was moved back to an ordinary hospital room. I said, "How dreary our culture is compared to the Jews'." But the hospital room was the ugliest thing I have ever seen. So unlike the Florentine room. Then, bored, I asked the nurses, "Would you like to work with me on organizing a film on Dostoevsky?" They worked, worked terribly hard. I felt: "Let's tell Hugo and we will find a producer for the film."

Dream: Too much sugar in the I.V. Doctor came in and saw I was in insulin shock—everything was distorted. Terribly hot, burning. Saw Jo…Jo. We talked, but I couldn't understand her. Fell asleep, blood transfusion going into my arm. Woke in a horrible sweat—swimming in water. Hands felt like a million cuts. Nurses would not tell me what was wrong, asked them to call Rupert—they refused. A friend came by and called Rupert. He called the doctor who called back and said not to worry—it was only a reaction to blood. The sweating stopped. I fell asleep.

Nightmare: I am an insect pinned to the wall. Nurses are doing things to the bags. One didn't want Dr. Martinson to see she did bad work.

Dream: Rupert went away. I am left alone in the hospital with a young doctor who squatted on my shoulder and caused intense pain. He said he didn't. Intolerable. Nurses said: "Your husband is there." Rupert came in and the bad dream dissipated.

Day I came home

I had dreamed all night long of coming home, but also of the fear of being parted from everything: I had said goodbye to Piccolino, to the house, to the pool, to everybody. Then after, the hospital preparation wore me out and the journey home (20 minutes) seemed endless. When I came into the room I had dreamed of returning to—I cried—because I had thought that I would never see all this again. I cried and cried. After much crying then I began to feel at peace. I did come back to the house— I became part of the house. As I went to bed I still couldn't believe my happiness.

LOS ANGELES, DECEMBER 16, 1976

Dream: I was tied to a wall with a chain. The wall was built of different pieces. When I finished I emptied the first wall—it was full of little huts where I put too much of everything. I wanted to cut the chain. I wanted to cut it off but felt overfull— feeling of clitter clatter—carrying feelings—burdens—pains. Everything attacking me. I wanted to fight.

Which thing do I want to remember? My greatest moment of pleasure is when the *mail* is brought to me. Unbelievably loving letters from those living my life and following me for guidance. Some mail comes from as far away as India, New Caledonia, and Michoutouchkine in the New Hebrides.

I asked Corita Kent whether I should prepare for death. She said, "Death will be especially easy for you because you have already transposed."

"What about my attachment to things and people?"

"You will find them on the other side."

Corita brought me a huge square silkscreen painting of a huge red heart and the word "Love" below in huge black handwriting—it seemed to fill the room with love. They (Corita and a nun) said I gave so much love to the world, their love would be waiting for me. All the love I had given to the world. Inside, I, myself, was weeping at the mere idea of separation from Rupert.

I want to go back to Paris—not to live—I want to sit with Rupert at a little bistro in Saint Germain-de-Prés. I feel I didn't show Rupert Paris properly. There is that little table—the only table on the sidewalk. I want Rupert to see that.

The first thing I noticed about Rupert was that he had intuition as well as a practical mind.

Anaïs Nin died at Cedars-Sinai Hospital, Los Angeles, on January 14, 1977.

ADDENDA

Tokyo, probably April 1968

Dear Anaïs:

You said your letter was written with love and understanding, and I felt it while reading. I felt it so much that I wept, and my husband, seeing my tears, was puzzled. I could explain nothing to him; he doesn't know.

Of course, you know, you must know, Anaïs, you are everything to Rupert, while I am almost nothing to him. Yes, Rupert said he loves me, but I don't know how much, whereas I know he loves you so much. I loved him most when he talked about you, said such beautiful things about you—Venus, your star, your tears in a Japanese soup bowl, your laughter, how he first met you at a party, how he asked you to come to California with him, how you put your purple scarf around your face when driving across the country in an open car…with such a beautiful expression on his face, expression of love, tenderness, admiration of you, and he told me you followed each other's heart. I have never seen a man who could talk about a woman like he does, and I loved him because he loves you, Anaïs, whom I love.

First I was in love with your stories, then, with you, and that's why I asked you to let me translate your novels, and I put all my heart into it, I have completed it; the result is, according to Nakada, sensitive and delicate and beautiful. (How I wish you could read Japanese!) Then, I wanted to find out the secret of the relationship you have with Rupert. I don't know if I found any secret, but I found there is mutual love constantly flowing between the two of you. I was amazed to see that such a flow of love can really exist between two individuals. I have never known that before except in the world of the imagination. I was amazed, struck—I didn't envy, but perhaps I wanted a little share of it.

Dear Anaïs, you have to know Rupert's last words spoken to me. It was "Now, be a good wife." I don't have to explain, then, where I stand in relation to Rupert, do I? I was preparing to see you both this summer, as a good wife, Mrs. Sugisaki, and I have completed the preparation. (Maybe I am like Matilda, I cannot but obey the word; but I am not Matilda, I obey because I know it's the best.) So, do come to Japan. I am begging you to come. I want to see you so much, so very much. Does it hurt you to see me? Yes, I know I hurt you. But try to think I am just a little foolish girl to whom Rupert might have given a little bit of his excess love once, but soon forgotten (how can I ever believe that I deserve any lasting love from Rupert?). Come with Rupert, I beg you. He would see me here and would realize how conventional I am, how terribly bound up with our social rules and obligations, how different I am than he thought I was.

Besides (let me be a practical joker), why should you give up all the beautiful places of Japan only because a tiny, foolish girl occupies a tiny spot of that country? Let me see you, and let me see Rupert. You and Rupert became one to me now that I am so far away from you. Loving you doesn't mean betraying Rupert, nor does loving Rupert mean betrayal to you. I wonder if you understand this feeling of mine.

I didn't understand it myself at first, but it is my true feeling. The more I love Rupert, the closer I feel to you.

I was translating your Café story, and *Children of the Albatross*, and there I came across the trinity you created in a Paris café between Michael, Djuna and Donald. I felt I found a key to my feeling in that trinity, then I met those people sitting at the round table, elbow to elbow and toes overlapping. I imagined you and Rupert were sitting there, and I was one of them, a member of a new kind of family, sitting at the same table. Please, Anaïs, let me sit there too. Don't turn away from me, don't leave me. Just let me sit there with you, that's all I ask, and maybe that's all Rupert wants. If you ever leave Rupert because of me, he will hate me for it, for the rest of his life. Please don't make him hate me, please don't!

I cannot leave Japan, for a few years anyhow; I have no excuse. I am not free. Even for love, I am not free. My only freedom allowed is to see you and Rupert in Japan. Please, Anaïs, don't deprive me of that freedom.

I am a little green fish swimming in the sea. I am always in the water, but once, only once in my life, I jumped above the surface. I saw the sky, I breathed the air, I saw my body reflecting the sun, phosphorescing. It was then I met you and Rupert. But the jump was momentary and the fish without wings sank deep down into the sea again. I am in the sea now, but I still remember the sensation of the jump when I imagined myself a bird. Am I asking you too much if I ask you to help me fly once again? The memory of the strength and hope would be enough to live on till finally, someday, I would be freed.

You and Rupert have been together for so long, and you will be together forever. I feel nothing can be more important than the relationship between you and Rupert. It's just so beautiful. Please forgive me for hurting you, for I must have hurt you, though I have no intention of doing so, and do understand that I (and, of course, Rupert too, for he told me so) could never be happy with Rupert if you went away, even for a few days, doubting Rupert's love for you.

I wrote this letter in duplicate, am sending one to L.A., the other to N.Y. so that wherever you happen to be first, you can read this.

Love,
Susie
P.S. I promise to keep it secret, secret from anyone else.

Tokyo, May 11, 1970

Dear Anaïs:

I received your letter of May 9. In reply to that, I am going to write a coarse and shrewish letter. Your illness is sad, very sad...and I know I have to be kind and tender to you, but no, not this time, I intend to be shrewish to make you forget your pain; I feel like I have to scold you, like little girls sometimes have to be scolded to be comfortably tucked in.

Please, Anaïs, how many times do I have to tell you that I have not meant, or do not, will not, mean to take your love away from you? You have to understand this. You and Rupert are one, and no one, no one ever can separate you two, not even death. Don't you know this, Anaïs? You must know, then, so what do you have to fear? Do not listen to Mrs. Ohnuki, please. She does not know anything about my plan or myself. She is a friend of mine, but not a confidential friend. Perhaps she heard about my coming from one of the Occidental [College] people whom I asked for some document. But nothing is definite yet. The Bank of Japan has to authorize something, and the American Embassy has to get clearance before they issue a visa, etc., etc. So, I don't know if or when I can come to the U.S. yet. But if all went well, and if I should come, then, my coming to Oxy has nothing to do with you or Rupert. Nothing really. I have to get the degree, this is all there is to it. You may not believe this from your way of looking at things. But Anaïs, you have to understand that I am different from you; I can be very business-like, shrewd and steady if I want to. When I decide that I have to get the degree, I do everything to get it. Only here in Japan, I cannot work, as there are so many other things to do, so many other things to worry about; that's why I want to be near Occidental where I can use their library books and where I can talk with professors when I need to.

I hope you do understand. So, really there is no reason for you to find pain in my presence in the U.S. If you want, I can arrange it so I do not have to see you, even though I feel so sad about it. Besides, I do not have any definite plan of coming.

I wrote a sort of farewell letter to Rupert...the end of something, like Hemingway's title.

My mother has cancer of the liver. She is in the hospital and I stayed with her.

Anaïs, darling, I want to do everything I can to make *you* happy, but most of all, I want to talk to you to make you understand that you and Rupert are the most beautiful couple that ever existed, and no matter what one of you does at times, the tie between you two can never be broken at all.

Love,
Susie

Dear Anaïs,
This is today's love letter…
The sun sweeps across the sea pulling
A net of draining diamonds
Gems of pure light, radiant,
More precious than the hard kind.
The essence of beauty is in the experience of it,
Not in the possession of it.

MEDICAL NOTES (Rupert Pole's handwriting)

Room 3813

Medicines:

Brompton's mix every 4 hrs. 4 teaspoons elixir 1 teaspoon syrup (phenothiazine)

Atropine morning and evening; Lomotil as needed

Konsyl (or Metamucil) 2 or 3 times a day as needed

2-3 aspirins at bedtime

Sleeping pills (injection) ad lib.

Vivonex and instant breakfast with egg if needed as supplement

24 hour therapy for bed sores: *most pain* now comes from bed sores

Valium if needed

Antacid after meals

CUNNINGHAM & O'CONNOR FUNERAL DIRECTORS

Date: January 15, 1977

For the funeral of: Anaïs Nin

10 certified copies: $20.00

Cemetery charges (cremation): $40.00

Professional services: $295.00

Use of hearse (to crematory): $45.00

Prepare, obtain certification permits, filing fee: $34.00

Scattering by airplane: $125.00

It seems appropriate, Rupert, that I should address a message to the shade of Anaïs care of you, since so often during the last years she told us (and when we were with you, we saw) how greatly your devoted magnanimity helped her surmount the ravages of her illness in order to continue her work on the diaries upon which her future renown will depend. I myself knowing her pretty well, and knowing how fragile her patrician spirit was—so easily hurt, so easily cast down by a rebuff by someone insensitive—could not help but marvel at the frightening tenacity and singleness of purpose which drove her on, kept her on course. In all this it was the stout right arm and the chivalrous self-abnegation of yourself, Rupert, which made possible this massive attack on the central citadels of art by this beautiful witch-like woman whom we called our third Musketeer. So we have lost our woman Musketeer, and the loss is psychically a heavy one for this small group of friends! She was our Aramis—the slim and delicate and aristocratic one, the born duelist. We lumbered about around her busy about our own work. But Anaïs was always there with some vital message, something which awoke and informed us, something which enriched us—she was quite inexhaustible when it came to giving; in a curious sort of way she managed to enrich herself by this constant dedication to her friends, and when there was no way in which she could be of use to someone she fell into a despondency.

She had the grand style in her life and in her work. She told me how she had at last learned the bitter lesson of mobilising her reserves of physical strength almost to a countdown of seconds. At Pasadena during a seminar which went on far too long she said to me under her breath, "Larry, I have about eleven minutes before I must simply lie down or collapse; let us wind this up. Don't worry, Rupert will be there to fix me up." And of course you were there. Meanwhile she had lectured and answered questions for nearly two hours, greeted students, performed several small acts of spontaneous kindness to timid pupils—in fact nobody could have noticed how ill she was, so splendid was her beauty and her bearing.

Her work is there now for us to read, in many languages, and her role in the modern world is a fruitful one. She taught that women must put a high price on themselves and demand the right to be free, but that in doing so they should not lose their femininity—for the whole civilised world of good values upon which our children will depend for their growth and mental well-being is precisely the work of the feminine element. And a world without real women in it to guide and nourish and inform its values will fall apart.

I am so happy to have lived in the same small moment of time with her; and I hardly dare to mourn her death—I seem to see that mischievous small smile with its sardonic edge, and hear that quiet laugh.

Larry

Letter from Hugh Guiler to Rupert Pole:
New York, February 23, 1977

Dear Rupert:

As we are going to be communicating with each other from now on, I think it is well that I do what I can to make things as easy as possible for us both, and I want to start by being quite frank with you.

First, I have been quite aware for more than ten years of your special relationship with Anaïs and I want you to know that I have not only respected that, but have been, and am grateful to you for having made her last years happy. There was a tacit understanding between Anaïs and me during those years, that we would allow each other to lead relatively independent lives and that this would in no way alter the deep devotion we felt towards each other, a devotion that became even stronger towards the end.

I am also grateful for all the help you gave Anaïs during her long illness. I wanted to share this burden with you, but Anaïs told me that my health would have broken if I had attempted to do this.

In the light of the above I hope you will feel at ease in communicating directly with me from now on.

Sincerely yours,

Hugo

Letter from Rupert Pole to Hugh Guiler:
Los Angeles, February 1977

My dear Hugo:

Please forgive a typewritten letter, but my handwriting (never very legible) became completely illegible during Anaïs's illness.

I am so grateful for your letter initiating our correspondence. I understand now why Anaïs loved and worshipped you so deeply. I cannot think of anything that would please Anaïs more than our close, sympathetic cooperation to carry on her work.

It has helped me greatly to recall an incident I'm sure you remember. In '66 Anaïs was in the hospital in N.Y. facing cervical surgery. The galleys of *Diary 1* were brought to her and she prayed that she might live long enough to know the reaction to her *Diary*. The gods granted her 10 years—years of fulfillment as an artist—years in which she was able to carry on a love affair with the world through the lectures and correspondence.

I am sending you a book, *Life After Life* [Raymond Moody, 1975], which more than any other convinced Anaïs that death is a joyous experience and helped so much prepare her for her "promotion to another realm."

The tribute here was just the right mood. There was a soft jazz combo with Cuban drums and bamboo wind chimes that would have delighted Anaïs. The University is making a tape and I will send you a copy as soon as it is completed. I have [heard wonderful things about] your program from Sharon [Spencer], John F[errone] and Joaquín. People were particularly awed at hearing Anaïs's voice in your beautiful film.

I will send an inventory of Anaïs's possessions as soon as I can manage it. In the meantime please rest assured that everything is insured and that nothing will be changed in my lifetime. The house will be kept as a working studio to carry on the writing. Right now I am drowned in work: getting materials ready for UCLA, for John Ferrone's memorial photo book (pictures of Anaïs), the Childhood Diary (the excellent translation is justified—Anaïs said: "I can't believe I didn't write it in English"), and Joaquín will write the preface; *Diary 7* (from 1966 to the present); and finally the '20s period from the end of the childhood diary when Anaïs was 17 to 1931, the beginning of vol. 1.

I suggested to John Ferrone that only you should write the preface for this diary. You are both the central figure and hero of this period. I hope you will accept.

Hugo, I know that you have moments of unbearable loneliness, as I do. It helps me to recall a line from the Bali diary (Anaïs wrote this as an ending for *Diary 7*):

"Let me think of death as the Balinese do, as a flight to another life, a joyous transformation, a release of our spirit so it might visit all other lives."

In these moments remember Anaïs's spirit is now free—free to be with you whenever you need her.

With profound sympathy,

Rupert

BIOGRAPHICAL NOTES

INGE BOGNER (1910-1987) was a New York psychiatrist whom Anaïs Nin and Hugh Guiler saw for decades.

RICHARD CENTING (1936-2017), a librarian at Ohio State University, was the first scholar to produce a periodical (*Under the Sign of Pisces*) based on Anaïs Nin's work.

ROSA CULMELL (1871-1954), Anaïs Nin's mother, was a classically trained singer whose career was thwarted by her husband Joaquín Nin and who struggled to support herself and her children after he left them in 1913. She lived with her younger son, Joaquín Nin-Culmell, until her death.

RENATE DRUKS (1921-2007) was a painter born in Vienna and was the protagonist of Nin's novel *Collages*. Her son, Peter, died of a drug overdose in 1967.

LAWRENCE DURRELL (1912-1990), was an English writer mentored by Henry Miller in the 1930s and who, with Miller and Anaïs Nin, was one of the "three musketeers," a literary group formed in the late 1930s. Durrell rose to fame upon the publication of his *Alexandria Quartet*.

JOHN FERRONE (1924-2016) was the Harcourt Brace editor of Anaïs Nin's diaries and erotica beginning in 1973 after the death of Hiram Haydn. Later, he edited Alice Walker's *The Color Purple* (1982) as well as several other successful titles.

FRANCES FIELD befriended Anaïs Nin in New York during the 1940s and was instrumental in maintaining Nin's affair with the young William Pinckard.

HUGH (HUGO) GUILER (1898-1985), Anaïs Nin's husband from 1923, was a banker and, under the name Ian Hugo, was an engraver and later an experimental filmmaker. He supported Nin, her mother and two brothers in Paris for years and financially backed several of Nin's publications.

JAMES LEO HERLIHY (1927-1993), an indefatigable supporter of Anaïs Nin's work and long-time friend, was the author of *Midnight Cowboy* (1965), upon which the Oscar-winning film of the same name was based.

EVELYN HINZ (1938-2002), a Canadian-born scholar, wrote about Anaïs Nin and was named her official biographer, although the biography was never completed.

HELBA HUARA (1900-1986) was a Peruvian dancer whose second husband was Gonzalo More. A near-invalid and hypochondriac, she was a burden on More and held a deep contempt for Anaïs Nin, More's lover for a decade.

MAX JACOBSON (1900-1979) was a German-born physician whose "energy shots" were a boost for Anaïs Nin and, later, Hollywood celebrities and politicians. Jacobsen gained a reputation as "Dr. Feelgood" or "Miracle Max," and when it was determined that he was using illegal drugs in his treatments, he lost his medical license.

WILLIAM BRUGH JOY (1939-2009), once a medical doctor, faced a life-threatening disease in 1974, which he claimed to have cured by meditation. He became an alternative healer, advocating cures by means of body energies, the chakra system, meditation, and higher levels of consciousness.

HENRY MILLER (1891-1980) was a groundbreaking American novelist who befriended Anaïs Nin in Paris during the 1930s and became her lover for ten years. His "Tropic" novels (*Tropic of Cancer*, *Black Spring*, and *Tropic of Capricorn*) are considered his best works. All three books were written during his relationship with Nin.

GONZALO MORE (1897-1959) was Anaïs Nin's Peruvian lover for a decade in Paris and New York. He was also her partner at the Gemor Press in the 1940s.

JOAQUÍN NIN (1879-1949), Anaïs Nin's father, was a Cuban-born pianist and composer who achieved professional success in Europe during the early 1900s. He left his family in 1913, married his young lover, and engaged in an incestuous relationship with Anaïs in 1933-34. He died penniless in Cuba in 1949.

THORVALD NIN (1905-1991) was the older of Anaïs Nin's two younger brothers. Unlike his parents and siblings, who were artists, his passion was for the sciences and business. He estranged himself from the family during the 1920s, pursuing a career in Latin America. In 1936 he had a brief incestuous relationship with Anaïs.

JOAQUÍN NIN-CULMELL (1908-2004) was the younger of Anaïs Nin's two brothers and studied piano in Paris. He became the head of American university music departments and was an accomplished concert pianist, director, and composer.

PETER OWEN (1927-2016), was Anaïs Nin's chief publisher in England.

RUPERT POLE (1919-2006), Anaïs Nin's "west coast husband," was born in Los Angeles to Reginald Pole and Helen Taggart. His mother divorced Pole and married Lloyd Wright when Rupert was a young boy. In the early 1940s, Rupert began a short and unsuccessful stage career, appearing in a few plays and on the radio. He was drafted into the army in 1943, refused to bear arms, got very ill in boot camp, and was medically discharged. Pole met Anaïs Nin at a party in February 1947 and became her lover. He invited her to drive from New York to California with him, and she accepted. Anaïs Nin bigamously married Pole in 1955, but the marriage was annulled in 1966 when she became a public figure. Pole went on to be Nin's literary executor and Trustee of the Anaïs Nin Trust, getting her work in print for many years after her death.

TRISTINE RAINER taught literature and writing in the English department at UCLA, where she co-founded the Women's Studies Program and created its first Women's Literature courses. Anaïs Nin wrote the preface to Rainer's book, *The New Diary* (1977).

SHARON SPENCER (1933-2002), professor of English and Comparative Literature at Montclair State University and friend of Anaïs Nin, was the author of *Space, Time and Structure in the Modern Novel* (1971) and *Collage of Dreams: The Writings of Anaïs Nin* (1977).

GUNTHER STUHLMANN (1927-2002) was the German-born New York literary agent who shepherded Anaïs Nin's career from obscurity to success over a twenty-year period. He continued to edit her work after her death and in 1983 established the longest-running literary publication dedicated to her, *ANAIS: An International Journal*, which consisted of 19 annual issues.

ALAN SWALLOW (1915-1966), owner of the Swallow Press, was the first American publisher to put all of Anaïs Nin's titles in print. In 1966, he was the co-publisher of the first volume of *The Diary of Anaïs Nin* and died shortly thereafter.

NOBUKO UENISHI, a Japanese-born writer and student of the Noh theater, is one of the subjects of Anaïs Nin's last work of fiction, *Collages* (1964). She was instrumental in getting Anaïs Nin published in Japan.

JEAN (YANKO) VARDA (1893-1971) was a Greek/French collage artist and friend of Henry Miller and Anaïs Nin.

EDGAR (EDGARD) VARÈSE (1883-1965), born in France, was an avant-garde composer befriended by Anaïs Nin.

LOUISE VARÈSE (1890-1989) was an American writer and translator who married Edgar Varèse in 1922.

GORE VIDAL (1925-2012), a writer who befriended Anaïs Nin in the 1940s, was instrumental in getting some of her fiction published by E. P. Dutton. His relationship with Nin was strained by an internal conflict between his attraction to her and his homosexuality. After Nin met Rupert Pole, she and Vidal became estranged, sometimes bitterly so.

ERIC WRIGHT (1929-2023), son of Lloyd and Helen Wright and half-brother of Rupert Pole, was the architect who designed Pole's and Anaïs Nin's house in Los Angeles. After Pole's death in 2006, he became the Trustee of the Anaïs Nin Trust.

HELEN TAGGART WRIGHT (1892-1977) was married to actor Reginald Pole when their son, Rupert, was born. She divorced Pole in 1923 and married architect Lloyd Wright a short time later.

LLOYD WRIGHT (1890-1978) was an architect and the son of Frank Lloyd Wright. After a divorce from his first wife, he married Helen Taggart, thereby becoming Rupert Pole's stepfather.

MARGUERITE YOUNG (1908-1995), writer and teacher, noted for her epic-length novel *Miss MacIntosh My Darling* (1965), was befriended and championed by Anaïs Nin.

INDEX

illnesses of 19, 21-22, 90-93, 140, 142, 143, 147, 172, 195, 205, 318, 321, 325

Haas, Madeleine 182
Haas, Robert 39, 124, 127, 144
Hadyn, Hiram vii, 1, 7, 20, 27, 32, 40, 43, 45, 49, 58, 65, 70-71, 73, 76-77, 83, 84, 106, 108, 141, 160, 222-23, 224
  letter from 51
  letter to 2-3
Hage, Virginia 149
Haggart, Stanley 24
Haines, Fred 32, 63, 97
Hakoshima, Yass 179, 203, 206, 246
Hamilton, Dran 262
Hamilton, Jennie 90, 216
Harcourt (publisher) vii, ix, x, xi, 1, 2, 4, 9, 24, 40, 41, 43-44, 45, 65, 66, 68, 71, 76, 77, 78, 81, 93, 105, 106, 107, 108, 112, 132, 145, 156, 158, 160, 166, 186, 196, 197, 213, 218, 222, 224, 226, 227, 232, 245, 250, 278, 280, 293
Hardwick, Elizabeth 234
Harms, Valerie 160, 167, 258, 261, 296, 298
Harrington, Jo 312, 313, 316, 317, 318, 319, 324
Harris, Beatrice 160, 166, 210, 258
Harshman, Tom 24
The Harvard Advocate (periodical) 161
Hauser, Marianne 46, 132, 161, 230
Hawkes, John 142, 157
Hedja (Nin) 185
Hemingway, Ernest 5, 10, 11, 204
Henderson, Olympia 218
Henry & June (Nin) xi
The Henry Miller Odyssey (film) 58, 83, 85, 86, 111, 152, 189, 263

Herlihy, James Leo ix, 178, 191, 196, 216, 223, 228, 260, 285, 309, 312
  letters from 283, 285
Herring, Bebe 167, 168
Herron, Paul xi
Hinz, Evelyn 158, 162, 166, 167, 168, 169, 228, 237, 240, 241, 248-49, 250, 300, 306, 310, 326
  letter from 158-59
History of Japanese Literature (Keene) 6
History of Medicine (Ibañez) 120
Hochman, Sandra 46, 52, 160
Hoffmann, Georges 108
Holiday (periodical) 173, 325
Holleff, Maxine 251, 263
Holt, Rochelle 120, 311, 320
  letter from 138-39
Honickman, Lynne 160, 195
Horowitz, Dave 180, 188
Horton, Millie 51
House of Incest (Nin) viii, 25, 42, 58, 75, 114, 119, 120, 124, 127, 128, 134, 136, 143, 150, 218, 221, 248, 258, 261, 266, 293, 315, 317, 320, 324
  Durrell's adaptation of 317, 320, 324
Hoy, Jody 237, 250-51, 266, 285, 286, 291, 301, 304, 310, 311, 315
Huara, Helba viii, 122, 152, 162
Hugo, Ian (see Hugh Guiler)
Hunderwasser, Friedensreich 297, 304
The Hunting Gun (Inoue) 50
Huxley, Laura 83
Hyde, Charlotte 224, 227, 238, 265, 299, 325

Ibañez, Félix Martí 17, 199
  letter to 120
In Favor of the Sensitive Man (Nin)

235, 297

Incest (Nin) xi

Interview (periodical) 201

Ippolito, Donna 296, 297

Isherwood, Christopher 83, 225, 306

Jackson, Glenda 191

Jaffe, Harold 120

Jaglom, Henry 175, 191, 193, 197,
    201-202, 210, 221, 228, 237, 260,
    284, 293, 305, 324

Japan, visit to 9-15

Jason, Philip K. 160, 214, 224
    letter to 185

Jean Racine (Knapp) 121

La jeune femme de 60 ans (Chalon)
    266, 268

Johan (partner of Ferrone) 211, 217,
    258

Johnson, Lyndon 1, 45, 50

Johnstone, Millie 245

Jones, Barry 161, 165, 174, 175, 243,
    244, 257, 270, 271, 277, 297, 299,
    300, 306, 312, 324

Jones, Jack 22, 56

Jones, Jennifer 158

Jouve, Pierre Jean 6

Jouvet, Louis 20

Jovanovich, William 40, 76-77, 245

Joy, Brugh 306, 307, 309, 310, 311,
    312, 316, 317, 318, 320, 321, 324,
    325, 326

Kannenstine, Lou 154

Kanters, Robert 101, 105

Karatani, Masako 50, 296
    letters from 122-23, 282
    letters to 126-27, 282-83

Kavan, Anna 71, 133, 304

Kawade Shobo (publisher) 6, 31, 40,
    42, 50, 56, 127, 128

Kawade, Tomohisa 10

Kazan, Elia 183, 306

Kazantzakis, Nikos 122, 195

Kennedy, John F. 262

Kennedy, Richard T. 47

Kennedy, Robert F. 45, 262

Kent, Corita 309, 310, 317, 328

Kerkhoven, Joseph 233

King, Martin Luther Jr. 52, 54, 81

Kirkus (periodical) 108, 113

Kirsch, Robert R. 32, 105, 112, 158,
    200, 239, 306, 319, 320

Knapp, Bettina 20, 58, 62, 121, 160,
    161

Knef, Hildegard 98, 99, 106

Knight, Derrick 203

Knopf (publisher) 251

Knopf, Alfred 47

Knox, Ronnie 26

Korn, David 118

Kort, Carol
    letter from 153

Kosinski, Jerzy 16, 29, 47, 124, 127,
    139

Kraft, Barbara 218, 235, 248, 285,
    292, 292, 297, 299, 301, 304, 311,
    330

Krementz, Jill 160, 225, 233, 279,
    280

Kurnick, Stanley 262

l'Abbé, France 172

L'Observateur (periodical) 278

Ladders to Fire (Nin) 25, 42, 84, 192,
    245, 267

Lahn, Ilse 73, 74

Laing, R. D. 134, 321

Lamy, Marthe 270, 274

Landfield, Timothy 162, 164

Larrocha, Alicia de 17, 159

Lartigue, Jacques H. 144, 145, 189

Last Tango in Paris (film) 185

Lawless, Joann

348

ALSO AVAILABLE FROM SKY BLUE PRESS

The Diary of Others: The Unexpurgated Diary of Anaïs Nin, 1955-1966 by Anaïs Nin (print, ebook)

Trapeze: The Unexpurgated Diary of Anaïs Nin, 1947-1955 by Anaïs Nin (print, ebook)

Mirages: The Unexpurgated Diary of Anaïs Nin, 1939-1947 by Anaïs Nin (print, ebook)

Reunited: The Correspondence of Anaïs and Joaquín Nin 1933-1940 by Anaïs Nin and Joaquín Nin (print, ebook)

Auletris: Erotica by Anaïs Nin (print, ebook, audiobook)

The Quotable Anaïs Nin by Anaïs Nin (two volumes; print, ebook)

The Portable Anaïs Nin by Anaïs Nin, ed. Benjamin Franklin V (print, ebook)

Letters to Lawrence Durrell 1937-1977 by Anaïs Nin (print, ebook)

D. H. Lawrence: An Unprofessional Study by Anaïs Nin (ebook)

House of Incest by Anaïs Nin (ebook)

The Winter of Artifice: 1939 Paris Edition by Anaïs Nin (print, ebook)

Winter of Artifice: American Edition by Anaïs Nin (ebook)

Under a Glass Bell by Anaïs Nin (ebook)

Stella by Anaïs Nin (ebook)

Ladders to Fire by Anaïs Nin (ebook)

Children of the Albatross by Anaïs Nin (ebook)

The Four-Chambered Heart by Anaïs Nin (ebook)

A Spy in the House of Love by Anaïs Nin (ebook)

Seduction of the Minotaur by Anaïs Nin (ebook)

Cities of the Interior by Anaïs Nin (ebook)

Collages by Anaïs Nin (ebook)

The Novel of the Future by Anaïs Nin (ebook)

Anaïs Nin: The Last Days, a Memoir by Barbara Kraft (ebook)

Henry Miller: The Last Days, a Memoir by Barbara Kraft (print, ebook)

Anaïs Nin's Lost World: Paris in Words and Pictures 1924-1939 by Britt Arenander (print, ebook)

Critical Analysis of Anaïs Nin in Japan (print, ebook)

Facts Matter: Essays on Issues Relating to Anaïs Nin by Benjamin Franklin V (print, ebook)

Anaïs Nin Character Dictionary and Index to Diary Excerpts by Benjamin Franklin V (print, ebook)

A Café in Space: The Anaïs Nin Literary Journal, Vol. 1 by Anaïs Nin, Janet Fitch, Lynette Felber… (print, ebook)

A Café in Space: The Anaïs Nin Literary Journal, Vol. 2 by Anaïs Nin, Benjamin Franklin V, Masako Meio… (print, ebook)

A Café in Space: The Anaïs Nin Literary Journal, Vol. 3 by Anaïs Nin, Gunther Stuhlmann, Richard Pine, James Clawson… (print, ebook)

A Café in Space: The Anaïs Nin Literary Journal, Vol. 4 by Anaïs Nin, Alan Swallow, John Ferrone, Yuko Yaguchi… (print, ebook)

A Café in Space: The Anaïs Nin Literary Journal, Vol. 5 by Anaïs Nin, Duane Schneider, Sarah Burghauser… (print, ebook)

A Café in Space: The Anaïs Nin Literary Journal, Vol. 6 by Anaïs Nin, Joaquín Nin y Castellanos, Tristine Rainer, Christie Logan… (print, ebook)

A Café in Space: The Anaïs Nin Literary Journal, Vol. 7 by Anaïs Nin, John Ferrone, Kim Krizan, Tristine Rainer…

A Café in Space: The Anaïs Nin Literary Journal, Vol. 8 by Anaïs Nin, Benjamin Franklin V, Anita Jarczok, Kim Krizan… (print, ebook)

A Café in Space: The Anaïs Nin Literary Journal, Vol. 9 by Anaïs Nin, Anita Jarczok, Joel Enos… (print, ebook)

A Café in Space: The Anaïs Nin Literary Journal, Vol. 10 by Anaïs Nin, Benjamin Franklin V, Kim Krizan, William Claire, Erin Dunbar… (print, ebook)

A Café in Space: The Anaïs Nin Literary Journal, Vol. 11 by Anaïs Nin, Henry Miller, Alfred Perlès, John Tytell… (print, ebook)

A Café in Space: The Anaïs Nin Literary Journal, Vol. 12 by Anaïs Nin, Kim Krizan, Benjamin Franklin V… (print, ebook)

A Café in Space: The Anaïs Nin Literary Journal, Vol. 13 by Anaïs Nin, Barbara Kraft, Danica Davidson… (print, ebook)

A Café in Space: The Anaïs Nin Literary Journal, Vol. 14 by Anaïs Nin, Jessica Gilbey, Joaquín Nin-Culmell… (print, ebook)

A Café in Space: The Anaïs Nin Literary Journal, Vol. 15 by Anaïs Nin, Rupert Pole, Steven Reigns… (print, ebook)

A Café in Space: The Anaïs Nin Literary Journal, Anthology 2003-2018 (print, ebook)

ANAIS: An International Journal, Anthology 1983-2001 (print, ebook)

Made in the USA
Monee, IL
05 March 2024

54108605R00219